D0948157

INTERNATIONAL SERIES IN
EXPERIMENTAL PSYCHOLOGY
General Editor H. J. EYSENCK

VOLUME 22

HUMAN MEMORY: THEORY, RESEARCH AND INDIVIDUAL DIFFERENCES

OTHER TITLES IN THE SERIES IN EXPERIMENTAL PSYCHOLOGY

HUMAN MEMORY: THEORY, RESEARCH AND INDIVIDUAL DIFFERENCES

by

MICHAEL W. EYSENCK, Ph.D.

*Department of Psychology,
Birkbeck College, University of London*

PERGAMON PRESS

OXFORD · NEW YORK · TORONTO · SYDNEY · PARIS · FRANKFURT

U.K.	Pergamon Press Ltd., Headington Hill Hall, Oxford OX3 0BW, England
U.S.A.	Pergamon Press Inc., Maxwell House, Fairview Park, Elmsford, New York 10523, U.S.A.
CANADA	Pergamon of Canada Ltd., 75 The East Mall, Toronto, Ontario, Canada
AUSTRALIA	Pergamon Press (Aust.) Pty. Ltd., 19a Boundary Street, Rushcutters Bay, N.S.W. 2011, Australia
FRANCE	Pergamon Press SARL, 24 rue des Ecoles, 75240 Paris, Cedex 05, France
FEDERAL REPUBLIC OF GERMANY	Pergamon Press GmbH, 6242 Kronberg/Taunus, Pferdstrasse 1, Federal Republic of Germany

First edition 1977
Reprinted 1978

Library of Congress Cataloging in Publication Data

Eysenck, Michael W.
Human memory.

(Pergamon international series in experimental psychology, vol. 22)
Bibliography: p.
Includes index.
1. Memory. I. Title. II. Series.[DNLM:
1. Memory. 2. Individuality. W1 IN835JE v.22
BF371 E98h]
BF371.E95   153.1'2   77-358
ISBN 0-08-020405-8

Printed in Great Britain by William Clowes & Sons Limited, London, Beccles and Colchester

To Chris

CONTENTS

PREFACE AND ACKNOWLEDGEMENTS

The commentator's classic remark on a football match that "It was a match of two halves" is applicable with slight modification to this book, for it basically comprises two halves. The main reason is that there are some psychologists who are interested in the processes of human learning and memory, and there are other psychologists who are interested in individual differences, but hitherto any attempt at communication between the two groups has resembled the dialogue of the deaf. My main aim in writing this book was to present the ideas and experimentation of both groups of workers, and to show the potential for cross-fertilization.

Part I of the book is largely concerned with current information-processing accounts of the various stages of processing involved in human learning and memory, whereas Part II deals primarily with individual differences. The work discussed in Part I has suffered from the prevalent assumptions that all individual differences can safely be relegated to the error term of the analysis of variance. The work discussed in Part II has suffered from a failure to utilize the conceptual and experimental advances that have transformed memory research over the past decade.

There have been some researchers who have successfully combined an interest in problems of learning and memory with an awareness of the importance of individual differences, and the work of three of them (Spence, Spielberger, and my father) is discussed in some detail in this book. Needless to say, my intellectual development owes much to each of them.

It is a pleasure for me to express my gratitude to several people who have in some way contributed to the book. Chris Cromarty provided expert assistance with the figures. My ideas on several points have been influenced by my students and friends, particularly Hilary Klee, Susan Bibby, Dave Riley, Chris Gillespie, Brian Clifford, and Harry Sacks, and by my colleagues, notably by David Legge and Vernon Gregg. I would also like to thank my parents, who have helped me in their very different ways. Above all, however, my greatest

debt of gratitude is to my wife, who has suffered patiently
during the long months when the manuscript was in
preparation, and who has been a source of inspiration.
Finally, thanks are due to Jemima, who was an enthusiastic
participator in the enterprise.   May her involvement in
psychology wax while her bird-catching proclivities wane.

CHAPTER 1

INTRODUCTION

The research literature in psychology is enormous, and increasing at a very fast rate. The psychologist determined to read every article that is published each year would need to read one article every 15 minutes, 24 hours of the day, 365 days a year. He would also need to be a polyglot. When one considers in addition the proactive and retroactive interference to which our sleep-deprived obsessionalist would be exposed, and the almost impossible task of integrating the disparate findings, it becomes clear that we are all extremely selective samplers of the literature in psychology. Even within the more modest boundaries of work on human memory, it has become essential to focus one's attention on certain phenomena to the exclusion of others. This book deals primarily with long-term memory, although there is some coverage of short-term memory. Little is said about the modality-specific stores into which it has been argued that information goes initially. The research on such stores, labelled iconic and echoic memory by Neisser (1967), has been capably reviewed by others. The interested reader is directed to recent articles by Crowder (1975) on echoic memory and by Coltheart (1975) and Holding (1975) on iconic memory.

The reader should be warned that the enormous recent proliferation of articles and books on human memory does not necessarily imply a commensurate increase in knowledge. It is difficult to disagree with the following somewhat pessimistic statement from Tulving and Madigan (1970): "Many inventions and discoveries in other fields would bewilder and baffle Aristotle, but the most spectacular or counter-intuitive finding from psychological studies of memory would cause him to raise his eyebrows only for an instant" (p. 437).

A more detailed analysis of current experimentation on human memory has been provided by Newell (1973) and Allport (1975). Their first point is that research tends to be phenomenon-driven, i.e., some finding, closely tied to a

1

particular experimental paradigm, is exhaustively analyzed
and investigated. Unfortunately, the usual consequence of
this thorough investigation is total obfuscation or
disappointment, or both. For example, consider the part-
to-whole transfer paradigm introduced by Tulving (1966).
Control and experimental groups of subjects learned two
lists of words, the second of which was twice as long as the
first. Retention was tested by free recall, with the
subjects recalling the words in any order. For the control
group, the two lists were unrelated, whereas, for the
experimental group, all the first-list words were included
in the second list. Counter-intuitively, the experimental
subjects had more difficulty than the control subjects in
learning the second list, in spite of the fact that the
experimental subjects had previously learned half the words.
Tulving argued that the experimental subjects had organized
the first-list words in order to learn them, and that this
organization was inappropriate to the second-list situation.

In subsequent work, Wood and Clark (1969) and Novinski
(1972) found that informing subjects in the experimental
group that the second list included all the first-list words
eliminated the slower learning of the experimental subjects
obtained by Tulving (1966). Slamecka, Moore, and Carey
(1972) argued that the experimental subjects would notice
that some of the words on the second list had come from the
first list, but they would not be certain that they had all
been included. Thus the experimental subjects might be
cautious in their recall in order to avoid possible intrusion
errors. In support of this contention, Slamecka et al.
found that inferior performance by the experimental group
was obtained with neutral instructions, but not with
instructions asking the subjects to adopt a lenient criterion
for response. The initial part-to-whole transfer
phenomenon, which was at first thought to provide strong
evidence for organizational processes in memory, is thus now
seen as a somewhat fragile and complex effect. Furthermore,
its relevance to important theoretical issues is now in doubt.

The concentration of effort on phenomena derived from
specific experimental paradigms carries with it the danger
of paradigm-specific theorizing. For example, theories have
been proposed on the basis of data collected solely or
primarily from a single experimental paradigm, such as free
recall, serial learning, or paired-associate learning. This
tendency is so strong that Murdock (1974), in his recent book,

discusses theories of association, serial order, and free recall in separate chapters. The danger, of course, is that theories formed on a narrow data base will have extremely limited applicability to the findings from other paradigms. Even in those cases where the same theoretical concept has been applied to data from various experimental situations, there have been remarkably few attempts to establish the identicality of the concept across situations. For example, as Watkins (1974) has pointed out, the concept of 'primary memory' has been applied to data from several paradigms, including free recall and probe experiments. A necessary but not sufficient test of the assumption that the same concept is applicable cross-situationally would be the demonstration that those with a relatively large (or small) primary-memory store in one situation should also have a relatively large (or small) store in other situations. This cross-situational generality has not as yet been systematically studied.

A further difficulty is that theoretical approaches have frequently involved the postulation of binary oppositions, such as the following: all-or-none versus incremental; serial versus parallel; peripheral versus central; continuous versus discontinuous; heredity versus environment; and so on. While it is surely true that many of these conceptual dichotomies relate to important theoretical issues, the actual consequence of these theses and antitheses has rarely been the desired Hegelian synthesis. Instead, it usually transpires that the dichotomy is either misleading or that one cannot safely favour either side of the opposition. If we continue our current practice of studying limited phenomena and proposing unhelpful binary oppositions, Newell (1973) argues, the future is unpromising:

> Another hundred phenomena, give or take a few dozen, will have been discovered and explored. Another forty oppositions will have been posited, and their resolution initiated. Will psychology then come of age? How will the transformation be accomplished by this succession of phenomena and oppositions?...It seems to me that clarity is never achieved. Matters simply become muddier and muddier as we go down through time (pp. 287-289).

A further, related, problem is the plethora of theoretical

concepts in recent work on human memory.   In the last decade
or so there has been an enormous increase in the number of
terms used to describe the workings of memory. Although
those who wield Occam's razor too recklessly are liable to
slit their own throats, more regard for Lloyd Morgan's (1894)
canon regarding parsimony would be appropriate. According
to the literature, we have iconic, echoic, active, working,
acoustic, articulatory, primary, secondary, episodic,
semantic, short-term, intermediate-term, and long-term
memories, and these memories contain tags, traces, images,
attributes, markers, concepts, cognitive maps, natural-
language mediators, kernel sentences, relational rules,
nodes, associations, propositions, higher-order memory units,
and features. While it is true that many of these concepts
have explanatory power in interpreting the experimental data,
it is also true that they are frequently used in senses other
than the rigorously scientific. The reader is warned that
we are far from having an established taxonomy of memorial
processes and structures.

    A final difficulty with contemporary approaches to human
memory is what Reitman (1970) referred to as the decoupling
problem. In order to simplify experimental work on memory,
laboratory tasks are frequently chosen in order to decouple
the memory system from the large system of cognitive processes
and problem-solving strategies. There is also an attempt,
implicit or explicit, to utilize experimental paradigms in
which individual differences in personality and motivation
will be minimized. The decoupling problem has several
aspects to it:-
            (1) It may not be possible to study memorial
processes separately from other cognitive processes.
            (2) Since the memory system usually operates
in interaction with other functional systems, we may well
obtain non-representative data in our attempt to decouple the
memory system.
            (3) Research questions involving the
interaction of the memory system with other processes are of
importance and require investigation. At the present time,
fewer than five per cent of all the studies on human memory
include any consideration of either motivational factors of
relevance or individual differences in personality.

    In spite of the various methodological and theoretical
problems associated with research on memory, there is no

doubt that much genuine progress has occurred over the past
ten to fifteen years. It is hoped that this discussion of
the problems will provide a critical framework for
evaluating the work considered in the following chapters.
The first part of the book deals with data and theory on the
major memorial processes, and the second part deals with the
relationship between memorial processes and ageing,
motivation, intelligence, and personality.

Summary

While our knowledge of the functioning of human memory
has increased considerably in recent years, there remain
a number of problems which beset research in this area.
Among the more consequential of such problems appear to be
the following:-
          (1) Paradigm specificity - the tendency for
generalizations and theoretical statements to be based
exclusively on findings obtained from a single, limited,
experimental situation.
          (2) Binary oppositions - the tendency for
theorists to assume that performance is determined by one or
other of two mutually exclusive processes, a tendency which
is limiting conceptually.
          (3) A plethora of concepts - several dozen
new concepts have been introduced into the research
literature over the past few years. Many of these concepts
overlap substantially with previous concepts, and several of
them have no unequivocal scientific meaning.
          (4) The decoupling problem - it is usually
tacitly assumed that experimentation on memory should
attempt to isolate the memory system from other systems.
The author doubts whether this is either possible or
desirable.

CHAPTER 2

INFORMATION STORAGE

Over the past twenty years, several attempts have been
made to describe what happens when people perceive and
retain information from the external environment. Two
different aspects of information processing have been
emphasized in recent theories: structure and process.
Those who emphasize structure have usually suggested that
the nature of the information-processing system imposes
limitations on the rate of flow of information through it.
It has commonly been assumed that there is a temporal
sequence to the flow of information, which passes from
modality-specific stores through a short-term store (STS) to
a long-term store (LTS). On the other hand, those theorists
stressing the importance of process have concentrated more on
the richness and variety of encoding and processing strategies
which can be applied to incoming information. While it is
convenient to distinguish between process and structure for
expository purposes, they undoubtedly interact and depend on
one another in a variety of complex ways.

Structural Theories: Boxology

The best and most detailed information-processing theories
of human memory put forward during the 1950s and 1960s were of
the structural variety. The theories in question were those
of Broadbent (1958), Waugh and Norman (1965), and Atkinson
and Shiffrin (1968). While these theories differ in points
of detail, it is nevertheless possible to construct from
them a 'modal model' (Murdock, 1967, 1972) incorporating the
substantial overlap among them (see Fig. 2.1). It is
assumed that information is initially held in a modality-
specific sensory store, but that information is rapidly lost
through decay unless attention is paid to it. Attended
items are passed on to a limited-capacity STS, where they are
rehearsed or displaced by further items. Rehearsal is used
both to maintain items in STS and to transfer (or copy)
information about the items to a semi-permanent LTS. Any
items in STS at the time of test can be recalled. The

6

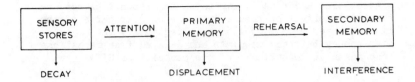

Fig. 2.1. The basic structural model of memory.

capacity of LTS is essentially unlimited, with forgetting
being determined by interference. Waugh and Norman (1965)
used the term 'primary memory' to refer to STS, and
'secondary memory' to refer to LTS. It has been
suggested (e.g., Baddeley, 1972a) that an important
distinction between STS and LTS is that information
processing is primarily phonemic (i.e., acoustic and/or
articulatory) in STS, but predominantly semantic in LTS.

   In order to distinguish between STS and LTS at an
experimental level, a much-used task has been that of free
recall. The subject is presented with a list of words, and
then has to recall as many as possible in any order. It is
usually found that the subject recalls well from the
beginning (the primacy effect) and the end (the recency
effect) of the list, with recall leveling out in the middle
of the list (the asymptote). Several variables affect the
asymptote, but have no discernible effect on the recency
portion of the recall curve. For example, the more items
in the list, the lower the asymptote (Postman & Phillips,
1965); the less frequent the words presented are in the
language, the poorer the recall of the middle-of-the-list
items (Raymond, 1969); and the faster the rate of
presentation, the lower the asymptote (Glanzer & Cunitz, 1966).
The fact that none of these variables affects the recency
effect suggests that different structures are involved in
different parts of the list. More specifically, the
assumption has been that recall from the initial and middle
portions of the list is from LTS, whereas recall from the
last few serial positions is predominantly from STS (see
Fig. 2.2). This assumption is supported by the finding that

a distracting task interpolated between the end of list
presentation and recall eliminates the recency effect, but
has little effect on recall from the earlier parts of the
list (Glanzer & Cunitz, 1966). Frequently, the
discrepancy between immediate and delayed free recall has
been taken as an estimate of the capacity of STS.

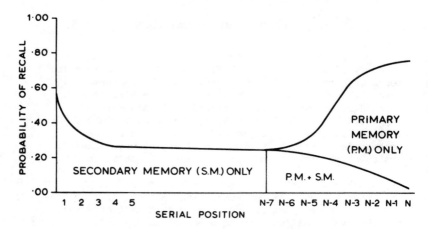

Fig. 2.2. The theoretical involvement of primary
memory and secondary memory in immediate free
recall as a function of serial position.

Since the structural models of human memory regard the
extremely limited capacity of STS as one of its prime
characteristics, several attempts have been made to provide
accurate estimates of its capacity (cf., Watkins, 1974).
Craik (1971a) discussed some of the methods which have been
used, most of which are based upon the free-recall paradigm.
Glanzer and Razel (1974) collated data from 21 free-
recall studies, and found that the mean estimate of STS
capacity was 2.2 words. As Glanzer and Razel pointed out,
the capacity of STS seems so small that it would appear to be
of extremely limited value in the processing of conversation.

It has usually been assumed that the capacity of STS is
appropriately measured in terms of the number of words
stored. For example, Craik (1968a) varied the number of

syllables per word in a free-recall list, and found that the
number of syllables had no effect on either STS or LTS.
This suggests that the subjects were processing a unit
consisting of a word, or something larger, in STS.   Glanzer
and Razel (1974) gave their subjects free-recall lists
consisting of proverbs, and estimated that 2.2 proverbs were
being held in STS.   The number of words represented by 2.2
proverbs is approximately nine, providing an estimate of
STS capacity considerably greater than conventional wisdom
would allow.   However, it is possible that subjects only
stored a single word from each proverb, and reconstructed
the proverb at test (e.g., 'broth' suggests the proverb
'Too many cooks spoil the broth').   This explanation is less
attractive in view of a further experiment by Glanzer and
Razel (1974), in which 1.5 unfamiliar sentences were
apparently stored in STS.   Thus STS is not as limited in
capacity or as restricted in its processing as has been
suggested.

The structural theories of human memory consider rehearsal
to be the process by which information is transferred from
STS to LTS.   However, it seems intrinsically implausible to
assume that rehearsal has much relevance to the retention of
visual, gustatory, tactile, and kinaesthetic information.
It should thus be noted that structural theories are limited
in potential applicability to studies of verbal learning.

Atkinson and Shiffrin (1968) hypothesized that information
about an item was transferred to LTS while, and only while,
it was being rehearsed in STS.   It follows that the longer
an item is maintained in STS via rehearsal, the higher will be
its recall probability.   The primacy effect in free recall,
i.e., the superior recall of the initial list items, might be
due to the fact that a disproportionate amount of rehearsal
is accorded to those items.   Fischler, Rundus, and
Atkinson (1970) instructed their subjects to repeat out loud
only the item currently being displayed during list
presentation, and found that this rehearsal-equalizing
procedure produced a substantial decrease in the primacy
effect.   In addition, Rundus and Atkinson (1970) and
Rundus (1971) investigated the processes involved in single-
trial free recall by means of an overt rehearsal technique,
in which the subjects were instructed to rehearse aloud any of
the list items they wished to during list presentation.   In
both studies, there was a close relationship between the
number of rehearsals an item received and its probability of

recall, with the initial items being rehearsed more often
than subsequent items, and being better recalled.

It seems likely that the overt rehearsal technique
distorts to some extent the encoding strategies used by
subjects. Kellas, McCauley, and McFarland (1975) compared
several aspects of learning and recall in subjects required
to rehearse the presented material either overtly or
covertly. Overt rehearsal produced a significant reduction
in efficiency, presumably because the attention-consuming
requirement to pronounce each of the list items in primary
memory restricted the use of more sophisticated mnemonic
strategies.

In other experimental situations, sheer quantity of
rehearsal appears to be less important. For example, Weist
(1972) used the overt rehearsal technique in a multi-trial
free recall study, and found that the number of rehearsals
of an item was correlated positively with the probability of
recall on the first trial, as Rundus had found. However,
the correlations were generally low thereafter. With
categorized lists, a more important determinant of recall was
the extent to which rehearsal was categorically organized.
This indicates that the patterning of rehearsal is of more
importance than the mere quantity. Furthermore, Craik
(1973) found that subjects instructed to make sure that they
recalled the last four items in a list accorded a
disproportionate amount of rehearsal to these items. In a
subsequent, unexpected test of recall of all words from all
the lists used in the experiment, subjects did not recall
these final items better than other, considerably less
rehearsed, items. Craik suggested that rehearsal could
either merely involve maintenance of information at one level
or might involve more elaborate processing of the material.
It is clear that rehearsal can function approximately in the
manner specified by Atkinson and Shiffrin (1968), but it
need not.

Baddeley (1972a, 1972b) has proposed that phonemic
similarity affects STS but not LTS, whereas semantic
similarity does the reverse. This suggestion seems
somewhat implausible, especially the notion that phonemic
similarity is irrelevant to LTS. However, there is some
reasonable supporting evidence (e.g., Kintsch & Buschke,
1969; Levy & Murdock, 1968). Shulman (1971) reviewed the
relevant evidence and concluded that many results were

inconsistent with Baddeley's position. Shulman's review
suffers from the disadvantage that he does not clearly
distinguish between STS and short-term memory tasks. Short-
term memory tasks are those which involve a short interval
of time between input and test; they may or may not involve
STS. Baddeley (1972b) argued that, in those experiments
where semantic coding has been found in STS, this was due to
the subject's utilization of rules of a semantic nature
stored in STS to retrieve phonemically coded material from
STS at recall.

It is obvious that phonemic information is stored in LTS;
if it were not, many common activities such as reading aloud
from a newspaper would be impossible. Woodworth (1938) and
Gruneberg and Sykes (1969) have obtained evidence that LTS
is susceptible to phonemic interference effects. Gruneberg
and Sykes found that, 20-25 minutes after the presentation of
a list of words, subjects were significantly more likely on a
recognition test to decide that words phonemically similar to
words in the presentation list had been presented than that
words phonemically dissimilar to words in the presentation
list had been presented. Logically, the transfer of
information from STS to LTS would be much more complex than
the single arrow pointing from STS to LTS in the modal model
implies if phonemic information resides in STS, and semantic
information in LTS. As Gruneberg and Sykes pertinently
stated, such a conception requires some additional mechanism
which can translate auditory coding into semantic coding,
and "such a mechanism would have to be as large as short snd
long term memory stores combined, which makes the
postulation of a short and long term memory separate from
compiler unparsimonious" (p. 296).

Shulman (1970) argued that, while subjects did not appear
to encode semantically in STS in most experimental situations,
this might be because successful task performance did not
require semantic coding in STS. Accordingly, he used a
task that required semantic processing for its successful
completion. Subjects received a list of words followed by
a probe word, to which the subject had to respond 'yes' or
'no'. A cue presented immediately after the list indicated
whether the subject was to respond 'yes' if the probe was
identical to one of the list words, was a homonym of a list
word (phonemic processing), or a synonym of a list word
(semantic processing). Performance under all conditions
was best at the last few serial positions, i.e., there was a

strong recency effect.   The existence of this recency effect
indicates that the last few items were in STS.   The
extremely good detection of synonyms from STS strongly
suggests that semantic coding is possible in STS.   While
such results could be explained by arguing that information
from LTS is retrieved at the time of presentation of the
probe item, the relatively fast reaction times to synonym
probes at the later serial positions (approximately one
second) appear to rule out that explanation.   Shulman also
found that subjects during list presentation took longer to
process semantically than phonemically.   Thus, in studies
using a fast rate of presentation, subjects may be unable to
process the information semantically.

    Several other investigators (e.g., Bruce & Crowley, 1970;
Glanzer, Koppenaal, & Nelson, 1972) have also indicated quite
strongly that the phonemic-semantic coding distinction is not
very relevant to the STS-LTS distinction.   For example,
Glanzer et al. reported several experiments on free recall in
which they manipulated phonemic and semantic similarity in
various ways.   It was found that both forms of similarity
were responded to by the subjects while the words were in
STS, both forms of similarity increased the number of items
that could be recalled from LTS, and neither type of coding
had any effect on the number of items in STS.   If STS and
LTS were specialized for different processes, one would
surely have expected some differential effects of phonemic
and semantic similarity on recall from these two stores.

    As the Shulman (1971) review made clear, much of the
earlier evidence that the processing in STS was phonemic in
nature merely tested for the subjects' retention of order
information, but not of item information.   This was done by
presenting the subject on test with the list words in a
random order, and requiring him to arrange them in the
appropriate order.   It is instructive to note that the more
recent evidence obtaining contrary findings has concentrated
on the retention of item information rather than order
information.

    It should be emphasized that the value of the STS-LTS
distinction does not depend critically on the discovery of
coding differences in the two stores.   Basically, the modal
model is concerned with structure rather than process.

    Wickelgren (1973) has argued that an important difference

between STS and LTS may lie in the form of the retention function from these two stores. His review of the relevant literature indicated that STS traces manifest exponential decay, whereas LTS traces cannot be so characterized, because their susceptibility to decay is continually decreasing. Wickelgren argued that LTS traces produce an exponential-power decay function, but he properly pointed out that the correct interpretation of this difference in retention functions is in doubt. Since forgetting can be caused by interference, since STS traces are more likely than LTS traces to be phonemic in nature, and since interpolated material between presentation and test is more likely to be phonemically similar than semantically similar to the learned material, the faster decay rates for STS traces might be attributable to the greater interference which they encounter.

Further evidence in support of a distinction between STS and LTS comes in work on neurological disorders of memory. Warrington (1971) has reviewed work on amnesic patients, who appear to suffer from LTS deficits. In one study, immediate free recall by amnesic patients showed reduced recall of the early items from the list, but the normal recency effect. Additional evidence indicates that at least part of the poor recall from LTS shown by amnesics is due to a retrieval rather than a storage difficulty. Other patients have been found who, on free-recall tasks, show a much reduced recency effect (i.e., small STS capacity) but a relatively normal asymptote and primacy effect. As Warrington (1971) pointed out, "these findings indicate that information need not be transferred from STM to LTM as is commonly supposed, but that the two systems can function in parallel" (p. 247).

In some respects, primary memory or STS seems to correspond to the 'contents of consciousness'. If so, it might be anticipated that information could be retrieved more rapidly from STS than from LTS. Waugh (1970) found that retrieval from STS was significantly faster than retrieval from LTS, but the experiment was suspect methodologically. There is some recent evidence that is hard to reconcile with the equation of primary memory and consciousness. Bjork and Whitten (1974) and Tzeng (1973) obtained large recency effects when word lists were presented at very slow rates, and the inter-item intervals were filled with arithmetic distractor activity. It is

unlikely that the subjects could have performed the
distractor task and still retained several items in
consciousness.

One further aspect of the structural model which has not
as yet been discussed is the assertion that items are lost
from STS by means of displacement. Glanzer, Gianutsos, and
Dubin (1969) found that the number of words intervening
between list presentation and free recall importantly
determined the size of the recency effect: the more
intervening items, the poorer the recall from the end of the
list. Since they also found that neither the information
load nor the similarity of the intervening task to the to-
be-recalled material substantially affected the recency
effect, they concluded that incoming items 'bumped out' items
from STS by the mechanism of displacement. However, other
work, reviewed by Broadbent (1971), has indicated that
similarity of interpolated material to to-be-remembered
material can affect the rate of loss of information from STS.

In sum, we have seen that a considerable body of
experimental evidence indicates the desirability of
distinguishing between short- and long-term stores.
However, there are strong grounds for believing that current
structural models are inadequate. More specifically, the
hypothesized flow of information from a sensory buffer,
through STS, to LTS is clearly a gross over-simplification.
Strictly interpreted, this would mean that all material
rehearsed in STS would seem to the subject to be novel, since
at that time no contact with LTS would have been made.
Moreover, the rehearsal of visually presented information in
STS requires the prior retrieval of phonemic information
from LTS. The placement of STS after LTS in the flow
diagram, as Morton (1970) has suggested, would obviate some
of these difficulties. The findings of Glanzer and Razel
(1974) indicate that the information-processing capacity of
STS is considerably greater than the modal model would allow.

The key process of rehearsal seems, in the light of the
experimental evidence, to be less important and more
versatile than it should be theoretically. It may, indeed,
be the case that rehearsal is a technique primarily used by
subjects who are unfortunate enough to be exposed to a
rapidly presented series of unrelated items which they have
to learn. Even under such circumstances, as West (1972)
has found, the quality or patterning of the rehearsal soon

becomes more important than the quantity, although
structural models of human memory have emphasized the
quantitative aspect of rehearsal. If STS is susceptible to
phonemic interference effects, and if information from STS
is merely copied into LTS, it is difficult to discern any
reason why LTS should be free from phonemic interference.
If the original is blurred, how can a copy be distinct?
Finally, and perhaps most importantly, an emphasis on the
structure of human memory tends to lead to a de-emphasis of
encoding processes and strategies. In other words,
structural models tend to postulate too rigid a system, and
fail to make sufficient allowances for the enormous
flexibility of encoding commonly displayed by human subjects.
There is merit in the proposal that STS represents some
small fraction of the information in LTS which is currently
being attended to, but there is none in the notion that STS
and LTS can only be connected by means of rehearsal in STS.
Clearly, the interconnections between STS and LTS are much
more complex and variegated than that. However, while it is
relatively easy to discover inadequacies in this type of
theory, it does have the inestimable advantage over many
theories of human memory that it has produced testable
deductions. As Popper (1935) has observed, an important
characteristic of a scientific theory is falsifiability, i.e.,
there should be some conceivable set of observations that is
demonstrably inconsistent with the theory.

The above discussion of structural theories of memory has
made it clear that the characteristics of STS must be more
complex than had originally been thought. Baddeley, in a
recent series of articles (Baddeley & Hitch, 1974;
Baddeley, Thomson, & Buchanan, 1975; Richardson &
Baddeley, 1975), has proposed in essence that the concept of
STS be replaced with the related concept of working memory.
The working memory system comprises a limited capacity
central processing space and a supplementary articulatory
rehearsal loop with a capacity of about three items.
Shallice and Warrington (1970) studied the case of a patient
(K. F.) who had a grossly defective STS, having a digit span
of only two items. In terms of the structural theories, it
would be expected that this deficit would cause dramatic
impairment of learning, memory, and comprehension, but this
was not found. Baddeley and Hitch suggested that the patient
had substantial impairment of the articulatory loop,
combined with an intact central processor.

Further evidence of the subdivision of working memory into two components was provided by Baddeley and Hitch (1974). In a series of experiments, subjects simultaneously retained a number of digits and performed a task (reasoning, comprehension, or free recall). On all three tasks, there was a substantial impairment in performance with six digits to be retained, but little or no performance decrement with three digits. This suggested that it was primarily the articulatory loop that is implicated when only three digits have to be retained, leaving the central processor free to handle the other task, whereas with more than three digits the capacity of the articulatory loop is exceeded, and the central processor has to recode and organize the digits as well as process the other task.

The distinction between the old and the new conceptualizations was made clearer by Richardson and Baddeley (1975). They investigated the effect on free recall of requiring subjects to utter a series of redundant speech sounds ('hi-ya') while memorizing a list of words. If the recency effect in free recall is based upon a phonemic store, then this articulatory suppression should reduce substantially the recency effect. In fact, articulatory suppression did not have a more detrimental effect on the recency effect than on the rest of the free-recall curve. It was argued that the recency effect might be due to an ordinal retrieval strategy, with the discriminability of ordinal position decreasing with increasing 'oldness' of the memory trace.

Additional evidence about the articulatory loop was obtained by Baddeley, Thomson, and Buchanan (1975). In a series of experiments, they discovered that the immediate memory span for words was affected substantially by the length of time required to read the words out loud. Thus fewer multi-syllable than single-syllable words could be retained, and subjects were only able to remember as much as they could read out in about two seconds. It seems likely on the basis of this evidence that the articulatory loop system is time-based, and has a temporally limited capacity. The smooth production of speech and the eye-voice span in reading (i.e., what the reader says when reading aloud lags consistently behind the point at which he is fixating) both seem to require something along the lines of the proposed articulatory loop system.

In sum, the fact that various factors such as phonemic

similarity and articulatory suppression have differential
effects on different short-term memory tasks indicates the
desirability of dividing working memory into two component
parts.   However, the nature of the interactions among these
components and the rest of the memory system is unclear as
yet, and the theory is most applicable to verbal-memory
tasks.   It may be the case that there is a single modality-
free central core, combined with several separate peripheral
memory components (e.g., articulatory, visual, tactile, and
so on).

Process Theories

Several researchers have independently espoused the
notion that word meaning is constituted from a large number
of attributes or features (e.g., Herriot, 1974;   Kintsch,
1970;   Morton, 1970;   Norman & Rumelhart, 1970;   Tulving &
Bower, 1974;   Underwood, 1969;   Wickens, 1970, 1972).
These attributes may be of several types, ranging from the
physical (e.g., graphemic and phonemic attributes) to the
semantic (e.g., denotative and connqtative aspects of word
meaning).   It is often assumed that psychologically
important word attributes can be identified, that words
comprise several attributes, and that the word attributes
are separable from the word itself.   No clear theoretical
formulation has emerged in this area;   the assumptions of
attribute theory are pre-theoretical and heuristic rather
than being incorporated into a hypothetico-deductive
network.

At an experimental level, the major problem has been the
difficulty of finding experimental situations which permit
a clear separation of attributes to be demonstrated. ｜ A
more detailed discussion of the paradigms used is given by
Tulving and Bower (1974).   One of the more successful
paradigms used was that introduced by Brown and McNeill
(1966).   They gave dictionary definitions of rare English
words to their subjects, and asked them to attempt to recall
the words defined.   The most interesting finding was that
subjects in the tip-of-the-tongue state (i.e., unable to
recall a word, but certain of knowing it) provided evidence
in their guesses that they possessed information about the
number of syllables in the word, the sound of it, and some of
its letters.   This clearly substantiates the assumption of
attribute theory that the attributes of a word are ｢

potentially separable from the word itself. In further
work, May and Clayton (1973) found evidence that subjects
could sometimes recall visual, or imaginal, information
about objects in spite of being unable to produce verbal
recall. These findings are of particular interest in that,
in most recall situations, recall is either all or none,
with the subject gaining access to most or none of the
attributes of a word.

A second experimental paradigm that has provided
information about word attributes involves the use of the
Brown-Peterson technique. On Trial 1, subjects are
presented with three words from the same class, followed by
a rehearsal-preventing task, followed by recall. The same
procedure is followed on Trials 2 and 3, with the words
continuing to be drawn from the same class. On Trial 4, the
control subjects receive three more words from the same
class, whereas the experimental subjects receive three words
drawn from a different class. Several different classes of
material have been used by Wickens (1970, 1972), including
words with a given number of phonemes, words of a
particular semantic category, and words belonging to one
language.

The general finding has been that the control subjects
show a progressive deterioration in recall performance over
trials, allegedly due to proactive inhibition, whereas the
experimental subjects show the same decline over the first
three trials, but an improvement in recall on the fourth, or
shift, trial. This improvement relative to the control
group is known as 'release from proactive inhibition'
(Wickens, Born, & Allen, 1963). Wickens (1970, 1972)
argued that the existence of the release effect when a
particular word attribute was changed between Trial 3 and
Trial 4 indicated that that attribute had been encoded by the
subject. If that attribute had not been encoded, then a
change in it could not affect performance.

Wickens (1972) has found the greatest release effects
where changes in semantic attributes were involved (e.g.,
taxonomic category shifts such as from 'door, window, cellar'
to 'bread, carrots, potatoes'), somewhat smaller release
effects with physical changes (e.g., syllable-number shifts
such as from 'bread, Main, nose' to 'rifle, spider,
airplane'), and no effect with syntactical changes (e.g.,
verb-noun shifts such as 'roam, destroy, listen' to 'earth,

house, pony'). Since subjects have only two seconds in
which to encode the three words presented on any trial, the
evidence suggests that subjects can extremely rapidly
encode information about a large variety of physical and
semantic attributes. Goggin and Wickens (1971) compared
the effects of single shifts (either from one language to
another or from one taxonomic category to another) with those
of double shifts (changing both the language and the taxonomic category), and found that the double shift produced a
greater effect than a single shift. This suggests that a
number of different attributes are normally encoded.

There are several interpretative difficulties with the
release effect. For example, since a substantial minority
of subjects commonly fails to show the release effect, it is
probable that some subjects do not encode the critical word
attribute. However, no method exists for determining which
subjects have or have not encoded appropriately.
Furthermore, it is likely that the results are affected by
'priming'. If a single word among the three presented on
each trial elicits the class or categorical response
common to all the words presented on that and the other
trials, this will prime the subject to perceive other words
in terms of their membership (or otherwise) in that category.

Another problem is that a shift between one class of items
and a second may not merely involve a change in the
attribute of interest, but may also involve a change in
correlated attributes undetected by the experimenter.
There is also the question as to the exact mechanism by which
the release effect is produced. Wickens (1970) concluded
as follows:-

> In the split second while the symbol is processed by
> the individual, it is granted a locus on many of these
> dimensions or aspects - encoded, in short, in a
> multiplicity of ways...The process of encoding symbols
> into these multiple dimensions is done - I believe -
> with tremendous alacrity and proficiency, the entries
> into many different attributes being achieved almost
> simultaneously, and with the deftness and automacity
> associated only with a highly practiced skill (p. 12).

An alternative interpretation of the release effect would
be that the initial storage of information is quite limited,
but that additional relevant attribute information is

retrieved from semantic memory at test.   Gardiner, Craik,
and Birtwistle (1972) found that a shift from garden flowers
to wild flowers, or vice versa, did not produce the release
effect, suggesting that information about the wildness or
otherwise of the flower names presented had not been encoded.
However, when an appropriate retrieval cue was presented at
recall on the shift trial (e.g., 'wild flowers'), a
significant release effect was obtained.

Another problem is that the results obtained by Wickens
(1970, 1972) seem somewhat strange in the light of his
interpretation.   Suppose, for example, that a subject
encodes ten dimensions or attributes of the word triads
presented on the first three trials, and that the words
presented on the fourth trial differ in terms of only a
single attribute.   Since the encoding overlap between the
earlier and last trials is ninety per cent, it seems
unreasonable that such a slight difference in encoding
should produce a large difference in recall.

A different kind of evidence is relevant to a determination
of the dimensions of encoding if we accept the basic tenet of
Tulving's encoding-specificity hypothesis.   This hypothesis
asserts that, "no cue, however strongly associated with the
TBR (to-be-remembered) item or otherwise related to it, can
be effective unless the TBR item is specifically encoded with
respect to that cue at the time of storage" (Thomson &
Tulving, 1970, p. 255).   In a sense, the hypothesis states
that a word attribute presented as a retrieval cue will only
facilitate recall when that attribute was encoded at input.
In studies where categorized word lists were presented to
subjects, it was frequently found that category names or
labels served as highly effective retrieval cues (see Wood,
1972, for a review).   Further evidence for the notion that
words are stored in terms of their category membership was
obtained by Rundus (1971) and by Weist (1972).   They used
categorized word lists for free recall with the words
presented in random order, and required subjects to rehearse
overtly during list presentation.   The subjects showed a
strong tendency to rehearse the members of a category
together, indicating that category membership was noticed at
input.   In addition, free recall from categorized lists
has almost invariably been found to proceed from category to
category, indicating the importance of category attributes.
However, it might be argued that such results are somewhat
contrived, in that few alternative methods of organization

were available to the subjects. Furthermore, the data
obtained from recording the temporal succession of responses
are necessarily somewhat limited, and are unlikely to reveal
the full richness of the subject's encoding techniques.

Mandler (1969) obtained interesting results with an
incremental method of presentation of categorized lists, in
which one item was added to the list on each trial. Under
such conditions, nearly forty per cent of the subjects
simply recalled the items in serial order, showing no
evidence of clustering the items by category. Even with
more traditional methods, there is evidence (e.g., Kintsch,
1970) that subjects tend to recall words in the order of
their presentation. On the other hand, Wood (1972)
showed the importance of semantic attributes in a study
utilizing a list of words that could be organized either
semantically or phonemically. Subjects were required to
sort the words into either semantic (e.g., 'parole',
kidnapping') or phonemic (e.g., 'foam', 'open') categories.
Those subjects encoding by semantic category recalled twice
as much as those encoding by phonemic attributes. Other
studies using retrieval cues, such as those of Shulman (1970)
and Bregman (1968) have found that phonemic, semantic, and
orthographic cues are all effective in improving performance.

A more formalized approach to attribute theory was
proposed by Bower (1967). He suggested that each nominal
stimulus in an experiment was able to give rise to N
possible elements, or attributes. When a nominal stimulus
is presented, s of the N elements are sampled. This
produces two sets of attributes, an active set of size s and
an inactive set of size N - s. During the retention interval
there is a certain amount of fluctuation, with conditioned
elements that move from the active to the inactive set being
replaced by unconditioned elements moving from the inactive
to the active set. Fluctuation is assumed to occur over
time as a Poisson process, i.e., in each small unit of time
there is a constant probability of an interchange. In a
recognition memory situation, new items have not previously
been presented, so that it might seem that they would have
no conditioned elements in their active set. However,
Bower (1967) assumed that some small number of their
attributes in the active set would be conditioned or
activated by the previous presentations of other items. On
a recognition test, the subject counts the number of
conditioned elements in the active set. If the number

exceeds the criterion, the subject indicates that that item
was presented previously; if it does not, he decides that
the item is a new one. While the theory has not been
tested in detail, it is clear that it can handle many of the
obtained findings. However, as Murdock (1974) pointed out,
the theory predicts that, as more and more items are
presented in a continuous recognition task, the greater will
become the number of conditioned elements among the new
items. In terms of recognition performance, the
discriminability of new from old items should decrease
during the experimental session. In fact, Donaldson and
Murdock (1968) found no deterioration in discriminability
or sensitivity, but there was a change in the response
criterion.

In sum, attribute theory emphasizes the notion put
forward by Underwood (1963) and others that a clear
distinction should be drawn between the nominal stimulus,
i.e., the stimulus as presented to the subject, and the
functional stimulus, i.e., the stimulus as encoded by the
subject. There are, however, considerable difficulties in
ascertaining what aspects of the stimulus have been encoded.
The next chapter is concerned to some extent with attempts to
distinguish between verbal and visual attributes and, as we
shall see, it has proved surprisingly difficult to decide
whether subjects are encoding visually, or verbally, or in
both these ways. Experimental work on the attributes of
memory has often involved fairly insensitive comparisons
between phonemic and semantic attributes. However, as the
chapter on semantic memory makes clear, there are in all
probability a large variety of semantic attributes
associated with any particular word or concept. For
example, as Barclay, Bransford, Franks, McCarrell, and
Nitsch (1974) have shown, a concept such as 'piano' has at
least the two semantic attributes of being a musical
instrument and of being something heavy. Indeed, it is
probable that most nouns have multiple semantic attributes,
and that a major function of adjectives is to bias one
semantic interpretation of the nouns they precede rather
than another (cf., Herriot, 1974).

If an attribute approach to human memory is to be
adequate, certain refinements are necessary. There is the
danger that we will soon have a list of several dozen
attributes apparently used by subjects in memory experiments.
For example, Turvey and Egan (1969) produced the release

effect by making the size of the display area for the to-be-
learned item smaller or larger on the shift trial than it
had been on the previous trials.   Does this indicate that
display-area size is a memorial attribute?   If so, a red
dot in the top left-hand corner of the screen would
probably also qualify as an attribute, and so on ad absurdum.

Two possible ways of preventing the proliferation of
attributes involve either the use of factor analysis or of
Tulving and Bower's (1974) reduction method.   Factor
analysis was used successfully by Osgood, Suci, and
Tannenbaum (1957) to put some order into analyses of the
connotative or affective component of word meaning.   While
there would appear to be a large number of connotative
attributes of words, Osgood et al. (1957) found through
factor analysis that the three major dimensions of affective
meaning were evaluation, potency, and activity.   It is
probable that other sets of word attributes would be found
to cluster together to form a manageable number of attribute
dimensions.

The reduction method (Tulving & Bower, 1974) stems from
Tulving's encoding-specificity hypothesis, which was
discussed earlier in this chapter.   The prime assumption is
that the effectiveness of a retrieval cue reflects the
informational overlap between the memory trace and the cue.
In the reduction method, subjects are given two or more
different retrieval cues in succession for probing each
memory trace.   For example, if the subject has learned the
word 'table', he might receive the retrieval cues or
attributes 'article of furniture' and 'starts with T',
either in that order or the reverse order.   The basic
prediction is that, if the informational content of one cue
(Cue X) is completely included in the information contained
in the second (Cue Y), then Cue Y will be totally ineffective
in producing recall if Cue X has failed to lead to recall.
On the other hand, if the information content of Cues X and
Y does not overlap at all, then they should exert separate,
additive, effects on recall probability.   The presence of
substantial or complete overlap between two attributes or
cues would indicate terminological redundancy.

Several investigators (e.g., Treisman, 1964) have
postulated that perceptual analysis involves a hierarchy of
levels or stages of analysis proceeding from the early
analysis of physical features to the later analysis of

semantic features.   Craik (1973) suggested that:

> the memory trace is one product of these perceptual
> processes, and trace persistence if a positive function
> of the depth of analysis...'Depth' is defined in terms
> of the number of analyses performed upon it...Greater
> depth usually implies more processing of the stimulus.
> Thus, with any one type of material it will take more
> time to carry out the further operations required for
> deeper levels of analysis.   When material is held
> constant, processing time is a correlate of depth of
> analysis and thus of subsequent memory performance
> (pp. 48-50).

Among the several factors leading to deeper processing,
Craik (1973) emphasized stimulus salience or intensity, the
amount of processing devoted to the stimulus, and the
compatibility of the stimulus with the analyzing structures.
Processing, however, can be divided into Type I processing,
which involves the maintenance of processing at any given
level of analysis, and Type II processing, which involves
further processing of the material to a deeper level.   It is
important to note that the term 'depth of processing' conveys
the impression that there is an invariant sequence of
processing stages, from physical to semantic and conceptual
analysis.   Craik (1973) and Craik and Lockhart (1972) were
careful to point out that they envisaged a greater degree of
flexibility in the order of processing analyses than was
implied by the terms 'depth' and 'levels'.   Primary memory,
or STS, is here defined as "the strategy of continued
attention to some aspects of the stimulus" (Craik, 1973, p.51).

At an experimental level, the major problem lies in the
identification of the processing strategies which the
subjects are using.   A direct comparison between the
memorability of information processed at different levels is
complicated by the difficulty in inducing subjects to
persevere with sub-optimal learning strategies (cf., Paivio
& Yuille, 1969).   An appropriate solution to that problem
lies in the use of incidental-learning paradigms, an
approach used in several recent studies (e.g., M. W. Eysenck,
1974d; Hyde, 1973; Hyde & Jenkins, 1969, 1973).   Subjects
were required to perform one of a number of orienting tasks
on a list of words, but were not told that they would
subsequently have to recall the words.   The orienting tasks
varied in terms of their processing requirements.   The most

important determinant of the level of subsequent recall was
whether the orienting task required that the subject
consider the meaning of the list words (i.e., a semantic
task). In general, semantic tasks led to considerably
greater recall than did non-semantic tasks, presumably
due to the greater depth of processing of the former.
However, an interpretation of such findings in terms of
qualitative differences in processing may not be warranted.
As Tulving and Bower (1974) have pointed out, the data could
equally well be explained by hypothesizing that semantic
tasks merely lead to a stronger memory trace than non-
semantic tasks. In other words, the detection of
quantitative variations in recall performance cannot be
taken as direct evidence for qualitative variations in
encoding.

Similar results using a different paradigm have been
obtained by Schulman (1971), who asked subjects to scan a
list of words for targets defined either structurally (e.g.,
words containing the letter A), or semantically (e.g., words
denoting living things). The subjects were subsequently
given an unexpected recognition test. Performance in the
semantically defined target condition was significantly
superior to that in the structurally defined conditions,
although scanning time per word was equivalent in the two
conditions.

The depth-of-processing approach has been successfully
applied to sentence memory, where the evidence indicates
that the more deeply sentences are processed, the higher the
level of recall (e.g., Anderson & Hidde, 1971; Bobrow &
Bower, 1969; Treisman & Tuxworth, 1974). Several other
studies of sentence memory (e.g., Johnson-Laird &
Stevenson, 1970; Sachs, 1967) have shown that sentence
meaning is much better retained than syntactical features
over a short retention interval.

However, other studies have produced results less
consistent with depth theory. Kolers and Ostry (1974)
presented several sentences visually to their subjects, half
in normal orientation and half inverted (the sentences, not
the subjects!), followed by a recognition test at an interval
of between three days and thirty-two days. The initial
instructions indicated that the experiment was concerned
with reading. In general, semantic information was better
retained than typographical information. However, the major

finding was that some information about typography was still
retained after thirty-two days.   Since encoding of
typographical information is an example of a shallow level
of processing, the longevity of such information is an
embarrassment to Craik and Lockhart (1972).   However, the
exact nature of the encoding processes is unclear.   Since
inverted sentences take longer to read and presumably
require greater effort than normal sentences, subjects may
retain information about the effort expended in reading
each sentence rather than about its typography.

Bregman (1968) also investigated the relative
memorability of information varying in depth.   He presented
a series of nouns interspersed with cued recall tests, and
found that phonemic, graphic, and semantic cues were all
equally effective.   However, while all three cue types
rapidly became less effective over time, there was an
indication that the semantic cues were less affected than the
other cue types by the retention interval.

Jacoby (1975) manipulated the study encoding of a list of
words so as to emphasize either the physical (i.e., sound
and spelling) or the semantic word attributes.   Subsequent
testing confirmed that the experimental manipulation had
been successful.   A recognition test indicated that
physical information was retained over the long term as well
as semantic information.   Jacoby concluded as follows:
"Since either semantic or physical information can be
retained over the long term, there must be some factor other
than the class of attributes chosen for encoding that
determines retention" (p. 251).

So far, we have seen that the prediction that material
processed at deep levels should be better retained than
material processed at shallow levels has been supported by
a number of studies (e.g., M. W. Eysenck, 1974d; Hyde &
Jenkins, 1973), but not by others (e.g., Bregman, 1968;
Kolers & Ostry, 1974; Jacoby, 1975).   The difficulty of
ascertaining the nature of a subject's processing
techniques has already been mentioned.   One approach is to
investigate the nature of the errors made on a recognition
test.   The basic procedure involves presenting subjects
with a list of words, followed by a two-alternative, forced-
choice recognition test.   Each pair of words comprises one
list word together with its synonym, its homophone, or an
unrelated word.   If only semantic information is retained,
the subject will find it easy to decide which of two

homophones was previously presented, but will have
difficulty in distinguishing between synonyms.   Conversely,
it would be easier to select the correct alternative from
synonym pairs than from homophone pairs if only phonemic
information were stored.   Studies using this paradigm
(e.g., Anisfeld, 1969; Buschke & Lenon, 1969) have found
that phonemic and semantic information is equivalently well
retained over relatively short retention intervals.   While
these investigators argued that they were studying phonemic
information by using homophone pairs, it should be noted
that there is a high correlation between pronunciation and
spelling.   This confounding of phonemic and orthographic
attributes (cf., Raser, 1972) requires investigation.
Furthermore, there are obviously many kinds of semantic
relationship that can exist between two words, and
synonymity merely defines one limited type of relationship.

Cermak, Schnorr, Buschke, and Atkinson (1970) also used
the same paradigm, and in addition instructed different
groups to remember the meaning, the sound, or the meaning
and the sound of the list words.   As Craik and Lockhart
(1972) would predict, the meaning subjects outperformed the

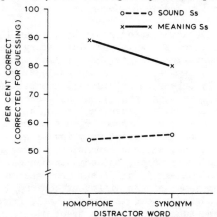

Fig. 2.3. Interaction between processing
instructions and recognition test pair type.
Adapted from Cermak et al. (1970).

sound subjects on all the recognition tests.   More
interestingly, there was a significant interaction between
instructions and recognition pair type: the meaning
subjects did better on the homophone pairs than the synonym
pairs, whereas the sound subjects did equally well on both

pair types (see Fig. 2.3). ⌡ While the main emphasis of the
Craik-Lockhart model concerns storage operations, it also
contains assumptions about the interaction between encoding
and retrieval that allow it to handle the Cermak et al.
results: "Although the distinction between availability and
accessibility (Tulving & Pearlstone, 1966) is a useful one,
the effectiveness of a retrieval cue depends on its
compatibility with the item's initial encoding or, more
generally, the extent to which the retrieval situation
reinstates the learning context" (p. 678). In other words,
deep levels of processing may or may not facilitate
retention, contingent upon the retrieval environment.

At this point, it is appropriate to consider whether
differences in retention as a function of phonemic and
semantic encoding (the two forms of encoding most commonly
compared) are really due to the fact that semantic
processing is deeper than phonemic processing. It is
possible that phonemic information is more poorly retained
than semantic information because it is exposed to more
highly similar interfering information during the retention
interval. This seems likely in view of the limited number
of phonemes in the English language.

A second alternative interpretation assumes that the
successful recall of words in most laboratory experiments
depends upon contextual tagging of the list words at input.
Since all the words presented to the subject are known to
him, he can only subsequently discriminate between the to-be-
remembered words and the other words he knows on the basis of
ancillary information, or contextual tags, stored with each
word. Jacoby (1974) has argued, with supporting evidence,
that phonemic encoding is relatively invariant across
different situations, whereas semantic encoding is context
dependent. In other words, the semantic encoding of a given
word in a given context is different from the semantic
encoding of the same word in different contexts, and so one
semantic encoding of a word is discriminable from prior
encodings of the same word. This trace discriminability
may be lacking in the case of phonemic encoding. An
interesting experiment to investigate this hypothesis would
be one in which subjects in an incidental-learning situation
were given a list of words whose pronunciation broke the
phonological rules of English (e.g., deny; subtle; sew).
Some subjects would be asked to read out the words, whereas
others would be told to read them as if they conformed to
phonological rules. The far greater distinctiveness of the
phonological encoding produced by the latter group of subjects

might produce superior retention.

A third interpretation of the results might be that
subjects spontaneously attempt to generate semantic rather
than phonemic retrieval cues when engaged in list recall.
It is essential to note that these three interpretations
emphasize quite different variables to the depth-of-
processing approach, and have not systematically been
compared with it in the research literature.

Craik (1973) predicted from his depth theory that deep
levels of analysis of the presented material would take
longer to complete than shallow levels of analysis. In
Experiment IV, Craik (1973) obtained evidence that
supported the prediction.   However, it is only strictly
necessary for deeper levels of processing to require longer
on the assumption that processing invariably proceeds from
physical to semantic, an assumption which Craik and
Lockhart (1972) rejected.   Shulman (1970), using a totally
different paradigm, also found that phonemic information was
more rapidly encoded than semantic information. On the
other hand, Gardiner (1974) asked subjects to search for
targets either containing particular phonemes or belonging
to a semantic category, and found that the semantic-
processing task was more rapidly performed than the
phonemic-processing task.

A third aspect of depth theory which has received
experimental investigation is the distinction between Type I
processing, involving the maintenance of the products of
analysis at one level, and Type II processing, involving
deeper processing of the material.   As Craik (1973) pointed
out, the high level of immediate recall combined with the
low levels of subsequent recall of the final items in a free-
recall list could be due either to their lack of re .earsal
(Rundus, 1971) or to their exposure to Type I proce 3ing
only.   In an experiment discussed earlier in this chapter,
Craik (1973) induced subjects to spend a disproportionate
amount of time rehearsing the last few items in a list, but
found that later recall of these items was still poor.
This indicates that the type of processing is more
important than the amount.   If the last few items in the
list were to receive Type II processing, then they should be
well recalled on a subsequent retention test.   As predicted,
Mazuryk (1974) found that subjects required to generate
verbal associates to the final items in a list showed

considerably better LTS recall of them than did subjects
who rehearsed overtly or engaged in silent learning.

Summary

   In sum, there is confirmatory evidence for all the
predictions of depth theory, but there are several
unresolved theoretical and methodological problems and some
negative evidence.   While it seems intuitively reasonable
that deeply encoded traces are usually more enduring than
superficially encoded traces, there is no adequate
theoretical conceptualization as to why this should be so.
Furthermore, the rationale underlying recent categorizations
of features and attributes into physical, linguistic, and
semantic is unclear.   There is no guarantee that these
are the optimal categories, or that it is appropriate to
equate the storage of physical characteristics with shallow
levels of processing.

   In the majority of studies, the decision to consider the
subjects' level of processing as deep or shallow was based
upon intuition rather than objective measurement.   For
example, pictorial stimuli are usually well recognized on a
retention test, suggesting that they have received a deep
level of processing.   This deep level of processing is
commonly thought of as involving imagery.   However, one
might equally well argue that imaginal processing of
pictorial stimuli merely involves the storage of some of the
physical attributes of the stimuli (i.e., the visual
characteristics) and so represents a shallow level of
processing.   There is the danger of using the retention-
test performance to provide information about the depth of
processing, and then using the alleged depth of processing
to 'explain' the retention-test performance, thus producing
a vicious circle.   Craik and Lockhart (1972) proposed a
partial solution to this problem, suggesting that deep
levels of analysis should take more time than shallow levels.
Unfortunately, as we have seen, there is much evidence that
this is an imprecise index of processing depth.   The
difficulty of ascertaining the nature of processing can be
illustrated with reference to work by Hyde and Jenkins (1973)
and by Mandler and Worden (1973).   Hyde and Jenkins argued
that judging the part of speech of words was a non-semantic
task, whereas Mandler and Worden considered the identification of words as nouns or verbs to be a semantic
processing task.

   Craik and Tulving (1975) have proposed some extensions of

the general theoretical approach, arguing that both the
depth of encoding and the spread or elaboration of encoding
within the various encoding domains are important
determinants of memory performance.   The more attributes of
a word that are encoded at input, particularly those at the
deep levels, the more elaborate will be the resultant memory
trace./ They concluded as follows: "Greater degrees of
integration (or, alternatively, greater degrees of
elaboration of the target word) may support higher retention
in the subsequent test.   Effective elaboration of an
encoding requires further descriptive attributes which are
(a) salient, or applicable to the event and (b) specify the
event more (sic) uniquely" (p. 282).

Relatively few attempts have been made to manipulate
experimentally the spread of encoding.   However, the seventh
experiment of Craik and Tulving (1975) included the technique
of asking the subjects whether or not a tachistoscopically
presented word fitted a given sentence.   The amount of
spread of encoding was manipulated by utilizing sentence
frames varying from the simple (e.g., "He dropped the ---")
to the complex (e.g., "The old man hobbled across the room
and picked up the valuable --- from the mahogany table").
Subsequent retention of the target words was significantly
affected by sentence-frame complexity.   However, while
these sentence frames differ in terms of the number of
semantic features they contain, they may also differ in their
relevance to the tachistoscopically presented word and in
imageability.

Further evidence that the spread of processing is an
important determinant of retentivity has been obtained in
studies using imagery instructions (e.g., Bower, 1970;
Morris & Stevens, 1974).   Morris and Stevens presented
their subjects with a list of words, and required them either
to form interactive images of groups of words or to produce
separate images of each word.   In spite of the fact that the
same depth of imaginal processing was presumably utilized
under both instructional sets, interactive imagery produced
much greater recall.

M. W. Eysenck (1977) has pointed to the lack of attention
to output processes as the major inadequacy of the depth
approach:

Craik and Lockhart (1972), in their attempt to describe

the memory trace, have focussed on input operations
such as the nature of the stimulus and the instructions
presented to the subject. However, the greatest
understanding of an intervening variable such as the
memory trace is likely to emerge from a simultaneous
consideration of input and output operations. Since
any single measure of retention is likely to provide us
with data representing an amalgam of memory-trace
variance and test-specific variance, it would seem that
the use of two or more retention measures is advisable.

   Since in many ways the attempt to specify more precisely
the nature of the memory trace is the fundamental problem of
theorists concerned with information storage, further
discussion of this issue seems warranted. A prevalent
assumption is that the major source of information about the
memory trace is the relationship between input to the memory
system and output from the system. Thus, for example, the
finding that word familiarity is positively correlated with
probability of recall has been taken as evidence that more
familiar words produce stronger memory traces. It has
already been pointed out that such an approach precludes
identification of qualitative differences among traces, since
the only available index is the quantitative one of recall
probability. Furthermore, Tulving and Watkins (1975) have
uncovered other major disadvantages associated with the
practice of inferring the characteristics of memory traces
on the basis of a single retention-test measure:-
             (1) Interpretative problems abound when it is
found that different patterns of memory performance are
obtained with different types of retention test. For
example, a simple strength theory cannot explain the common
finding that familiar words are better recalled but less
well recognized than rare words. In order to avoid such
embarrassments, many experimenters have quite unwarrantedly
used invariant retrieval conditions.
             (2) Since so little information is obtained
about the characteristics of the memory trace, there is a
natural tendency to regard the memory trace as a pallid copy
of what was presented to the subject.
             (3) The fact that the trace is defined as a
relationship between input and output means that its
characterization includes a description of input conditions.
Such an approach makes it difficult to conceptualize
important qualitative differences between what is presented
at input and the memory trace.

Tulving and Watkins (1975) argued that the best method of ascertaining the nature of the memory trace was to engage in the successive probing of a given trace with two or more different types of retrieval cue. The assumption that any retrieval cue is effective only to the extent that its informational contents match the information contained in the memory trace, an assumption known as the encoding specificity principle, is made by Tulving and Watkins. It then follows that the observed effectiveness of different retrieval cues can be taken as evidence about the characteristics of the trace. It also follows that the greater the variety of retrieval cues utilized, the more complete will be the resultant description of the trace. If memory traces consist of structural aggregates of trace elements or attributes, then some kind of successive probe retention test seems essential if a satisfactory account of the memory trace is to be provided.

M. W. Eysenck (1977) proposed that the recall of information from memory involves at least five different stages or processes, which are assumed to occur serially:
   (1) Presentation of a retrieval cue;
   (2) Rule or strategy formulation, including a determination of the size of the search set to be used;
   (3) Item search, in which the search process operates on the specified search set and produces one or more items;
   (4) Evaluation, in which any responses generated by the search process are evaluated in terms of the current rule or strategy and the experimental requirements;
   (5) Emission, in which items positively evaluated are produced.

A plausible hypothesis is that the depth of processing primarily affects the stage of item search rather than the stages of rule formulation or evaluation. This could explain the results of some of the studies already discussed (e.g., Bregman, 1968; Jacoby, 1975; Kolers & Ostry, 1974). In all these studies, all of which obtained small or no differences between physical and semantic information, retention tests were used that minimized the importance of the search process (e.g., recognition tests and certain cued-recall tests). Furthermore, Nelson and Brooks (1974) found that rhymes and synonyms were equally effective as retrieval cues, and Light (1972), utilizing quasi-recognition tests, found that homophones were actually superior to synonyms as retrieval cues.

✓ Further evidence that deep levels of processing do not
necessarily facilitate evaluation comes in a study by
Bransford, Barclay, and Franks (1972), who found that
people could not discriminate on a recognition test between
a to-be-remembered sentence such as "The woman stood on the
stool and the mouse sat on the floor beneath it" and a
similarly worded inference (e.g., "The woman stood on the
stool and the mouse sat on the floor beneath her"). While
there was evidence that the subjects used deep levels of
processing at input, this obviously did not facilitate
recognition performance.

The importance of the rule or strategy formulation stage
can be seen in recent work by Morton (1975). Subjects were
asked to say as many colour names as possible, and there
were noticeable individual differences in performance.
Some subjects tended to recall the more familiar colour
names, and seemed to be merely looking for strong associates
of the word 'colour', whereas other subjects recalled
systematically the colours of the rainbow and failed to
recall some common colour names. Those who recalled the
colours of the rainbow were more likely to recall 'indigo'
than 'brown', in spite of the presumably stronger memorial
representation of 'brown'. An implication of this result
is that memory performance frequently depends more on the
retrieval strategy adopted than on the encoded depth of
stored information.

Lockhart, Craik, and Jacoby (1976) have recently
suggested some amendments to the depth-spread theory.
While they continue to argue that, "both recall and
recognition are superior when 'deeper', 'richer', 'more
semantic' traces are formed at input" (p. 86), they now feel
that two basic modes of retrieval should be distinguished:
reconstruction and scanning. Reconstruction involves
attempting to construct an encoding corresponding to an
encoding produced at the time of learning, whereas scanning
involves searching recent traces for the presence of some
salient feature. While the factors determining which
retrieval mode is utilized are unclear, Craik et al. propose
that scanning for some distinctive feature is more feasible
when short retention intervals are used. Their major
prediction is that depth of processing is an important
determinant of the probability of successful reconstruction,

but is less relevant when scanning is used.

As support for their modified theory, they cited a study by Craik and Jacoby (1975), in which subjects were instructed to encode information structurally, phonemically, or semantically.   Recognition tests at relatively short retention intervals were interspersed with presentation trials, and revealed no differences in recognition memory as a function of encoding instructions, possibly because the scanning mode of retrieval was used.   However, on a subsequent, unexpected recall test, semantically processed material was much better recalled than phonemically or structurally processed material, possibly due to the fact that subjects used the reconstruction mode of retrieval.

As Craik and Tulving (1975) noted, their theoretical approach forms a part of the general shift of interest in memory research from external, or situational, stimuli to internal mental events and processes:

> In the experiments we have described here, these important determinants of the strength of associations and traces were held constant: nominal identity of items, pre-experimental associations among items, intralist similarity, frequency, recency, instructions to 'learn' the materials, the amount and duration of interpolated activity.   The only thing that was manipulated was the mental activity of the learner, yet, as the results showed, memory performance was dramatically affected by these activities (p. 292).

Their general approach has the advantage of offering an alternative to the prevalent obsessional devotion to relatively minor paradigms and phenomena (Newell, 1973). It is almost certainly the case that there are important inter-paradigm similarities in the mental processes used by laboratory subjects, and Craik and Lockhart (1972) have encouraged us to consider these processing commonalities. On the other hand, as we have seen, there is a variety of difficulties with the Craik-Lockhart viewpoint: neither depth nor spread can be satisfactorily indexed;   some of the experimental evidence is inconsistent with the model; retrieval processes are under-emphasized;   the proposed classification of word attributes into physical, phonemic, and semantic is ad hoc;   and alternative theoretical accounts can explain many of the findings.

In sum, it appears that the greatest strength of depth
theory is the source of its greatest weakness. The attempt
to focus on the stimulus-as-encoded rather than the
stimulus-as-presented is surely correct. However, our
present experimental techniques only supply us with
tantalizing glimpses of what is encoded. If someone throws
a sackful of money into the middle of a hedge on a dark
night, it has been argued, the psychologist will insist on
looking for it under the nearby street light. The
psychologist's reason for this is that he can only see
clearly what he is doing while in proximity to the light.
Analogously, memory psychologists in the past have too
frequently concentrated on what is simple but irrelevant:
the stimulus-as-presented.

Summary

The research literature contains a mass of evidence
indicating the value of distinguishing theoretically between
STS and LTS. However, while there is consensus that a
prime characteristic of the short-term store is its limited
capacity, agreement is less marked with respect to its other
characteristics. On the one hand, Glanzer and Razel (1974)
have found that the capacity of STS is appropriately measured
in terms of the number of sentences that it can hold,
indicating that high-level cognitive processing occurs in
STS. On the other hand, Baddeley et al. (1975) found that
the memory span for words was constrained by the time
required to articulate the words, suggesting that the
capacity of STS should be measured in terms of phonemic or
similar units. From this finding, STS is a relatively
primitive mechanism that stores the results of rather low-
level processing.

Baddeley has proposed a solution to some of the problems
of STS in his concept of working memory. Working memory
comprises a central processor, that is capable of high-level
cognitive functioning, and an articulatory loop, that
involves more primitive processing. Many of the
contradictions in the literature seem capable of resolution
within this new framework.

While an understanding of the structural limitations of
the human information processing system is one prerequisite
of an adequate account of information storage, the

qualitatively and quantitatively different processing strategies applied to incoming information must also be considered.   Several theorists assume that the memory trace consists of a variety of qualitatively distinct attributes or features (e.g., phonemic, semantic, visual), and the processes generating the trace have been assumed to vary in their depth and spread.   It is clear that memory traces do differ in terms of their encoded features, and it is also obvious that the number and variety of encoded features importantly determine subsequent memory performance. However, the search continues for improved methods of determining more precisely the nature of the memory trace, with the reduction or successive probe method introduced by Tulving and Bower (1974) being the currently most successful approach.   As they pointed out, the more varieties of retention test and retrieval cue used in connection with each memory trace, the more complete and accurate will be the resultant description of the memory trace.

In sum, a reasonable conceptualization of the structural and processing components of the information processing system is available in recent research, but more empirical and theoretical precision is required for the key concepts: STS, LTS, attributes, depth, spread, and memory trace.

CHAPTER 3
IMAGERY

The previous chapter dealt, among other issues, with the nature of the encoding processes used by people when storing information. While the major theoretical emphasis in that chapter was on the depth of such processing, it is clearly important to distinguish among the varieties of processing at any given level. One of the more important of such distinctions is that between verbal and imaginal processing, both of which are frequently assumed to represent deep levels of processing (e.g., Bower, 1972; Paivio, 1971a). There are several developmental theories which emphasize the importance of the imaginal and verbal modes of representation (e.g., Bruner, Olver, & Greenfield, 1966; Piaget & Inhelder, 1966). Bruner et al. (1966), for example, hypothesized that children exhibit the sequential emergence of three modes of representation, starting with the enactive, or motor, proceeding through the ikonic, or imaginal, and concluding with the symbolic, which is largely verbal in nature.

In spite of the widespread theoretical and empirical interest in imagery as a form of processing qualitatively distinct from verbal processing, the evidence is more equivocal than one would like. However, considerable progress has been made over the past ten years or so, and the intractable methodological problems that have been encountered are those that follow from any determined attempt to discover what intervenes between the presentation of a stimulus and the emission of a response.

The study of mental imagery received an initial impetus from the early investigations of Galton (1883). In one approach, he asked several people to imagine their breakfast table that morning, and to decide how clearly they could visualize it. As subsequent researchers have found, there were substantial individual differences, and some people reported that they had no conscious mental imagery. Galton also found out, in studying his own associations to words, that words varied considerably in terms of the amount of imagery they evoked. The behaviourist revolution in the

early years of the twentieth century led to the rejection of
mentalistic concepts such as 'imagery', but recent years
have witnessed a dramatic return to favour of work on
imagery, which has been ably documented by Paivio (1971a).

Several rather different definitions of the concept of
'imagery' have been suggested, but most of them point to a
close, although unclear, relationship with perception (e.g.,
Segal, 1971). Evidence for this relationship was obtained
by Segal and Fusella (1970). They asked their subjects to
form both auditory and visual images, and also to detect
both auditory and visual signals. The main finding was that
auditory images interfered more with the detection of
auditory signals than with the detection of visual signals,
whereas visual images interfered more with the detection of
visual signals. A reasonable conclusion is that visual
perception and visual imagery share common processes, as do
auditory perception and auditory imagery. Shepard and
Chipman (1970) asked American subjects to rank fifteen
American states from memory for degree of similarity,
followed by the same ranking in the presence of outline
drawings of the same states. The correlation between the
rankings under the memory condition and the picture condition
was positive and highly significant, the data seeming to
indicate that it was mainly the geometrical or pictorial
properties of the shapes which formed the basis for
judgement.

Evidence of this kind has led to definitions such as that
of Neisser (1972): "A subject is imaging whenever he employs
some of the same cognitive processes that he would use in
perceiving, but when the stimulus input that would normally
give rise to such perception is absent" (p. 245). However,
several problems remain. For example, Pylyshyn (1973) has
raised a number of important questions which have as yet
received no satisfactory answer at an empirical level. How
similar is a visual image to some conceivable picture? If a
visual image does resemble a picture in some of its
characteristics, must it always be a picture of some specific
instance, or can it be generic? Do images necessarily have
to be conscious? Is an entire image available at once, or
do parts of it come and go?

Basic Experimental Findings

Stimulus Attributes

At an experimental level, the main finding has been that concrete, or high-imagery words are better retained than abstract words, this result having been obtained in studies of paired-associate learning, free recall, serial learning, and recognition memory (Paivio, 1969; Paivio, 1971a). In most studies, decisions about word concreteness and word imagery have been based upon norms prepared by Paivio, Yuille, and Madigan (1968). These norms list subjects' ratings of several hundred nouns on the dimensions of imagery, i.e., the extent to which each word evokes imagery, and concreteness-abstractness, i.e., the extent to which each word refers to sense experience. They found that word concreteness and word imagery correlated +.83 with each other, so that both sets of ratings have commonly been used as equivalent indices of the imagery-evoking characteristics of nouns. However, there is recent evidence (e.g., Richardson, 1975a, 1975b), discussed in detail later in this chapter, indicating the non-equivalence of concreteness and imagery.

In a major study, Paivio (1968) obtained data from nouns on a total of 30 variables, including scores on free recall and paired-associate learning, and a selection of word characteristics thought to be relevant in verbal-learning tasks (e.g., frequency, imagery, concreteness, interest, meaningfulness, familiarity, emotionality). Noun imagery and concreteness correlated more highly with performance on the paired-associate and free-recall tasks than did the other word characteristics, thus indicating that imagery is a particularly important determinant of recall. However, purely correlational studies suffer from a number of disadvantages, and a variable such as word frequency, which has been found to be a good predictor of retention in dozens of studies, cannot be overthrown on the basis of a single study.

Accordingly, Paivio then carried out a series of more systematic studies of which we shall take the Paivio and Madigan (1970) study as an illustration. They noted that word imagery and word frequency tend to be highly correlated, so that it is difficult to decide whether to attribute one's results to the operation of imagery or of frequency. Their strategy was to select four classes of nouns (viz., high

imagery, high frequency;   high imagery, low frequency;   low
imagery, high frequency;   and low imagery, low frequency)
and to compare the recall performance of nouns in these
various categories.   The results of this study indicated
that imagery was a powerful predictor of recall, but that
word frequency per se was of marginal significance.

While a large number of studies have found that concrete
words are better remembered than abstract words, the proper
interpretation is in doubt.   The essential difficulty stems
from the existence of correlated attributes.   In an
experiment on imagery, we may select two groups of nouns, one
group concrete and the other group abstract.   We can only
assert with confidence that any performance difference
between the two groups of nouns is due to the concreteness-
abstractness variable if there are no other systematic
differences between the two groups of nouns.   However,
several other word attributes, such as word frequency and
meaningfulness, are known to correlate with concreteness-
abstractness.   Accordingly, we can select groups of concrete
and abstract nouns in such a way that they are equivalent in
terms of word frequency and meaningfulness.   It is, however,
logically impossible to ensure that the concrete and abstract
words do not differ importantly in terms of yet further
correlated attributes.

Kintsch (1972b) argued that abstract nouns were more
likely than concrete nouns to be lexically complex.   A
lexically complex item is one that can be decomposed
lexically into a simpler form (e.g., 'wisdom' can be
decomposed into 'wise').   Kintsch found that lexical
complexity had highly significant effects on paired-associate
learning, but that there was a residual effect of word
imagery even when lexical complexity was controlled.
Similar results with free recall were reported by
Richardson (1975a).

The implicit assumption has been made by most researchers
that the image-arousing capacity of nouns is unaffected by
the context in which they occur.   This assumption has been
shown to be invalid by Begg and Clark (1975).   They found
that words were rated as higher in imagery and were better
remembered when they were presented in a high-imagery
context than a low-imagery context.   Thus, for example, the
word 'view' was rated as higher in imageability in the phrase
'view from the balcony' than in the phrase 'in view of the

evidence'.   Begg and Clark also found that imagery ratings
of words presented in isolation, as in the Paivio et al.
(1968) norms, were based on subject-produced contexts.   The
selection of a particular context depended on the relative
frequency with which that context had been encountered.   An
important implication of this study is that the image-evoking
capacity of any given word may be a more complex and flexible
matter than has hitherto been assumed.

Other studies have considered memory for pictorial
stimuli.   Shepard (1967) presented his subjects with 540
words, 612 sentences, or 612 coloured pictures, followed by
an immediate two-alternative, forced-choice recognition test.
The percentages of correct choices were 88 per cent for the
words, 89 per cent for the sentences, and 97 per cent for the
pictures.   Other subjects who were tested three or seven
days after learning obtained correct percentages of 92 per
cent and 87 per cent respectively on the picture stimuli.
However, it should be noted that the superiority of the
pictures could be due to the use of easier distractor items
with pictures than with the other types of material.

Even more striking evidence of the memory capacity for
pictures was provided by Standing, Conezio, and Haber (1970).
They presented subjects with 2,560 slides over a period of
four successive days, and gave a two-alternative, forced-
choice recognition test one hour after the completion of the
presentation trials.   The percentages correct were 95, 93,
and 85 per cent for the three subjects.   Unlike the pictures
in Shepard's (1967) study, which were selected for low
confusability, many of the pictures used by Standing et al.
came from the same categories (e.g., there were 300 pictures
of male adults and 200 pictures of female adults).

The nature of the pictorial stimuli is obviously an
important determinant of performance.   For example,
Goldstein and Chance (1971) asked their subjects to view
faces, ink-blots, or snow crystals.   On a subsequent
recognition test, performance was considerably better for
faces than for ink-blots, and worst of all for snow crystals.

Other studies have directly compared recognition memory
for concrete words and their pictorial equivalents.
Snodgrass, Volvovitz, and Walfish (1972) presented subjects
with words and drawings, and found that recognition
performance after a retention interval of two minutes was

considerably better for the drawings than for the words.

There are several differences between verbal and pictorial stimuli, any of which might account for the memorial superiority of pictures. One obvious possibility is that the recognition results are due to the fact that pictorial stimuli contain extra details which are not contained in the verbal stimuli. In order to investigate this hypothesis, Nelson, Metzler, and Reed (1974) presented their subjects with one of the following types of stimulus: black-and-white photographs, verbal descriptions of the main theme of the photographs, unembellished line drawings of the main theme of the photographs, or main-theme line drawings embellished with extra details from the photographs. Recognition tests were given both seven minutes and seven weeks after the items had been studied. All the pictorial and drawing conditions produced significantly better short- and long-term recognition memory than the verbal-description condition, and the rate of recognition loss between the two retention intervals was greater for the verbal-description condition than for the other conditions. All of the picture and drawing conditions produced equivalent findings, suggesting that the amount of detail contained in the stimulus is not a critical factor.

On the other hand, Loftus and Bell (1975) used the same stimuli as Nelson et al. (1974), but found that recognition memory was significantly better for photographs than for drawings. Since Loftus and Bell presented the stimuli at a much faster rate than Nelson et al., it seems that the rate of extraction of information from pictures is quicker than from drawings.

Paivio's (1971a) hypothesis that pictures are encoded primarily by imaginal processes was investigated by Wyant, Banks, Berger, and Wright (1972). Subjects were given a two-alternative, forced-choice recognition test one hour after viewing a set of pictures for either three or ten seconds each. The recognition test pairs had previously been rated by other subjects for visual similarity and for the ease with which the differences between them could be verbally described. The main finding was that picture recognition was considerably higher where verbal describability of the differences between the members of the recognition test pair was high than when it was low. In addition, recognition following the three-second presentation rate was slightly affected by the visual similarity of the test pairs, though

less than would have been anticipated on Paivio's (1971a)
hypothesis.

Instructions

A second approach to the investigation of the effects of
imagery on learning and memory is by means of variations in
instructions.   This work is particularly associated with
the work of Bower (e.g., 1972).   In a typical experiment,
Bower and Winzenz (1970) required subjects to learn a list of
paired associates after receiving one out of four sets of
instructions: (1) repetition condition: repeat each pair
silently during the study time; (2) sentence-reading
condition: the stimulus and response words were embedded in
a sentence which the subject was to read aloud; (3) sentence-
generation condition: the subject was asked to make up and
say aloud a meaningful utterance relating the two words of
each pair; (4) imagery condition: the subject was to form
an image in which the two referents (denoted by the words)
were in some kind of vivid interaction.   The percentage
correct recall was 37 per cent for the repetition condition,
54 per cent for the sentence-reading condition, 77 per cent
for the sentence-generation condition, and 87 per cent for
the imagery condition.   The general finding in other studies
has been that imagery instructions lead to as high or higher
levels of recall than other types of instructions.

Bower (1970) argued that the efficacy of imagery
instructions in paired-associate learning might be due to the
greater distinctiveness of imaginal representation compared
to other forms of representation, or it might be due to a
stronger stimulus-response association.   Some subjects were
instructed to learn a list of paired associates by
constructing interactive scenes in imagery, while others
were told to form images of the objects non-interacting and
separated.   Interactive imagery led to recall that was
considerably higher than that obtained under the separation-
imagery instructions; indeed, separation imagery led to
retention as poor as that of a rote repetition control group.
Bower (1970) concluded that, "the fact that separation-
imagery subjects recall so poorly is evidence that the
customary benefit of imagery in paired associates learning is
in the associative part, not the stimulus differentiation
part" (p. 532).

Anderson and Bower (1973) proposed an alternative

of these results, pointing out that an interactive image of
A and B can be represented as the abstract proposition 'A
verbs B', whereas separation imagery would only be
represented as 'A and B'. Thus the effectiveness of
interactive imagery may be due to the resultant semantic and
conceptual integration.

Paivio and Foth (1970) combined the stimulus-attribute and
the instructional approaches. They argued that imagery
instructions should have a greater facilitatory effect on the
learning of concrete paired associates than on the learning
of abstract pairs. However, earlier studies had failed to
obtain this result (see Paivio, 1969), possibly because
subjects are reluctant to utilize sub-optimal processing
techniques. Paivio and Foth asked subjects to generate
either images or verbal mediators to assist them in the
learning of a list of paired associates. The subjects were
also required to draw their images on paper, and to write
down their verbal mediators, in order to exert more
experimental control over the subjects' strategies.
Relative to the verbal mediation condition, imagery
instructions facilitated the recall of concrete items, and
had a detrimental effect on the recall of abstract items.

The basic problem with attempts to manipulate encoding
processes by means of different sets of instructions is that
one cannot be sure that the instructions have produced the
intended effect. For example, Paivio and Yuille (1969)
found it was extremely difficult to induce subjects to use
sub-optimal learning strategies. A partial solution to
this problem lies in the use of incidental rather than
intentional learning instructions.

Individual Differences
A third approach to the problem of determining the effects
of imagery on learning has considered individual differences
in imagery ability. The tests used to measure imagery
ability have been of two basic kinds: (a) verbal report
tests, in which the subject indicates how vivid, colourful,
and so on his images are (e.g., the Betts Vividness of
Imagery Scale, Betts, 1909; the Gordon Test of Visual
Imagery Control, Gordon, 1949); (b) tests of spatial ability
(e.g., the Revised Minnesota Paper Form Board, and the Space
Relations test of the Differential Aptitude Test Battery,
Bennett, Seashore, & Wesman, 1963).

There have been several studies in which high-imagery
subjects performed more effectively than low-imagery
subjects on those tasks hypothesized to favour imaginal
mediation, whereas low-imagery subjects outperformed high-
imagery subjects on tasks favouring verbal mediation.
These results have been obtained both where verbal report
tests were used (e.g., Sheehan, 1966a, 1966b), and where
tests of spatial ability were used (e.g., Hollenberg, 1970;
Klee & M. W. Eysenck, 1973; Kuhlman, 1960; Stewart, 1965).
However, many investigators have failed to find significant
performance differences between subjects classified as low
and high in imagery ability.

Strong evidence that the verbal report and spatial ability
tests are not measuring the same imaginal processes was
obtained by DiVesta, Ingersoll, and Sunshine (1971). They
factor analyzed data from tests of verbal ability, spatial
ability tests, and verbal report tests. Three factors were
extracted, with the verbal report tests of imagery ability
and the spatial ability tests loading on different factors,
i.e., the spatial ability tests did not correlate with the
verbal report tests. Interestingly, scores on the verbal
report tests of imagery ability were highly correlated with
scores on the Marlowe-Crowne Social Desirability Scale
(Crowne & Marlowe, 1964), possibly because the ability to
produce images is a culturally desirable trait. However,
unpublished work by one of my students (Susan Bibby) has
failed to replicate this finding. An obvious limitation of
the verbal report method is that it assumes that all imagery
is necessarily conscious, which is an unduly restrictive
assumption.

Theoretical Implications

Findings such as those discussed in the previous section
have been incorporated into a major theory by Paivio (1969,
1971a, 1971b). He has drawn a distinction between verbal
and imaginal codes or processes. The precise defining
characteristics of these two forms of processing are unclear,
as can be seen in the following quotation from Paivio (1971b):

> One mode is related directly to speech itself; that is,
> we can think in terms of words and their interrelations
> and these implicit verbal processes can mediate our
> language behaviour. The other code is nonverbal and is

presumably tied closely to the private experience that
we call imagery (p. 7).

While Paivio (1971a) postulated that there were rich and
complex relationships between the two codes, he also
assumed that different kinds of stimulus material had
differential access to the two codes, as indicated in Fig.
3.1.   The greater the number of plus signs, the greater the
availability of the appropriate code.

TYPE OF STIMULUS	CODING SYSTEM(S) USED	
	IMAGINAL	VERBAL
PICTURE	+ + +	+ +
CONCRETE WORD	+	+ + +
ABSTRACT WORD	−	+ + +

Fig. 3.1. Availability of imaginal and
verbal processes as a function of type
of stimulus.   Adapted from Paivio (1971a).

The evidence reviewed above has indicated that pictures
are better remembered than concrete words, which in turn are
better remembered than abstract words, as predicted by the
dual-coding model.   Pictorial information is commonly
processed thoroughly both imaginally and verbally, whereas
concrete and abstract words are weakly processed at an
imaginal level, if at all.   However, while imaginal coding
enhances information storage, there may be problem of
decoding the imaginal representation into the appropriate
verbal form on a subsequent recall test.   A final
assumption of the dual-coding model (Paivio, 1971a) is that
visual imagery is specialized for parallel processing in a
spatial sense, but not for sequential processing, whereas
verbal memory codes are specialized for serial or
sequential processing because of the essentially sequential

nature of the auditory-speech system.

A major difficulty with Paivio's theory is the imprecise
description of the two main processes, imaginal and verbal.
The evidence relating to attribute theory and the levels-of-
processing approach indicates that there is a considerable
variety of verbal processes, and the same is surely true of
imaginal processes. For example, Bower, Karlin, and Dueck
(1975) asked subjects to study nonsensical pictures. Half
the subjects received no interpretation of the pictures,
whereas the other half heard clarifying phrases. For
example, Fig. 3.2 shows the rear end of a pig disappearing
into the fog.

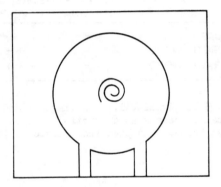

Fig. 3.2. The rear end of a pig. Adapted
from Bower, Karlin, and Dueck (1975).

In spite of the probable use of imagery by all subjects,
recall was considerably higher where an interpretation was
provided, indicating that one must distinguish between
interpreted and uninterpreted images. The process which
interprets the product of the imaginal process is
presumably some non-imaginal process of an abstract and
conceptual nature. The point at issue has been clearly
expressed by Humphrey (1951), who argued that, while the
process of thinking "may involve some sense-resembling
processes of a particular modality...this is the cart, not
the horse. The primary 'work' when one thinks a
proposition such as 'Russia is East of Britain' is

imageless" (p. 106).

The argument can be extended to the paired-associate
learning situation, which has frequently been used to test
Paivio's hypotheses.   It is assumed that subjects learn
paired associates such as 'child-brick' by forming an image
of a small boy sitting on the ground constructing a tower of
bricks with his hands.   The problem, as Pylyshyn (1973) has
indicated, is to explain why the subsequent presentation of
the word 'child' leads the subject to respond 'brick' rather
than 'ground', 'tower', 'hands', 'boy', or any of the other
responses that are suggested by the image.   The answer
presumably is that the stored representation of a paired
associate is much closer to being a description of the scene
suggested by the pair of words than it is to a picture of it.

As was mentioned earlier in the chapter, common
assumptions are that word concreteness and imagery are
equivalent measures, and that both reflect the image-arousing
capacity of words.   However, there are several recent studies
that show that both these assumptions are incorrect.
Increasing emphasis is being placed on a distinction between
concreteness, defined as a fundamental semantic feature of a
word, and imagery, defined as an encoding strategy applied to
incoming material.   Richardson (1975a), in a free-recall
study, included some words that were high in imagery and low
in concreteness (e.g., fantasy, happiness) and other words
that were low in imagery and high in concreteness (e.g.,
charlatan, socialist).   Two findings pointed to the non-
equivalence of word imagery and concreteness: (1) recall was
significantly related to imagery but not to concreteness;
and (2) there was a significant interaction between
concreteness and imagery, with the enhancement effect of high
imagery being obtained only with abstract words.   In a
second study, Richardson (1975b) found that word imagery but
not concreteness was related to free recall when imagery
instructions were given.   This finding suggests that the
subject's use of imaginal processing is largely unrelated to
the concreteness-abstractness dimension.

Baddeley, Grant, Wight, and Thomson (1975) investigated
the processing of concrete and abstract material in more
detail.   In their initial experiment, they required
subjects to learn either easily visualized material or
non-visualizeable material concurrently with the performance
of a visual tracking task, which involved the subjects in

tracking a light moving along a circular track.   They
discovered that the tracking task had a highly detrimental
effect on retention of the easily visualized material, but
not on retention of the non-visualizeable material.   The
most natural interpretation of this finding is that subjects
were using imaginal processing with the visualizeable
material.   In a subsequent experiment using concrete and
abstract paired associates, Baddeley et al. found that the
tracking task produced an equivalent decrement in recall of
the concrete and abstract pairs.   This indicates quite
strongly that concrete material was not more likely than
abstract material to be processed imaginally.

More evidence that matters are more complex than was
originally assumed was obtained by Griffith and Johnston
(1973).   Their subjects performed a paired-associate task
and a simple reaction-time task concurrently.   The amount
of the subject's processing capacity expended on the paired-
associate task was inferred from his reaction-time
performance: the slower his reaction time, the greater the
amount of processing capacity expended.   The major finding
was that imagery instructions reduced expended processing
capacity only during list study, whereas high item-imagery
reduced expended processing capacity only during attempted
recall.   Thus imagery instructions affect imaginal encoding
at input, whereas item imagery affects ease of retrieval, but
does not affect encoding processes.   This would explain the
numerous studies cited by Paivio (1971a) in which an
interaction between imagery instructions and concreteness was
sought in vain.

Richardson (1975b) attempted to demonstrate more clearly
that concreteness is a basic semantic attribute.   He asked
subjects to sort words into two semantic categories, and
noticed that the sorting performance of most subjects was
determined by word concreteness, but not by word imagery.

In sum, it is clear that concreteness should be
conceptualized as a lexical feature rather than as a measure
of the image-arousing capacity of verbal material.
Enhancement effects of imagery on retention may be due either
to the use of imaginal encoding processes or to the presence
of additional features or attributes in semantic memory, and
the conceptual distinction between these two factors is an
important one.

The fact that people can readily move in their thinking
from mental words to mental pictures and vice versa suggests
that there must be some form of representation or common
format which encompasses both. As Pylshyn (1973) pointed
out, the alternative assumption that there are direct
associative links between mental words and mental pictures
runs into the problem that there are an essentially infinite
number of pictures to which a particular word applies:
"When the mental word 'rectangle' is elicited by the mental
picture of a rectangle, it cannot be by virtue of an
associative link between the two, since this would require
that we postulate an infinite number of such links (one for
each possible picture)" (p. 5).

The fundamental difficulty with Paivio's hypothesis can be
seen in the light of its historical antecedents. Thorndike
and Woodworth (1901) and the early behaviourists argued that
transfer of training from one task to another was dependent
upon the number of 'identical elements' that were common to
the two tasks. This emphasis upon the high degree of
specificity of stored information seems to find an echo in
Paivio's hypotheses about the highly specific nature of the
images formed in verbal learning tasks. As an interesting
speculation, the relatively greater success of Paivio's
theory when applied to verbal learning than when applied to
sentence learning may be due to the much greater
specificity of the information stored in verbal learning.

It is likely that images correspond to specific
photographic representations only when subjects are
confronted with relatively novel situations. For example,
de Groot (1966) found that chess masters could recall an
authentic game position much better than novice players after
viewing it for a few seconds, even though their visual
memories were no better. Presumably the novices formed
simple, relatively uninterpreted images of the board, whereas
the masters produced much richer mental configurations which
went well beyond simple images.

Binet (1966), on the basis of observations of blindfolded
chess games and interviews with the players, reached a
similar conclusion. He found that the rank amateurs
"imagine the chessboard exactly as if they were actually
looking attentively at the board and the pieces. They
retain a veritable mental photograph in which the board
appears clearly with its black and white squares, and all the

pieces are present in colour and with their characteristic
shapes" (p. 156).   On the other hand, visual imagery is much
less useful to those with more expertise: "The experienced
player leaves the concrete visual image of the chessboard to
the mere amateur; to put it mildly, such a view is useless
and naive.   In general, the good player depends surely on
abstract memory" (p. 161).   Obviously the retrieval of
information would be extremely difficult if storage usually
consisted of highly specific, uninterpreted images.   The
attempted retrieval of information about one of the events of
the day with such a storage system would be analogous to
trying to find one specific photograph in a trunk full of
randomly distributed photographs.

An assumption of dubious validity that appears to have
been made by, among others, Bower (1972), Bugelski (1970),
and Paivio (1971a) is that the only forms of mental
representation are the verbal and the imaginal.   While it
may be true that our conscious thought deals exclusively
with words and images, it would be extremely naïve to deny
the possible existence of other important processes of which
we are not consciously aware.   For example, when lecturing
the author finds it reasonably easy to evaluate the extent to
which the words that he is using to express himself provide
an accurate account of some concept of which he has but vague
conscious awareness.   Such introspective evidence indicates
that thinking consists of far more than mere words and images.

The thrust of the argument so far has been that imaginal
processes may be considerably more limited in their ability
to facilitate learning and thinking than has been implied by
Paivio (1971a) and others.   Supporting evidence is
available from a consideration of day- and night-dreaming.
Most people, if questioned shortly after a dream, report
considerable use of imagery in dreaming.   However, people
tend not to remember their dreams for long periods of time,
indicating that the use of imagery does not necessarily
facilitate learning and retention.   Furthermore, the
thought processes in dreaming tend to be of a somewhat
primitive nature, as would be expected if imagery were
limited in its powers.   In addition, Paivio (1971a)
reviewed the literature on eidetic imagery, and came to the
conclusion that it is particularly prevalent among young
children and in primitive societies.   For example, Doob
(1964, 1965, 1966) found a large number of eidetikers in some
non-literate African cultures.   This is to be expected,

since eidetic imagery is of a simple, uninterpreted kind
which is unlikely to be of much general value in thinking.
Indeed, 'S', the famous eidetiker researched by Luria (1968),
complained that the wealth of highly specific information
contained in his images had a considerable interfering effect
on his normal thought processes.

In sum, much of the theory and experimentation on imagery
assumes that all processing is either verbal or imaginal,
that there is something especially potent or valuable about
imaginal processing, and that imagery is commonly of a
highly specific and relatively uninterpreted nature.   All
these assumptions are wrong.   Fuller discussion of these
issues will follow a further consideration of the relevant
experimental evidence.

Additional Findings

The question as to whether the differences between verbal
and imaginal processes are quantitative or qualitative has
recently been investigated by means of the selective
interference technique.   This technique, which is
discussed by Woodworth (1938), involves observing the effects
of visual and verbal interference tasks on the retention of
different kinds of information.   If verbal and imaginal
processes do differ qualitatively, then verbal interference
should exert a greater detrimental effect on verbal processes
than on imaginal processes, whereas visual interference
should have the opposite effect.   Atwood (1971) presented
subjects with a set of concrete and abstract phrases, each of
which was immediately followed by visual or verbal
interference.   On the subsequent recall test there was a
highly significant interaction between the type of phrase
and the type of interference task.   Abstract phrases were
recalled better after visual than verbal interference,
whereas concrete phrases were better recalled after verbal
than visual interference.   Although several subsequent
studies have obtained similar findings (Bower, 1970;   Brooks,
1967, 1968, 1970;   den Heyer & Barrett, 1971;   Klee & M. W.
Eysenck, 1973;   Murray & Newman, 1973), there have been some
negative results (e.g., Baddeley et al., 1975;   Bower, Munoz,
& Arnold, 1972;   Brooks, 1972).   Baddeley et al. pointed
out that Atwood confounded type of material with
instructions by telling the subjects given concrete material
to form visual images, whereas the subjects given abstract

material were told to 'contemplate the meaning' of each
phrase.   They argued that Atwood's results were due more to
the instructional variable than to variations in the type of
material.

Salthouse (1974) has reported a particularly interesting
study, in which subjects had to perform two tasks.   The
recall task involved remembering either the positions or the
identities of seven target items in a 25-item array.   During
the retention interval of the recall task, subjects were
given a recognition task for either aeroplanes or words.   On
the recall test, position information was more detrimentally
affected by the aeroplane recognition task than by the word
recognition task, with the opposite result for identity
information.   On the recognition task, aeroplane recognition
was more affected by the position-information recall task
than by the identity-information task, with the opposite
result for word recognition.   Salthouse concluded that the
position-recall and aeroplane-recognition tasks were
mutually interfering because they both involved imaginal
processing, whereas the identity-recall and word-recognition
tasks were mutually interfering because they both involved
verbal processing.

The selective-interference technique has produced several
interesting findings, but it does suffer from a number of
limitations.   Unequivocal interpretation of the results from
studies using the technique would require knowledge about the
exact processes involved in the performance of interference
tasks.   Furthermore, the technique has as yet merely
indicated the probable importance of visual processes to the
comprehension and retention of some types of stimulus
material, but has not led to a fuller understanding of the
complexity and specificity-generality of those visual
processes.   Some of the problems are illustrated by the work
of Byrne (1974).   Subjects were tested for speed of recall of
previously acquired information by means either of a vocal-
response test or a visually-guided response test.   On the
assumption that the visually-guided recall test interferes
with imaginally processed material, one might expect slower
rates of recall with concrete than with abstract items.
The results did not support this prediction, but it was
found that visual conflict at recall occurred where the
presentation conditions and stimulus materials led to the
storage of spatially-organized information.   Byrne
concluded that "the presence or absence of spatial

organization is an important characteristic of stimulus
material when it comes to predicting whether the material
will be coded imaginally and needs to be considered
separately from item concreteness" (p. 58).

A major attempt to separate out the effects of verbal and
imaginal processing was made by Paivio and Csapo (1969, 1971).
They argued that fast rates of presentation (5.3 items per
second) would restrict subjects to imaginal coding of
pictorial stimuli and to verbal coding of concrete and
abstract words, whereas both forms of coding would be
available for pictures and concrete words at slower rates of
presentation (2 items per second).   In addition, it was
argued that verbal processes are specialized for serial
processing, whereas imaginal processes are specialized for
parallel processing and spatial representation.   To
investigate these hypotheses, Paivio and Csapo (1969) used
two tasks apparently requiring serial processing (memory
span and serial learning) and two tasks not requiring serial
processing (free recall and recognition).

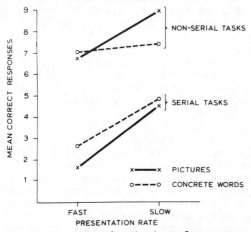

Fig. 3.3. Retention test performance as
a function of rate of presentation, task
processing demands, and type of stimulus.
Adapted from Paivio and Csapo (1969).

The major findings, which are presented in Fig. 3.3, are
consistent with the hypotheses.   For example, the common
superiority of pictorial information over concrete-word

information should be (and was) reversed on the serial tasks,
which depend upon verbal-symbolic processes.   Furthermore,
pictures should also show a relative decrement where the rate
of presentation does not allow for dual coding of pictorial
information, and this prediction was confirmed.   A
substantial methodological difficulty is that performance at
the fast rate was undoubtedly influenced by purely perceptual
factors such as masking.   If there were more perceptual
interference with pictures than with words, this would
explain some of the results.   These perceptual difficulties
are highlighted by the fact that the mean memory span at the
fast rate was approximately two items.

Some recent studies of paired-associate learning by
Nelson and Brooks (1973a, 1973b) have considered the effects
of phonemic similarity of the stimulus items.   The
conventional finding, replicated by Nelson and Brooks (1973b),
is that phonemic similarities among stimulus items produce
interference that has a detrimental effect on performance.
In addition, they employed lists of picture-word paired
associates, with the stimulus pictures in one list comprising
pictorial representations of phonemically-related words.
The main finding was that the phonemic similarity of the word
labels corresponding to the pictured objects had no effect on
performance.   However, other subjects who were presented
with the same picture-word pairs, but who had to articulate
overtly the names of the picture stimuli, produced some
effect of phonemic similarity.   Nelson and Brooks (1973b)
concluded as follows:

> The null effect of similarity within the Picture
> condition suggests that easily recognized nonverbal
> representations of meaningful phenomena can function
> effectively as memory codes independently of their
> corresponding verbal representations.   The verbal
> report data appear to corroborate this inference.
> Although verbal labels for most of the pictures were
> readily supplied upon request, the great majority of
> subjects reportedly did not name any of the stimuli or
> utilized a label for only one of them during acquisition
> (p. 47).

In an earlier study, Nelson and Brooks (1973a) found similar
effects of phonemic similarity with concrete and abstract
words, and with imagery and neutral instructions.

The studies reviewed so far in this section have indicated that a number of variables exert differential effects on concrete and abstract material: type of interference, speed of presentation, phonemic similarity, and parallel versus sequential tasks. These results suggest that the processes involved in encoding concrete and abstract material may differ qualitatively. The parallel-sequential variable has been further investigated in a number of recent studies, to which we now turn.

The notion that the verbal system is primarily a serial processing system, whereas the visual imagery system is a parallel processing system (Bower, 1972; Paivio, 1971a), has been considered by Kosslyn (1973). He investigated the time required to scan left to right or right to left through information learned after verbal or imaginal instructions. Verbal and imaginal instructions led to equivalent left-to-right scanning rates, but the subjects using imagery were much faster at right-to-left scanning. The conclusion was that there is a strong left-to-right serial order encoding bias for verbal material that is largely absent from imaginal encoding.

Castillo and Gumenik (1972) investigated serial processes in a study in which subjects had to arrange familiar and unfamiliar visual forms in their order of presentation. Presentation was either fast (5.3 items per second) or slow (2 items per second). On the assumption that verbal processes are more useful than imaginal processes in storing sequential information, it was argued that recall of serial order should be low with stimulus material having no verbal equivalent (e.g., unfamiliar visual forms) and with visual stimuli presented at a rate too fast to allow for verbal encoding. As predicted, serial-order recall was extremely low in all conditions, except where familiar visual forms were presented at a slow rate, the only condition permitting verbal encoding.

Snodgrass and Antone (1974) presented subjects with pairs of pictures and pairs of concrete words which were shown either in a spatial (left to right) or a temporal sequence, the task being to remember either the spatial or the temporal order of the stimuli. On Paivio's (1971a) hypothesis, it was predicted that spatial memory would be better for pictures than for words, but that temporal memory would be equivalent for words and pictures. In fact, pictures were

superior to words on both the spatial and the temporal
memory tasks, and the difference between performance on
pictures and words was the same regardless of whether spatial
or temporal memory was being measured.

Further evidence that the imagery system represents
information in a spatially parallel manner was obtained by
Weber and Harnish (1974).   Subjects looked at or formed an
image of a short word, and were then asked to indicate as
quickly as possible whether the letter at a specified
position within the word was vertically large or not.
Images and percepts did not differ significantly in the
speed with which spatial information was extracted from them.
Furthermore, the effects of probe position were relatively
slight, particularly with the shorter words.   Weber and
Harnish concluded that the evidence pointed to a limited-
capacity visual image system that could represent short words
in a spatially parallel manner as efficiently as they could be
represented in a visual percept system.

Summary

While the majority of researchers investigating the
relationship between imagery and learning have compared the
retention of concrete and abstract words, we have seen that
there are considerable interpretative problems with the
evidence.   However, there is a good deal of experimental
evidence, especially that obtained from the use of selective
interference techniques, demonstrating that there is a valid
distinction between imaginal and verbal processing.

It is probable that subjects can process any particular
nominal stimulus in several different ways (cf., Craik &
Lockhart, 1972).   A very interesting demonstration of this
encoding flexibility was provided by Tversky (1969).
Initially subjects learned to associate schematic faces with
their associated nonsense names.   They then received a
series of trials, with a name or face being followed one
second later by a name or a face.   The subjects were to
respond 'same' as rapidly as possible where the stimuli had
the same name, and 'different' otherwise.   The subjects'
expectations crucially affected performance.   When the
majority of the second stimuli were pictorial, subjects
responded faster to second stimuli that were pictorial,
irrespective of the modality of the first stimulus.   When

the majority of the second stimuli were verbal, subjects
responded faster to verbal than to pictorial second stimuli,
irrespective of the first stimulus modality. Furthermore,
the subjects were faster in saying 'different' when the
stimuli were more dissimilar, where similarity was defined
in terms of the number of attributes in common in the second
stimulus modality. The modality of the first stimulus did
not affect performance. These results clearly show that the
first stimulus was either verbally or visually encoded
contingent upon the anticipated modality of the second
stimulus.

The evidence suggests that several rather separate
processes are commonly considered conjointly under the term
'imagery'. A good example comes in recent work by Morris
and Stevens (1974). They compared the free recall of
subjects instructed to form images linking together the items
to be recalled in groups of three, subjects told to form a
separate image of each word, and those given conventional
learning instructions. The main finding was that the
linking-image subjects recalled considerably more words than
the separate-imagery subjects, who, indeed, recalled at the
same level as the control subjects. Paivio (1971a) has
claimed that imagery facilitates recall either by providing
a second means of storage in addition to the verbal, or
because retrieval from a visual store is more efficient than
from a verbal store. Neither of these explanations handles
the large difference in observed recall between the two
imagery groups. A possible interpretation of the findings
is that there was more semantic and conceptual integration of
the material under the linking-image condition than under the
separate-image condition. It may be the case that
instructions to use imaginal processing usually produce good
memory performance by inducing people to process more of the
available conceptual features.

It has been argued in this chapter that the term
'imaginal processing' encompasses an enormous variety of
processing activities. The results of imaginal processing
range from relatively uninterpreted, quasi-photographic,
representations to complex, abstract, conceptualizations.
Some of this variety was recognized by Piaget and Inhelder
(1966), who distinguished between reproductive and
anticipatory images. Anticipatory images first occur at
around the age of seven or eight, compared with reproductive
images that are found between one-and-a-half and two years.

Future researchers are likely to make similar distinctions
between imaginal processing involving deep and shallow levels
of processing.

Theoretically, the analysis of the salient characteristics
of verbal and imaginal processing has been inadequate in
other ways. For example, it may be true that problems
involving the calculation of the ordering of three objects or
people (e.g., subjects are given two premises, such as 'A is
leading B'; 'C is followed by A', and then the question
'Who is first?' or 'Who is last?') commonly lead to the use
of imaginal processing (Huttenlocher, 1968). However, to
ascribe successful solution of the problem simply to imagery
is to engage in pure mysticism. By analogy, to 'explain'
the existence of a magnificent palace by pointing out that
its construction involved the use of bricks is a true but
woefully partial explanation. In terms of human thought,
we can decide whether or not an image or verbal ideas is
accurate, appropriate to a current problem, and so on, which
implies that some type of processing other than the purely
verbal or imaginal must be postulated. One possibility is
that information from the environment is processed verbally
and imaginally to provide input to a central conceptual
processing system, the products of which are consciously
expressed in images or words.

CHAPTER 4

RETRIEVAL I

The conceptual distinction between storage and retrieval
is an important one. This is so, even though it is obvious
that there can be no retrieval of information which has not
been stored, and even though the more adequate the storage of
information is, the higher will tend to be the probability of
retrieval. The distinction can be seen when we consider
that the forgetting of information previously acquired could
logically occur in two separate ways:

(1) A storage deficit, in which there is a loss of
information from the traces of experienced events;
(2) A retrieval deficit, in which the information
remains in store, but the retrieval environment does not
suffice to gain access to the information.

This chapter discusses the possibility that much
forgetting is attributable to problems of retrieval rather
than of storage. This concern with retrieval necessarily
involves some discussion of the processes of retrieval, and of
the various forms of retention test, primarily recall and
recognition. Since the literature on these topics is
enormous, we shall focus attention in this chapter on a few
of the major experimental and theoretical approaches. In
the following chapter, the problems of retrieval will be
considered from the viewpoint of research on speed of
retrieval.

The Permanent-memory Hypothesis

Several prominent theorists have argued that a considerable
proportion of all apparent forgetting is due to some form of
retrieval deficit rather than any deterioration in the stored
traces. William James (1892), for example, believed that
some people had permanent storage of information:

The persistence or permanence of the paths is a
physiological property of the individual, whilst their

61

> number is altogether due to the facts of his mental
> experience.   Let the quality of permanence in the paths
> be called native tenacity, or physiological
> retentiveness.   This tenacity differs enormously from
> infancy to old age, and from one person to another.
> Some minds are like wax under a seal - no impression,
> however disconnected with others, is wiped out.
> Others, like a jelly, vibrate to every touch, but under
> usual conditions retain no permanent mark (p. 293).

Sigmund Freud (1943) held that most forgetting was due to
repression, with the original memory traces stored
permanently in the unconscious, which "knows no time limit"
(p. 174).   More recent theorists who have stated, in
rather different terms, the case for permanent storage are
Shiffrin and Atkinson (1969) and Tulving (1974).   Shiffrin
and Atkinson, for example, considered the fact that most
people have extremely limited recollections of early
childhood, much to the distress of their parents!   They
speculated that what is involved is a retrieval deficit, due
to the changing organization of memory that occurs with
increasing age.

Direct experimentation on this topic is lacking, but
Adams (1967) has cited with approval Penfield's work on brain
stimulation.   Penfield (1955, 1959, 1968) has performed over
one thousand craniotomies, in which there was unilateral
removal of a portion of the temporal lobes and adjacent areas
in an attempt to relieve focal epilepsy.   The patients were
conscious during the operation, and in 520 cases Penfield
explored one or other of the temporal lobes by means of
gentle electrical stimulation.   Forty of these patients,
representing 7.7 per cent of those stimulated, reported
'flashbacks' during stimulation.   These flashbacks
consisted of remembered experiences from the past.   The most
interesting finding was that the electrical stimulation
sometimes produced detailed re-enactments of a single
experience that had for a long time been unavailable to
normal recall.   The implication is that far more information
about events and experiences has been stored than we can
retrieve under normal circumstances.   However, it appears
that several of the recollections produced by stimulation
could quite easily have been recalled without stimulation:
for example, patient J. T., when stimulated, could hear his
two cousins Bessie and Ann Wheliaw laughing.   Penfield did
not have any independent verification of the events which

subjects claimed to remember during electrical stimulation.
In addition, it should be noted that 92.3 per cent of the
epileptic patients did not experience these flashbacks, so
that it may only have been the more suggestible patients who
reported them.

If we now turn more specifically to Freudian theory, there
have been several experimental attempts to demonstrate the
importance of repression in producing forgetting.   However,
most investigators have not appreciated the variety of
interpretations which Freud assigned to the concept of
repression.   It is commonly assumed that repression means
motivated forgetting, and certainly Freud did sometimes
employ the term in this sense.   However, as Madison (1956)
pointed out, at least three other meanings of the concept can
be found in Freud's writings:

(1) Freud (1915): "The essence of repression lies
simply in the function of rejecting and keeping something out
of consciousness" (p. 86).   This definition is extremely
general, and would seem to include many things apart from the
specific recollection of past events.
(2) Freud also used 'repression' as a term
synonymous with 'defence', as Madison (1956) clearly shows.
Freud was basically interested in defences that achieved ego-
protection by some form of unawareness, i.e., by some form of
repression.
(3) The final sense in which Freud used the term
'repression' was as the inhibition of the capacity for
emotional experience.   In essence, Freud is here
distinguishing between ideas and affects, or emotions.
Repression can occur even where there is conscious awareness
of cognitive ideas, provided that these ideas are deprived of
their emotional content.

Researchers have usually assumed that repression involves
the motivated inability to recall stored information.   The
inability to be aware of the emotional content of remembered
ideas has not been investigated experimentally.   One of the
studies which has been taken to indicate the existence of
repression in memory (although not by the authors
themselves) was conducted by Levinger and Clark (1961).
They gave subjects a free-association test, and asked them to
respond as rapidly as possible.   The GSR to each item on the
list was recorded.   After the completion of the test,
subjects received the items of the free-association test for a

second time, and had to try to remember their original associations. The major indication that emotional factors can produce forgetting came from a comparison of the GSRs occurring to those items subsequently forgotten and remembered. Forgotten associations had produced significantly greater GSRs than remembered associations on the initial free-association test. A major problem is that this experiment provided no evidence that the items associated with large GSRs were as well learned as those associated with small GSRs. Subjects took longer to respond to the more emotional items on the free-association test. It is possible that the more emotional items led to the implicit generation of a number of responses prior to the overt vocalization of one of them, and that subjects at recall found it difficult to distinguish between the overt and the covert responses. Furthermore, the results can be accounted for in terms of an entirely different theory proposed by Walker (1958), which is discussed at length later in the book. This theory states that high arousal leads to a strong process of consolidation, but an initial inhibition against responding.

Much of the research on repression effects in memory has utilized a paradigm introduced by Zeller (1950a, 1950b, 1951). He argued that there were three requirements for a study attempting to demonstrate repression. The first was to ensure that the material in question has been learned by the subjects. The second was to demonstrate that the introduction of some inhibiting factor causes a significant decrease in the recall of the material, and the third was to show that the removal of the inhibiting factor results in the reinstatement of the ability to recall the material.

In practical terms, the 'inhibiting factor' has usually consisted of failure information given to the subjects when performance is occurring on some task, and the 'removal of the inhibiting factor' has either involved reassurances that the failure information was not genuine, or the introduction of success information on the task previously associated with failure. In a typical study, Penn (1964) asked subjects to learn paired associates. They then performed a tapping task, either associated with failure or with no information. The first retention test was then given, followed by some more tapping associated with no information, failure information, or success information. Finally, there was a second retention test. The most interesting group is the

one given failure information before the first retention
test but given success information before the second
retention test.   Relative to the appropriate control groups,
these subjects had a very low level of recall after the
failure information (repression), and a high level of recall
after the subsequent success information (return of the
repressed).   While the purist might complain that being
told that your performance on a tapping task is poor is not
comparable to the major traumata producing clinically
observed repression, the finding is a reasonably robust one.

Considerable doubt as to the validity of the original
interpretation of data such as those of Penn (1964) has been
engendered by the studies of D'Zurilla (1965) and Holmes
(1972).   D'Zurilla did an experiment similar to that of
Penn, but asked his subjects post-experimentally what they
had thought about immediately after the failure or success
information had been given.   The failure subjects reported
more thoughts than the success subjects that were quite
irrelevant to the subsequent task of recalling the words.
He suggested that the increase in amount of conflicting
cognitive events could have reduced the efficiency of recall
in the failure group.

Holmes (1972) investigated this hypothesis further.
Subjects were presented with a list of forty words in an
incidental-learning paradigm, followed by recall.   They then
received a personality test incorporating the same words.
On this test, subjects were given either ego-threatening,
ego-enhancing, or neutral feedback.   Following this, they
were tested for recall again, told that the personality test
feedback was not genuine, and tested for recall for the third
time.   The ego-threatened subjects showed the common
pattern of relatively poor recall after the threatening
feedback, and a substantial improvement in recall after the
debriefing.   Conventionally, these findings would be
interpreted as evidence for repression, and for the return of
the repressed, respectively.   However, the main finding of
the study was that the ego-enhanced group showed the same
recall changes as the ego-threatened group.   It is unlikely
that ego-enhancement would cause repression.   Holmes
favoured the hypothesis that both ego-enhancement and ego-
threat caused a relative lack of attention to the immediately
following recall test, and that thinking about the positive
or negative feedback produced interference.   However, it
should be noted that the equivalent performance of the threat

and enhancement groups does not prove that repression was not
occurring in the threat group.

While the concept of repression has not as yet been
conclusively demonstrated experimentally, there is recent
evidence that high levels of emotion or motivation can have a
detrimental effect on the retrieval of information.   Common
examples are the failures of recall that students experience
under the stress of writing examinations, and the unexpected
recall of some items of information after one is relaxing
after strenuous attempts at recall.   Further evidence that
high levels of arousal can be detrimental to retrieval has
been obtained in several studies by M. W. Eysenck (e.g.,
1974a, 1974d, 1975b, 1975c).   This work is discussed in
detail in Chapters 8 and 9.

Encoding Specificity Hypothesis: Endel Tulving

We saw in the previous section that it is difficult to
demonstrate that forgetting is importantly attributable to
problems of retrieval.   However, a series of interesting
studies by Endel Tulving has clearly established that at
least some forgetting is not simply due to a weakening of the
stored trace.   One paradigm which he has used requires two
groups of subjects to learn the same information under the
same conditions.   This ensures that equivalent storage of
the to-be-remembered material has occurred in the two groups.
All subjects then receive a retention test, with the nature
of the retention test given to the two groups differing in
some important characteristic.   If one group has
significantly poorer retention-test performance than the
other, it is assumed that the inferior group was affected, to
some extent, by a problem of retrieval rather than of storage.
It should be noted that the term 'retrieval' is being used in
a somewhat special sense in this context.   It is, of course,
just as appropriate to attribute recall failure to
inappropriate initial coding of the to-be-remembered material
as to the use of an inadequate retrieval cue.   The
important factor in determining successful retention-test
performance is a match between the information in the trace
and in the cues provided on the test.

A concrete example of this approach comes in a study by
Tulving and Pearlstone (1966).   In essence, two groups of
subjects received identical lists of words belonging to
various categories, such as four-footed animals, articles of

furniture, and so on.   The members of each category were
presented adjacently, and were preceded by the category
label.   Since the two groups of subjects were treated
identically until the time of recall, there cannot have been
any systematic difference between them in terms of the
information stored.   The subjects then attempted to recall
as many of the category instances as possible, one group
under conditions of cued recall, in which the subjects were
given a list of the category labels, and the other group
under normal conditions of non-cued recall.   The cued recall
group recalled considerably more words than the non-cued
recall group, three or four times as many words under some of
the conditions.   While this finding seems to demonstrate
that the non-cued group must have stored several words that
they could not retrieve without the appropriate cues, one
problem must be considered.   It is possible that the cued
subjects, presented with category labels such as 'Articles of
furniture', might simply have produced guesses, some of which
would correspond to list words.   In that case, the findings
would be of minor consequence.   However, if the cued recall
subjects had been merely guessing, they would presumably have
produced many intrusion errors.   In fact, the relatively
small number of intrusion errors means that a guessing
hypothesis cannot explain the results.

A particularly striking example of the discrepancy between
storage and retrieval was found in a study by Tulving and
Psotka (1971).   Subjects learned between one and six
categorized word lists.   Each list comprised four words
belonging to six conceptual categories.   After the
presentation of each list, the subjects attempted non-cued
recall of the words from that list, a test of original
learning.   After the subjects had learned their last list,
and attempted to recall it, they were asked to provide free
recall of all the words from all the lists they had seen, a
test of non-cued recall.   Finally, the subjects were given a
test of cued free recall of all the words from all the lists,
in which they were given the names of all the conceptual
categories used in all the lists, a test of cued recall.

The main results of interest can be seen overleaf in Fig.
4.1.   The curve representing performance on the overall
non-cued recall test is a typical example of retroactive
interference, with the number of words forgotten from a list
being directly related to the number of other lists
interpolated between the learning of the list and recall test.

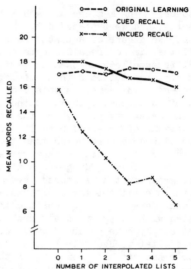

Fig. 4.1. Original learning, and cued and
non-cued recall as a function of the number
of lists between acquisition and test.
Based on data in Tulving and Psotka (1971).

Is this substantial deterioration in recall performance due
to some kind of storage deficit or is it due to a retrieval
deficit?   Modern interference theory, with its concept of
'unlearning' (Postman & Underwood, 1973), appears to suggest
that retroactive interference reflects a storage deficit.
However, more insight into the nature of the poor non-cued
recall performance is afforded by a consideration of the
results for cued recall.   The cues restored recall to about
its original level, and show clearly that the subjects'
difficulty on the non-cued recall task was not due to a
complete loss of stored information.

One might suppose that retrieval deficits would be found
primarily in studies of recall.   With recognition, it has
frequently been assumed that there is no retrieval problem.
For example, Bower, Clark, Lesgold, and Winzenz (1969) stated
quite categorically: "Recognition tests, which directly
provide the test word, clearly bypass the search and retrieval
processes by which the subject generates his recall" (p. 329).
The basic procedure required to investigate retrieval
problems in recognition is to have two groups of subjects

attempt to learn a list of words under identical conditions,
so that the amount of information stored is the same for both
groups.   Then a recognition test is given under two
conditions, and a difference in performance is taken to mean
that the group performing worse is experiencing retrieval
problems.   A number of studies along these lines have been
published (e.g., Light & Carter-Sobell, 1970; Tulving &
Thomson, 1971).   Tulving and Thomson presented a long list of
words, in which each word either appeared by itself or
together with a semantically related word.   The subjects
were told to pay close attention to each word, since their
memory for these words would be tested in a subsequent
recognition test.

On the recognition test, subjects were given list words and
distractors presented both singly and as pairs of words.
Some words originally presented singly were tested as one
member of a pair, while others were tested singly.   Whether
the words were tested singly or in pairs, the subjects had to
decide whether each word had occurred in the presentation
list.   When singly presented words were tested as single
words, the corrected recognition percentage score was 46 per
cent, but when singly presented words were tested together
with a new word on the recognition test, the corrected
recognition score was 35 per cent, significantly lower.   For
example, if the word 'baby' was presented by itself at input,
then the subject would be more likely to recognize it if the
recognition test had the word 'baby' presented by itself than
if the pair of words 'grasp' and 'baby' were presented
together at test.   Since the word 'baby' was equally well
learned in either condition, it appears that the additional
word 'grasp' somehow interfered with retrieval.   More
generally, Tulving and Thomson (1971) came to the following
conclusion: "With availability of stored information held
constant, recognition of a previously seen item depends upon
its context at the time of test, recognition being higher if
test context matches the input context than if the input
context is introduced at the time of test" (p. 122).

Tulving (Thomson & Tulving, 1970; Tulving & Osler, 1968;
Tulving & Thomson, 1973; Watkins & Tulving, 1975; Wiseman &
Tulving, 1975) has put forward what he calls the encoding
specificity hypothesis or principle.   It was expressed by
Wiseman and Tulving (1975) in the following words: "A
retrieval cue is effective if its informational content
matches and complements the information contained in the

trace of the to-be-remembered event" (p. 371). In more detail, it is proposed that the initial presentation of to-be-remembered stimulus material leads to a specific encoding, and that the subsequent presentation of a retrieval cue on the retention test also leads to a specific encoding, whether a recall or a recognition test is used. Memory performance depends upon the overlap or similarity of encoding processes at presentation and at test.

An immediate difficulty with this theory is that it is extremely hard to establish the nature of the encodings at input and at test, and the specification of how great the overlap needs to be for successful memory performance has not been made. Tulving himself admits that the principle constitutes a general conceptual framework rather than a testable hypothesis. The principle does not indicate how encodings are produced, so that it can only provide a partial analysis of many retrieval situations. For example, subjects in a free-recall situation in some unspecified manner produce a series of encodings; the encoding specificity principle merely argues that successful free recall necessitates the production of several encodings resembling those generated by the list words at input. In practice, Tulving has usually attempted to control the encodings at input and at test by means of manipulating the context in which the to-be-remembered words are encountered. The argument is that words are typically encoded not as separate entities, but in combination with contextual information.

One of the predictions of the encoding specificity principle is that, if a retrieval cue fails to be encoded at test in a manner approximating the encoding of the to-be-remembered word, then it will prove ineffective, even if there is a strong pre-experimental association between the retrieval cue and the sought-for item. Thus, a to-be-remembered word like 'black', if presented at input along with the contextual word 'train', will presumably be encoded in terms of dirt, smut, smoke and so on. According to the encoding specificity principle, the retrieval cue 'white' may well be unsuccessful in leading to recall of its strong associate 'black', because 'black' was not originally stored simply as a colour name. A provocative assumption of the encoding specificity principle is that the effectiveness of a retrieval cue is far more dependent upon the manner in which the to-be-remembered words are encoded in the laboratory situation than

it is on pre-experimentally acquired associations between
cues and to-be-remembered words.

This assumption was directly investigated by Thomson and
Tulving (1970). In their second experiment, they presented
lists of to-be-remembered words, with each word accompanied
by the same weak associate both at input and at output.
Thus a subject might receive a pair such as 'blow COLD' at
input and 'blow' at output, and he had to try to recall the
word 'cold'. On the third list, three groups of subjects
again received a list of words together with weak
associates. Recall was tested either in the presence of
strong associates of the to-be-remembered words, in the
presence of the same weak associates as at input, or in the
presence of no retrieval cues. As predicted, recall was
high in the presence of the weak associate input cues (19.8
words), was greatly reduced when no cues were present (7.1
words), and was even worse in the presence of strong
associate cues (5.5 words). The implication is that a
strong associate (e.g., 'ice') is useless as a retrieval cue
unless it is encoded with the to-be-remembered word (e.g.,
'cold') at input.

A disturbing aspect of the methodology employed in the
study by Thomson and Tulving (1970), and in other studies by
Tulving, is the fact that subjects are unexpectedly, and
without explanation, switched from recall in the presence of
weak associates to recall in the presence of strong
associates. As Santa and Lamwers (1974) have pointed out,
subjects switched from weak to strong cues are likely to be
confused. They may either ignore the cue, which would
explain the low level of recall, or they may continue their
previous strategy of generating weak associates of the
retrieval cues. Santa and Lamwers essentially replicated
the Thomson and Tulving study, but they also included a
further condition. In this condition, subjects were
switched from weak cues at input to strong cues at output,
but they were informed about the relationship between the
cues.

Exactly as Thomson and Tulving had found, recall was
higher when the retrieval cues were the same weak associates
presented at input (about ten words), than when either no
retrieval cues (5.4 words) or strong retrieval cues without
explanation (5.3 words) were given. The key finding was
that those subjects who switched from weak associates to

strong associates, but were informed about the nature of the
new retrieval cues, recalled an average of 10.1 words,
significantly more than those subjects switched from weak
associates to strong associates without explanation.   It
thus appears that the subjects in Thomson and Tulving's (1970)
study may have been confused, and that a change in cues need
not have the drastic effects predicted by the encoding
specificity hypothesis.   However, if pre-experimental
associations were of primary importance, one would expect
strong associates to be better retrieved than weak associates,
which was not found.

    The reader may have noticed that recall and recognition
are handled similarly by the encoding specificity principle.
The effectiveness of a retrieval cue depends upon the
congruence of encoding operations at input and output, and
this applies even when the retrieval cue is the same word
presented at input, as is the case with a recognition test.
The basic similarity between recall and recognition was
forcefully argued by Tulving and Thomson (1973).   They
pointed out that most theories of retrieval, including the
popular generation-recognition theory, argue that
recognition involves simpler processes than recall.   The
generation-recognition theory basically assumes that
retrieval comprises the two stages of (1) implicit
generation or production of possible responses; and (2)
recognition of one of the generated alternatives as meeting
certain criteria of acceptability.   Recall involves both
stages, whereas recognition only involves the second stage.

    The above theory, subscribed to by Bahrick (1969), Bower
et al. (1969), Kintsch (1970), and many others, appears to
predict that recall cannot be higher than recognition.   In
fact, the overwhelming majority of studies comparing recall
and recognition have found recognition to be higher than
recall.   However, the encoding specificity principle allows
for the possibility that recall could be better than
recognition, and this surprising finding has now been
obtained several times (e.g., Tulving, 1968b; Tulving &
Thomson, 1973; Watkins, 1973).

    The basic procedure adopted by Tulving and Thomson (1973)
was to require subjects initially to study and recall lists
of words in the presence of weak associates, in order to set
subjects to encode with respect to the weak associates.   A
final list of to-be-remembered word plus weak associate pairs

was presented, and subjects were then required to perform a
series of recall and recognition tests.   Their first task
was to recall some of the list words in the presence of
strong associates not present at study.   They then had to
generate free associations to the strong cues, followed by
an attempt to recognize any list words that had been
produced on the free-association test.   Finally, the
subjects were given a test of cued recall, with the weak
associates presented at input constituting the cues.

The results were similar in all three experiments
reported by Tulving and Thomson (1973).   In their first
experiment, for example, recall as measured by the final cued
recall test was 63 per cent.   While the strong associates
enabled subjects to generate 74 per cent of the list words on
the free-association test, the subjects only managed to
recognize 24 per cent of these list words.   There was thus
an enormous advantage of recall over recognition.   In the
first two experiments, the number of words that were recalled
but not recognized exceeded the number of words that could be
recognized but not recalled by a ratio of approximately 15:1.

Tulving and Thomson (1973) claimed that the above results
were inconsistent with most theories, including the
generation-recognition hypothesis.   Let us consider that
claim in more detail.   This hypothesis assumes that recall
involves the generation of responses and decision making,
whereas recognition only involves decision making.   Recall
is likely to be worse than recognition, since the subject
must first retrieve the desired information before making a
decision as to its appropriateness.   Recognition, on the
other hand, merely requires a decision.   However, the
assertion that this hypothesis does not allow for the
possibility of recall exceeding recognition is only true if
the decision phase of recall is identical to the decision
phase of recognition.   As Santa and Lamwers (1974) have
pointed out, the comparison of recall and recognition
provided by Tulving and Thomson is only appropriate if the
decision phases of recall and recognition both involve the
same number of alternatives, and if the alternatives on both
tests are equally discriminable.   In fact, the decision
phase of recognition in the Tulving and Thomson study
involved several highly similar alternatives, and it is well
known that recognition performance is poor under such
circumstances.   Since we do not know the number and
discriminability of the alternatives considered by subjects

in cued recall, we cannot confidently reject the
generation-recognition hypothesis on the basis of these data.

Recently, Watkins and Tulving (1975) have attempted to
deal with some of the issues raised by Santa and Lamwers
(1974). They performed a series of experiments
representing modifications of the paradigm used by Tulving
and Thomson (1973), and found that recall was still superior
to recognition even when the distractor items on the
recognition test were associatively unrelated to the list
words. In addition, the superiority of recall was
maintained when the number of recognition alternatives was
reduced to three and subjects had to make forced choices.
This finding seems to rule out explanations of the poor
recognition performance in terms of excessive response
caution.

Another attempt to demonstrate that recall can be
superior to recognition was made by Wiseman and Tulving
(1975). They presented a series of to-be-remembered words
accompanied by weakly associated contextual words, followed
by a recognition test and by a cued recall test using the
weak associates as cues. Overall, recall was superior to
recognition: 62 per cent versus 45 per cent. This was in
spite of the fact that the distractor items on the
recognition test were semantically unrelated to the target
items in order to facilitate recognition performance, and,
more importantly, the entire procedure was repeated four
times so that the subjects were not confused or unaware of
what would be required of them.

Thus the encoding of a stimulus and the resultant memory
trace are rather specific, so that only a restricted set of
retrieval cues can provide access to the trace. As Wiseman
and Tulving (1975) pointed out, "The cues that on pre-
experimental grounds can be thought to be closely related to
and associated with the words to be remembered, such as strong
semantic associates (Thomson & Tulving, 1970) or nominal
copies of to-be-remembered words (Tulving & Thomson, 1973;
Tulving, 1974) are not always effective" (p. 370).

However, it is still not clear whether Tulving has as yet
demonstrated conclusively the existence of recall superiority
over recognition. In connection with the Wiseman and
Tulving (1975) article, Santa and Lamwers (1976) have noted
that recognition performance depends critically upon the

subject's response criterion.   Since Wiseman and Tulving's
subjects produced extremely few false alarms (i.e.,
erroneously selecting words as having being presented), the
implication is that their subjects were rather cautious.
Furthermore, it is usual when both recall and recognition
tests are used to give the recall test first to avoid the
confounding effects of the recognition test, whereas the
Tulving paradigm uses the opposite sequence.

The finding that recall of stored information can exceed
recognition is non-intuitive, but it is consistent with the
encoding specificity principle.   In spite of the fact that
the to-be-remembered item is identical with its nominal copy
in the recognition test, it is possible for the specifically
encoded trace of that item to differ significantly from the
copy cue to preclude recognition, while permitting recall.
Recently, some investigators have found that the existence of
recall superiority over recognition in the Tulving paradigm
depends critically on the stimulus materials used.   Reder,
Anderson, and Bjork (1974) found recall superiority was only
obtained with high-frequency target words, and Salzberg
(1976) noticed that recall superiority occurred with concrete
noun encoding cues, but not with other kinds of cues.   The
implication is that the encoding specificity principle has a
rather restricted range of applicability.

In answer to these points, Wiseman and Tulving (1976)
conceded that recall superiority over recognition is a rather
infrequent finding.   However, they argued that the existence
of recognition failure of recallable words was the most
critical finding in support of the encoding specificity
principle, and pointed out that many studies (e.g., Salzberg,
1976) had found evidence of recognition failure of
recallable words even though recall was not superior to
recognition.   A characteristic of many studies obtaining
both recall and recognition measures is that the recognition
test has preceded the recall test, and there is clearly the
possibility that recall performance has been affected by
prior recognition.   Wiseman and Tulving argued that the
probability of unsuccessful recognition combined with
successful recall would be unaffected, since the first test,
when unsuccessful, does not change the information stored
about a given word's occurrence in the list.   In a series of
experiments, Wiseman and Tulving demonstrated the existence of
recognition failure of recallable words in the absence of
confounding factors.

The approach proposed by Tulving can be regarded from a
slightly different viewpoint.   If we accept, on the basis of
evidence presented in this and previous chapters, that the
memory trace is multi-dimensional, comprising an amalgam of
encoded attributes or features, then the use of a single
retention-test measure is hardly to be recommended.   While
thousands of memory studies have used only one retention
index (e.g., probability of recall), such studies have been
extremely uninformative about the complexity of the stored
trace.   For example, consider a word concept that has the
four attributes A, B, C, and D.   Four different subjects
might encode different members of the attribute set (e.g.,
ABC; ABD; ACD; BCD), and might reveal the same
probability of recall, in spite of very important differences
in the memory trace.   More accurate information about the
memory trace would be obtained if A, B, C, and D were each
used in succession as retrieval cues: retrieval cue A would
probably produce recall from memory traces ABC, ABD, and ACD,
but could not lead to recall from memory trace BCD.   Tulving
has consistently (and with justification) argued for the
importance of multiple retention tests.   We may regard
encoding operations as establishing a ceiling on potential
memory performance, with retrieval cues serving to determine
the extent to which that potential is realized.   Due to the
specific nature of the encoded trace, only certain retrieval
cues will be effective in producing successful retention.

It is probable that successful retention depends on
factors in addition to the overlap between input and output
encodings emphasized by Tulving.   Muscovitch and Craik
(1976) required subjects to process words either
phonemically or semantically in response to questions.   They
manipulated encoding uniqueness by either using the same
question for only one word, or by using each question with
ten different words.   Phonemic processing led to low and
equivalent levels of recall under either condition, whereas
semantic processing led to much higher levels of recall when
there was a unique link between the question (used as a
retrieval cue) and the encoded word.   Ausubel (1962) argued
that well-remembered events must be compatible with the
subject's store of past experiences, and that they must also
be discriminable from such past experiences.   Tulving has
emphasized the former point at the expense of the latter.

In recognition experiments, the overlap between input and
test encodings of a word's phonemic characteristics would

appear to be greater than the overlap in the encodings of
semantic characteristics, and yet recognition is usually
superior following semantic encoding.   M. W. Eysenck and
M. C. Eysenck (in preparation) have argued that phonemic
processing leads to poor retention partly because the
phonemic encoding of any given word in the experimental
situation cannot be discriminated from prior phonemic
encodings of the same word.   The discriminability of
semantic encodings of a word is much greater due to the
increased variability inherent in semantic processing.   In
two separate experiments, subjects were instructed to
process words semantically or phonemically in a typical or
atypical manner.   Typical semantic processing involved
discovering an adjective commonly found with the target noun,
whereas atypical semantic processing required thinking of an
adjective less commonly encountered in the context of the
target noun.   Typical phonemic processing involved simply
saying the word as it is normally pronounced, and atypical
phonemic processing meant pronouncing phonemically irregular
words (e.g., denial, glove, knee, monarch) as if they were
phonetically regular.   For example, 'glove' would be
pronounced to rhyme with 'drove'.   The basic hypothesis was
that atypical phonemic processing would produce a unique
encoding that could be discriminated from previous phonemic
encodings of any given word.   In both experiments, atypical
phonemic processing produced much higher levels of
recognition than typical phonemic processing, approaching the
level attained by semantic processing.   The implication is
that successful retention requires (a) overlap between input
and test encodings, and (b) discriminability of these
encodings from previous encodings of the same stimulus
material.

Tulving's encoding specificity principle is a
significant contribution to our understanding of retrieval
processes.   It is true that any given stimulus can be
encoded in a number of different ways, and that the exact
form of the encoded representation will importantly determine
the success or otherwise of retrieval cues.   However, the
theoretical analysis of the retrieval process seems
inadequate.   Tulving appears to assume that the crucial
determinant of performance on a retention test is the overlap
between encoding at input and encoding at test.   However, is
there a single encoding at test?   Is it not likely that
retrieval can be more variegated and flexible than Tulving
implies?   The point at issue has been well expressed by

Reitman (1970):

> To what extent can we lump together what goes on when
> you try to recall (1) your name, (2) how you kick a
> football, and (3) the present location of your car
> keys?   If we use introspective evidence as a guide,
> the first seems an immediate automatic response.   The
> second may require constructive internal replay prior
> to our being able to produce a verbal description.
> The third...quite likely involves complex operational
> responses under the control of some general strategy
> system.   Is any unitary search process, with a single
> set of characteristics and input-output relations,
> likely to cover all these cases? (p. 485).

One of the main implications of the encoding specificity
principle was expressed in the following way by Watkins and
Tulving (1975): "There is no fundamental difference between
the processes of recognition and recall; the term
recognition is used to describe a retrieval environment in
which a nominal copy of the encountered word is physically
present, and the term recall when it is not" (p. 5).   The
major evidence for this assertion seems to be that
contextual change between the input and output
environments exerts similar detrimental effects on recall and
recognition.   However, there are several other factors (e.g.,
word frequency and interference) which have differential
effects on recall and recognition.   These factors are
discussed in more detail later in this chapter; they
indicate that there are important differences between recall
and recognition.

The existence of context effects in recognition memory, and
the low levels of recognition when a list word is presented
with a cue word but tested in the presence of other words
does not necessarily require an explanation in exactly the
terms used by Tulving.   Light, Kimble, and Pellegrino
(1975) discussed an attribute theory that can handle the
data.   The encoded version of an item in memory represents
some subset of its potential attributes, and the context in
which the item is presented (e.g., a cue word) partially
determines the particular subset of encoded features.   A
different context on the recognition test could lead to a
sampling of unencoded features of the to-be-remembered item
and thus to recognition failure.   A deduction from this
theory is that those list words most susceptible to encoding

variations as a function of differing contexts would be most
detrimentally affected by contextual changes between input
and test.   Reder, Anderson, and Bjork (1974) investigated
this hypothesis using high-frequency and low-frequency
words, claiming that the high-frequency words were more
likely than low-frequency words to allow multiple semantic
interpretations.   As predicted, recall and recognition were
impaired by changes in the cues between presentation and
test for high-frequency words but not for low-frequency words.
It should be noted that the Light et al. hypothesis
constitutes a more specific version of Tulving's encoding
specificity principle.

An important question about retrieval cues which merits
further research is whether, in any particular experiment,
they are affecting the retrievability of information, or the
decision process, or both.   For example, suppose subjects
are attempting to recall only the names of three wild
flowers recently presented to them, having previously been
presented with the names of garden flowers.   The retrieval
cue 'wild flowers' has been found to enhance recall in such a
situation (Gardiner, Craik, & Birtwistle, 1972).
Theoretically, this enhancement effect could be due to the
fact that the retrieval cue afforded a basis for the
discrimination between current and previous items, or to the
fact that the retrieval cue facilitated the search process in
some way.

An additional complication is that the studies
investigating the encoding specificity principle have used
experimenter-produced retrieval cues.   Our knowledge about
the subject-produced retrieval cues normally used to
facilitate performance is quite limited.   The distinction
between experimenter-produced and subject-produced retrieval
cues can be seen in the light of a hypothetical experiment.
If all the words in a free-recall list were two syllables in
length, and the first syllable of each word were used as a
retrieval cue, it is probable that these retrieval cues
would enhance recall compared to a suitable control.
However, such a finding would not demonstrate that subjects
normally utilize the first syllable of words as retrieval
cues, and it would also provide little information about the
nature of the retrieval cue which enables the non-cued
subject to recall the first syllable.

A final difficulty with Tulving's hypothesis is that

retrieval cues may facilitate recall in ways other than
those specified by the encoding specificity principle.   As
Tulving (1974) has admitted, it is possible that "the
retrieval cue somehow changes the trace, by updating the
information it contains, by restoring some of the
information lost from it, or, in some other manner, by
'strengthening' it" (p. 81).

In sum, the primary advantage of Tulving's approach is
that it requires us to focus on the stimulus-as-encoded both
at input and at test, rather than on the stimulus-as-
presented.   In general terms, poor recognition can be
produced by inducing the subject to encode one and the same
stimulus differently at input and at test.   The significance
of such findings is currently in doubt.   As Wickelgren
(1975) argued,

> It may well be that the probability that a subject
> thinks of the same meaning or sets of meanings at the
> time of retention as he did at the time of original
> learning is so high in most learning and memory tasks
> that these potentially significant retrieval
> interference effects can, in practice, be completely
> ignored" (p. 251).

Furthermore, it seems unlikely that the encoding specificity
principle can account for the typical forgetting observed as
a function of retention interval in recognition tests,
unless the probability of interpreting the stimulus in a
different manner at test from the interpretation given at
input increased as a function of retention interval.   No
unequivocal evidence of this has been produced, and it seems
more likely that retention of the input encoding decreases
over time.

Generation-recognition Models
    While Tulving denies that the processes underlying recall
and recognition differ importantly from each other, several
theorists (e.g., Anderson & Bower, 1972b, 1974; Bahrick,
1969, 1970; James, 1890; Kintsch, 1970; Müller, 1913) have
proposed that there are important qualitative differences
between them.   The general conception is that recall
involves a retrieval or search process, followed by a
decision or recognition process to adjudicate on the
appropriateness of what has been retrieved, whereas

recognition primarily involves the latter process.   It has commonly been assumed that any differences observed between recall and recognition are due solely to differences in the retention tests, i.e., subjects will store the same information whether they anticipate a recall or a recognition test.   However, the evidence indicates that what is stored is dependent upon the anticipated form of the retention test, so that many of the differences found between recall and recognition may be either due to storage differences or may be more directly related to the retention test.   Relevant evidence is available in Frost (1972) and Tversky (1973, 1974).

Interesting evidence about the ways in which subjects prepare themselves for recall and recognition tests was obtained by Broadbent and Broadbent (1975).   They found that subjects expecting tests of both free recall and recognition were more likely to report linking together different list words than linking list words to symbolic events outside the list, whereas the reverse was the case for subjects expecting only a recognition test.   They also found that non-recalled items were not necessarily poorly recognized.   Both these findings point to the existence of qualitative differences between recall and recognition, with Broadbent and Broadbent emphasizing differences in the type of information retrieved: "Can we not say that both processes (i.e., recall and recognition) involve the presentation of event A and the retrieval of event B; but in recall B is the to-be-remembered item and A is a cue for recall, whereas in recognition A is the item and B the circumstances in which it was last experienced?" (p. 589).

If recall and recognition differ qualitatively, a major prediction is that it should be possible to find experimental variables that have a differential effect on recall and recognition.   For example, a variable that only affects retrieval processes should exert a discernible effect on recall, but not on recognition.   Although several variables, such as presentation rate and retention interval have similar effects on both tests, Kintsch (1970) considered some that have a differential effect.   For example, high-frequency words have been found to be better recalled than low-frequency words (e.g., Hall, 1954), whereas low-frequency words are better recognized than high-frequency words (e.g., Shepard, 1967).   However, there are some exceptions (see

Gregg, 1976).   Recall is usually higher when subjects are
given intentional rather than incidental learning
instructions, whereas recognition is equally good under
intentional and incidental learning conditions (e.g., Estes
& DaPolito, 1967).   Furthermore, proactive and retroactive
interference effects are much more frequently obtained in
studies using recall tests (e.g., Postman, 1961) than in
studies employing recognition tests (e.g., Bower & Bostrum,
1968; Postman & Stark, 1969).

The structure or organization of the material has been
found to have differential effects on recall and recognition.
For example, Kintsch (1968) presented either a highly
organized or a poorly organized list, followed by recall or
recognition.   In accord with several previous findings,
subjects recalled about 50 per cent more from the organized
list.   However, recognition performance was the same for the
two lists.   In other studies, usually involving greater
opportunity for learning, organization has been found to
enhance both recall and recognition (e.g., Mandler,
Pearlstone, & Koopmans, 1969).   Finally, Hogan and Kintsch
(1971) gave subjects either four presentations of a list, or
one presentation followed by three successive recalls.   Two
days later, recognition was significantly better where there
had been more item-exposure time, whereas recall was
significantly better where there had been more opportunity
for retrieval.

One of the best statements of a generation-recognition
theory is that of Anderson and Bower (1972b).   During
presentation of a list, they assumed that the subject performs
a series of operations of which the most important are tagging
or labelling pre-existing associative pathways among the list
items with a tag specific to that list, and tagging the
memory nodes (corresponding to the words being presented) with
a list marker.   The original article should be consulted for
full details.   However, the basic assumptions are that
retrieval depends heavily on the extent to which appropriate
associative pathways among the words have been tagged,
whereas recognition depends on the extent to which items have
been tagged with list markers referring to the most recent
list.

The distinctions are clearer in the light of the
experimental situation used by Anderson and Bower (1972b).
From a master set of 32 words, they presented a different

quasi-random selection of 16 words on each of 15 successive
lists, so that all lists after the first had partial overlap
in membership with earlier lists.   Since every list provides
further opportunities for tagging associative pathways, the
ability to retrieve the full set of 32 words should improve
over lists.   However, recognition or discrimination or those
items that appeared on the most recent list is a different
matter.   While discrimination may be relatively easy
initially, the problem of recognition should increase as the
number of lists presented increases.   If, for example, the
word 'flower' occurs in the first, third, and fifth lists,
the subject will tag each occurrence with the appropriate
list marker.   Thus he learns something like 'flower-list 1',
'flower-list 3', and 'flower-list 5'.   It seems reasonable
to assume that interference would increase as more list
markers were associated with each word: the subject would
know that the word 'flower' had been presented several times
during the course of the experiment, but would become
confused as to whether or not it had been presented on the
most recent list.

When subjects were tested for free recall, performance
increased over the first few lists, and then declined.
Anderson and Bower (1972b) assumed that this was because
initially the main factor was the increase in item
retrievability, whereas subsequently, after item
retrievability had reached its ceiling, problems of
discrimination or recognition continued to increase.   While
that sounds very speculative, they did a further experiment
in which subjects were invited after each list to recall all
the words presented to them during the course of the
experiment.   This provided a measure of retrievability of
information.   Recall of the words from the most recent list
could be examined, and it was found that this increased with
negative acceleration to an asymptote, indicating that there
was a systematic improvement in retrievability (see Fig. 4.2
overleaf).   On each trial, subjects were asked to look
through the words they had retrieved, and to indicate whether
or not they thought that each word came from the most recent
list.   This recognition measure revealed a decrease in
performance over lists (see Fig. 4.2).   It thus appears that
free recall divides up into independent processes of
retrieval and recognition.

Since their theory assumes that the processes underlying
the recognition phase of free recall are the same as the

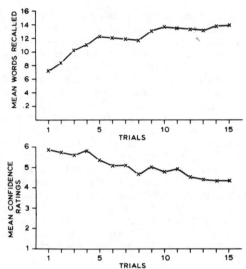

Fig. 4.2. Recallability and recognition
of information as a function of trials.
Adapted from Anderson and Bower (1972b).

processes underlying performance in a pure recognition task,
Anderson and Bower (1972b) repeated the experiment using
recognition as the only retention measure.   As predicted,
recognition declined continuously throughout the experiment.

Anderson and Bower also considered another interesting
theoretical possibility.   If the subject, on a recognition
test, encounters a word which is not directly tagged with
information about its list membership, it is possible that a
more inferential process is used.   The subject may use the
recognition test item as a basis for retrieving associated
list words.   If these other words are tagged with the
appropriate list marker, then the subject may conclude that
the test item was probably in the most recent list.   A
similar inferential process was probably operative in several
other studies in the literature.   For example, Light and
Carter-Sobell (1970), in their third experiment, presented
nouns biased towards one interpretation by their context
(e.g., 'sliced ham') and biased towards a second
interpretation on the recognition test (e.g., 'radio ham').
While recognition performance for the nouns was worse than
under conditions which emphasized the same meaning at

presentation and test, as predicted by Tulving (1974), there
was nevertheless clear evidence that some of the nouns could
be recognized in spite of the change in interpretation.
Perhaps the subjects look initially for a memorial match for
'ham' in the sense of 'radio ham', but, failing to obtain
such a match, attempt a second encoding of the word 'ham'.
Stronger evidence for inferential processes in recognition
would be obtained if correct recognition latencies under the
changed semantic context were longer than under the unchanged
semantic context.

M. W. Eysenck (unpublished data) required subjects to
learn sentences containing homographs to criterion, followed
by a recognition test in which either the same or different
meanings of the homographs were used. On half the trials,
homographs not contained in the presentation sentences were
given; the subjects had to respond 'yes' if the homograph
were from one of the presentation sentences and 'no'
otherwise. Surprisingly, recognition latencies were no
longer with the different semantic context than with the same
semantic context. However, subjects presented with different meanings of the homographs were much more likely to make
a rapid no-response followed shortly by a slower yes-
response correcting their mistake. It appeared that
subjects used both a rapid decision process based on
semantic overlap of the input and test encodings and a
slower, inferential, process.

Mandler (1972) has distinguished between direct
recognition, based upon list or occurrence tags stored with a
recognition test item, and indirect recognition, in which, if
the information stored with the item is weak, the subject
uses organized retrieval processes in order to facilitate
recognition. One might predict that the longer the
retention interval, the more likely that the list or
occurrence information stored with an item will be weak, thus
necessitating the longer, indirect method of recognition.
As Mandler pointed out, "It is intuitively appealing to
suggest that the face of somebody met yesterday is
recognized on the basis of occurrence information, but that
somebody one has not seen for years is appropriately
recognized only after extensive retrieval and search
involving contexts and categories" (p. 141). Since
organizational factors are only involved in indirect
recognition, but not direct recognition, and indirect
recognition is more extensively utilized at longer retention

intervals, the correlation between organization and
recognition should increase as the retention interval
increases.   Mandler reported exactly this finding.

The greatest weakness of the Anderson and Bower (1972b)
formulation is that their one-process model of recognition
incorporates the fallacious assumption that presentation of a
stimulus provides automatic access to its trace in memory.
The work of Tulving has demonstrated the inadequacy of such
an assumption.   Accordingly, Anderson and Bower (1974) have
revamped their hypothesis, so that it is now admitted that
retrieval processes operate in recall and in recognition.
They described four types of retrieval:

> (a) the associative chaining through long-term memory
> during free recall, examining idea after idea, searching
> for senses of words that occurred in the list; (b) the
> examination of list markers or contextual propositions
> from a sense or idea in the attempt to determine whether
> that sense occurred in the list; (c) the generation of
> a lexical realization of the sense in recall; (d) the
> access to a sense from a word.   Recall of a word
> involves retrieval aspects a, then b, then c; on the
> other hand, word recognition involves d then b (p. 411).

They still maintain that their original hypothesis, which
assumed that retrieval processes c and d were infallibly
accurate, is a reasonable simplifying assumption to make when
words are not presented in special semantic contexts.   This
revised hypothesis appears potentially capable of handling
most of the data, and it allows for the possibility of fairly
complex processes in recognition.   However, this all-
encompassing coverage seems to have been obtained at the
expense of rendering the hypothesis somewhat untenable.

A conceptualization that has a number of points of
similarity with that of Anderson and Bower (1972b, 1974) has
been put forward by Underwood (1969, 1972).   He asserted
that the stored representation of an event consists of a
number of attributes, and he identified temporal, spatial,
frequency, modality, orthographic, acoustic, visual,
affective, contextual, and associative attributes.   He
suggested that recall and recognition differ in terms of the
attributes which are necessary for successful performance.
The basic conception is that discriminative attributes are

required for recognition tests, whereas retrieval attributes
are required for recall tasks.   While it is difficult to
decide whether some attributes are better characterized as
discriminative or retrieval attributes, frequency of
occurrence information would appear to facilitate the
discrimination of list items from distractors, but would not
seem to influence retrieval in any way.   On the other hand,
associative attributes are crucial to the success of retrieval
rather than to item recognition.

It is clearly no easy matter to investigate the various
attributes at the experimental level.   However, some
relevant evidence was collected by Zechmeister and
McKillip (1972).   On Underwood's assumption that spatial
attributes are essentially discriminative, they argued that
providing spatial information would not facilitate retrieval.
In their second experiment, subjects were given a long prose
passage on pages that were clearly divided into quadrants.
As expected, it was found that telling some subjects the
quadrant location of a particular fact did not enhance
recall.

A reasonable prediction from the assumption that different
attributes underlie recall and recognition is that the
correlation between recognition and recall scores for
subjects given both types of task should be reasonably low.
Underwood (1972) has confirmed this prediction.

A further prediction from the type of theoretical
approach towards recall and recognition taken by Anderson and
Bower and by Underwood is that relatively shallow levels of
processing may suffice for successful recognition but not for
recall.   Recognition only requires the storage of list-
marker information (Anderson & Bower, 1972b) or frequency of
occurrence information (Underwood, 1969).   Some (but not
all) of the data discussed in Chapter 2 supported this
prediction.

A relevant study was done by Schwartz and Humphreys
(1974), using a list learning task.   Half the subjects were
given conventional learning instructions; the remaining
subjects were required to rehearse aloud only the item
currently being presented, thus reducing the opportunity to
organize the material by means of associative links.   The
rehearsal-constraining instructions had no effect on
recognition, but resulted in a highly significant decrement

in recall.   Underwood would presumably explain these results
by pointing out that both instructional conditions allowed
the encoding of the frequency-of-occurrence information
necessary for recognition, whereas only the condition using
conventional instructions allowed full scope for the
encoding of the associative attributes necessary for recall.

   Underwood (1969) suggested that a particularly important
associative attribute in some circumstances would be the
category name.   Of the studies considered in this chapter,
those of Tulving and Pearlstone (1966) and Tulving and
Psotka (1971) have shown that category names can be
extremely effective retrieval cues.   In addition, several
studies have investigated free recall for a list of randomly
presented words belonging to various semantic categories.
Shuell (1969) and Wood (1972) have reviewed such studies,
which usually find that the words are recalled category by
category.   This suggests that the subject is, in some sense,
using the category names as retrieval cues.

   An attribute approach to memory encourages us to consider
other, non-semantic, types of retrieval cue.   If other
attributes of presented material (orthographic, phonemic,
visual) are stored, it would seem likely that various non-
semantic cues could enhance recall.   Bregman (1968)
investigated this hypothesis by presenting a long series of
nouns interspersed with recall tests.   He found that
semantic, graphic, and phonemic cues were of equivalent
efficacy.   It should be noted that the subjects were aware
of the types of retrieval cues they would receive, so that
the experiment indicates that appropriate phonemic, semantic,
and graphic information can be stored, rather than that it is
normally stored.

   The major role played by word attributes in semantic
memory is exemplified by studies of word fluency.   In such
studies, subjects can readily recall large numbers of words
starting with a specified letter, comprising a certain
number of syllables, belonging to a particular semantic
category, and so on.   Brown and McNeill (1966) offered the
following simple but interesting hypothesis: "We will
suppose that words are entered on keysort cards instead of
pages, and that the cards are punched for various features of
the words entered.   With real cards, paper ones, it is
possible to retrieve from the total deck any subset punched
for a common feature by putting a metal rod through the

proper hole. We will suppose that there is in the mind
some speedier equivalent of this retrieval technique" (p. 333).
Unfortunately, physiologists have as yet been unable to
locate this metal rod.

The general assumption of attribute theory that the memory
trace comprises multiple inter-related attributes and that
retrieval occurs when one or more of the trace's component
attributes is presented as a cue is intuitively plausible.
However, detailed specifications of the processes involved are
rare. For example, consider the effects of multiple cueing.
Is the probability of recalling Attribute A when given
Attribute B as a retrieval cue the same as that of recalling
Attribute B given A? This is the problem of cue symmetry.
What is the effect of providing two independent cues for
recall, as instanced by comparing the probability of recalling
Attribute A when given both B and C as cues with that of
recalling A given either B or C alone?

In a recent study, Jones (1976) investigated these
questions. Subjects were presented with naturalistic
pictures, each incorporating the four components of colour,
object type, location, and sequential position. They were
subsequently cued for recall by the provision of one or more
attributes of each item. With the exception of data
involving the sequential-position attribute, there was
evidence for cue symmetry. In addition, the use of two (or
more) cues for recall instead of just one produced
surprisingly little improvement in recall. Jones argued
that these results supported his fragmentation hypothesis,
according to which the memory trace corresponds to a
fragment of the stimulus situation, and may consist of any
combination of attributes. Any attribute contained in the
fragment, when used as a retrieval cue, gives access to the
remainder of the fragment. In other words, recall of the
memory trace is all-or-none. The failure of multiple cues
to produce substantial increments in recall over single cues
was accounted for by assuming that many fragments contained
several attributes. For example, if a memory trace
comprises Attributes A, B, and C, then the fragmentation
hypothesis predicts that A, B, or C as single cues would each
permit retrieval of the remainder of the fragment. Use of
two retrieval cues (A and B, A and C, or B and C) would be
completely redundant, and would not increase the probability
of recall.

While the fragmentation hypothesis offers an attractively
simple account of the effects of cueing on retrieval
probability, it seems probable that the existence of encoding
specificity means that the relationship between a particular
retrieval cue attribute and its memorial representation in
the trace is more complex than is allowed for on the
fragmentation hypothesis. There is also evidence that
cueing asymmetry occurs with other kinds of material.
Horowitz and Manelis (1972) found that nouns generally
acted as better cues for adjectives than vice versa.
Salzberg (1976) found that the more concrete member of a
paired associate was the more effective cue in providing
access to the unit. He argued that, if each pair of words
was encoded as a unified image, then the word that is the most
salient part of that image should provide the most reliable
access to it. Cueing asymmetry is found when the trace
elements interact together to form a Gestalt-like trace,
whereas cueing symmetry occurs when, as in the Jones (1976)
experiment, the trace elements are more independent.

Output Interference: Verbal Fluency

The work discussed so far in this chapter has been largely
concerned with the processes involved in recalling and
recognizing single words. While the same processes
undoubtedly occur in situations where subjects are required
to recall a long series of words, there are additional factors
involved. The nature of these additional factors is
discussed in connection with the paradigms of verbal fluency
and free recall.

In studies of verbal fluency, subjects are required to
produce as many words as possible from semantic memory
belonging to some specified conceptual category (e.g., animal
names; words starting with the letter A). Since the
requested information has been learned some years previously,
such tasks provide a good method of investigating problems of
retrieval. A common observation is that the rate of
retrieval of items decreases greatly over time, and that,
even with plentiful time available, the subject fails to
produce several items that he knows (Bousfield & Sedgewick,
1944; Bousfield, Sedgewick, & Cohen, 1954). Lazar and
Buschke (1972) suggested that subjects retrieved only about
20 per cent of the category members which they knew on the
basis of their observation that the average subject recalled
about one-fifth of the total number of different items

produced by all the subjects.   It is likely that this is an
under-estimate, but it is clear that such tasks involve a
substantial retrieval problem.

A hypothesis that fits some of the data has been proposed
by Brown (1968).   If a subject is attempting to recall items
from some category, such as four-footed animals, we may
assume that the subject initially selects a search set which
comprises only four-footed animals - intrusions are rare in
verbal fluency tasks.   Then he samples at random from the
items in the search set, and produces any items which he has
not previously produced.   The sampling is with replacement,
so that the subject may well find himself retrieving some of
the stronger items several times, and this frequent re-
retrieval of some items may inhibit, or interfere with, the
retrieval of weaker items.   Results consistent with such a
hypothesis were reported by Brown.   He found that study of a
list of half the English county names had a detrimental
effect on subsequent retrieval of the non-list county names.
Since Brown was unable to detect the use of any strategies
when he considered the order of recall of the English county
names, he concluded that the evidence was consistent with the
notion of random sampling, and that the poor performance of
the group that had studied the list of county names was due
to frequent re-retrieval of the studied names during recall.
It is possible that the subjects who studied the list of items
merely spent a disproportionate amount of the available
retrieval time in attempting to recall the items on the
studied list.

Shiffrin (1970) introduced a needed flexibility into
Brown's hypothesis when he proposed that the subject might
select a series of search sets rather than a single, global,
search set.   For example, the recall of four-footed animals
might proceed by considering four-footed animals found in
England, then those found in the rest of Europe, and so on, or
by considering domesticated animals followed by wild animals.
Shiffrin, however, retained the notion of sampling with
replacement, and was able to demonstrate logically that
sampling with replacement is more effective if the subject
systematically varies his search set than if he retains a
single search set.   Thus a systematic search for county
names based upon geographical or alphabetical information can
lead to an enhancement of retrieval (Rawles, unpublished
data).   Furthermore, the usual rapid reduction in the number
of items produced can be eliminated if the subject is given a

systematic search strategy.   For example, Indow and Togano
(1970) asked their subjects to list Japanese cities starting
with those in the north of Japan and working southwards.   The
rate of production of cities was constant over time.

The weakest assumption of the Brown-Shiffrin hypothesis as
applied to verbal fluency tasks is that of random sampling.
Several findings indicate that the sampling is not random.
For example, Bousfield and Sedgewick (1944) asked their
subjects to write down the names of quadrupeds, and found
that several subjects recalled domesticated animals together,
wild animals together, commonly exhibited species together,
and so on.   While Shiffrin's hypothesis can handle such
findings on a post hoc basis, it is unable to predict their
occurrence.   Bousfield and Barclay (1950) found a fair
degree of inter-individual consistency in the order of
recall, with those items recalled by most of the subjects
tending to be recalled early in the retrieval period.   The
extent to which retrieval is organized may well be an
important determinant of recall performance.   M. W. Eysenck
(1974a) required his subjects to recall words from five
different categories, and they were free to change categories
at any time.   He found a highly significant positive
correlation of .55 between the extent to which recall was
organized or clustered by categories and the number of words
recalled.

The notion of random recall is fallacious, but the idea of
sampling with replacement may well be important, since it
represents a major limitation of human retrieval processes.
As yet, however, no definitive proof of the existence of
sampling with replacement in verbal fluency tasks has been
provided.   A simple experiment in which subjects were invited
to produce any words belonging to a specified category,
whether they had been produced previously or not, might be
most instructive.   The verbal fluency task is a particularly
interesting one because of the apparent scope it offers the
subject to utilize a variety of retrieval strategies.   The
other side of the coin, however, is that it is extremely
difficult to do tightly controlled experiments with this task.
Accordingly, some of the ideas developed so far will be
extended to another body of experimentation which is similar,
at least superficially, and which offers greater opportunity
for experimental control.

Output Interference: Free Recall

Roediger (1974) has reviewed the relevant evidence
indicating the existence of output interference in studies of
free recall.   For example, Slamecka (1968, 1969) compared
recall for subjects who received some of the items from a
previously-presented list as retrieval cues with that of
subjects recalling under conditions of free recall.   Since
it has frequently been assumed that inter-item associations
are formed during learning, one might expect the list items
to serve as effective retrieval cues.   In fact, Slamecka
found that presenting various proportions of a list as
retrieval cues not only failed to facilitate recall of the
remainder of the list, but actually exerted a slight
inhibiting effect on recall, as compared to normal free
recall.

Unfortunately, there were several inadequacies in
Slamecka's work.   In some of the experiments, subjects in
the conditions receiving part-list retrieval cues were
deprived of recall from primary memory, whereas the control
subjects were not.   The suspicion is that the
ineffectiveness of the retrieval cues was due to the fact
that the subjects only learned as many higher-order units or
clusters of items as they were capable of retrieving unaided,
so that the list cues provided redundant information.
Roediger (1973) extended this line of reasoning, and put
forward a two-factor hypothesis of the effectiveness of
retrieval cues:

> Retrieval cues which allow access to more higher-order
> units than a subject could recall without the aid of
> cues will lead to benefits in cued over noncued (free)
> recall, but when more retrieval cues than are needed to
> produce access to higher-order units are provided (for
> example, other instances from the higher-order unit)
> recall of items from the higher-order unit will be
> impaired (p. 654).

An elaboration of Roediger's position was proposed by
Rundus (1973).   He suggested that a subject, when required to
free recall a list of words, would attempt to retrieve a
retrieval cue representing an organizing idea used at input
to form a grouping of items (e.g., a category name).   Words
associated with that retrieval cue are retrieved, then the
subject attempts to find a second retrieval cue, and
retrieves any words associated with it.   He assumed that the

probability of retrieving a particular word on a given
retrieval attempt with a retrieval cue is determined by the
ratio rule (i.e., the probability of retrieving a given item
is equal to the strength of association of that item to the
cue, divided by the sum of strengths of association of all
items to that cue). Further crucial assumptions are that
sampling is with replacement, and that retrieval of an item
increases the strength of association between that item and
its retrieval cue.

Rundus (1973) tested some of the above assumptions in an
experiment in which subjects were presented with categorized
word lists, followed by a test for recall. Differing
numbers of list words belonging to the various categories
were presented on the recall test, and the subjects were
invited to recall the non-given members of each category. If
presentation of list items as cues is functionally equivalent
to the retrieval of these items by the subject, then these
items should tend to be re-retrieved, and should interfere
with recall of the additional list members. More precisely,
as the number of items in any category presented as cues
increases, the proportion of additional list items
recallable should decrease. Rundus obtained evidence in
line with this prediction, as did Roediger (1973). While
the hypothesis proposed by Rundus appears to handle intra-
category interference effects satisfactorily, Roediger has
provided evidence of output interference effects due simply
to the total number of items previously presented or
retrieved which appears to be inexplicable on Rundus' theory.

If retrieval limitations are importantly due to sampling
with replacement, it then seems to follow that, at a given
stage of learning, subjects will only be able to retrieve a
limited <u>number</u> of items, but the exact items actually
recalled might be variable. Tulving (1967) presented an
unrelated word list followed by three successive attempts at
free recall, and found that, of all the words recalled at
least once within a given set of recall attempts, only
approximately 50 per cent were recalled all three times.
Patterson (1972) obtained similar findings with a categorized
word list.

More direct evidence for the notion of sampling with
replacement comes from a study by Bousfield and Rosner (1970).
They asked subjects to recall lists of unrelated words either
under standard free recall conditions or under conditions of

'uninhibited' recall.   Uninhibited recall involved telling
the subjects to report any words that occurred to them during
the recall period, whether or not they knew the word to be a
repetition or some other kind of error.   The uninhibited
subjects produced several more words than the control
subjects, and most of the difference was accounted for by the
greater tendency to repeat previously-recalled items of the
uninhibited subjects.   While the difference in the number of
repetitions was smaller than might have been anticipated,
this study does point to the existence of sampling with
replacement.

In sum, retrieval cues are sometimes ineffective in
enhancing recall, probably because they are supplying
redundant information.   The finding that retrieval cues can
actually interfere with, or reduce, recall can be described
as 'output interference', but the term is not explanatory.
While the evidence is suggestive rather than conclusive, it
does indicate that retrieval of a long series of items can be
detrimentally affected by sampling problems.   One danger
with such hypotheses is that they may explain too much.   It
is difficult to see any sampling-with-replacement problem
when an actor effortlessly recites hundreds of lines of
Shakespeare.   Furthermore, a careful consideration of
Rundus' model suggests that perfect retrieval of long lists
of words should be almost impossible, due to the limitations
of the retrieval system.

Summary

In general terms, the probability of successful recall or
recognition of a previously-presented word depends on the
extent to which mental events and processes on the retention
test approximate to those occurring during input.   This
emphasis on mental proficiency in processing is necessitated
by several findings, most notably those of Tulving.   He has
found that, under some circumstances, subjects are less
likely to recognize an identical copy of a list word than
they are to recall that word when given another word as a
retrieval cue.   This result seems inexplicable if one
concentrates on the nominal stimulus, or the stimulus-as-
presented, rather than on the functional stimulus, or the
stimulus-as-encoded.

Tulving's encoding specificity principle, while providing

a useful conceptual framework, is uninformative about what
the crucial mental processes might be. One common
suggestion is that the initial encoding of information at
presentation involves the storage of a subset of a word's
attributes, with the probability of successful memory
performance depending primarily on the extent to which the
attributes encoded on the retention test match those encoded
at storage. It is probable that the semantic attributes
are of particular significance in determining retention-test
performance, but this has not been clearly demonstrated.

In spite of the applicability of Tulving's encoding
specificity principle to both recall and recognition, it is
probable that there are important differences in the
information used and the processes required on the two types
of retention test. There is obviously merit in the
proposal that recall and recognition both involve a decision
process, but that recall also involves a search process.

It has proved difficult to provide a precise elaboration
of the mechanics of these search and decision processes. It
is possible, however, that some light could be thrown on
search and retrieval processes by the use of physiological
recording techniques. For example, Kahneman (1973) has
argued that pupillary dilation is a good measure of effort.
Kahneman and Peavler (1969), in a study of paired-associate
learning, found that the dilation which occurred during
retrieval was four to six times as large as the dilation
which occurred during learning. The degree of effort
involved in retrieval as a function of the number and
relevance of the retrieval cues available could be assessed,
and the moment by moment changes in pupil size during
retrieval might be revealing.

While the tip-of-the-tongue phenomenon demonstrates that
it is possible to retrieve some word attributes separately
from others, it has not yet been shown whether word retrieval
normally involves the successive retrieval of attributes or
the simultaneous retrieval of attributes in an all-or-none
fashion. Retrieval cues consisting of attributes of the to-
be-remembered word could be presented at different points
during the retrieval period. If the retrieval of attributes
is successive, then more attributes will have been retrieved
later in the retrieval period. On this hypothesis,
retrieval cues presented later in the retrieval period are
less likely to speed up recall than cues presented at the

start of the retrieval period.

The work on free recall and verbal fluency has provided at
least one insight into the nature of search processes.
While the subjects are instructed to recall each word once
only, i.e., to sample without replacement, it seems that
people inevitably sample with replacement.

An obvious deficiency in most of the work on retrieval has
been the use of experimental paradigms that only require
limited retrieval processes on the part of the subject.
Morton and Byrne (1975) asked subjects to provide suggested
menus fulfilling certain constraints, or to indicate the food
and furniture required by a honeymoon couple living in a
small cottage.   The resultant protocols indicated that
retrieval can involve complex cognitive processes that are
usually unexplored by psychologists.

CHAPTER 5
RETRIEVAL II

In the previous chapter, we considered some of the factors involved in retrieval. The studies dealt with in that chapter utilized probability of a correct response as the major dependent variable. In this chapter, on the other hand, we will discuss those studies employing latency of a correct response as the dependent variable. While the naïve might imagine that data and theory deriving from these two approaches might dovetail neatly together, such is not the case. One reason for the discrepancy is that probability is only a useful measure where performance falls substantially short of perfection, whereas latency tends to be used in essentially error-free situations. Since response latency is greatly affected by a subject's preference for speed or accuracy, comparability of performance across the various conditions of an experiment is maintained by ensuring that subjects emphasize accuracy to the point where errors occur on no more than five to ten per cent of all trials.

A major subdivision within studies of search latency is between those that investigate recognition, in which the subject has to indicate as rapidly as possible whether a given item corresponds to one of the learned items, and those considering recall, in which the subject's task is to retrieve a learned item upon the presentation of some cue.

Recognition
The paradigm which has been most investigated is one introduced by Sternberg (1966, 1969). In essence, the subject memorizes a short set of items, the positive set. He then receives a probe item, to which he must make a yes-response only if it belongs to the positive set. The enormous literature using this paradigm has been reviewed by Corballis (1975) and by Shiffrin and Schneider (1974). The most explored variable that has been used by researchers is size of the positive set, i.e., the number of items learned.

Typical findings are presented in Fig. 5.1.   As can be seen,
both the positive and negative functions are linear and
parallel, and the negative function is consistently slower
than the positive function.   However, other investigators
have reported functions which are negatively accelerated, and
more closely approximated by a logarithmic function than by a
linear one.   Corballis (1975) pointed out that linear
functions tend to be obtained when individual items appear in
the positive set on some trials but in the negative set on
other trials, whereas logarithmic functions are more common
when none of the items included in any positive set ever
appears in the negative set.

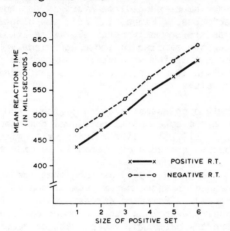

Fig. 5.1. Recognition reaction time as a function
of the number of items learned (hypothetical data).

Sternberg (1969) proposed a four-stage model to explain
the typical findings.   Stage 1 involves stimulus encoding, in
which sensory information is transformed into a stable form;
stage 2, serial exhaustive comparison, involves the
comparison of the probe stimulus with each member of the
positive set in memory;   stage 3, response decision, consists
of determining which response is appropriate;   and stage 4,
response selection and evocation, involves the actual
execution of the response.   Sternberg argued that stage 2,
the serial exhaustive comparison, is of crucial importance in
explaining data such as those in Fig. 5.1.   The fact that
the function relating reaction time to set size is linear is

consistent with the notion that the subject conducts a
serial search through the positive set: the greater the
number of items in the positive set, the longer this search
will take.   However, it seems intuitively more likely that
the search would be self-terminating, i.e., ending when the
probe item is located in the positive set, rather than
exhaustive.   Sternberg claimed that if the search process
were self-terminating, then, on average, only about half the
items in the positive set would be searched through on yes-
decision trials, whereas all the items would apparently need
to be examined prior to a no-decision.   The natural
deduction from a self-terminating search model is that the
slope for yes-decisions should, on average, be about half
that for no-decisions.   Since, in fact, the slopes for yes-
and no-decisions are commonly parallel, it is likely that the
search processes are similar for both decisions.   Sternberg
thus concluded that serial exhaustive searches at the rate of
approximately 25-30 items per second were performed on both
positive and negative trials.

If Sternberg's hypothesis is correct, then recognition
memory can involve a substantial retrieval component.
However, several well-known difficulties exist with respect
to this hypothesis, and some of them will be discussed:-

(1) Sternberg (1969) assumed that the set-size
variable influenced only the memory-comparison stage of the
recognition process.   However, Kirsner (1972b) ran an
experiment closely resembling those conventionally done
within the Sternberg paradigm, except that he required the
subjects to name the probe as rapidly as possible rather than
to provide a yes- or no-decision.   There was a significant
effect of set size on naming latency, with the naming latency
advantage for positive set items over negative set items
increasing as set size decreased.   These findings suggest
that set size can affect stage 1, stimulus encoding, in
addition to the memory-comparison stage.

(2) The notion of an exhaustive search appears
implausible in most situations.   For example, consider the
fact that people can extremely rapidly decide that
'mantiness' is not a word in their vocabulary.   If subjects
performed a serial exhaustive search through their entire
vocabularies, the search process would take nearly half-an-
hour!   Even with much smaller sets of words, exhaustive
scanning is unlikely.   For instance, Atkinson and Juola

(1972) conducted a Sternberg-type experiment using positive sets of 16, 24, and 32 words. The slopes of the reaction-time functions worked out at 4.12 milliseconds per item on yes trials, and half a millisecond per item on no trials. It is unlikely that the fast rates of search implied by these figures actually occur. Furthermore, exhaustive searches do not seem to occur when the to-be-learned material can be organized. When the items in the positive set are not members of the same category but can be grouped perceptually (Crain & DeRosa, 1974; Williams, 1971), semantically (Naus, 1974; Naus, Glucksberg, & Ornstein, 1972), symbolically (Milles, 1969), or syntactically (Clifton & Gutschera, 1971), subjects appear to be able to utilize the categorization in order to obviate the need for an exhaustive search.

(3) An exhaustive-scan hypothesis has difficulty in accounting for the frequent finding that a logarithmic function describes the data more adequately than a linear function (e.g., Briggs & Swanson, 1970; Simpson, 1972). Possible counter-arguments are discussed by Corballis (1975).

(4) Sternberg's theory predicts that the time taken to make yes responses should not depend on the probe item's serial position in the positive set. However, several researchers have obtained substantial serial-position effects (e.g., Burrows & Okada, 1971; Corballis, 1967; Corballis, Kirby, & Miller, 1972; Morin, DeRosa, & Stultz, 1967). In most cases, there was a recency effect, with faster response latencies for the last item or two in the positive set, but sometimes there was a small primacy effect. Sternberg's model could account for these serial-position effects by assuming either the encoding or response stages are affected by the serial position of the probe item.

(5) It is becoming increasingly clear (e.g., Townsend, 1971) that it is extremely difficult to obtain experimental evidence that will unequivocally distinguish between parallel and serial search models. Aube and Murdock (1974) interpreted several results obtained with the Sternberg paradigm in the light of Murdock's parallel processing model. According to this model, all items are processed simultaneously, but at different rates. The processing rates vary as a function of serial position. For a self-terminating model, the processing time for positive probes is the average over all serial positions of the different items tested, whereas the processing time for

negative probes depends on the time taken to process the
slowest item.   Additional assumptions allow Aube and
Murdock to account for many of the major findings.
Insufficient work has been done to assess the tenability of
this particular parallel-processing model;   the main point is
that complex parallel-processing models certainly could
generate predictions as accurate as those of the serial-
processing models favoured by Sternberg.

    Some of the preceding difficulties with the Sternberg
model can be suitably viewed within the framework of direct-
access strength theory (e.g., Banks, 1970;   Egan, 1958;
Norman & Wickelgren, 1969;   Pike, 1973).   It should be
noted that this 'theory' is more a general orientation to
recognition memory than a single, detailed set of hypotheses.
The basic assumption is that the subject consults the memory
location corresponding to the probe item, and bases his
decision on the strength, or familiarity, of the trace that
is stored there.   The subject erects a criterion at some
point along the familiarity scale, and responds 'yes' if the
familiarity of the item is above the criterion, and 'no'
otherwise.   As Pike has suggested, the further the probe
item's familiarity deviates from the criterion, the faster
the response should become.   Effects of set size could be
handled by assuming that increasing the size of the positive
set would reduce the average familiarity of the items in it,
thus placing the items closer to the criterion and increasing
the response latency.   Serial-position effects are accounted
for by assuming that early and final items are more familiar
than those in the middle of the memory set.   Baddeley and
Ecob (1970) predicted on the basis of direct-access theory
that reaction times should be faster for items that were
repeated in the memory set, which is what they found.
However, there are various difficulties with direct-access
strength theory.   A major problem is that the theory does
not, in the absence of additional assumptions, predict
specifically whether the reaction-time functions should be
either linear or logarithmic.   Further problems with the
theory are discussed by Corballis (1975).

    Reed (1976) has argued that a potentially fruitful
experimental approach to the problem of differentiating
among the various explanations of the Sternberg effect is to
make processing time an independent, rather than a dependent,
variable.   In his response-signal method, there is a lag
between the onset of the probe item and a signal instructing

the subject to respond.   The performance measure is the
accuracy of the subject's reaction as a function of the lag,
or processing time.   Since this new paradigm may lead to
rather different retrieval strategies to those produced by
the conventional Sternberg paradigm, Reed compared results
obtained from the two paradigms.   He found sufficient
similarity to indicate that very similar processes are
probably involved in both cases.

In terms of Sternberg's exhaustive scan model, the
simplest assumption is that no information is available
before the scan is completed, and complete information
thereafter.   This should produce a step function, in which
accuracy increases dramatically at some critical processing
time.   The shapes of the time-accuracy curves should be the
same for different list lengths.   Furthermore, the processing time at which this step function produces the step
should increase by about 30 milliseconds per extra item.
In fact, Reed's results were inconsistent with all these
predictions.   There was no step function, and the time-
accuracy curves for the various list lengths had different
shapes, rather than the same shape horizontally displaced.
Although the exhaustive-scan model predicts a difference of
approximately 90 milliseconds in processing time between the
arrival of the curves for one-item and four-item lists at the
terminal level, the actual difference was well over 300
milliseconds.

Strength or direct-access models typically predict that
the average item strength varies inversely with the number of
items in the list.   This implies that the asymptotic level
of accuracy at the longer processing times should decrease
rapidly with increasing list length.   In fact, the results
showed that accuracy of performance with long processing
intervals varied little, if at all, as a function of list
length.

The findings were most consistent with a theory proposed
by Theios, Smith, Haviland, Traupmann, and Moy (1973).   In
essence, they argued that the subject engages in a self-
terminating search through a stack containing entries for all
the items in the population from which the members of the
positive set may be drawn.   Members of the positive set are
marked as positive and placed at the head of the stack, with
negative markers being attached to the remaining items in the
stack.   The subject then compares the probe to successive

items in the stack, until an item matching the probe is
located.   However, in spite of the success of this model in
accounting for the results, it is clear that such a theory is
inapplicable where the potential set of positive items is
either unknown or extremely large.

One possible solution to the problem of accounting for
all the relevant data is to attempt to amalgamate the best
aspects of two or more models.   Atkinson, Herrmann, and
Wescourt (1974), Atkinson and Juola (1973), Corballis (1975),
and Forrin and Cunningham (1973) have all argued that a
theory incorporating an amalgam of the assumptions of the
serial-search and direct-access models can provide a more
adequate account of recognition-latency data than either
model considered separately.   The subsequent discussion will
concentrate on the Atkinson and Juola (1973) model, and its
elaboration by Atkinson et al. (1974), since this is the most
developed of the two-process models.

Atkinson and Juola (1973) assumed that each probe word
presented on a recognition test has associated with it a
familiarity value that can be considered as a value on a
continuous scale.   The familiarity value of a word would be
determined by such factors as the frequency and recency with
which that word has accurately been accessed.   It is further
assumed that the familiarity values for items from the
positive set (target items) have a higher mean than is the
case for non-list probes (distractor items), as indicated in
Fig. 5.2.

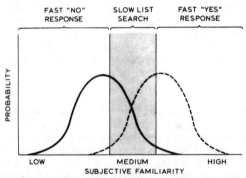

Fig. 5.2. Recognition-memory decision making
as a function of probe word familiarity value.
Adapted from Atkinson and Juola (1973).

The subject establishes a low criterion and a high criterion which correspond to two different points along the familiarity continuum. There are then three major possibilities. The first is that the probe item has a low familiarity value which lies below the low criterion. In this case, the subject makes a rapid no-decision. The second is that the probe item has a high familiarity value which lies above the high criterion. In this case, the subject makes a rapid yes-decision. The third is that the probe item has a moderate familiarity value which lies in the area of uncertainty between the low and high criteria. In this case, the subject will be less confident about which response to choose, and will make a more extensive search through the memorized list. Since serial and parallel search processes are often mathematically indistinguishable (cf., Townsend, 1971), the model is not dogmatic about the nature of this search process. Whether the search process is serial or parallel, the inclusion of a search component will inevitably lead to slow responses.

In sum, subjects can rapidly decide whether a probe item does or does not belong to the positive set provided that its familiarity value is low or high enough. If its familiarity value is intermediate, a decision cannot be based upon familiarity, and a search process is instigated. If the experimenter's instructions emphasize speed, then the low and high criteria will be placed closer together, and subjects will usually respond solely on the basis of familiarity. If accuracy is emphasized, then the criteria will be placed further apart, and the subject will more frequently engage in the slower memory search. In other words, the low and high criteria for judging familiarity are set on the basis of the speed-accuracy trade-off deemed preferable. The above sketchy account is amplified by Atkinson et al. (1974).

Atkinson and Juola (1973) discussed the results of several experiments in which subjects initially learned a list of between 16 and 32 words, followed by a long series of test trials. During the course of these test trials, each of the target and distractor words was presented a number of times. On their initial presentation, targets (yes-decision items) were responded to more slowly than distractors, whereas the reverse was the case on subsequent presentations. Theoretically, the argument is that the repeated presentation of targets and distractors leads to increases in

their familiarity values.   For target items, the major
effect will be to increase the probability that these items
will receive a fast yes-response, and decrease the
probability of an extended memory search, i.e., mean latency
should decrease.   For distractor items, repetition will
lead to an increased probability of an extended search, with
a consequent increase in response latency.

Interesting support for the type of theory proposed by
Atkinson and Juola (1973) comes from the subjects'
introspective reports.   They sometimes found themselves
making immediate responses to a probe without 'knowing for
sure' whether or not it was a target item.   Theoretically,
such decisions are based solely on the probe's familiarity
value.   In addition, subjects are usually aware of their
errors.   This suggests that errors involve responding on the
basis of familiarity, although the subjects continue
processing by searching memory and thereby check their
decision.

The fact that strong evidence for search processes has
been found by Sternberg and by others can be accounted for by
considering in more detail their experimental procedure.   A
small pool of items, such as digits, has frequently been
used, with items belonging to the positive set on some
trials and the negative set on other trials.   Under such
circumstances, there would be negligible differences in
familiarity between targets and distractors, so that subjects
would have to utilize the extended search process in order to
make accurate decisions.

The Atkinson-Juola model predicts that speed instructions
will lead the subject to make most of his recognition
decisions on the basis of the familiarity value of the probe.
Since the increase in reaction time as a function of set
size is said to be due to the memory-search process, it
follows that the reaction-time slope will be reduced under
speed instructions.   Exactly this result was obtained by
Banks and Atkinson (1974), who also noted that the standard
procedure of requiring almost perfect accuracy in the
Sternberg·paradigm means that information is obtained from
only one end of the speed-accuracy continuum.   The Atkinson-
Juola model is one of the few theories to account for speed-
accuracy trade-off.   While some of the data obtained by
Banks and Atkinson were not entirely consistent with the
Atkinson-Juola model, Banks and Atkinson provided plausible

extensions of the theory that would enable it to handle the discrepancies.

The Atkinson-Juola model assumes that errors occur either when a distractor has a high familiarity value or a target has a low familiarity value. If a probe has an intermediate familiarity value, and thus is given an extended memory search, it is assumed that the subject never makes an error. The prediction is that error latencies will be fast, since they are based upon familiarity only. Data reported by Atkinson and Juola (1973) are consistent with this prediction. However, some studies have reported slow errors, presumably due to imperfect learning of the positive set or to instructions emphasizing speed of response.

Atkinson et al. (1974) reported recognition memory latencies for short-term store and long-term store searches. The same basic model appears to handle data in both cases, although there are some quantitative differences. For example, the fact that the slopes of the memory set functions are much steeper with small memory sets than with large ones suggests that search processes are more likely in short-term than in long-term store. In addition, some comparisons implied that it takes longer to initiate the search process in long-term store, but that the subsequent search rate is faster.

In another experiment, subjects memorized 30 words to mastery (the long-term set). On each of the test trials, the subject was presented with between zero and four words (the short-term set), followed by a probe word. A yes-decision was required if the probe word came from either the short-term or the long-term set. If the probe came from the short-term set, then mean reaction time was a function of short-term set size. If the probe word came from the long-term set, mean latency was not a function of short-term set size, except that mean latency was less if there was no short-term set. In general, responding was faster from short-term store than from long-term store. If one assumes that short-term store search is followed by long-term store search, then it would follow that reaction times to long-term store items should be affected by the size of the short-term set. Since this was not supported by the data, Atkinson et al. (1974) concluded that short-term and long-term stores are searched in parallel; if a match is found in either store, a positive response is made.

The Atkinson-Juola model seems to provide a useful integration of previous theoretical formulations, and is of more general applicability than the earlier hypotheses in this area. However, theories of memory which emphasize concepts such as 'trace strength' and 'item familiarity' tend to ignore the multi-dimensional nature of the memory trace. For example, it is possible that somewhat different memorial attributes are accessed when determining the familiarity values of items in short-term and long-term store. Consider a thought experiment in which the subject is presented with a particular word dozens of times prior to the experiment proper, and that this word is never subsequently used as a member of the positive memory set. According to the Atkinson-Juola model, the subject should rapidly respond 'yes' if the word initially presented many times occurred as a probe word; common sense indicates that this result would not be obtained. There seems to be a need for deeper analysis of the concept of 'familiarity value'.

A second criticism of the work on speed of recognition is the almost total lack of attention paid to individual differences. There are at least two studies (Anders, 1973; Clifton & Birenbaum, 1970) which indicate important effects of individual differences. Clifton and Birenbaum ran 12 subjects in a typical Sternberg task, and found that nine subjects produced linear positive and negative functions of approximately the same slope. This, of course, is the typical result and consistent with the notion of a serial-exhaustive scan. However, the remaining three subjects produced functions for no-responses that were twice as steep as their functions for yes-responses, a finding suggesting that these subjects were using a self-terminating strategy.

Anders (1973) also used the Sternberg paradigm, but included ten items in each memory set. He asked subjects to verbalize the nature of the search processes that they used, and found a correlation of +.80 between the number of items subjects said they encountered during the search and response latency. While there was a general tendency for the subjects to adopt a strategy of self-termination on 'yes' trials and of exhaustive scanning on 'no' trials, there were some pronounced differences among the four subjects. Two subjects divided each list into smaller groups or sub-lists, and searched group by group, one subject placed the number stimuli in their numerical order, and the remaining subject adopted a variety of strategies. It is thus probable that

individual differences of considerable importance are
obscured by the conventional procedure of reducing the data
to group means.

Recall

Much of the work on speed of recall has been capably
reviewed by Mandler (1975).   The emphasis has tended to be
on the effects of organizational variables on speed of
recall.   In free recall of categorized word lists, subjects
tend to recall the words category by category, even if they
were originally presented in a random order (see Wood, 1972,
for a review).   Some investigators (e.g., Kellas, Ashcraft,
Johnson, & Needham, 1973; Patterson, Meltzer, & Mandler,
1971; Pollio, Richards, & Lucas, 1969) have looked at
temporal aspects of recall by recording inter-word response
times (IRTs) in categorized free recall.   A major finding
is that members belonging to a common category are
characterized by relatively short IRTs, whereas words which
mark the boundaries of different categories are
characterized by relatively long IRTs.   In addition, there
is a more noticeable increase in between-category IRTs than
in within-category IRTs during the course of retrieval.

The interpretation of the above findings, as Patterson et
al. (1971) have pointed out, is complicated by the fact that
between-category IRTs represent a combination of three
factors: time to exit from one category, time to access a
second category, and time to access a word belonging to the
second category.   The increase in between-category IRTs
during retrieval appears to be due largely to the increased
difficulty of accessing the second category, since no
increase was observed when subjects were given all the
category names as retrieval cues during recall.   Many of the
results obtained by researchers investigating the temporal
characteristics of free recall from categorized word lists
were replicated by McCauley and Kellas (1974), in a free
recall study in which subjects were instructed to form
groupings of unrelated words during input.

Patterson et al. (1971) proposed a theoretical model based
upon random sampling with replacement, similar in some ways
to the Rundus (1973) and Shiffrin (1970) models discussed in
the previous chapter.   According to such a model, retrieval
of additional categories becomes progressively more difficult,
a prediction confirmed by the finding that between-category

IRTs sometimes show an exponential growth function across category output positions (e.g., Pollio et al., 1969; Patterson et al., 1971). However, Kellas et al. (1973) and McCauley and Kellas (1974) found a linear function rather than an exponential growth function, and their data are more difficult to reconcile with the Patterson et al. (1971) model.

Kellas et al. (1973) argued that memory trace strength was an important factor neglected by the sampling-with-replacement models. Rundus (1971), who required overt rehearsal of categorized word lists, found that initial category members were rehearsed more than terminal items in each category, and Wood and Underwood (1967) found that the initial items in each successive category had higher recall probabilities than terminal items. The implication is that the members of a category vary considerably in trace strength as indexed either by amount of rehearsal or recall probability. The increase in IRTs as subjects recall the members of a category could be due to the fact that subjects initially recall the strongest items. As Kellas et al. indicated, the general similarity of the IRT patterns within and between categories suggest that a strength model could also account for the increasing between-category IRTs observed during recall. If categories recalled late in the output sequence are more weakly represented in memory, one would predict that fewer items from them should be recalled. Although this result was obtained, it is possibly due to output interference from items previously recalled (cf., Smith, D'Agostino, & Reid, 1970).

There are important similarities between free recall from categorized word lists and studies of verbal fluency in which subjects simply recall as many items belonging to a specified category as possible. Mandler (1975) discussed the common finding that subjects in verbal fluency tasks frequently produce short 'bursts' of items in rapid succession. The items within these bursts tend to be characterized by a high level of inter-item associations (Pollio, 1964). Dean (1971) defined fast IRTs as those falling within the top 25 per cent of the distribution, and found that 91 per cent of sequences comprising fast IRTs contained five or fewer items. This indicates an important limitation on retrieval processes, as does an observation reported by Mandler (1975). He asked subjects to name common objects (e.g., those to be found in an office) as rapidly as possible, and found that there was frequently a discernible pause after four to six items had been named that was embarrassing to the subject.

An obvious interpretation of the above findings stems from the assumption (Atkinson & Shiffrin, 1968; Shiffrin & Atkinson, 1969) that exit from long-term memory is through primary memory or the short-term store. If primary memory can hold only four or five items at any one time, this could provide an explanation for the limited size of most response bursts. However, Patterson (1971) obtained data indicating that exit through primary memory may not be an important determinant of retrieval from long-term store. She presented subjects with a categorized list or a list of unrelated words, followed by standard free recall or free recall in which the subject counted backwards for 15 seconds after recalling each word. While one would expect that the counting task would seriously affect primary memory storage, the two recall conditions did not differ in terms of items recalled, repetitions, or intrusions. Furthermore, the categorized lists showed no differences in clustering or in the size of the first cluster recalled.

Mandler (1975) rather speculatively proposed that the reason why retrieval from long-term memory is limited to about five items at a time is due to storage limitations:-

> I assume that at the time of original storage, the system must make a decision as to the items or categories with which a particular new item must be stored. At the time the decision to store is made the organism needs to have available within his attention span or consciousness the other items which belong to the same group. That decision is reached on a single dimension and is limited to about 5-7 values of that dimension (p. 511).

A few studies have compared speed of recall from short-term store with speed of recall from long-term store. For example, Waugh (1970) presented lists of words, each list followed by a probe word. The probe word was one of the list words, and the subject's task was to recall the word that had followed the probe word in the list. The results indicated that retrieval from primary memory took significantly less time than retrieval from secondary memory. Freedman and Loftus (1974) required subjects to learn categories of varying size, and then asked subjects to

HM—I

produce a member of one of the categories starting with the letter. Response latencies increased as a function of category size up to a size of seven items, but then showed no further increase up to the largest category size of thirty-two items. This finding, reminiscent of recognition latency findings reported by Atkinson et al. (1974), may indicate that an extended memory search is more likely when retrieving from short-term store than from long-term store. Anders (1971) used a somewhat different paradigm, in which subjects had to recall the location of a probe item, and noticed that the search rate was approximately twice as fast in primary memory (8 items per second) as in secondary memory (4.5 items per second).

There are substantial individual differences in the strategies used to recall well-learned items of information. Anders (1971), in the study referred to above, presented 12 numbers followed by a probe number, and asked his subjects to indicate the presentation location of the probe number. Response latency correlated +.94 with the number of items which the subject reported searching prior to responding, indicating the value of verbal reports. Most of the subjects reported grouping the list into three groups of four items or four groups of three items during input. In either case, subjects most frequently reported gaining access to memory through the initial item of one of their subjectively-formed groups. Some subjects relied upon a single access position, whereas others distributed their entry points more randomly among the main alternatives. It is clear that group data involving means based upon these varied strategies would inaccurately reflect the performance of any specific subject.

Seamon (1972) asked his subjects to recall the item from a specified location, using a total of up to six locations. After responding, subjects were asked to indicate whether they had responded automatically or after accessing one or more of the other locations. Response latencies were longer, the greater the number of locations from which the probe could come, but this effect was much more pronounced on those trials where the subject reported accessing other locations. Once again, important data would have been lost by averaging across strategies.

Summary

The literature on decision latencies in recognition tasks suggests that recognition decisions are either rapid decisions based upon an item's familiarity or slower decisions based upon a search process. This distinction is similar to the one made by Mandler (1972) between direct and indirect recognition. However, the work discussed in the previous chapter suggested that the retrieval process might involve more than simply searching through the list items.

A second similarity between the recognition data discussed in this and the previous chapter is the indication that the nature of the encoded attributes determines both the probability of recognition and the latency of the recognition response. Light, Kimble, and Pellegrino (1975) argued that the overlap between the word attributes encoded at presentation and at test determined the probability of recognition, and several investigators (e.g., Naus, 1974) have found that recognition latencies are reduced when list items can be organized in terms of their attributes.

A major finding in studies of free recall and verbal fluency is that recall tends to consist of a number of short bursts of related items. There are several possible reasons why retrieval from long-term memory is limited to about five items at a time. Mandler (1975) suggested that limitations on the span of attention at the time of storage were responsible, and other plausible notions are that retrieval is through the limited capacity primary memory, or that sampling with replacement occurs for any set of words sharing common attributes. Mandler's theory implies that the important limitation is one of storage rather than retrieval, whereas the other hypotheses emphasize constraints on retrieval.

Relevant data were collected by Dean (1971). He used a verbal fluency task, and subsequently gave his subjects all the words they had recalled, and asked them to sort the words into categories that belonged together. There was clear evidence that the order of recall in the verbal fluency task was determined by the conceptual categories formed by the subjects. However, while the median category size was seven, the mean number of words in each burst was between three and four, implying that retrieval constraints were operating.

CHAPTER 6

SENTENCE MEMORY

At one time, it seemed to many researchers that sentence memory represented the promised land. At last it would be possible to look at memory in a more naturalistic way, rather than forcing subjects to perform the highly artificial tasks used previously. However, while it is indisputable that people in their everyday lives are more likely to encounter sentences than lists of nonsense syllables, it is now less clear that the promise will be fulfilled. While we typically deal with sentential material in the form of connected discourse, and attempt to understand the meaning and retain it over long periods of time, the laboratory experiment commonly involves intentional learning of unrelated sentences with recall of the wording required after a short retention interval.

The importance of some of the above findings in determining the nature of the processing accorded to sentential information has been discussed by Aaronson (1976). She hypothesized that tasks with great memory demands would produce a strategy of coding serially through the stimulus sentence in order to form integrated chunks for efficient storage. The successive integration of the entire sentence would mean that coding time would increase over the phrase, the clause, or the sentence. In terms of the resultant memory trace, high memory demands would produce a stored representation that reflected the lexical items and the surface structure.

On the other hand, the greater the comprehension demands, the more likely that coding units are centred on semantically important anchor points. More specifically, coding is focussed on the subject noun, the verb, and the object noun, and their inter-relationships. With comprehension tasks, coding time should decrease over the phrase, the clause, or the sentence, as linguistic predictability increases.

Aaronson (1976) discussed some of the evidence supporting

114

these hypotheses.   For example, Foss and Lynch (1969)
required their subjects concurrently to memorize speech and
to monitor it for a target phoneme.   Reaction times to
phoneme detection were longer when the phonemes occurred
late rather than early in the sentence, suggesting that
coding effort increased during sentence presentation.   In
contrast, in a task more concerned with comprehension,
Mehler, Bever, and Carey (1967) obtained eye-fixation data as
subjects read stories.   Fixations occurred more frequently
on the first rather than the second half of each constituent
at all levels of structure: two-morpheme words, short
phrases, subject-predicate clauses, and the whole sentence.

Further evidence was obtained by Aaronson and Scarborough
(1976).   Either a memorization or a comprehension task was
used, and subjects controlled the word-by-word presentation
rate for each sentence.   There were several large
differences in the reading time data for identical linguistic
stimuli as a function of task.   Reading times for the
memory task reflected the syntactical structure of the
sentence, with prolonged pauses at phrase boundaries.
Comprehension-task subjects showed prolonged reading times for
important content words, with reading time decreasing as
contextual redundancy increased.

While studies of verbatim recall of sentential material
indicate that people can retain information about the exact
wording of sentences, it is very unlikely that this occurs
under more naturalistic conditions.   For example, Johnson-
Laird and Stevenson (1970) asked two groups of subjects to
comprehend a short spoken passage.   The intentional-learning
group was told that there would be a subsequent test for
memory, whereas the incidental-learning group was not.   An
almost immediate recognition test indicated that both groups
retained information about the meaning of the passage, but
retention of the wording was significantly better for the
intentional group than for the incidental group.

The finding that meaning is retained much better than
wording even when subjects are attempting to remember the
precise wording of sentences was obtained in a classic study
by Sachs (1967).   Subjects were given a passage followed by
a sentence.   The sentence was either identical to one of the
sentences from the passage, or differed from one of the
original sentences syntactically (e.g., by changing the
active to passive, or vice versa) or semantically (e.g., by

exchanging subject and object).   The task was to indicate
whether the test sentence was identical to one of the
original sentences.   With 80 or 160 syllables of sentential
material interpolated between the original and test sentences,
subjects were very good at detecting semantic changes in the
material, but were quite poor at detecting grammatical, or
syntactical, changes.

The remainder of the chapter is concerned with the
evaluation of various theoretical approaches to sentence
memory.   Initially, those theories concerned with the
syntactical aspects of sentences are discussed, followed by a
variety of theories emphasizing different components of
meaning.   In spite of the distinction between syntax and
meaning, it is probable that a close relationship exists
between the two, and that syntax serves primarily as a
preliminary step in the semantic interpretation of a sentence.

Memory For Syntax

The most influential theorist who has emphasized
syntactical factors is Chomsky (1965).   His complex
theoretical position has been explicated in several places
(e.g., Anderson & Bower, 1973; Greene, 1972).   His crucial
assertion is that every sentence has both a deep structure
and a surface structure.   The surface structure is related
to the physical form, or sound pattern, of the sentence, and
it determines the phonetic interpretation of the sentence.
Deep structure refers to the underlying abstract structure,
which determines the semantic interpretation of the
sentence.

It is important to note that different deep structures can
underlie identical surface structures.   For example, the
sentence 'The shooting of the hunters was awful' would be
given the same surface structure analysis, regardless of
whether the hunters were taken as the subject or the object
of the verb 'shoot'.   However, the two interpretations of
the sentence would be differently represented at a deep
structure level.   In one deep structure representation, the
first noun phrase would be re-written as 'The hunters shoot',
and in the second interpretation as 'Someone shoots the
hunters'.   Conversely, the two sentences 'The boy is hitting
the girl' and 'The girl is being hit by the boy' clearly
differ in terms of the superficial, or surface, grammatical
structure, but incorporate highly similar meanings, a fact

which is reflected by similar deep structure representations.

Kennedy and Wilkes (e.g., 1969) and N. F. Johnson (1965) have investigated the effects of surface structure on retention. They used paradigms which would seem to maximize the probability of surface structure involvement, since short-term verbatim recall was required. However, even these studies have produced several findings quite inconsistent with the notion that surface structure is importantly involved in sentence memory. Even if it were to be conclusively demonstrated that sentences are segmented in the ways stipulated by surface-structure theorists, this would clearly constitute only a modest beginning to an adequate theory of sentence memory. The inability to handle the semantic aspects of sentences necessarily invalidates this approach. We may well concur with Johnson-Laird (1974): "It is difficult to see why any syntactic property should ordinarily be relevant to the retention of intelligible sentences, unless it is being deliberately used as an aid to memory" (p. 150).

Some indirect evidence for deep structure analyses of sentences comes from Levelt (1970), who asked subjects to make judgements about the degrees of syntactic relatedness between pairs of words in sentences. One of his sentences, 'Carla takes the book and goes to school', would be analyzed into two strings in deep structure: 'Carla takes the book' and 'Carla goes to school'. Levelt's subjects indicated that they considered 'Carla' and 'goes' to be as closely related as 'Carla' and 'takes', which follows from the deep structure analysis, but not from the surface structure analysis. In the surface structure analysis, 'Carla' only appears in close relationship with 'takes'.

Related work involving sentence memory was done by Wanner (1968). Subjects were presented with a number of sentences, followed by various items in the sentences as prompts for recall of the complete sentence. He hypothesized that the effectiveness of a prompt word should vary directly with the number of times that word was present in the deep-structure representation. Thus, in the example from Levelt's study, the word 'Carla' appears twice in the deep-structure representation (but only once in the surface-structure representation), and should thus be a good prompt. Two of the sentences used by Wanner were as follows: 'The governor asked the detective to cease drinking' and 'The

governor asked the detective to prevent drinking'.   In the
former sentence, the word 'detective' appears in three
different deep-structure propositions, against two in the
latter sentence.   As predicted, the prompting effectiveness
of the word 'detective' was greater in the former case.
This result cannot be handled by considering only surface
structure, since the word 'detective' occurs just once in the
surface-structure analysis of each sentence.

Similar results were obtained by Blumenthal (1967) and
Blumenthal and Boakes (1967).   Blumenthal compared full-
passive sentences, such as 'Gloves are made by tailors',
with agent-replaced (truncated) passives, such as 'Gloves are
made by hand'.   On a deep-structure interpretation, it might
be expected that the last word of full-passive sentences
would be a more effective cue for sentence recall than the
last word of a truncated passive sentence.   The results bore
this out.   However, Danks and Sorce (1973) replicated this
work, and also manipulated the imagery value of the cue or
prompt.   They confirmed Blumenthal's findings with low-
imagery prompts, but found no effects of deep-structure
differences with high-imagery prompts.   They concluded that
subjects must rely on the syntax of an abstract sentence to
remember that sentence, but in the high imagery condition
they may use other forms of coding, such as imagery.

While it is possible that deep structure plays an
important part in the initial comprehension of sentences, it
would seem of minor consequence relative to more purely
semantic considerations.   A finding favourable to deep-
structure theory has been the high degree of effectiveness as
retrieval cues of those words in sentences that are centrally
implicated in a deep-structure analysis.   However,
discovery of thematically important concepts often requires
some appropriate knowledge of the world, a factor more
honoured in the breach than the observance by Chomsky.   For
example, in the sentence, 'For the crucial World Cup game
in 1976, Don Revie picked the team, and the England team
manager was well satisfied with their midfield mastery', 'Don
Revie' and the 'England team manager' refer to the same
individual, but it is one's knowledge of the world rather
than of deep structure that allows us to see the equivalence.

In sum, it is probable that syntax facilitates the process
of extracting the meaning from sentential material, but that
memory for syntactical features of thematic material fades

rapidly after comprehension has occurred.   While one
certainly can retain syntactical information for long periods
of time, this is the exception rather than the rule.

Imagery Hypotheses

The major imagery hypothesis was proposed by Paivio
(1971a, 1971b).   The details of this hypothesis and the
relevant experimental evidence will be discussed shortly.
It may be noted, however, that there are at least two sorts
of conceptual confusion inherent in most of the work in this
area.   The first was pointed out by Pylyshyn (1973), who
noted that most psychologists, including Paivio, have
assumed that information must be represented either
imaginally or verbally.   Little consideration has been given
to the possibility that other, more abstract, forms of
representation may be important.

The second confusion centres around the concept of
'imagery'.   Although few psychologists would argue that the
images formed by people are like photographic representations,
the experimental literature suggests that this equivalence is
implicitly assumed by many of them.   If it were true, then
attempting to recall a specific image would be like searching
for a particular photograph in a trunk full of photographs.
Obviously, the images must be fully integrated into the stock
of related past knowledge if they are to be retrieved
subsequently.   But if the images must be interpreted to be
useful, is this not tantamount to suggesting that imaginal
representation is merely a means to an end, rather than an
end in itself?

The notion that sentences can be stored either imaginally
or verbally has been put forward by Paivio (1971a, 1971b).
In essence, he suggested that concrete sentences such as 'The
fat boy kicked a girl' would tend to be imaginally processed,
and a complex image representing the sentence's meaning
stored.   However, while the meaning will be well stored, the
subjects may find it difficult to remember the wording, since
this must be decoded from the image, with the obvious
possibility of errors.   On the other hand, abstract
sentences such as 'The theory has predictive power' would
normally be processed as a series of sequentially organized
verbal units, and would tend to be stored as strings of words.
Paivio (1971b) claimed that, "The meaning of abstract material
is tied to the wording itself, and to remember the meaning is

to remember the specific wording" (p. 24). The most
interesting prediction from this hypothesis is that
sentence meaning will be better retained than sentence
wording with concrete sentences, whereas wording will be
better remembered than meaning with abstract sentences.
Begg and Paivio (1969) presented several concrete and
abstract sentences, followed by recognition tests, on which
either a sentence identical to one of the presentation
sentences, a semantically changed sentence, or a sentence
with changed wording was given. As predicted, detection of
meaning changes exceeded detection of wording changes with
concrete sentences, with the opposite occurring with
abstract sentences.

While the Begg and Paivio study appeared to provide
strong evidence for qualitative differences in the nature of
the encoding strategies for concrete and abstract sentences,
a complicating factor was uncovered by Johnson, Bransford,
Nyberg, and Cleary (1972). They asked subjects to rate the
comprehensibility of the concrete and abstract sentences used
by Begg and Paivio, and found that the abstract sentences
were significantly more difficult to comprehend than the
concrete sentences. It thus seems likely that the subjects
in the Begg and Paivio study could not detect changes in the
meaning of abstract sentences simply through lack of
comprehension, rather than because of the nature of the
encoding process.

Tieman (1972) performed a series of experiments on
recognition memory for concrete and abstract sentences, but
used relatively simple sentences that appear easier to
understand than those of Begg and Paivio. As expected on
Paivio's hypothesis, those subjects instructed to use
imagery during presentation tended to remember meaning at the
expense of wording, and did so to a greater extent than
subjects told to remember the meaning or gist. However,
retention of sentence meaning was consistently better than
retention of sentence wording, just as much for abstract as
for concrete sentences, and this result is inconsistent with
Paivio's imagery hypothesis.

Klee and M. W. Eysenck (1973) looked at speed of
comprehension. In an attempt to ascertain whether there are
qualitative differences in the processing of concrete and
abstract sentences, they presented the sentences auditorily
under conditions of visual or verbal interference, and found

that there was a highly significant interaction between
interference and sentence concreteness (see Fig. 6.1). In
this interaction, concrete sentences were comprehended more
rapidly under verbal interference than under visual
interference, whereas abstract sentences were comprehended
faster under visual interference conditions. While this
finding represents good evidence for Paivio's dual-coding
hypothesis, it could still be the case that the ultimate form
of storage for concrete and abstract sentences is similar.

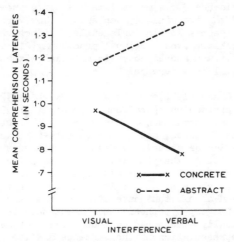

Fig. 6.1. Comprehension time as a function
of sentence type and interference type. Based
on data in Klee and M. W. Eysenck (1973).

Another study on interference effects was done by Sasson
(1971), who presented concrete sentences, and required free
recall after two minutes or three days. Interference was
investigated by presenting the subjects with a neutral task,
with pictures related or unrelated to the to-be-learned
material, or with sentences related or unrelated to the
to-be-learned material during the interval between sentence
presentation and test. Picture presentation was apparently
rapid enough to preclude verbal processing. The unrelated
pictures had a detrimental effect on immediate retention,
whereas the related pictures had a facilitatory effect, but
there was no effect of picture interpolation on delayed

retention after three days.   This can be taken as evidence
for imaginal coding of concrete sentences, if we are prepared
to assume that there was predominantly imaginal processing of
the interpolated pictures.   Sasson and Fraisse (1972)
replicated these findings, and found that the immediate and
delayed retention of abstract sentences was not affected by
interpolated concrete or pictorial material, but was
detrimentally affected by interpolated abstract material.
The discovery that interpolated pictures had a differential
effect on retention of concrete and abstract sentences is
reasonable evidence for some qualitative differences in
processing of the two kinds of sentence.   However, some of
these results seem a little implausible.   Since we spend so
much of our waking lives in visual processing, it is
miraculous that any stored concrete material withstands this
continual visual interference!

   Clark and Chase (1972) and Chase and Clark (1972) have
investigated processing operations in a situation involving
sentence-picture comparisons.   In essence, the subject is
shown a simple sentence, and then a picture (or vice versa),
and has to decide as quickly as possible whether the
statement is true of the picture.   Since in all cases the
picture only contained two symbols, one above the other, the
sentences 'A is above B' and 'B isn't above A' were identical
in meaning, and should thus have produced the same image.
Since, on an imagery hypothesis, both sentences would be
stored identically, the subsequent comparison process between
the stored representation of the sentence and the picture
would be the same in either case.   Any difference in reaction
time would be due solely to the difference in the time
required for image formation from positive and negative
sentences.   In fact, when the picture is false with respect
to the sentence, reaction is a little slower for the
negative sentence ('B isn't above A') than for the positive
sentence ('A is above B'), but when the picture is true with
respect to the sentence, reaction time is considerably slower
for the negative sentence than for the positive.   This
interaction between the form of the sentence and its truth
value is not readily explicable in terms of imagery
hypotheses.   Clark and Chase assumed that pictures and
sentences are both represented in terms of elementary
propositions, but it is possible that they are represented in
some more semantic form.

   Anderson and Bower (1973) have discussed several

difficulties with the imagery approach to sentence memory,
and carried out some experiments. In one of their
experiments, subjects received a series of sentences such as
'The lieutenant signed his signature on the cheque'. On the
subsequent recognition test, subjects had to pick out the
originally presented sentences from among several distractor
sentences, some of which would presumably evoke similar
imagery to presented sentences (e.g., 'The lieutenant forged
his signature on the cheque'). Such imaginally similar
distractors were chosen incorrectly with only slightly greater
frequency than imaginally different but syntactically similar
distractors. Since it could be argued that the images
evoked by the imaginally similar distractors might not be
very similar (e.g., the lieutenant forging his signature may
have an evil grin on his face which he would not have when
signing his signature), a further study was done by Kosslyn
on pairs of sentences which had been pre-rated according to
the similarity of the images they evoked. Kosslyn used only
pairs of sentences that were rated as having extremely
similar images (e.g., 'George picked up the pen to write on
the paper' and 'George picked up the pen to doodle on the
paper'). A recognition test indicated that subjects could
preserve a conceptual distinction between such sentences.

In their second and third experiments, Anderson and Bower
presented sentences of the form, 'The hippie touched the
debutante who sang in the park'. When the sentences had
been presented, the subjects received an incremental cueing
procedure, in which progressively more of the original
sentence was presented, with the subject attempting to
recall as much as possible of the rest of the sentence. A
vast number of word recall probabilities conditional upon the
recall of other words and the presentation of different cues
were obtained. The same paradigm was used in the two
experiments, the only difference occurring in the
instructions. In one experiment, the subjects were given
conventional instructions; in the other, instructions to
form an image of the situation described by the sentences
were given. It might have been anticipated that the use of
imagery would produce more integrated storage of the
sentence, leading to a smaller effect of sentence structure
on recall, and to a tendency to recall the sentence in an
all-or-none fashion. In fact, the imagery instructions led
to a higher overall level of recall, but had no effect on any
of the other quantitative or qualitative aspects of the data.

In sum, the major issue appears to be whether it is possible to demonstrate qualitative differences in storage corresponding to separate verbal and imaginal processing systems. If the differences are merely quantitative, then parsimony would suggest adopting Anderson and Bower's hypothesis that the use of imagery instructions or concrete sentences simply leads subjects to encode a greater number of propositions than they do when given conventional instructions or abstract sentences. Several studies have failed to obtain qualitative differences (e.g., Anderson & Bower, 1973; Chase & Clark, 1972; Tieman, 1972). Of those studies finding qualitative differences, one (Begg & Paivio, 1969) is methodologically suspect, and the others (Klee & M. W. Eysenck, 1973; Sasson, 1971; Sasson & Fraisse, 1972) found such differences only during comprehension or shortly thereafter.

The evidence thus seems to indicate that imagery is a relatively transient process that can occur for a relatively short period of time after sentence presentation. The exact length of time has not been established. In recent research, Davies and Proctor (1976) found that recall of abstract sentences was much worse following verbal interference than visual interference, whereas the opposite was the case with concrete sentences. The effects of interference were comparable whether the interference occurred immediately after sentence presentation or after a number of seconds, suggesting that imaginal and verbal processing both require several seconds for completion. An interesting hypothesis is that imagery primarily serves the function of maintaining a quasi-perceptual representation of external events for sufficient time to allow interpretation of the events to occur. Imagery would thus be more used in those cases where interpretation was difficult. Exactly in line with that prediction, Klee and M. W. Eysenck (1973) discovered that visual interference, which was assumed to affect imaginal processing, lengthened the comprehension time of anomalous sentences more than of meaningful sentences.

If the considerable memorial superiority of concrete sentences does not depend critically on imagery, on what does it depend? Klee and M. W. Eysenck suggested that concrete sentences were likely to have a single dominant interpretation which could be readily comprehended, whereas abstract sentences tended to incorporate several potential

interpretation, and so could only be interpreted
unequivocally in the presence of a disambiguating context.
This suggestion was supported by the work of Pezdek and Royer
(1974), who noted that the presentation of a disambiguating
context at input enhanced recognition memory for abstract
sentences, but not for concrete sentences. Klee (1975)
presented phrases to her subjects, and required them to
supply as many responses as possible in 90 seconds that would
complete the sentence. The greater interpretative
variability inherent in the abstract sentences was revealed by
two of the findings: (1) phrases containing abstract verbs
produced responses belonging to a larger number of
independent conceptual groupings than did phrases containing
concrete verbs; (2) there was more response variability
across subjects with abstract phrases than with concrete
phrases.

Reconstruction Hypotheses: World Knowledge
   The general notion that the encoded representation of
sentential information incorporates a considerable amount of
information not immediately present in the stimulus material
has become increasingly popular. More specifically, the
memory traces formed as a result of exposure to connected
discourse are seen as the resultant of a dynamic interaction
between the presented information and the subject's store of
relevant information.

   Bartlett (1932) was the first psychologist to put forward
a theory along these lines. He argued that the central
meaning of a prose passage is stored in schematic form, with
subsequent recall being achieved by a process of reconstruction from the underlying schema. The central concept of the
'schema' was defined as "an active organization of past
reactions, or of past experience, which must always be
supposed to be operating in any well-adapted organic response"
(p. 201).

   A rather similar hypothesis was proposed by Neisser (1967).
It suffers from the same vagueness as Bartlett's theory.
Neisser expressed his hypothesis in the following way:

   The analogy being offered asserts only that the role
   which stored information plays in recall is like the role
   which stimulus information plays in perception.   In
   neither case does it enter awareness directly, and in

> neither case can it be literally reproduced in
> behaviour, except after rather special training.   The
> model of the palaeontologist...applies to memory: out
> of a few stored bone chips, we remember a dinosaur
> (p. 285).

The most obvious way to investigate the reconstruction
hypothesis is to ask people to learn material that induces a
conflict between what is presented and the reconstructive
processes based on knowledge of the world.   If, for example,
stories from a foreign culture are presented, the prediction
is that the reconstructive processes will distort the
information in the story, rendering it more conventional and
acceptable from the standpoint of the subject's cultural
background.

This approach was adopted by Bartlett (1932).   In his
best-known study, subjects brought up in England were asked
to memorize a story, 'The War of the Ghosts', which is a tale
taken from the North American Indian culture.   The subjects
gave a series of attempted recalls of the passage, and
showed a tendency to distort and change the style and
content.   There was some evidence that the distortions and
changes increased over successive reproductions.   As
predicted, many of the errors in recall involved changes
which made the passage read more like a conventional English
story.   For example, in the original passage, as the Indian
died, 'something black came out his mouth'.   One subject
recalled this as 'foamed at the mouth'.   Unfortunately,
Bartlett did not provide exact figures for the amount of
distortion obtained, although it seems to have been
substantial.

It is of importance to determine whether the changes
introduced by Bartlett's subjects were genuine memorial
distortions, or whether they were rather the result of
deliberate inventions on the part of the subjects in order to
smooth out, or facilitate, the telling of the story.   Since
Bartlett did not give any very specific instructions to his
subjects ('I thought it best, for the purposes of these
experiments, to try to influence the subjects' procedure as
little as possible'; p. 78), it is probable that the
subjects did not always limit themselves solely to what they
could definitely remember from the passage.

Gauld and Stephenson (1967) presented their subjects with

'The War of the Ghosts', followed by instructions putting
varying degrees of stress on the need for accuracy.   The
error rate was 41 per cent less under the strictest
instructions than under the most lenient instructions, a
highly significant difference.   The subjects were taken back
over their written recall and invited to indicate any phrases
they had written down that they thought had possibly not been
in the original passage.   This produced an average
reduction of 39 per cent in the error rate.   While the
evidence indicates that some of the distortions noted by
Bartlett were due to conscious guessing and confabulation,
it should be noted that incorrect additions were still found
even under the most stringent conditions.   Furthermore, they
used an immediate recall test, and it is likely that more
evidence for genuine memorial distortions would have been
found at longer retention intervals.

   Experiments using more conventional material do not always
produce evidence of substantial recall distortion.
Gomulicki (1956) presented various short passages to his
subjects.   He instructed them to repeat orally as much as
they could, using the original words where possible, but
reproducing all retained ideas as well as they were able.
He found, on average, that 55.5 per cent of each passage was
reproduced verbatim, 32.7 per cent was omitted, and 11.8 per
cent was changed, e.g., through transposition.   Additions
were equivalent to 6.2 per cent of the passage.   Thus
additional material was rarely incorporated into the recall of
these passages, and the nature of the recall process appeared
to be abstractive rather than constructive.   The subjects
abstracted and recalled the most important theme-related parts
of each passage, while omitting those aspects (adjectives,
short descriptive phrases) which were incidental to the main
theme.

   The above interpretation of the findings is strengthened
by the work of Gomulicki (1953).   He asked judges to attempt
to distinguish between a precise written by one subject while
looking at a passage with an immediate reproduction of the
same passage written by a second subject, and found that the
judges' performance was poor.   As Zangwill (1972) has pointed
out, this suggests that "intentional and unintentional
abstracts of the same material are virtually indistinguishable" (p. 128).   The nature of the material is of critical
importance.   Zangwill (1956) presented a 44-word passage
containing odd and unusual features, and found that there was

considerable distortion on an immediate recall test, the
subjects having been instructed to be as accurate as
possible.

Some recent work has confirmed the importance of
abstractive processes.   De Villiers (1974) compared the
recall of sentences low and high in imagery as a function of
whether or not they appeared to form a connected story.
High imagery only enhanced recall for unrelated sentences.
For the connected story, sentence centrality to the theme of
the story was highly correlated with both immediate and long-
term recall.

Sulin and Dooling (1974) investigated Bartlett's hypothesis
in a study obviating the methodological problems that have
plagued research in this area.   The subjects received a
short biographical passage in which the main character was
either a famous or a fictitious person (e.g., Adolf Hitler or
Gerald Martin).   The tendency to think that a non-presented
but thematically related sentence had been presented when
given a recognition test was greater with passages concerning
a famous character.   Moreover, as Bartlett would predict,
these memory distortions were more pronounced at longer
retention intervals.

The evidence considered so far has suggested that people
will sometimes assimilate presented information to their
stock of relevant knowledge, and that this can cause memorial
distortions.   However, work by Bransford and his associates
has led to the stronger conclusion that the stored
representation will usually consist of an elaborated and
extended version of what was actually presented.   Bransford's
basic hypothesis was that we typically draw one or more
inferences from sentential stimuli, and that the sentence
information plus inferences are stored as an integrated unit.
The main deduction is that subjects should find it difficult
to discriminate on a recognition test between presented and
inferred information.

Bransford, Barclay, and Franks (1972) gave subjects
sentences such as (1) 'Three turtles rested beside a floating
log, and a fish swam beneath them', or (2) 'Three turtles
rested on a floating log, and a fish swam beneath them'.
They suggested that most subjects presented with sentence (2)
would store away the inference that the fish swam beneath the
log, an inference not strongly implied by sentence (1).   It is

important to note that the information that the fish swam
beneath the log is not directly supplied by the sentence
presented, but seems to be derivable from our knowledge of
spatial relations.   If this analysis is correct, then it is
probable that subjects hearing sentence (2) should be far
more likely than those hearing sentence (1) to assume
incorrectly on a subsequent recognition test that they heard
(3) 'Three turtles rested (beside/on) a floating log, and a
fish swam beneath it'.   Exactly as predicted, they found
that subjects were unable to distinguish between sentences
such as (2) and (3), whereas they could distinguish between
sentences such as (1) and (3).

In order to ensure that the results were not attributable
to the method of test, they ran another experiment, in which
recall was required.   With sentences such as (2) that allow
a strong inference, recall of the final pronoun was
significantly inferior to recall of the final pronoun in
sentences such as (1) that do not appear to have a strong
inference.

While the experiments discussed so far have strongly
indicated that subjects create semantic products that are a
joint function of input information and prior knowledge, it is
not clear from these studies whether the integration of past
and present information takes place during comprehension,
during subsequent storage, or at the time of retrieval.
Relevant evidence was obtained by Bransford and Johnson
(1972).   They presented rather obscure passages to their
subjects.   Some of the subjects received appropriate
contextual information (a picture or the topic of the
passage), which was given either before or after the passage.
Soon after the passage had been presented, subjects tried to
recall it as accurately as possible.   Contextual information
only increased recall when it was given prior to the passage.
This indicates that the integration of past knowledge with
present input is particularly important during initial
comprehension, and, indeed, subjects given the context prior
to the passage rated their comprehension higher than subjects
given the context after the passage.

Different kinds of inference may be required in different
situations.   In everyday conversation, an extended process of
inference may be required to arrive at adequate comprehension.
For example, the wife who says to her husband, "Would you mind
opening the window, dear?" is likely to become irate if he

responds yes or no.   Clark and Lucy (1975) have put forward
a three-stage model to account for the process by which the
listener arrives at the intended meaning of a sentence.
The initial stage involves the calculation of the literal
meaning of the sentence.   This is then tested against the
immediate context to see whether or not it is plausible.   If
it seems appropriate to the context, then it is taken to be
the intended meaning.   If it does not seem appropriate, the
literal meaning is combined with a suitable rule of
conversation, and this produces the intended meaning.   The
model is especially relevant to an understanding of rhetori-
cal devices such as irony, sarcasm, and understatement, in
which the listener must recognize the inappropriateness of
literal meaning in context and must compute the conveyed
meaning based on implicit rules of conversation.

Clark and Lucy found that statements with both literal and
intended meanings were nearly always interpreted in terms of
their intended meaning, as the model predicts.   There was
some evidence that subjects at some point constructed the
literal interpretation of the sentences.   The sentences 'I'll
be very happy if you make the circle blue' and 'I'll be very
sad unless you make the circle blue' have the same intended
meaning, and yet the latter sentence took much longer to
comprehend.   Clark and Lucy argued that this was due to a
difference in their literal interpretations, with 'unless'
having the inherent negative meaning of 'if not'.

Thorndyke (1976) has argued that the generation of
inferences during the comprehension of discourse occurs in at
least two ways.   The first occurs when a sentence in
isolation requires the identification of a situational
context or 'frame'.   The verb in the sentence 'John gave
Mary the book' is interpreted differently from the same verb
in the sentence 'John gave Mary the lesson', because the
former sentence is identified as an example of a 'transfer'
frame, whereas the latter sentence involves a 'teaching'
frame.

The second way occurs when an incoming sentence cannot be
interpreted in any currently active frame, i.e., the events
described appear inconsistent with expectations.   In that
case, the subject engages in 'bridging', using backward
inferencing to establish an appropriate context.   Thorndyke
found that subjects frequently believed that those inferences
required to make sense of presented information had actually

been presented, suggesting that backward inferencing had
occurred.

A reasonable prediction from this general theory is that
the comprehension of a sentence should occur rapidly if it is
consistent with a current context, since backward inferencing
is not necessary. When no satisfactory context has been
established, the subject must initiate backward inferences to
a previous context, a time-consuming process. Haviland and
Clark (1974) obtained this result using comprehension
latencies for sentences.

The evidence is now very strong that the sentence-as-coded
may differ substantially from the sentence-as-presented.
More specifically, the situational context and past
knowledge are both utilized in an attempt to understand
sentential material as fully as possible. The final
sentence-as-coded is the result of processing designed to
integrate information from the sentence, the context, and
past knowledge. While this approach is a useful one, it is
not always clear what determines the nature of the inferences
drawn. In many studies, there is clear evidence of
circularity. It is argued that certain inferences have been
drawn because of recognition errors, and recognition errors
are 'explained' by reference to inference drawing. What is
lacking is any clear account of the psychological processes
involved. Part of the problem is that 'previous knowledge'
is an experimentally intractable factor, even though it is
obviously an important determinant of performance.
Manipulation of situational context allows better experimental
control over the type and amount of relevant additional
information possessed by subjects when comprehending a given
sentence.

Configural Theory

An interesting but relatively neglected problem is the
relationship between isolated words and words embedded in a
sentential context. A frequent assumption is that the
encoding of words is unaffected by including them in
sentences. For example, Anderson and Bower (1973) proposed
a neo-associationistic theory of sentence memory that
explicitly eschewed a Gestaltist approach (i.e., the whole is
greater than and other than the sum of its parts) in favour
of a theory in which the encoding and retrieval of sentential
information involves considering the sentence as a series of

functionally independent associations. Since associationism
is the basis of several models of sentence memory, it is
important to obtain empirical evidence to distinguish
between a Gestaltist or configural approach and an
associationistic one. It should be noted that Tulving's
work, discussed in Chapter 4, has provided strong evidence
for the notion that the specific encoding of a given word is
heavily affected by the immediate context in which that word
is encountered. On Tulving's theory, the rest of the
sentence should provide a strong contextual determination of
the encoding of each word in the sentence.

     Anderson and Bower (1971, 1972a) introduced an ingenious
technique in which pairs of sentences such as 'The child hit
the landlord' and 'The minister praised the landlord' were
presented. The subject was then given various cues or
prompt words, of which the two most important were Same Cues
(e.g., 'The child hit the ---') and Cross-over Cues (e.g.,
'The child praised the ---'). The Same Cues preserve the
form of one of the original sentences, and thus should
mediate better recall of the object noun than the Cross-over
Cues, which combine parts of two different sentences. On
the other hand, associationistic theory postulates only a
series of independent associative links, and predicts that
the two cues will be equally effective or even that the
Cross-over Cues will be superior. While Anderson and Bower
found in some of their experiments that Cross-over Cues were
slightly superior, the generality of that finding is now in
considerable doubt.

     Foss and Harwood (1975) used the same paradigm, but
instructed their subjects to rate the sentences for
meaningfulness. The Same Cues produced much better object-
noun recall than the Cross-over Cues. It is probable that
the associationistic prediction will be upheld only when the
sentences are poorly integrated and when the subjects treat
the sentences as if they were strings of words. Under more
natural conditions, it is clear that sentences are processed
as configurations.

     There are several other sources of evidence supporting a
configural approach to sentence memory. For example, Begg
and Clark (1975) found that the rated imagery and the
retention of concrete and abstract nouns were determined by
the phrase context into which they were placed. Norms of
imagery and concreteness are based upon ratings of words in

isolation, and so tend to reflect their most familiar
meanings.   However, configural theory would anticipate that
sentential context would affect word imagery, and this was
found.

   Barclay, Bransford, Franks, McCarrell, and Nitsch (1974)
found that a cue such as 'something heavy' produced better
recall of the noun 'piano' when subjects had previously
received the sentence 'The men lifted the piano' than when
the sentence had been 'The musician played the piano'.   The
implication is that the two sentential contexts had led
subjects to process different semantic attributes of the word
'piano', thus producing differential effectiveness of various
retrieval cues.

   Johnson-Laird, Robins, and Velicogna (1974) provided
additional evidence that sentences can be remembered
configurally rather than as a series of associations.   Under
incidental learning conditions, subjects could not distinguish
on a recognition test between a presented sentence (e.g., 'The
owner of the magic staff dispatched the ship') and a
distractor sentence of similar meaning (e.g., 'The dispatcher
of the ship owned the magic staff').   While several memory
models (e.g., Anderson & Bower, 1973) propose that sentences
are processed into a subject noun, verb, and object noun,
Johnson-Laird et al. have shown that subjects can remember
the meaning of a sentence without retaining information about
syntactical categories.

   Halff, Ortony, and Anderson (1976) argued for the
importance of contextual effects in determining the
representation of word meaning.   They selected several
sentences containing the word 'red', and presented them two at
a time to their subjects.   The task was to decide whether the
red object in one sentence was definitely redder than the red
object in the other sentence, or whether the two objects could
be equally red.   As expected, the degree of redness
associated with the word 'red' was affected substantially by
sentential context.   More specifically, the meaning of red
in each context was best represented as a real interval, i.e.,
there was a discernible distance between the upper and lower
furthest limits of possible redness in each context.
Furthermore, the widths of the intervals between the upper
and lower limit varied from sentence to sentence.   Thus,
'red' in the sentence 'The boy with red hair stood out in the
crowd' covered a wider range of the redness continuum than did

'red' in the sentence 'As the sun set the sky turned red'.
The hypothesis that sentential context operates to narrow the
possible representations of a word concept to an appropriate
interval is plausible and of far-reaching consequence. At
present, concepts are frequently represented as context-
invariant points rather than context-sensitive intervals.

In sum, there are several converging lines of evidence
that sentences are encoded as configurations. More precisely
it is probable that the subset of semantic memory attributes
for each concept in a sentence that is actually activated
during sentence processing is strongly determined by
contextual factors. Context is to be thought of as
operating both forwards and backwards in the sentence, rather
than merely left-to-right (cf., Miller & Selfridge, 1950).
The configuration that is formed may incorporate semantic
attributes only indirectly related to those defining the
words in the sentence (e.g., Bartlett, 1932). It seems
likely that future research will concentrate on more precise
delineations of this configural approach.

Summary

In most studies, sentences are regarded as sources of
information. This means that people are typically most
interested in extracting the gist or meaning from sentences,
merely using syntax to facilitate the extraction of semantic
information. While specifically verbal or imaginal
processes may be involved in the initial attempt to
comprehend the stimulus material, it is probable that
sentential information is stored in a modality-free, conceptual fashion.

The process of coding sentential material semantically is
facilitated by the immediate frame or context in which it is
encountered, and by the utilization of relevant information
from semantic memory. The varying contributions of these
several factors in determining the sentence-as-coded means
that there is a large variety of possible encodings for each
sentence. The frequent misinterpretations of everyday
conversation are evidence for this encoding flexibility.

If we consider the encoding of an individual word in a
sentence, it is clear that this is importantly affected by the
encoding of the other sentence words, to remove ambiguity.

CHAPTER 7

SEMANTIC MEMORY

In the terminology introduced by Tulving (1972), the great majority of experiments on human memory have been concerned with episodic memory, which consists of an experiential record of events and occurrences. For example, if a subject is asked to learn a list of words including the word 'door', he does not learn the concept 'door', but rather that the word door, which he already knows, was presented in a particular experimental context. Episodic memory thus has an autobiographical flavour, and refers to the storage of specific events and episodes. Semantic memory, on the other hand, is defined in the following manner by Tulving (1972):

> It is a mental thesaurus, organized knowledge a person possesses about words and other verbal symbols, their meanings and referents, about relations among them, and about rules, formulas, and algorithms for the manipulation of these symbols, concepts, and relations. Semantic memory does not register perceptible properties of inputs, but rather cognitive referents of input signals (p. 386).

The most popular experimental approach to the study of semantic memory is to interrogate subjects about facts which are presumably part of their general knowledge, and see how fast they can answer the questions posed to them. The hope (unrealized as yet) is to discover the ways in which information is organized in semantic memory. It is at least clear that semantic memory is highly organized. For example, Smith, Shoben, and Rips (1974) found that subjects, on average, could decide that a sparrow was a bird in 975 milliseconds; Rubenstein, Lewis, and Rubenstein (1971) reported that subjects could decide that 'rolt' was not an English word in 918 milliseconds; and Loftus and Suppes (1972) found that subjects could recall a fruit starting with the letter 'P' in 1,170 milliseconds. On such tasks, accurate performance with response latencies of approximately one second would manifestly be impossible unless semantic memory were structured in some way.

Two important general points should be borne in mind as we
turn to a discussion of the research and theory in this area.
The first is that much of the work has been restricted to
certain aspects of the semantic component of language.
Relatively little attention has been paid to the grammatical,
affective, and imaginal aspects of semantic memory.   The
second point is that many of the findings and theories seem
highly specific to a particular experimental situation.   For
example, Loftus and Suppes (1972) required subjects to think
of words belonging to designated categories starting with
specified letters.   Their theoretical explanation of the
results relied heavily on assumptions about the nature of the
retrieval process used by the subjects.   On the other hand,
Smith et al. (1974) asked subjects to decide whether or not a
word was a member of a designated category.   Their theory
makes no direct reference to retrieval processes.   The
difference in the importance attached to retrieval processes
in these two theories tells us more about the differences in
the two tasks than about the organization of semantic memory.

Verification Technique

Collins and Quillian (1969, 1970) introduced an
experimental technique, and proposed a theory which has
served as the stimulus of much of the later work.   They
presented their subjects with sentences such as 'A canary has
wings' and 'Coca-cola is blue', and asked them to indicate as
quickly as possible whether the sentence was true or false.
They argued that the characteristics of canaries (e.g., they
have wings, they have skin, and they are yellow) could either
be stored in semantic memory with the concept 'canary' or
might be stored at some higher level of a hierarchy.   Since
essentially all birds have wings, they claimed that it would
be cognitively uneconomical to have information about the
possession of wings stored with each bird name.   A process
of **inference** could be used, in which the subject would verify
the sentence 'A canary has wings' by retrieving the
information that a canary is a bird, and that birds have
wings.   Information about the possession of skin would be
stored still further up the hierarchy, since nearly all
animals have skin.   At an empirical level, it should take
longer to verify a sentence, the greater the separation of
subject and predicate in the hierarchy.   Thus 'A canary is
yellow' should be verified quickly, since the predicate 'is

yellow' would be stored with the concept canary, 'A canary
has wings' should be verified somewhat slower, because one
step in the hierarchy (from canary to bird) has to be
traversed, and 'A canary has skin' should take still longer
to verify, because two steps (canary to bird to animal) are
involved.

The results supported this hypothesis, but some more
recent work has rendered it untenable. The basic difficulty
is that, while the various sentences above may differ in the
distance between subject and predicate, they undoubtedly
differ in several other salient characteristics. For
example, it is probable that the reader is more familiar with
the sentence, 'A canary is yellow', than with the sentence,
'A canary has skin', and Conrad (1972) has confirmed the
importance of this factor. She found no effect of
hierarchical distance, but a substantial effect of sentence
familiarity. She concluded that properties are stored with
every word which they define, and that inferential processes
are not used. However, as Anderson and Bower (1973) noted,
some unusual sentences such as 'Spinoza had an elbow' or
'Hugh Scanlon has a brain' may indeed require inferential
thinking (and some guesswork) in order to be verified (e.g.,
Spinoza was a man, and men have elbows).

A different problem for the Collins and Quillian model was
uncovered by Schaeffer and Wallace (1969, 1970). They were
particularly concerned with negative judgements. In their
first experiment, they presented subjects with word pairs
composed of trees, flowers, birds, and mammals, and asked
them to respond 'same' to those pairs consisting of two
members of the same category, and to respond 'different' to
all other pairs. The different pairs were either
semantically similar (e.g., 'walnut' and 'daisy') or
semantically dissimilar ('walnut' and 'parrot'). The most
natural assumption on the Collins and Quillian model is that
semantically dissimilar 'different' pairs would be responded
to slower than semantically similar 'different' pairs, since
the hierarchical distance that must be traversed is less in
the latter case. In fact, the results were the exact
opposite of this. However, as predicted by Collin and
Quillian, semantic similarity did facilitate 'same'
judgements. The explanation favoured by Schaeffer and
Wallace (1970) was that the subjects considered the degree of
attribute or concept overlap between the two members of a
pair. A substantial overlap of attributes facilitates the

judgement that the words are from the same category, but has
a detrimental effect on the 'different' judgement.

An important generalization to have emerged from work on
the verification task is as follows: "The greater the
similarity in meaning between words, the easier it is to make
a positive judgement, and the harder it is to make a negative
judgement, about a semantic relation between them" (Johnson-
Laird, 1974, p. 141).   However, there are exceptions to this
generalization (e.g., Glass & Holyoak, 1975).   One theory
that has attempted to interpret this generalization is an
extension of the Schaeffer and Wallace hypothesis proposed by
Rips, Shoben, and Smith (1973) and by Smith et al. (1974).
Their initial assumption is that the meaning of a word is not
an unanalyzable unit, but can be represented as a set of
semantic features.   Moreover, these semantic features may be
divided into defining and characteristic features.   For
example, some of the defining features of the concept 'robin'
are having wings, having distinctive colours, and being a
biped, whereas perching in trees and being undomesticated
appear to be characteristic features.   For more abstract
terms such as 'bird', it is possible that we commonly think
in terms of a typical bird having among its characteristic
features a specific size and ferocity (Rosch, 1974).   A
sentence such as 'That bird is big' is evaluated in terms of
our conception of the average size of a bird.

Reasonable linguistic evidence for the distinction between
characteristic and defining features comes in work by Lakoff
(1972).   We say that a robin is a <u>true</u> bird because the two
nouns share both defining and characteristic features, but
that a chicken is <u>technically speaking</u> a bird, since the two
nouns share defining but not characteristic features, and a
bat is <u>loosely speaking</u> a bird, because the two nouns share
characteristic but not defining features.   Evidence
reviewed by Smith et al. (1974) seems to indicate that
birdness is, in a sense, a matter of degree: members of the
bird category rated as typical birds are those taking the
modifier 'a true', whereas those judged to be atypical are
those taking the modifier 'technically speaking'.   This
approach has some disadvantages.   It seems to predict that a
sentence such as 'Loosely speaking, a robin is a canary'
should be acceptable.

In a task in which subjects have to decide the truth of
statements such as 'A robin is a bird', Smith et al. (1974)

assumed that subjects would retrieve both characteristic and
defining features of the two nouns, and determine the overall
degree of feature similarity. If the overall similarity is
high, the subject rapidly responds 'true', while if the
overall similarity is low, the subject rapidly responds
'false'. However, if the degree of overall similarity falls
in the intermediate range, a second comparison occurs on the
basis of the defining features only of the category and test
instance. Thus, for 'true' sentences, the greater the
degree of semantic relatedness, the faster the response
latency should be, since highly related nouns will only
require the first comparison process. For 'false'
sentences, the opposite should be the case, with low degrees
of semantic relatedness facilitating fast responding.

The above predictions were confirmed by Smith et al.
(1974), and their model is in many ways superior to previous
hypotheses. However, the model is not without difficulties:

(1) The model apparently leads to the prediction
that subjects would rapidly decide that a sentence such as
'A bird is a robin' was true!
(2) The concept of 'semantic relatedness' is
hard to measure unambiguously, and is probably confounded
with familiarity, i.e., pairs of nouns judged to be
semantically related are probably those frequently
encountered together. A further confounding variable is
that of production frequency, i.e., the frequency with which
the instance is produced as an association to the category
name, as measured by association norms such as those of
Battig and Montague (1969). Smith et al. (1974) found that
production frequency was a better predictor of reaction time
than were relatedness judgements.
(3) Problems of the retrieval of information seem
to be de-emphasized. For example, it seems probable that
subjects confronted with the sentence, 'A robin is a bird',
will not retrieve information about 'bird' in the sense of a
young female, but the theory does not say why not.
(4) Since larger, more abstract, categories
logically have fewer defining features than small categories,
fewer comparisons should be required during the second
comparison based on defining features only. It follows
that, if the probability that the second comparison occurs is
held constant by controlling semantic relatedness, then an
increase in category size should be associated with a
reduction in reaction time. In fact, Smith et al. (1974)

found that the effect of category size per se was not
significant.

(5) Glass and Holyoak (1975), in work discussed
later in the chapter, have obtained evidence inconsistent
with the prediction of the Smith et al. model that low
degrees of semantic relatedness should facilitate fast
responding with false sentences.

(6) The model seems remarkably restricted in terms
of its potential applicability to situations other than
verification times of 'An S is a P' sentences. As Glass and
Holyoak (1975) noted, the model has little to say about
simple sentences such as 'The man has a car'. The abstract
relationship of possession expressed by 'has' cannot easily
be expressed by combining sets of features.

It is intuitively reasonable that subjects may use
several different strategies to decide whether a word does or
does not belong to a particular category. One method that
subjects use in falsifying statements such as 'A collie is a
cat' was investigated in a study by Anderson and Reder (1974).
They found, in agreement with the hypothesis of Smith et al.
(1974), that the rated similarity of the two nouns correlated
positively with the time to falsify untrue statements
(correlation coefficient = +.35), but they also found that
other variables correlated more strongly with falsification
time. The evidence indicated that subjects were deciding
that statements such as 'A collie is a cat' were untrue by
means of an inferential process in which they generated the
propositions 'A collie is a dog' and 'A dog is not a cat'.
In other words, subjects falsify As are Cs by (a) retrieving
a superordinate B of A; (b) attempting to verify that Bs are
Cs. Anderson and Reder found that the time to generate B to
A, and the time to falsify Bs are Cs, were both correlated
with the time to falsify As are Cs. The notion that
negative information is likely to be stored at large
categories rather than small ones seems plausible in the
light of the learning experiences of young children. They
are more likely to learn the distinction between the concepts
'cat' and 'dog' than between 'collie' and 'cat'.

A further variable that has been used to explain performanc
-e on the instance-category verification task is that of
category size (Landauer & Freedman, 1968; Landauer & Meyer,
1972). Some of the hierarchical effects reported by Collins
and Quillian (1969, 1970) and others may be due to the fact
that it takes subjects longer to find the test instance among

the contents of large categories.   However, it should be
noted that a test instance may be located early in the search
of a large category, but very late in the search of a small
category.   Evidence that category size is an important
variable was obtained by Meyer and Ellis (1970), who found
that subjects took longer to decide that a non-word item like
'mafer' was not a member of a large category like 'structures'
than to decide that it was not a member of a smaller category
like 'buildings'.   Such a finding does not seem explicable
in terms of semantic relatedness, frequency of occurrence of
the sentences, or hierarchical distance.   However, the
difference in response latency was under 40 milliseconds, and
inappropriate statistical procedures were used (Clark, 1973).
If the correct analysis had been done, it is likely that the
effect of category size would have been reduced to non-
significance.

While Landauer and Meyer (1972) presented several findings
indicative of a category-size effect, Smith et al. (1974)
have obtained good evidence that the category-size variable
is not of great importance in verification tasks.   They
investigated the effects of category size and semantic
relatedness, and found that only semantic relatedness
significantly affected verification latencies (see Fig. 7.1).

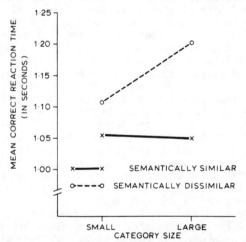

Fig. 7.1. Verification time as a function of
category size and semantic relatedness. Based
on data in Smith, Shoben, and Rips (1974).

The Landauer-Meyer hypothesis predicts that subjects will verify 'A chimpanzee is a primate' more rapidly than 'A chimpanzee is an animal', whereas Smith et al. predicted the opposite, since the degree of semantic relatedness is greater for the pair of words chimpanzee and animal than for chimpanzee and primate. The Smith et al. prediction was confirmed.

In some ways, the notion that subjects search through categories looking for the test instance seems implausible. For example, subjects could presumably decide rapidly that a cliff was not a living organism, but hardly by searching through all the names of living organisms known to them. The search rate would need to be incredibly fast, at least 1,000 items per second. In addition, the methods of assessing category size have not always been suitable: those used include reference to norms, numbers of category instances that can be recalled, and numbers of category instances that can be recognized. Clearly these methods provide different estimates, and only the method most relevant to any particular experiment should be used.

A recent theoretical analysis of the verification task by Glass and Holyoak (1975) seems to obviate many of the problems that have plagued other theories. Their marker-search model has affinities with the Collins-Quillian approach but it avoids the rigid hierarchical search process proposed by Collins and Quillian. Glass and Holyoak assumed that most common words (e.g., 'dog') are directly associated with a single marker (e.g., canine) in a marker structure, and that the order in which markers are searched is the prime variable determining reaction times in the verification task. Unlike Collins and Quillian, Glass and Holyoak argued that the order of marker search must be determined empirically rather than by fiat. The method adopted was to require subjects to provide true one-word completions to incomplete sentences of the type, 'All/Some S are ---'. They assumed that the production frequency with which a word appeared as a completion reflected the probability with which its corresponding defining marker was accessed from the defining subject marker. As predicted, reaction times to true sentences were faster where the object noun had a high production frequency to the subject of the sentence. However, this result could also be explained in terms of semantic relatedness.

The same general strategy was also used by Glass and

Holyoak (1975) in the attempt to explain reaction times to false statements. False production frequency norms were obtained by asking subjects to supply false completions to sentences of the type 'All/Some S are ---'. As predicted, false statements having high production frequency were rejected more rapidly than false statements given with low frequency in the norms. Thus, a sentence such as 'All birds are dogs' was rapidly rejected, in spite of the fact that the concepts 'bird' and 'dog' are semantically related. Indeed, in complete antithesis to the predictions of the Smith et al. (1974) model, false sentences of high semantic relatedness were rejected faster than false sentences of low semantic relatedness.

In sum, it now appears that performance on verification tasks is based on ordered, but non-hierarchical, search procedures, rather than upon the feature comparisons emphasized by Smith et al. (1974). Furthermore, the marker-search model can readily account for an interesting finding obtained by Loftus (1973) that is inexplicable on a feature-comparison account. She obtained measures of the production frequency of a category given an instance, as well as of the frequency of the instance given the category as a stimulus. She then measured reaction times in a verification task in which either the instance preceded the category (e.g., 'canary-bird') or the category preceded the instance (e.g., 'bird-canary'). As the marker-search model would predict, the instance-to-category production frequency determined reaction time when the instance preceded the category, whereas the category-to-instance production frequency determined reaction time when the category preceded the instance. With a feature-comparison model of the type proposed by Smith et al., it is impossible to account for the effects of presentation order.

The simple form of the marker-search model presented here requires some elaboration in order to explain performance with anomalous false sentences (e.g., 'All birds are chairs'). Such sentences are usually rejected rapidly, in spite of the fact that the production frequencies (e.g., of 'chairs' given 'All birds are ---') are extremely low. Glass and Holyoak argued that this was due to the fact that many markers in their marker structure do not correspond to single common English words. Thus, the subject and predicate nouns in the sentence, 'All birds are chairs', differ at the level of an abstract marker such as living-versus-nonliving. In other

words, while production frequency is the main index of the
order in which markers are searched, the index may be very
inadequate when one is dealing with markers which do not
correspond directly to single words. The introduction of
such additional factors into the Glass-Holyoak model has the
disadvantage that unequivocal predictions are hard to make.

At this point, it seems desirable to consider some of the
methodological and interpretative problems posed by research
into semantic memory. The basic difficulty stems from the
fact that the experimenter is highly constrained in his
choice of stimuli. The usual technique, as we have seen, is
to assign stimulus materials to conditions on the basis of
some property they possess such as category size or semantic
relatedness. Even if highly significant differences are
found between, for example, pairs of stimuli high and low in
semantic relatedness, one does not know whether the results
are due to the effects of semantic relatedness or to some
other variable that is correlated with semantic relatedness.
A major reason for the proliferation of theories has been the
existence of several variables that correlate highly with
each other: semantic relatedness, hierarchical distance,
familiarity, category size, and production frequency. As
Anderson and Reder (1974) pointed out, "the underlying logic
of a semantic memory experiment is not that of a true
experiment with controlled manipulation of an independent
variable; rather, it is correlational" (p. 665). The need,
then, is for careful experimentation in which the effects of
some factors are investigated while an attempt is made to
control for as many extraneous factors as possible. More
specifically relevant to the literature on the instance-
category verification task, Johnson-Laird (1974) has made an
excellent point. He noted that comprehension and
verification of a sentence such as 'A dog is an animal' are
very closely related. If experimenters were to use slightly
different sentences such as 'A dog is expensive to keep', the
distinction between comprehension and verification would be
much clearer, since one can understand this sentence without
knowing whether or not it is true.

The Mantiness Problem: Word Recognition
One method of investigating semantic memory is to present
strings of letters to the subject, and to ask him to decide
as rapidly as possible whether each string is an English
word. 'The mantiness problem', a phrase used by Norman

(1969), refers to the difficulty of explaining how subjects
can decide in approximately one second that an item such as
'mantiness' is or is not one of the 20,000-100,000 words
known to them.   An initial attempt to uncover some of the
relevant variables was made by Rubenstein, Garfield, and
Millikan (1970), in a study in which subjects had to
distinguish between English and nonsense words.   They found
that response times were faster for English words than for
nonsense words, for high frequency words than for low
frequency words, and for homographs (i.e., words with more
than one meaning) than for non-homographs.   While the data
did not suffice for a thorough explanation of the findings,
Rubenstein et al. made the reasonable, if obvious,
assumption that word recognition requires consultation of the
internal lexicon.   The faster response times for homographs
would thus be due to the fact that there are more entries in
the internal lexicon for homographs than for non-homographs.

Several subsequent investigators have proposed a phonemic-
encoding hypothesis (e.g., Meyer, Schvaneveldt, & Ruddy,
1974).   The hypothesis assumes that visually presented items
are encoded phonemically.   If the phonemic representation is
illegal (e.g., because it is unpronounceable), the subject
decides immediately that the item is not an English word.
If the phonemic representation is legal, the subject then
searches his internal lexicon, and attempts to locate an
appropriate lexical entry.   If he does so, he concludes that
a word has been presented; if he does not, he concludes that
a nonsense string has been presented.

In a general sense, it is clear that the phonemic
attributes of presented items are important in determining
reaction time.   Among non-words, responses are fastest for
unpronounceable items (e.g., 'brakv'), slower for
pronounceable items (e.g., 'blean'), and slowest for items
(e.g., 'brume') that are homophonic with English words
(Rubenstein, Lewis, & Rubenstein, 1971).   They also found
that reaction time was longer for words, such as 'weak', that
are homophonic with other words of different spelling (e.g.,
'week').   Further evidence of the importance of phonemic
attributes was obtained by Meyer et al. (1974).   Subjects
were presented with pairs of items and had to respond 'yes'
if both items were English words and 'no' otherwise.   A
graphemically similar pair of words was responded to rapidly
if the words were also phonemically similar (e.g., 'bribe'
and 'tribe'), but was responded to slowly and with many

errors if the words were phonemically dissimilar (e.g.,
'couch' and 'touch').

One difficulty with the phonemic-encoding hypothesis is
that it is often hard to distinguish empirically between
effects due to the graphemic and the phonemic attributes of
presented material.   The unpronounceable non-words used by
Rubenstein et al. (1971) may also have looked less like
English words than the pronounceable non-words.   A second
difficulty is with the assumption that phonological
evaluation precedes a search of the internal lexicon.
Subjects should thus be able to reject phonemically illegal
consonant-consonant-consonants (CCCs) without any
consideration of their meaning.   It follows that the reaction
times to nonsense CCCs (e.g., JRK) should not differ from the
reaction times to meaningful CCCs (e.g., JFK, LSD).   In
fact, Novik (1974) found that the reaction times to the
meaningful CCCs were significantly longer than those to the
nonsense CCCs, suggesting that phonological evaluation and
memory search may operate in parallel rather than
sequentially.   Baron (1973) obtained evidence for the
importance of graphemic attributes in a study in which
subjects had to decide whether or not phrases sounded
meaningful.   In spite of their phonemic identicality, the
phrase 'My new car' was responded to faster than the phrase
'My knew car'.

It is important to note that the particular word-
recognition paradigm considered here does not explicitly
require the subject to process the semantic attributes of the
stimulus material, and does not supply any semantic context.
Thus the importance of phonemic and graphemic information may
be over-emphasized by the nature of the task, and, indeed,
relatively small changes in procedure can make semantic
information a critical determinant of reaction time (e.g.,
Schvaneveldt & Meyer, 1973).

The Tip-of-the-tongue Phenomenon

Some of the work on the tip-of-the-tongue phenomenon was
reviewed in Chapter 4.   The basic method is to give the
dictionary definitions of rare English words to subjects
(e.g., 'a small boat used in the river and harbour traffic of
China and Japan'), and ask them to supply the word defined.
Subjects in the tip-of-the-tongue state, in which they
cannot think of the word, but feel that it is on the point of

coming back to them, appear to have some knowledge of the
number of syllables in the missing word, the sound of the
word, the location of the primary stress, and some of the
letters (Brown & McNeill, 1966), as well as information
about its visual characteristics (May & Clayton, 1973).

A similar phenomenon was investigated by Hart (1965,
1966). Subjects were presented with general knowledge
questions and allowed a few seconds for recall. Interest
centred on those questions for which the subject was unable
to supply the correct answer; for such questions, subjects
made feeling-of-knowing judgements, in which they indicated
whether or not they felt they knew the correct answer.
Finally, subjects were given a multiple-choice recognition
test for the items which had not been recalled. The critical
finding was that the feeling-of-knowing judgement was a
relatively good predictor of recognition success, i.e., among
unrecalled items, those which subjects felt they knew were
more likely to be correctly recognized than items which
subjects did not feel they knew. An important
methodological point is whether or not the unrecalled items
were in fact unrecallable. Hart (1965) allowed only ten
seconds for recall, and Gruneberg, Smith, and Winfrow (1973)
found that 75 per cent of items for which subjects reported
'blocking' were subsequently recalled, with over half
requiring more than ten seconds for correct recall to occur.
In addition, Hart (1966) obtained evidence that subjects
sometimes withheld responses in the recall situation due to
overcautiousness.

A further difficulty is that some of the recognition
decision success rate is spurious: for example, it does not
take an expert in English literature to select the author of
'The Tempest' from Moliere, Jonson, Strindberg, and
Shakespeare. Better than chance recognition scores will be
achieved if subjects know that 'The Tempest' was written by
an English playwright.

Theoretically, the implications of the work on the tip-of-
the-tongue phenomenon are exciting. It appears that words
in semantic memory are stored in terms of their several
attributes (phonemic, graphemic, visual, and semantic), and
that the attributes of a given word are discriminable to the
extent that some attributes of a word can be retrieved in the
absence of retrieval of the remaining attributes. Gardiner,
Craik, and Bleasdale (1973) provided dictionary definitions

to subjects, and asked them to produce the words defined.
If they could not do so within one minute, the experimenter
supplied the word.   At the end of the experiment, the
experimenter unexpectedly asked the subjects to recall all
the words whose definitions had been given.   If the subjects
in the tip-of-the-tongue state are processing some of the
attributes of the sought-for word whereas those who disclaim
knowledge of it are not, one might expect superior recall from
the former subjects, as Gardiner et al. found.   In addition,
words producing the tip-of-the-tongue state were better
recalled than the target words produced by subjects within
the one minute period.

One of the unfortunate aspects of the tip-of-the-tongue
paradigm is that, since the definitions provide the semantic
attributes of the sought-for information, one cannot
investigate the subjects' ability to retrieve semantic
attributes separately from other attributes.   However, M. W.
Eysenck (in preparation) has made use of a paradigm that
overcomes this difficulty.   The subject attempts to define a
number of rare words, and indicates the extent to which he
feels he knows the meaning of each word.   On a subsequent
semantic-differential test for the three dimensions of
evaluation, activity, and potency, subjects' feeling-of-
knowing judgements for words they could not define were
strongly related to the accuracy of semantic-differential
performance, a finding referred to as the 'reverse tip-of-the-
tongue' phenomenon.   Theoretically, it was argued that the
feeling-of-knowing judgement was based upon the number of
semantic attributes of each word that could be accessed, as
was performance on the semantic differential.   A definite
implication is that word concepts in semantic memory consist
of discriminable or separable semantic features.

Koriat and Lieblich (1974) have suggested that accurate
guessing of the attributes of sought-for information could be
based either on the subjects' knowledge of the characteristics
common to the class of item of which the target is a member or
on their knowledge of the characteristics specific to the
target in question.   Workers in this area have assumed,
possibly erroneously, that accurate guessing is an indication
of specific information about the target.   However, we
certainly can use more general sorts of information in these
tasks: for example, the reader would probably guess that the
name of a new medical drug contains more syllables than the
nickname of a famous British football player.   Koriat and

Lieblich obtained evidence that both general and specific
sorts of information were available to subjects in the tip-
of-the-tongue state. Interestingly, even subjects who
responded 'don't know' to the definitions showed some
evidence of general and specific information about the
number of syllables and the first and last letters of the
target word, although they did have less information than
tip-of-the-tongue subjects.

The Method of Incomplete Definitions

It is probable that information in semantic memory is
primarily organized in terms of semantic attributes. While
some of the theories we have considered so far, such as that
of Smith et al. (1974), have emphasized the importance of
semantic attributes, little clarification of the exact nature
of these attributes has been achieved. Miller (1972) has
attempted to investigate these semantic attributes by means
of the method of incomplete definitions. An incomplete
definition of a word is a substitutable phrase which has a
more general meaning than the word it replaces, but which
expresses some important semantic aspect of the word. For
example, an incomplete definition of 'dog' might be 'warm-
blooded animal'. The definition is incomplete in the sense
that a thing cannot be a dog without being a warm-blooded
animal, but it can be a warm-blooded animal without being a
dog. Elephants, cats, and kangaroos are also warm-blooded
animals, so that all four (i.e., dog, cat, elephant, and
kangaroo) share the semantic attribute of warm-bloodedness.

Miller (1972) applied his method of incomplete definitions
to 217 verbs of motion, and located 12 major semantic
components of these verbs. Sample components are
instrumental (i.e., by foot, by boat, by plane, etc.), and
velocity (i.e., slowly, rapidly). It should be pointed out
that these components were identified subjectively by Miller.
He has also obtained evidence that people are capable of
finer semantic discriminations than is indicated by the
method of incomplete definitions. Miller (1969) formed ten
sentences by using each of ten verbs (walks, strolls, runs,
tiptoes, sprints, jogs, trots, goes, rides, and swims) in the
frame 'John verbs to school'. Subjects were asked to sort
the ten sentences into piles 'on the basis of similarity of
meaning'. The major clusters of verbs identified by the
sorting procedure were 'walks-strolls-tiptoes' and 'runs-
sprints-jogs-trots', indicating that subjects distinguished

among the travel-on-land-by-foot verbs in terms of velocity.
Approximately one-sixth of the subjects placed all the ten
verbs into one pile.

The work of Miller does appear to have identified some of
the important semantic similarities and dissimilarities among
English verbs of motion. The major problem lies in the
implicit assumption that each verb has a fixed and unchanging
set of semantic components. The possibility that the
context can determine which aspects of a word's meaning are
salient should be considered. For example, the verbs 'hop',
'step', and 'jump' would seem to be more semantically
related in the context of the Olympic Games than in other
contexts. In the Miller (1969) study, inserting the verb
'runs' into the sentence 'John runs to school' is clearly
contextually biasing one meaning of the verb 'run' over
others (e.g., 'John runs a temperature', 'John runs up
against trouble', 'John runs scared'). A suitable procedure
might involve subjects initially generating sentences to
embody all the different meanings which they know of a given
verb, and then using the method of incomplete definitions.

Retrieval from Semantic Memory: The Fruit-P Task
A technique emphasizing retrieval processes has been used
in several recent studies (e.g., M. W. Eysenck, 1974c, 1975b;
Freedman & Loftus, 1971; Loftus, Freedman, & Loftus, 1970;
Loftus & Suppes, 1972). The basic procedure involves the
presentation of a category name followed by a single letter
(e.g., 'fruit-P'). The task for the subject is to respond
as quickly as possible with a member of the specified
category starting with the designated letter (e.g., 'plum').
The most thorough attempt to determine the variables
affecting response time in this situation was made by Loftus
and Suppes (1972), in a study investigating the effects of
twelve variables. In spite of the fact that the subjects
were young adults, the three most important variables were
frequency of the stimulus category in children's vocabulary,
frequency of the most likely response in children's
vocabulary, and dominance in the category of the most
dominant appropriate response. Dominance was determined by
reference to the Battig and Montague (1969) norms, in which
subjects were asked to name words that belonged to a
particular category. The relative frequency of the most
frequently given word in a category that satisfies a
category-letter pair defines the dominance rating. For

example, in the Battig and Montague norms of responses to the
category label 'fruit', the most frequently given word
satisfying the pair 'fruit-P' is 'pear', which is the third
most frequently given word to the category 'fruit'. The
concept of dominance corresponds to that of production
frequency emphasized by Glass and Holyoak (1975).

Several other studies have confirmed that category-letter
pairs that have an appropriate response of high frequency and
of high dominance produce the fastest responses.
Theoretically, Anderson and Bower (1973) have proposed that
the subject performs a serial search through the members of
the specified category, starting with those of greatest
frequency and dominance. The relatively slow mean response
latencies for some category-letter pairs (e.g., 2.17 seconds
for country-A; Loftus & Suppes, 1972) would certainly allow
time for a serial search, but direct evidence is lacking.
An interesting, although unexplored, question is whether the
subject necessarily initiates the search with items of high
dominance and frequency. If he were instructed that all
appropriate responses to the next category-letter pair were of
low dominance and few-per-million frequency, could he re-
organize his search process? It may be that the search
usually proceeds in the way it does merely because that is
the most generally successful method.

Some of the implications of the serial-search hypothesis
have been explored by Loftus (1973) and Loftus and Loftus
(1974). They presented a series of category-letter pairs to
their subjects, and sometimes repeated a category after zero,
one, or two intervening items. Thus, subjects might receive
'colour-B' on trial one and 'colour-G' on trial three. If
the serial search for a colour starting with the letter 'B'
activates other colour names starting with different letters,
then some facilitation of performance might be expected when
the category is repeated. As predicted, the immediate
repetition of a category had a facilitatory effect on reaction
time which declined as the number of intervening items
between the two appearances of the same category name
increased. A similar, but more complex, experiment was done
by Loftus and Loftus (1974), who discovered that the
decrease in response latency when a category was repeated was
due to a reduction in the time taken to search the category
rather than to a reduction in the time taken to retrieve and
enter the category.

A matter of some interest is whether or not the processes used to retrieve the name of a category member starting with a particular letter are similar to those used in other situations.   Grober and Loftus (1974) and Loftus and Cole (1974) compared performance on category-letter pairs (e.g., fruit-P) with performance on category-adjective pairs (e.g., fruit-yellow), with the subjects having to produce an item from the specified category having the designated characteristic.   On some trials, subjects could predict whether a letter or an adjective was going to be presented. The major finding was that performance on letter trials was significantly faster when the subjects knew that a letter cue was to be presented, but performance on adjective trials was unaffected by prior information.   This differential effect of predictability indicates that some important difference exists between category-letter and category-adjective trials, possibly due to the fact that the set of possible letters is better defined and more obvious than the set of possible adjectives.

M. W. Eysenck (in preparation) has argued that there may be an important distinction between discriminative attributes or features, i.e., those that differentiate one semantic memory trace from another and facilitate recognition memory judgements, and retrieval attributes, i.e., those that facilitate the search component of recall.   It is probable that semantic characteristics are of most importance as retrieval attributes, it commonly being assumed that subjects attempting to retrieve members of a category starting with a particular letter effectively limit their search processes to that category alone.

The distinction between discriminative and retrieval attributes in semantic memory may be clarified by considering an analogy drawn by Broadbent (1971).   He suggested that the organization of information in semantic memory might well resemble in some ways the structural characteristics of a library, with a filing system providing a variety of methods of accessing the individual concepts, words, or books.   In a library, some information about a particular book can only be obtained by a perusal of the book itself, whereas other information about the book (e.g., title, author, topic area) can be obtained from the filing system alone.   Similarly, some information about words (i.e., discriminative attributes) can be discovered only by retrieving the word itself from semantic memory, whereas other information (i.e.,

retrieval attributes) appears to be accessible _prior_ to item
retrieval.

As already indicated, some semantic aspects such as
category membership are best thought of as retrieval
attributes, but the status of other attributes (e.g., initial
letters) is unclear. M. W. Eysenck (in preparation) asked
subjects to write down all the words belonging to a particular
category starting with a specified letter that they could
think of as rapidly as possible. Over trials, the category
size (i.e., the number of instances in the entire category)
and the target size (i.e., the number of category members
that began with the specified letter) were both varied. If
subjects could utilize first letters to act as retrieval
attributes, this would imply that subjects effectively
limited their memory searches to members of the target set.
It would then be predicted that the speed of recall of items
would be determined by target-set size but would be
unaffected by category size. The results were entirely
consistent with this prediction, suggesting that subjects can
use initial-letter information to limit their search sets to
appropriate items. Subsequent research indicated that third
and final letters could not be used in the same way. In
sum, it is likely that a fuller understanding of semantic
memory will come from systematic investigation of word-
concept features to determine whether they are discriminative
or retrieval features.

Free Association

It is reasonable to argue that some of the techniques for
investigating semantic memory that we have discussed so far
have produced paradigm-specific data that are more a
reflection of the methods used than of the functioning of
semantic memory itself. A method that, at least
superficially, obviates this problem is the method of free
association, in which the subject is asked to respond with
the first word that comes into his mind after being presented
with a word by the experimenter. The lack of structure in
the situation might lead one to suppose that the data
obtained by this method would be particularly valuable.

In a series of studies, Deese (1961, 1962, 1965) has
investigated the mean relative frequencies with which all the
words in a list tend to elicit each other in tests of free
association. The greater this relative frequency for any

list, the greater is its inter-item associative strength.
Several experiments have obtained significant relationships
with inter-item associative strength.   Pollio (1964) taped
the responses of subjects as they produced continuous
associations to a single word for a period of four minutes.
He found that the subjects sometimes produced a burst of
rapid responses from semantic memory, and that the responses
in such bursts tended to be highly associated according to
free-association data.   Deese (1965) found that the number
of words that could be recalled from a list correlated very
highly with his index of inter-item associative strength, and
he also (1959b) noted that intrusion errors in free recall
tended to consist of words having strong associations with
list words.

Deese (1962) argued that, as well as direct associative
links among words, there are additional indirect links.   For
example, 'symphony' and 'piano' do not elicit each other as
associates, but they do share several common associates (e.g.,
'note', 'sound', 'music', 'noise', and 'orchestra').   Deese
claimed that two major determinants of association among
words were a sharing of common attributes of meaning (e.g.,
bees, flies, bug) and contrast in terms of position along
some attribute (e.g., hot, cold).

While a number of replicable findings have emerged from
these studies, there are several problems of interpretation.
As Tulving (1968a) has pointed out, "the concept of
association is a descriptive concept, not an explanatory one.
Association is a name for the fact that one event leads to
another, and as such it carries no theoretical implications"
(p. 19).   In other words, associations are merely indices of
underlying patterns of relation.   A prime defect of many
hypotheses based upon associations is that the main aspect of
the associative relationship between two words that is
considered is its strength.   The work of Miller (1969, 1972)
has shown that words may be related in terms of several
different semantic relationships.   As Kintsch (1972a) has
noted, 'insect' and 'wing' are equally common as responses to
'butterfly', so that the associations 'butterfly-insect' and
'butterfly-wing' are said to be equivalently strong.
However, two different semantic relationships are
represented in these associations, one a class relationship
and the other a part-of relationship.

The greatest single difficulty with the use of free

association normative data as an index of the organization of
semantic memory is that the free association technique is
likely to measure only relatively strong semantic
relationships among words.   When someone interprets and
responds to an isolated word, as happens in free association,
his interpretation probably reflects only the subset of its
semantic properties which are most frequently emphasized in
familiar contexts.   For example, Geis and Winograd (1974)
asked subjects to provide a single association to each of
several homographs.   Ninety-nine per cent of the subjects
gave an association to the word 'bank' that emphasized its
semantic interpretation as a financial establishment, and
only one per cent gave an association related to the other
major meaning of 'bank', i.e., 'water's edge'.
Nevertheless, it is presumably true that the latter semantic
interpretation of 'bank' is stored in semantic memory for all
the subjects used by Geis and Winograd.   The tendency of the
free association technique to measure only the strongest
semantic attributes was noted by Barclay, Bransford, Franks,
McCarrell, and Nitsch (1974).   For example, most responses
to the word 'piano' in a free association situation would
emphasize its musical characteristics, but not its weight.

Inferences

    While the majority of studies investigating semantic
memory have been concerned with individual words and their
attributes, it is also important to consider those aspects of
semantic memory that underlie the retention of sentential
information.   Studies of sentence memory by, for example,
Bartlett (1932) and Bransford, Barclay, and Franks (1972),
have indicated that subjects frequently remember both the
information actually specified in sentences and information
that can be inferred from that provided.   Presumably such
inferences are stored in semantic memory.   Kintsch (1972a)
has studied this aspect of semantic memory in some detail.
He presented subjects with simple sentences, and asked them
to specify any information that the sentences conveyed to
them that was not explicitly stated.   There was reasonable
agreement among the subjects as to the inferences that could
be drawn from each sentence.   The two major inferences made
by the subjects dealt with (a) missing grammatical cases;
and (b) semantic implications.   For example, consider one of
the sentences used by Kintsch: 'Fred was murdered'.
Grammatically, the implication is that someone (the missing
subject) must have murdered Fred;   semantically, the

implication is that Fred is now dead.   The exact method by
which we comprehend complex utterances, and then proceed to
draw complex inferences from them, is unknown.

General

It is obvious that we possess a wealth of information
about the words and concepts stored in semantic memory.   The
evidence reviewed in this chapter has indicated that we have
information about the pronunciation and spelling of words
(Brown & McNeill, 1966), the visual characteristics of
concrete words (May & Clayton, 1973), and the semantic
attributes of concepts (Miller, 1972).   In addition, however,
we possess information about the frequency of occurrence of
words in the language (Shapiro, 1969, found that familiarity
ratings correlated substantially with frequency data), and
about the appropriate contexts in which to use certain words
(e.g., the synonymous terms 'loo', 'lavatory', 'bog',
'toilet', 'throne', and 'smallest room in the house' are not
used entirely interchangeably).   The contextual factor is
particularly apparent in bilinguals and polyglots, whose use
of the terms 'le chat', 'the cat', and 'der Kater' is
situationally determined.

A limitation on many of the experimental techniques that
have been used to study semantic memory is that they focus
almost exclusively on the most dominant semantic information
about words and concepts.   The verification technique, the
method of incomplete definitions, the free association
technique, and Kintsch's work on inferences, are all examples
of methods to which this criticism applies.   These
techniques have been relatively uninformative about non-dominant semantic information.   For example, while the dominant
semantic information about 'piano' is that it is a musical
instrument, most people also know that pianos tend to be
heavy, black, have white and black keys, are kept indoors,
and so on.   This richness of semantic knowledge has not been
explored thoroughly as yet.

Many of the experimental paradigms involve an emphasis on
the speed with which decisions about information contained in
semantic memory can be taken, rather than on the correctness
of the decisions themselves.   Performance is usually nearly
error-free, and it is assumed that errors reflect either
momentary inattention or lack of storage in semantic memory.
Since analysis of the number and nature of errors in

performance is frequently useful in facilitating an
understanding of the operation and limitations of the memory
system, it would seem that there is scope here for future
research.   The tip-of-the-tongue paradigm provides a good
example of the value of considering error data.   One
potentially fruitful area of research would be the
investigation of the stored representations in semantic
memory of those words whose meaning can be both recalled and
recognized compared with the representations of words whose
meaning can only be recognized.   There are several thousand
words in most people's 'passive' vocabularies that are not in
their 'active' vocabularies, and yet the experimental bias
has been towards an explication of active vocabulary only.

A final point is that performance on most semantic memory
tasks is likely to be determined by interactive effects of
episodic and semantic memory.   For example, Buschke (1975)
used a verbal fluency task in which subjects had to retrieve
all possible members of a semantic category on two separate
occasions.   While the initial, relatively poor and
unorganized retrieval may have reflected the storage
characteristics of semantic memory, the second retrieval
clearly involved episodic memory.   Performance was much
better, and subjects tended to recall the words given in the
first retrieval at the start of the second retrieval.
Furthermore, when given a recognition test, the subjects were
good at recognizing which items produced during the second
retrieval period had also been produced during the first.
While the confounding of episodic and semantic memory effects
is obvious in this case, the problem arises in more subtle
ways in most work on semantic memory.

Summary

It is obvious that all theories are inadequate to account
for the sheer size and complexity of semantic memory.   One of
the problems with the literature which has been referred to a
number of times is the tendency for experimenters to
concentrate on the most dominant semantic attributes of the
words used in their experiments.   It is customary to present
words in contexts that emphasize their dominant semantic
aspects (e.g., 'A robin is a bird').   In view of the analysis
by Tulving and Watkins (1975), the best method of discovering
the nature and extent of the information stored in semantic
memory would be to utilize a series of different probes or

contexts for each word rather than a single context as
currently favoured.

At the level of the individual word, theoretical and
empirical approaches that have viewed word concepts as
aggregates of features or attributes have been quite
successful (e.g., the tip-of-the-tongue paradigm and Miller's
method of incomplete definitions).   An alternative method
was adopted by Caramazza, Hersh, and Torgerson (1976).
Subjects rated the similarity of animal terms selected from
the categories of fish, birds, and mammals.   Application of
a multi-dimensional scaling technique indicated that the
similarity ratings were determined by class membership, as
well as the features of size and ferocity.   These features
were also identified by Rips et al. (1973), and thus seem to
be particularly salient for some kinds of words in semantic
memory.

At the level of inter-relationships among words, however,
an account based primarily upon feature analysis seems less
adequate.   We have seen the various problems with the Smith
et al. (1974) model that attempted to do this, and it is now
clear that feature-comparison models are unlikely to prove
satisfactory.   Network models of the type proposed by Glass
and Holyoak (1975) presently offer the best approach to
accounting for inter-relationships among words, but as yet
suffer from an excess of theoretical flexibility.   Production
frequency is an important determinant of performance in recall
and recognition tasks, and is more naturally incorporated into
a network model.   However, as with the related measure of
association strength, further theoretical examination of the
production-frequency index is required.

CHAPTER 8

AROUSAL AND MEMORY

One of the more immediately obvious facts about human learning and memory is that there are enormous individual differences. The intelligent layman would probably imagine that an explication of these individual differences would be one of the primary targets of psychologists interested in learning and memory. In actuality, the emphasis throughout the history of psychology has been on devising materials and paradigms that will minimize individual differences in performance, from the use of nonsense syllables by Ebbinghaus (1885) to the current search for simple paradigms (e.g., Peterson & Peterson, 1959; Sternberg, 1966). Cofer (1967) expressed one of the major reasons which deter psychologists from undertaking research into individual differences: "I remain to be convinced... that there are but a few basic processes underlying individual differences in learning, and that the interactions of specific task characteristics with highly specific individual propensities are not the basis of the enormous individual differences which everyone finds in most learning tasks" (p. 139). The theories and data to be presented in this and subsequent chapters indicate that there are several consistent, replicable, differences in learning and memory between those low and high in arousal, between introverts and extraverts, between those low and high in anxiety, and between young and old. Furthermore, some of these differences hold across a variety of different paradigms, indicating that Cofer may have been unduly pessimistic when he emphasized the specificity of the relationships likely to be found between learning scores and individual-difference variables.

A second line of argument advanced by those opposed to work on individual differences (cf., several of the chapters in Gagne, 1967), is that the student of learning and memory is attempting to obtain data on the cognitive processes involved in learning. The discovery that there are reliable individual differences in learning does not, in and of itself,

159

further our understanding of information processing.   Such
an argument might be persuasive if all subjects utilized the
same processes and strategies, and if the performance
differences among subjects were all quantitative in nature.
In fact, some of the differences appear to be qualitative,
with different subjects using quite different approaches to
the storage and retrieval of information.   In many cases,
no theory ignoring individual differences could possibly be
accurate.   For example, Clifton and Birenbaum (1970)
presented subjects with between one and seven items, followed
by a probe item.   The subject's task was to respond 'yes' as
rapidly as possible if the probe corresponded to one of the
items on the learned list, and 'no' otherwise.   As usual in
experiments of this type (cf., Corballis, 1975), the 'yes'
and 'no' response latencies both increased linearly as the
number of items in the learned list increased (see Fig. 8.1).
In addition, the slope of the negative reaction-time function
was somewhat greater than the slope of the positive reaction-
time function.

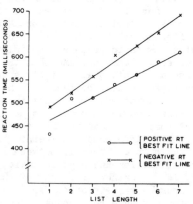

Fig. 8.1.   Recognition reaction time as a function of
set size.   Adapted from Clifton and Birenbaum (1970).

   A theoretical model could presumably have been proposed
that would explain the curious indication of a difference
between the positive and negative functions.   However,
Clifton and Birenbaum looked at the individual results, and
found that none of the subjects produced results like those
shown in Fig. 8.1.   Instead, three-quarters of the subjects

produced parallel positive and negative functions, and the
remaining subjects produced negative functions that were
twice as steep as their 'yes' functions. It is surely naïve
to imagine that a process model based on group data will
provide a complete account of any set of data, particularly
where the subjects within each group are utilizing
qualitatively different strategies.

A second experimental demonstration of this point comes in
a study by Howarth and H. J. Eysenck (1968). They found
that paired-associate recall was apparently unaffected by the
length of the retention interval, for periods of time between
a few minutes and a week. It would certainly be possible to
account for these data theoretically, although most theories
would predict a performance decrement over time. However,
once again, the group data are misleading. Fuller analysis
of the data indicated that the recall of extraverts
declined considerably over the retention interval, whereas
that of introverts increased substantially. In the face of
such findings, a refusal to consider individual differences
at all seems obtuse.

A third line of argument against the consideration of
individual-difference variables is the problem of confounded
variables. In a typical experiment, the researcher will
select extreme scorers on some personality questionnaire, and
will then attempt to obtain significant differences between
these two groups on some aspect of learning or memory.
However, even if significant differences are obtained, there
are considerable interpretative problems. The two groups of
subjects may well differ in several respects other than the
one of interest to the experimenter. For example, high-
anxiety subjects frequently show inferior learning to low-
anxiety subjects (e.g., Spence & Spence, 1966). However,
there is evidence (Grice, 1955; Kerrick, 1955) that high-
anxiety subjects are less intelligent than low-anxiety
subjects, so that there is some confounding between anxiety
and intelligence. In addition, high-anxiety subjects tend
to be more introverted than low-anxiety subjects (H. J.
Eysenck, 1973). Thus, in order to obtain an unbiased
comparison between low- and high-anxiety groups of subjects,
it would be necessary at least to equate the two groups on
intelligence and extraversion. In fact, there are probably
several other, as yet undiscovered, respects in which high-
and low-anxiety subjects differ. Another way of expressing
the same point is to note that the normal experimental control

over the independent variable is lacking in the case of
personality variables.   Two possible approaches to this
problem are to attempt to affect personality characteristics
either by situational manipulation (e.g., introducing
stressful stimuli in order to increase anxiety) or by drug
administration (e.g., use of alcohol to increase extraversion
and to decrease anxiety).

This chapter is devoted to an examination of the work on
arousal and learning.   The concept of arousal has assumed
considerable significance in the major theoretical
statements in the entire area of individual differences.
Differences in arousal or emotional responsiveness are
assumed to provide the basis for individual differences in
extraversion (H. J. Eysenck, 1973), and in anxiety (Spence
& Spence, 1966), and there may also be important changes in
arousal in old age (e.g., Eisdorfer, 1968).

A noticeable deficiency in the work to be reported is the
general use of somewhat outmoded and imprecise learning
paradigms.   This is probably due to the fact that the
majority of psychologists attempting to build a bridge
between individual differences and memory have been
primarily interested in individual differences.   If more
psychologists interested mainly in memory participated in
this enterprise, a less lop-sided structure might eventuate.
It is obvious that Melton (1967) was right when he wrote:

> The sooner our experiments and our theory on human
> memory and human learning consider the differences
> between individuals in our experimental analyses of
> component processes in memory and learning, the sooner
> we will have theories and experiments that have some
> substantial probability of reflecting the fundamental
> characteristics of these processes (pp. 249-250).

The concept of Arousal

In the history of psychology, 'arousal' is one of the
concepts which has caused the most controversy.   In spite of
its apparent applicability to a large number of problems, it
is not satisfactorily anchored to observables at either the
stimulus or the response end.   At various times, it has been
argued that several factors such as heat, noise, incentive,
and stimulant drugs all contribute to increasing arousal,
while sleeplessness, sensory deprivation, and depressant drugs

(e.g., alcohol) reduce the level of arousal. In addition,
personality factors such as introversion-extraversion and
anxiety are alleged to act as determinants of arousal.
However, Broadbent (1971) has convincingly shown that these
several variables cannot simply be regarded as contributing
to the same arousal factor. For example, noise and
sleeplessness usually cancel each out if applied together,
suggesting that their effects are opposite, but they are
alike in that they both have their greatest detrimental
effects on performance towards the end of a work-period.

A second example comes in a study by Wilkinson and
Colquhoun (1968). Theoretically, the effects of alcohol
and of incentive should be antagonistic and thus nullify
each other, but Wilkinson and Colquhoun found that incentive
actually increased the adverse effect of alcohol. In spite
of such results, it is worth emphasizing that there are
dozens of experiments in which the various stimulus factors
did interact with one another as anticipated on a model
employing a unitary concept of arousal.

On the response side, various physiological measures of
sympathetic dominance, including pulse rate, skin
conductance, pupil diameter, and the EEG, have been proposed
as indices of arousal. The concept of a unitary dimension of
arousal implies that the correlations among these measures
should be substantial. However, the observed correlations
are usually quite modest, although positive. There are some
situations in which one autonomic variable may indicate
sympathetic dominance while another variable displays a
typically parasympathetic response. Lacey (1967) has used
the term 'directional fractionation' for such discrepant
patterns. Part of the problem may be that these
physiological measures reflect both arousal and effort
(cf., Kahneman, 1973).

A further difficulty is that arousal is sometimes used as
a psychological concept, and sometimes as a physiological
concept, and even as an amalgam of the two. Broadbent
(1971) has argued persuasively that the current state of
knowledge requires us to use separate physiological and
psychological concepts of arousal, since "the physiological
concept of arousal is certainly of interest and of ultimate
relevance to the one found in behaviour, but at this stage
the connection of any suggested physiological measure and the
psychological state is too remote to make it practical to

attach one concept directly to the other" (p. 413).

It seems probable that the unitary concept of arousal will need to be replaced by a number of more specific concepts, but the precise nature of these concepts is unclear. Lacey (1967) has argued for a separation of arousal into electrocortical arousal, autonomic arousal, and behavioural arousal. Broadbent (1971), on the other hand, suggested an upper and a lower mechanism, with the lower-level one concerned with the execution of decision processes, and the higher-level one monitoring and altering the parameters of the lower level so as to maintain a constant level of performance. Sleeplessness and noise affect the lower mechanism, whereas alcohol and extraversion affect the higher. This formulation certainly handles more of the findings than can be done using a unitary concept of arousal, but there is little directly relevant evidence available.

It is possible that there is a reasonable analogy with the concept of 'intelligence', where the generally positive but low inter-correlations among response measures indicate the desirability of postulating a general factor of intelligence together with other, smaller, factors (e.g., verbal, spatial). Similarly, it may be appropriate to postulate a general factor of arousal, an intervening variable representing an elevated physical state, together with a number of more specific arousal-related factors.

Evidence about the number and nature of the arousal concepts that we should use could come from large-scale studies involving several situational variables and several behavioural measures. Many studies have attempted to investigate arousal either through the introduction of a single stressor or the recording of a single physiological variable. Such studies are unrevealing about the status of the arousal concept. Since most studies investigating the relationship between arousal and memory are of this type, and since they have commonly relied upon a unitary concept of arousal, the term 'arousal' will frequently be used in this and succeeding chapters in accord with custom. That is to say, it will be assumed that arousal refers to some elevated state of bodily function, that it represents a non-specific increment in physiological activity, and that it is non-informational.

Partial reviews of the experimental literature have been

prepared by M. W. Eysenck (1976a), Levonian (1972), and
Uehling (1972).   Accordingly, a brief summary of the
findings and relevant theories will be given here.

The various sources of arousal which might be involved
in the learning situation include arousal induced by the
material presented to the subject (item arousal) and the
arousal level of the subject (subject arousal).   It is clear
that both of these sources of arousal could affect any or all
of the three stages of trace formation, trace storage, and
trace utilization.

Item Arousal at Input

The most influential theory of arousal and memory was
proposed by Walker (1958).   He argued that any psychological
event would establish a perseverative trace lasting for some
length of time.   During this period of time, long-term
memory is laid down, but there is a temporary inhibition of
retrieval (or action decrement) which preserves the trace
and protects it against disruption.   The further assumption
is made that high arousal has the effect of producing a
longer lasting active trace, with the result that high levels
of arousal should lead to greater long-term memory, but a
larger initial inhibition of retrieval.   The major
predictions at an experimental level have been that low-
arousal items should be better recalled than high-arousal
items at short retention intervals, that the opposite should
occur at longer retention intervals after consolidation has
been completed, and that there should be an interaction
between item arousal and retention interval.   It is
important to note that studies in this area have frequently
used the term 'short retention interval' to refer to
retention up to about 15-20 minutes after presentation of the
material, with the term 'long retention interval' being used
to refer only to longer periods of time.   These time periods
suggest that it would be extremely misleading to identify the
term 'short retention interval' with primary memory, which
characteristically has a much shorter duration.

The predictions of Walker's action-decrement theory have
most frequently been tested in studies of paired-associate
learning, with each subject's items being assigned to a high-
or a low-arousal category on the basis of the GSR to the
items at presentation.   In a typical study using this
approach, Kleinsmith and Kaplan (1963) found the predicted
interaction effect between arousal and retention interval

(see Fig. 8.2).   Several other investigators have obtained
comparable results (e.g., Butter, 1970; Walker & Tarte,
1963).

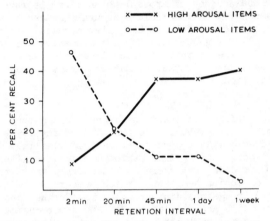

Fig. 8.2. Recall performance as a function
of item arousal and retention interval.
Adapted from Kleinsmith and Kaplan (1963).

Other studies have exerted experimental control over the
assignment of items to high- and low-arousal categories by
pairing some of the items with white noise, which has been
found to increase the level of physiological arousal
(e.g., Magoun, 1963).   Most of the relevant paired-associate
studies have produced findings in line with Walker's
hypothesis (e.g., Berlyne, Borsa, Craw, Gelman, & Mandell,
1965; McLean, 1969).

On the other hand, most of the studies of free recall have
produced results inconsistent with the predictions of Walker.
For example, several researchers have found that high arousal
facilitates immediate free recall (e.g., Corteen, 1969;
Maltzman, Kantor, & Langdon, 1966; Schönpflug, & Beike,
1964).   However, the prediction that there should be an
interaction between arousal and retention interval was
supported by, among others, Corteen (1969) and Haveman and
Farley (1969).

There have been relatively few studies concerned with

arousal and recognition, but Archer and Margolin (1970),
Schwartz (1974), and Wesner (1972) all found that items
presented in white noise showed better performance than
items presented in quiet on an immediate recognition test.
However, Levonian (1967) obtained more expected results, with
high-arousal items showing poorer short-term and better long-
term recognition than low-arousal items.

   Since the relationship between item arousal and retention
appears to depend on the type of retention test, it is
obvious that some modification of Walker's theory is
necessary. In addition, there are several other difficulties
with that theory:-

        (1) The only convincing evidence for Walker's
theory derives from the item arousal by retention interval
interaction. However, it is somewhat speculative to
interpret this interaction as indicating the existence of
consolidation processes with varying time courses. The
theory would become more tenable if factors thought to affect
consolidation processes, such as electroconvulsive shock and
various drugs were systematically incorporated into the
experimental paradigms, since they should theoretically have
different effects on low- and high-arousal items.

        (2) An implication of Walker's hypothesis is that
memory traces differ from one another quantitatively, i.e.,
high arousal merely makes traces stronger than they would
otherwise have been. The recent findings of Hamilton,
Hockey, and Quinn (1972) and Schwartz (1975a) have indicated
that high arousal may affect qualitatively the resultant
memory trace. Hamilton et al. tested for recall of paired
associates either by using the same order of the pairs as at
presentation or by randomizing the order of the pairs.
While the arousal variable had no effect upon performance
when the random order of testing was used, noise produced a
significant improvement over the no noise condition when the
fixed order was used. They concluded that high arousal led
to the storage of more information about the presentation
order of the pairs.

   Schwartz (1975a) considered the implications both of the
Hamilton et al. study and of one by Hörmann and Osterkamp
(1966), who found that white noise led to a decrease in
semantic category clustering in free recall. Schwartz
proposed the following hypothesis: "Given that arousal

reduces semantic clustering but facilitates verbatim, ordered
recall, it seems plausible to hypothesize that arousal
facilitates recall based on the actual physical properties of
verbal stimuli but adversely affects memory for semantic
features" (p. 2).

In one experiment, Schwartz (1975a) presented subjects
with normal sentences, anomalous strings, and anagram strings,
and random words, either in silence or accompanied by white
noise.   On an immediate recall test, the major finding was
that the noise by sentence type interaction was significant,
with the detrimental effect of white noise being greatest for
normal sentences, the type of material presumably containing
the most semantic features.   In a second experiment, Schwartz
tested free recall of either unrelated words, phonemically
related words, or semantically related words.   Arousal was
manipulated by varying the intensity of white noise during
list presentation.   There was a highly significant
interaction between arousal and type of material, with high
arousal improving recall on phonemically related material,
but having no effect on semantically related words.
Schwartz argued that the differential effects of arousal on
memory for phonemically and semantically related material was
due to processes operating at retrieval, but the paradigms
which he used only involved the manipulation of arousal at
the time of input.

        (3) Insufficient attention has been paid to the
reasons why some items produce larger GSRs than others.
Items which differ in terms of the GSRs which they evoke may
well also differ in terms of meaningfulness, familiarity, and
other important characteristics.   An intriguing hypothesis
is that those items producing large GSRs tend to be the ones
that are processed the most fully and to the greatest depth.
Since Craik and Lockhart (1972) have found evidence that
material processed to a greater depth is better retained over
long periods of time than material processed shallowly, this
hypothesis could account for significant arousal by retention
interval interactions.   Kahneman (1973) has suggested that
the GSR is a good index of processing effort, and it is even
possible that the GSR represents the elusive index of
processing depth for which Craik and Lockhart have been
searching.

Indirect evidence for this hypothesis is available in
serial-position data, since Craik (1973) found that the

early items in a list were likely to be most fully processed, whereas the last few items were least adequately processed. In line with the hypothesis, Walker and Tarte (1963) observed that GSRs declined continuously throughout the presentation of a list.   It is known that the last items in either a paired-associate or a free-recall list are the best recalled on an immediate-retention test, but are the worst recalled subsequently.   It thus appears that those items showing the greatest forgetting over time will be those from the end of the list, and they will be low-arousal items.   However, Kaplan and Kaplan (1968) found that two out of three studies re-analyzed in terms of serial position produced no signifi- cant pattern at different retention intervals, and Kleinsmith and Kaplan (1964) obtained little evidence of any contaminating effects of serial position.   On the other hand, Walker (1967) presented evidence indicating that the increased retention over time of high-arousal items was largely due to the fact that the initial item, which was usually a high-arousal item, showed poor short-term recall, but good long-term retention.

(4) Walker's (1958) theory assumes that the groups of subjects at the various retention intervals differ primarily in the extent to which the process of consolidation is still continuing.   However, it is possible that habituation effects may be such as to make subjects at the longer retention intervals less aroused than subjects at the shorter retention intervals (cf., Christie, 1974).   Some evidence that the level of subject arousal is important is contained in an article by Kaplan and Kaplan (1969).   They reported that the instructions given to subjects in their earlier experiments were 'ego-oriented', i.e., arousing. When an effort was made in the instructions to relax the subjects, Kaplan and Kaplan found a considerable reduction in the interaction between arousal and retention interval.

(5) The finding that item arousal is frequently directly related to immediate free recall but inversely related to immediate paired-associate recall is inconsistent with Walker's theory.   While the nature of the differences between the processes involved in free recall and in paired- associate learning is unclear (cf., Postman, 1972), it is probable that free recall is much less affected than paired- associate learning by response competition.   An alternative, although related, viewpoint is that paired-associate learning comprises the processes of response learning and association

learning, whereas free recall basically involves the learning
of responses.   At short retention intervals, high arousal
may facilitate the retrieval of responses, but hinder the
retrieval of appropriate associative links.   The hypothesis
that high levels of arousal can have an enhancing effect on
retention at short retention intervals, provided that the
subjects do not have to retrieve specific associative links,
is also supported by studies involving immediate recognition
tests, in which high arousal has been found to lead to
superior recognition performance (e.g., Archer & Margolin,
1970; Schwartz, 1974).

        (6) Although Walker argued that arousal was
inversely related to memory performance at short retention
intervals but positively related at long intervals, Berlyne
(1967) proposed that an intermediate level of arousal was
optimal.   Most of the studies have divided items into only
two categories (low and high arousal), which means that
little clarification of the true arousal-memory relationship
can be achieved due to the limited number of points along the
arousal continuum which have been sampled.   A few studies
have obtained an inverted-U relationship between arousal and
short-term recall (e.g., Berry, 1962; Kleinsmith, Kaplan, &
Tarte, 1963), but such a relationship cannot be demonstrated
with only two data points.

Subject Arousal at Input

    The work looking at the effects of individual differences
in arousal level on memory performance has relied heavily on
Walker's (1958) action-decrement theory and on the Yerkes-
Dodson Law (Broadhurst, 1959).   The Yerkes-Dodson Law
asserts that there is a curvilinear relationship between
arousal and task performance, with optimal performance
occurring at some moderate level of arousal or motivation.
In addition, the Law claims that the optimal level of arousal
will be lower on difficult than on easy tasks.   In spite of
the definitional problems with the notion of task difficulty,
Broadhurst concluded that evidence from a diverse collection
of experiments provided support for the theory or Law.

    Several of the studies have made the assumption that the
arousal level of introverts is chronically higher than the
arousal level of extraverts (H. J. Eysenck, 1967, 1973).
Much of the relevant work has been reviewed by Gale (1973),
who cited seven experimental studies finding evidence that

introverts are more highly aroused than extraverts on the
EEG.   However, he also cited three studies finding the
opposite, and six studies where there were no significant
EEG differences between introverts and extraverts.   Blake
(1967) obtained evidence for a complex relationship between
introversion-extraversion and arousal, with introverts
having a higher body temperature than extraverts during the
earlier part of the day, but a lower body temperature during
the evening.   The evidence, discussed in more detail in the
next chapter, is unclear.   A reasonable hypothesis is that
the optimal level of arousal is lower in introverts than in
extraverts, which would explain why introverts perform as if
highly aroused even when they do not appear to be highly
aroused physiologically.

As predicted by the Yerkes-Dodson Law, the nature of the
learning task is an important factor in determining the
relative memory performance of introverts and extraverts.
For example, McLaughlin and H. J. Eysenck (1967) measured
arousal by means of the extraversion and neuroticism scores
on the Eysenck Personality Inventory (EPI), and required
their subjects to learn either an easy or a difficult list of
paired associates to criterion.   The results indicated that
the optimal level of subject arousal was lower on the
difficult than on the easy list.   Other studies have also
found that tasks which are difficult in the sense of involving
response competition or the retrieval of relatively
inaccessible information produce a greater advantage of low-
arousal (extraverted) subjects than is the case with tasks
involving minimal response competition (e.g., Allsopp & H. J.
Eysenck, 1974; Bone, 1971; Howarth, 1969a, 1969b).

H. J. Eysenck (1967, 1973) has proposed, in an extension of
Walker's theory, that the period of consolidation takes
longer for introverts than for extraverts.   He thus
postulated that the short-term retention of extraverts would
be higher than that of introverts, with a reversal at longer
retention intervals.   The first part of the prediction was
confirmed by most of the studies discussed in the previous
paragraph, in which extraverts usually showed superior memory
performance to introverts at the short retention intervals
used.

Howarth and H. J. Eysenck (1968) tested for recall of
paired associates at retention intervals up to one day.   The
results showed that extraverts were superior at the short

retention intervals, but inferior at the long retention
intervals (see Fig. 8.3).   While this interaction was
exactly as predicted, the recall measure used was a
combination of intentional and incidental learning, and it is
not clear which form of learning was responsible for the
obtained interaction.   The same kind of interaction has been
obtained in some other studies (McLean, 1968; Osborne,
1972; Skanthakumari, 1965), but there have been some
negative findings (McLaughlin, 1968; McLaughlin & Kary,
1972).

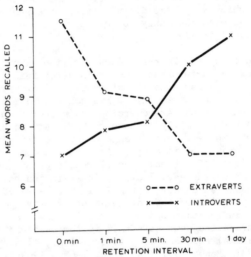

Fig. 8.3. Recall as a function of retention
interval and introversion-extraversion.
Adapted from Howarth and H. J. Eysenck (1968).

The hypothesis proposed by Schwartz (1975a), arguing that
arousal enhances retention based on the physical properties
of stimulus material, but adversely affects retention of
semantic attributes, has been further explored by Schwartz
(1975b).   His subjects were assigned to different arousal
groups on the basis of their neuroticism and introversion
scores on the EPI.   They learned a paired-associate list
where the response words were either all phonemically similar
or semantically similar.   The triple interaction involving
neuroticism, extraversion, and list type was highly

significant (see Fig. 8.4).   In this interaction, high-
arousal subjects were not adversely affected by semantic
similarity, theoretically because they were concentrating on
the physical attributes of the presented material, and low-
arousal subjects, who concentrated on the semantic
characteristics, were not deleteriously affected by
phonemic similarity.

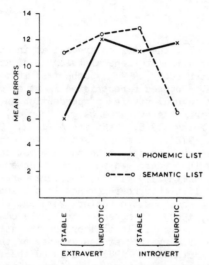

Fig. 8.4.   Errors in recall as a function
of list type, introversion-extraversion, and
neuroticism.   Adapted from Schwartz (1975b).

In a second experiment, Schwartz (1975b) presented a
categorized word list in a random order, and found that high-
arousal subjects recalled the list in a less semantically
organized fashion than did subjects with lower levels of
arousal, and also showed a tendency to recall the words in
the order in which they were presented.   The implication is
that high-arousal subjects concentrated on the physical
aspects of verbal material, whereas low-arousal subjects
utilized semantic attributes.

A major difficulty with the work reviewed above is that one
cannot determine whether the results obtained are a function
of subject arousal at input, subject arousal at test, or both.

The extremely limited evidence suggests that arousal both at
input and at test is important.   Berry (1962) found that
those subjects with moderate levels of skin conductance
during learning performed better on a short-term retention
test than did those with either low or high levels of skin
conductance.   He also found that moderate levels of
conductance in the first minute of the recall period were
optimal for recall.

Easterbrook's Hypothesis

It is strange that the work on arousal at input has had
so little contact with more general theories of arousal.
For example, Easterbrook (1959) hypothesized that high
levels of arousal produced a restricted range of cue
utilization, and several studies of perception and attention
have supplied supporting evidence (e.g., Bruning, Capage,
Kozul, Young, & Young, 1968; McNamara & Fisch, 1964;
Reeves & Bergum, 1972).   A major finding has been that
aroused subjects pay less attention to information in the
visual periphery than unaroused subjects.   However, as was
pointed out by Hockey (1970, 1973), the peripheral visual
cues usually had little or no relevance to the subject's
primary task.   When these two factors were unconfounded
(e.g., Cornsweet, 1969), it appeared to be the case that the
main effect of high arousal is to increase the attentional
bias towards the primary task at the expense of the
secondary task.   Broadbent (1971) concluded that, "the
aroused system devotes a higher proportion of its time to
the intake of information from dominant sources and less from
relatively minor ones" (p. 433).

Bacon (1974) pointed out that it has typically been
assumed that the reduced responsivity to peripheral stimuli
under high arousal is due to an actual attenuation of
sensitivity to the signal.   However, the same results could
have been obtained if arousal only produced an increase in
the subjective decision criterion, so that there was a
reduced probability that peripheral signals would exceed this
stricter criterion.   Subjects concurrently performed a
pursuit-rotor tracking task and an auditory signal detection
task, and high arousal was produced, in line with a great
tradition, by means of extremely painful electric shocks.
The data indicated that (for the survivors) the stimulus
loss under high arousal resulted from a reduction in
sensitivity to the signal rather than from response criterion

changes.   In addition, this effect of arousal was observed
when several seconds intervened between stimulus
presentation and report, but not when the report was
requested within one second of presentation.   This suggests
that arousal does not impede perception of stimulus input,
but rather that it interferes with the subsequent
maintenance of information in short-term storage (e.g.,
rehearsal processes, Folkard, 1976).

Hockey and Hamilton (1970) and Davies and Jones (1975)
have investigated Easterbrook's hypothesis in a short-term
memory situation.   In both studies, loud noise during
presentation of the material had the effect of reducing
incidental learning of the locations on the slides of the
list words.   Since there was also evidence that ordered
recall of the material was improved by noise, the results of
these two studies are consistent with Easterbrook's
hypothesis, with attention being allocated to the high-
priority task component (words) and away from the low-
priority task component (locations) to a greater extent in
the noise group.

Even if Easterbrook's hypothesis is essentially correct,
there is still the question as to the mechanism whereby
arousal produces a reduction in cue utilization.   Walley and
Weiden (1973), in an extremely interesting article, have
proposed such a mechanism.   They argue that pattern
recognition is achieved by means of a hierarchical network of
feature analyzers, and that encoding represents the function
of the highest level of the pattern-recognition network.
While encoding is potentially a parallel process, the
encoding of one input interferes with the concurrent encoding
of additional inputs, this interference effect being termed
'cognitive masking'.   Cognitive masking is thought to be
due to inhibitory interactions among cortical neurons at the
highest levels of the hierarchical pattern recognizers.   Of
most immediate importance, Walley and Weiden also argued that
the degree of lateral inhibition in the cortex is related to
arousal, so that increases in arousal (whether tonic or
phasic), will produce increases in cognitive masking.   As a
consequence, while parallel or shared processing would be
possible at low levels of arousal, it would become
decreasingly so as arousal increased.

In spite of the fact that the physiological data are not
conclusive, there is good evidence that a state of arousal

produces both excitatory and inhibitory effects.   For
example, Steriade (1970) reviewed several studies of the
responsiveness of the thalamus and cortex during arousal,
and concluded that although there is a facilitation of
thalamic excitability during arousal, a state of tonic
arousal is accompanied by a reduction in the responsiveness
of the cortex.

Demetrescu, Demetrescu, and Iosif (1965) found that the
state of arousal produced by activity in the brain-stem
reticular formation involves both inhibitory and
facilitatory influences on cortical responsiveness, and that
these influences depend upon anatomically and physiologically
separate systems.   The evidence suggested that, in addition
to the reticular activating system, there was a diffuse
ascending inhibitory system originating in the ventral
pontine reticular formation.   This inhibitory system
activates an intra-cortical inhibitory network which is
excited by specific input to the cortex, and may be
responsible for cognitive masking.   In addition, Demetrescu
et al. also noted that the caudate nucleus exerted an
independent inhibitory effect on cortical functioning.

Walley and Weiden (1973) have not only suggested a
physiological mechanism capable of producing a narrowing of
cue utilization under high levels of arousal, but have also
considered the effects of the transient, or phasic, arousal
produced by encoding.   In general, it is assumed that tonic
and phasic arousal both lead to an increase in cognitive
masking.   The extent of the increase in arousal produced by
attention or encoding is related to the complexity of the
encoding process: the greater the complexity of the task,
the greater the phasic arousal produced, and the narrower
the range of cue utilization.   In other words, very simple
tasks should permit more parallel processing than more
difficult tasks (Kahneman has put forward a similar theory
and supporting data in his 1973 book).   The finding that
cognitive masking is apparently reduced in highly practiced
and skilled subjects (e.g., Moray, 1967; Mowbray &
Rhodes, 1959) can be explained if one assumes that practice
leads to the development of more efficient encoding
techniques, resulting in smaller increases in phasic arousal
and thus less cognitive masking.

Experimental evidence that the phasic arousal produced by

encoding processes leads to cognitive masking was obtained
by Kahneman, Beatty, and Pollack (1967). Subjects
listened to a four-digit sequence, having been instructed to
add one to each digit, and to repeat back the resulting
digits one second after the final digit had been presented.
Pupil diameter gradually increased during the listening
phase, reached a maximum during the early stages of response
emission, and then decreased. Concurrently with the digit-
transformation task, subjects also watched a visual display
and attempted to detect presentations of the letter 'k'.
Errors on the letter-detection task increased during the
listening phase of the transformation task, reached a
ceiling near the start of the response-emission phase, and
then declined. Subsequent work has shown that heart rate
and skin resistance produce similar effects to pupil
diameter during the digit-transformation task (Kahneman,
Tursky, Shapiro, & Crider, 1969), indicating that increased
processing demands generate increased levels of phasic
arousal. Kahneman et al. also found that the peak level of
response on each of the physiological measures was directly
related to the complexity of the digit-transformation task,
subjects having to add either 0, 1, or 3 to each digit.
Thus Kahneman has found that increases in complexity of the
encoding process lead to increases in phasic arousal, and
that there is a close correspondence between phasic arousal
and cognitive masking (indexed by performance on the letter-
detection task).

Levels of Processing

    Many of the experimental findings can be interpreted by
assuming that arousal affects, and is affected by, the nature
of the encoding process. In connection with the
interaction between item arousal and retention interval
(e.g., Kleinsmith & Kaplan, 1963, 1964), it is usually the
case (Craik & Lockhart, 1972) that semantic processing of
material takes longer and is more effortful than shallow
levels of processing. A large GSR to an item may indicate
that that item is being processed to a deep, semantic, level,
whereas small GSRs to an item reflect a shallow level of
processing. In view of the evidence discussed by Craik and
Lockhart indicating that deep levels of processing lead to
enhanced retentivity, it would be predicted that the
forgetting curve for high-arousal items would be less steep
than for low-arousal items. Although this hypothesis
cannot explain reminiscence effects, such as the improved

recall of high-arousal items over time, it does handle the
puzzling interaction between item arousal and retention
interval.   Moreover, it can account for the superior long-
term recall of high-arousal items, and the beneficial effects
of arousal on short-term recognition and free recall.

The notion that high levels of arousal lead to reduced
cue utilization (Easterbrook, 1959) seems to imply that
high arousal might reduce the number of attributes of
presented material that are processed.   More specifically,
Schwartz (1975a, 1975b) has argued that high arousal leads
to increased selection of information about the physical
characteristics of stimulus information and to decreased
processing of semantic information.   Some confirming
evidence was discussed earlier in the chapter, and there
seems little doubt that high arousal frequently reduces
semantic clustering in free-recall tasks.

A similar hypothesis was proposed by Dornic (1975).   He
distinguished between a lower storage mechanism, relying
primarily on physical features, and a higher storage
mechanism, involving identification of stimuli according to
their names or meaning.   In data on free recall of digit
and consonant strings, he found that 'more difficult'
conditions (including stress and white noise) led to
reasonable retention of order information but to poor item
retention.   He implied that arousal and stress led to the
use of the lower, more rudimentary, storing mechanism;   in
other words, arousal led to 'parrotting back'.

The relationship between level of arousal and type of
processing has also been investigated in studies of phonemic
and semantic generalization, in which the degree of
generalization from previously reinforced words to
homophones and to synonyms is measured.   Rather contrary to
Schwartz' hypothesis, Levy and Murphy (1966) found that
alcohol increased phonemic generalization and reduced
semantic generalization, and Schalling, Levander, and
Wredenmark (1975) found that extraverted subjects showed
considerably greater generalization to homophones than to
synonyms, whereas introverted subjects showed equivalent
generalization to both kinds of stimulus.

Folkard (1976) has produced additional findings that are
difficult to reconcile with Schwartz' hypothesis.   He
argued that an important factor in experiments on STM may be

that subvocal activity is reduced under high levels of
arousal.   The model of STM proposed by Baddeley and Hitch
(1974) involved the postulation of two processes: a central
work space of limited capacity, and a peripheral
articulatory loop.   While Schwartz' hypothesis would seem
to imply that high arousal would reduce use of the work
space and increase that of the articulatory loop, Folkard
hypothesized that high arousal would reduce the utilization
of the articulatory loop, but would have little effect on
the work space.

    In one study, Folkard (1976) compared digit-span
performance of subjects under conditions of muscle tension or
no muscle tension.   In agreement with most of the research
literature, he found that arousal (i.e., muscle tension) had
a detrimental effect on performance under normal conditions.
However, when an attempt was made to minimize subvocal
rehearsal by requiring the subjects to say 'the' every time
they saw a digit, there was no effect of arousal on
performance.   The greater decline in performance under the
subvocal-suppression condition shown by the low-arousal
subjects indicates that they usually rely more heavily on
subvocalization than do high-arousal subjects.   This
finding has some generality, in that Folkard obtained the
same pattern of results in a study using time of day to
manipulate arousal and using a free-recall task rather than
digit span.

    Folkard (1976) obtained rather more direct evidence for
his hypothesis in a further study in which subjects
performed a verbal syllogisms test under conditions of high
arousal (noise) or low arousal (quiet).   During task
performance, three independent judges rated the subjects'
level of subvocal activity on the basis of their lip
movements.   Noise significantly reduced the observed
subvocal activity level.

    A reasonable deduction from Schwartz' hypothesis is that
high levels of tonic arousal should be associated with poor
long-term retention, since relatively few semantic attributes
have been encoded.   However, there are several personality
studies in which the long-term retention of high-arousal
subjects exceeded that of low-arousal subjects (e.g.,
Howarth & H. J. Eysenck, 1968; McLean, 1968;
Skanthakumari, 1965).   Folkard, Monk, Bradbury, and
Rosenthall (1977) investigated the effects of time of day on

LTM in a study in which they read a story to children.
While low arousal (i.e., morning presentation) led to
superior immediate recall than high arousal (i.e.,
afternoon presentation), the results were reversed for those
children whose recall was tested at a retention interval of
one week.

It is probable that people actually possess much greater
flexibility of encoding than the simple equation of low
arousal with semantic processing and high arousal with
physical processing implies.   M. C. Eysenck (in preparation)
required subjects to process a list of words either
phonemically or semantically in an incidental-learning
situation.   They were then unexpectedly given a recognition
test involving synonym pairs (i.e., a list word together with
its synonym) and homophone pairs (i.e., a list word together
with its homophone).   Semantic instructions led to
equivalent semantic processing for introverts and extraverts,
indicating that high arousal does not necessarily inhibit
semantic processing.   On the other hand, with phonemic-
processing instructions, introverted subjects showed
significantly less semantic processing than extraverted
subjects.

While the limited and equivocal research findings preclude
any definitive theoretical statements, some speculation is
possible.   If, as Walley and Weiden (1973) have hypothesized,
high arousal generates increased lateral inhibition and
cognitive masking, then high arousal will produce a switch
from parallel or shared processing to serial processing.   In
a learning situation in which the to-be-remembered material
is rapidly presented, the highly aroused subject will be
under more severe time pressure than the less aroused subject,
since for him encoding of each item's set of attributes or
features must occur seriatim rather than concurrently.   The
experimental evidence on the speed with which different kinds
of encoding occur (e.g., Craik, 1973; Craik & Tulving, 1975)
indicates that physical or phonemic processing typically
requires less time than semantic processing.   Accordingly,
the highly aroused subject under time pressure may often opt
for physical over semantic processing because there is a
greater probability of successful completion of physical
processing in the time available.   Several studies have
obtained results consistent with this analysis (e.g., Dornic,
1975; Hörmann & Osterkamp, 1966; Mueller, 1976a, 1976b;
Schwartz, 1975a, 1975b).   The studies of phonemic and

semantic generalization, which produced rather different
results, did not involve time pressure.   The hypothesis
proposed here suggests that a major effect of high arousal is
to reduce the probability of concurrent processing of several
word attributes, a finding obtained by M. C. Eysenck.
Proper investigation of this hypothesis would require the use
of experimental situations permitting some assessment of the
extent of parallel or serial processing, such as the paradigms
used to investigate the psychological refractory period and
the Sternberg effect (cf., Kahneman, 1973).   Furthermore,
rate of presentation of to-be-learned material is seen as a
critical variable.

Arousal at Output

A frequent observation is that high levels of arousal have
a detrimental effect on retrieval.   For example, students
commonly claim that the stress of taking important
examinations causes them to forget information which they
know well.   In addition, people are sometimes unable to
retrieve some desired item of information when they are
highly motivated to do so, followed by recall soon after
abandoning the attempt (James, 1890).

The experimental findings have not always supported the
notion that memory performance is detrimentally affected by
high arousal.   Uehling and Sprinkle (1968) introduced white
noise at the time of test, and found that it facilitated
recall.   However, Berlyne et al. (1965) did not find any
effects of white noise presented at test on recall performance
and Wickelgren (1975b) found that white noise during a
recognition test did not affect performance.   On the other
hand, Pascal (1949) observed that relaxation instructions
given immediately prior to recall led to superior recall
performance.   Birenbaum (1930) obtained some interesting
results that may be of relevance.   She instructed her
subjects to sign their work sheets upon completion of each of
a series of tasks.   The instruction was apparently learned
and retained by the subjects, since they remembered to sign
their names when the tasks were of a homogeneous nature.
However, when strikingly different tasks followed a number of
homogeneous tasks, the excited (aroused?) subjects showed
more forgetting of the intention to sign than the quiet
subjects.   An element of competition concerning task
performance appeared to increase excitement (arousal?) in all
groups of subjects, and also increased forgetting of the

intention.

It is possible that the results of the above studies were contaminated by the effects of continuing consolidation. Accordingly, the author has investigated the effects of arousal on semantic memory, defined by Tulving (1972) as "a mental thesaurus, organized knowledge a person possesses about words and other verbal symbols" (p. 386). In various experiments, arousal has been indexed by the extraversion scale of the EPI, white noise, and the General Activation scale of Thayer's (1967) Activation-Deactivation Adjective Check List (ADACL). The ADACL is an objective self-report measure of transient levels of activation, or certain aspects of mood, requiring the subject to indicate the extent to which certain adjectives apply to him at that moment (e.g., tense, activated, vigorous, energetic). In several studies, Thayer (1967, 1970) has found that the General Activation scale derived from the ADACL correlated substantially (about +.6 to .7) with a physiological index representing the pooled data from various physiological measures.

M. W. Eysenck (1974a) asked his subjects to produce spontaneously as many words from five different categories as they could. Intermediate levels of subject arousal produced the best performance. M. W. Eysenck (1974c, 1975b) investigated this finding further in two studies of semantic memory incorporating both recall and recognition. On recall trials, subjects had to produce a word from a specified category starting with a particular letter (e.g., 'fruit-A'). On recognition trials, they had to respond 'yes' if a category name was followed by a member of that category, and 'no' otherwise. In both cases, subjects were instructed to respond quickly and accurately, and the response speed of correct responses was the main dependent variable.

On recognition trials, the high-arousal subjects responded faster than the other groups of subjects. On recall trials, the relationship between arousal and speed of responding was affected by the dominance of the item pair, which was determined by reference to the Battig and Montague (1969) norms. 'Cat' is clearly a more dominant or strong member than 'yak' of the category 'four-footed animal', and so response speed is higher for the pair 'four-footed animal-C' than for the pair 'four-footed animal-Y'. Intermediate levels of arousal produced the greatest response speeds on high-dominance recall trials, whereas arousal was negatively

related to response speed on low-dominance recall trials.
Thus, the relationship between subject arousal and retrieval
depends critically on the nature of the task.

The results obtained by M. W. Eysenck (1974c, 1975b) can
be seen within the context of the Yerkes-Dodson Law. If one
takes speed of response as an index of task difficulty, then
recognition was the easiest task and low-dominance recall was
the most difficult. As expected, the optimal level of
arousal was high on the easy recognition task but low on the
difficult low-dominance recall task. However, it is
important to note that the Yerkes-Dodson Law is merely a
descriptive statement of the relationship between two
variables, and it does not provide an explanation of this
relationship.

Broadbent (1971) has provided a more adequate account of
the effects of arousal in his hypothesis that a crucial
characteristic of the aroused system is that it devotes a
higher proportion of its time to the intake of information
from dominant sources than does the unaroused system. If
one assumes that on recognition trials the storage locations
to be accessed are directly given to the subject, then they
constitute dominant sources of information, and the findings
are consistent with Broadbent's hypothesis.

The effects of subject arousal on speed of retrieval from
secondary storage have also been considered by M. W. Eysenck
(1975c, 1975d). Subjects learned lists of words to
criterion, followed by probed recall tests, and subjects of
intermediate arousal level responded faster than those of
either low or high arousal (M. W. Eysenck, 1975d). In a
study of paired-associate learning, M. W. Eysenck (1975c)
found that high-arousal subjects tended to recall the
responses from highly associated pairs faster than low-
arousal subjects, whereas intermediate subject arousal led to
the fastest production of responses from a second list
involving response competition. Once again, high arousal
facilitated the retrieval of relatively dominant information
but had a slowing effect on the retrieval of non-dominant
information.

In sum, any adequate theory of the effects of arousal on
memory must allow for the existence of effects of arousal on
the processes involved in the retrieval of information. In
general terms, it appears to be the case that the somewhat

variable effects of arousal at output are due to the
difficulty of the task and the extent to which dominant
sources of information are involved: high arousal at output
facilitates the retrieval of dominant information, but
increases the difficulty of retrieving non-dominant
information.

The hypothesis that high arousal has the effect of
biasing the subject's search process towards readily
accessible information more than is the case with lower
levels of arousal may have application to some of the other
findings. For example, as would be predicted on this
hypothesis, high arousal is more detrimental to the short-
term retention of 'difficult', inaccessible, information,
such as in tasks involving response competition than to the
short-term retention of 'easy', accessible, information
(e.g., Allsopp & H. J. Eysenck, 1974; Howarth, 1969a, 1969b;
Siegman, 1957).

While the various findings of highly significant effects of
arousal on speed of recall (e.g., M. W. Eysenck, 1974c, 1975b,
1975c, 1975d) are most naturally interpreted in terms of the
effects of arousal on the search process, it is possible that
arousal affects the subject's degree of caution. Indeed,
Schwartz (1974) found that noise-induced arousal led to
increased caution on a recognition test for common names,
and to decreased caution for rare names. However, M. W.
Eysenck (1974c) argued that a caution hypothesis would
predict that arousal would affect the incidence of errors,
but found no relationship between arousal and errors.

A rather different way of considering arousal and retrieval
was adopted by Beatty and Kahneman (1966) and by Kahneman and
Peavler (1969). They measured pupillary dilation while the
subject attempted to retrieve information. In spite of the
fact that pupillary dilation appears to measure some
combination of arousal, mental effort, processing load, and
anxiety, interesting results have been obtained. For
example, Beatty and Kahneman (1966) found that retrieval from
long-term memory induced a greater increase in pupil size
than did retrieval from short-term memory, and Kahneman and
Peavler (1969) found that pupil dilation on a recall test was
several times greater than pupil dilation during the
presentation trial. Kahneman and Peavler also noticed that
overt vocalization was not a necessary condition for the
occurrence of a large dilation at test, since the pupil size

increased substantially even when the subject failed to
respond.   The inter-relationships among subject arousal,
arousal induced by the specific retrieval task, and
probability of retrieval, are well worth exploring.

On a more speculative note, the reader may have noticed
a certain similarity between the findings and hypotheses
concerning the effects of arousal at input and at output.
This may well be no coincidence.   As we saw in an earlier
chapter, Tulving argues that the success or otherwise of
retention-test performance depends upon the overlap between
the encoding produced at input and the encoding produced at
output.   This suggests there are important commonalities
between the processes occurring at input and at output, and
it is clear that at input retrieval of attribute-information
occurs, and at output encoding and storage of information
occur (cf., Gardiner & Klee, 1976).

It thus becomes possible that the cognitive-masking
hypothesis of Walley and Weiden (1973) may be applicable to
some of the retrieval data.   They assumed that high arousal
produced cognitive masking, thus reducing the likelihood of
shared or parallel processing.   Let us consider this
hypothesis with respect to the findings on speed of retrieval
of information from permanent storage (M. W. Eysenck, 1974c,
1975b).   If recall from permanent storage involves the
processing of a number of categorical instances prior to the
encountering of the appropriate response, then heightened
arousal should generate increased cognitive masking, and the
processing of initial instances would interfere with the
processing of subsequent items.   Furthermore, in line with
the empirical evidence, low-dominance items would be the ones
most detrimentally affected by this increase in cognitive
masking.   On the other hand, with recognition items,
cognitive masking might reduce extraneous processing and
enhance performance.

The cognitive-masking hypothesis may also be applicable to
paired-associate studies of response competition.   In such
studies, response competition has often been induced by means
of the A-B, A-Br transfer paradigm, in which the stimuli and
responses of the first list are re-paired to form the second
list.   The typical finding is that high arousal is associated
with inferior performance only on the second (or transfer)
list, which would presumably involve response competition
(e.g., Bone, 1971; M. W. Eysenck, 1975c; Jensen, 1964).

If subjects on the second list tend to retrieve the
inappropriate first-list response to a stimulus prior to the
appropriate second-list response, then the retrieval of the
first-list response should cognitively mask the retrieval of
the second-list response. This cognitive masking should be
greater for high-arousal than for low-arousal subjects, thus
explaining the inferior recall performance of high-arousal
subjects. Furthermore, high-arousal subjects should have
longer response latencies than less aroused subjects to emit
the correct second-list responses, and this result has been
obtained in my research (M. W. Eysenck, 1975c).

Other Theories

We have already seen that Walker's action-decrement
theory is unable to account for several of the findings,
including the differential effects of arousal on paired-
associate, free recall, and recognition tasks. In addition,
the hypothesis is not equipped to explain subject-arousal
effects or the effects of arousal at test. The evidence
does not unequivocally implicate consolidation, the key
concept in Walker's hypothesis, as being an important
determinant of arousal-related effects on memory performance.
However, Berlyne (1967) and Levonian (1972) have also put
forward general theories of arousal and memory, and these
will now be considered.

Berlyne (1967) argued that an intermediate level of
arousal was optimal for performance, and that changes from
either high arousal to intermediate or low arousal to
intermediate levels would be reinforcing. In order to
explain the differential effects of arousal on short-term and
long-term retention, Berlyne suggested that different
inverted-U shape functions relate arousal to performance and
to learning. At relatively short retention intervals,
high-arousal items are said to be further from the optimal
level of arousal than low-arousal items, whereas the opposite
is the case with long retention intervals. However, the
assumption that items which differ in their arousal-inducing
properties at presentation will continue to differ at long
retention intervals is contrary to the findings of Kaplan and
Kaplan (1968).

Evidence for a curvilinear relationship between arousal
and short-term retention has been obtained in a number of
studies (e.g., Berry, 1962; Kleinsmith et al., 1963;

McLaughlin & H. J. Eysenck, 1967).   Furthermore, arousal at
output frequently seems to be related in curvilinear fashion
to recall performance (e.g., M. W. Eysenck, 1974a, 1975c,
1975d).   The evidence for a curvilinear relationship
between arousal and performance is greater at relatively
short retention intervals, and in studies dealing with
subject rather than item arousal.   A partial explanation for
this might be that variations in subject arousal are likely
to be greater than variations in item arousal.

A further difficulty is that good evidence for a
curvilinear relationship requires sampling several points
along the arousal continuum.   If only three points are
sampled, there are six different possible orderings, and only
two of these would be incompatible with Berlyne's hypothesis.
Unfortunately, very few studies have sampled more than three
points along the arousal dimension, so that the exact nature
of the arousal-performance and arousal-learning relationships
remains unclear.

Additional problems have been discussed by M. W.
Eysenck (1976a):

> The failure to specify precisely the differences
> between the arousal-performance and the arousal-learning
> functions means that it is extremely difficult to test
> the hypothesis.   The evidence of M. Eysenck (1974c,
> 1975b) indicates that, even using very long retention
> intervals, we cannot investigate effects of arousal on
> learning uncontaminated by performance factors, so that
> the conceptual distinction drawn by Berlyne (1967)
> between learning and performance seems clearer than the
> empirical distinction.   The theory is somewhat
> descriptive in nature, and provides little in the way of
> explanation of the causal factors underlying the arousal-
> performance and the arousal-learning functions (p. 399).

Levonian (1972) distinguished between an item's
retentivity, or storage strength, and its accessibility, or
retrieval strength.   The effects of arousal on retentivity
and on accessibility are said to be different.   On the one
hand, arousal is directly related to storage strength, with
storage strength at all levels of arousal increasing for
approximately one minute, followed by a slow decrease.   On
the other hand, arousal is related in curvilinear fashion to
retrieval strength at short retention intervals, with

moderate levels of arousal being associated with the
greatest retrieval strength; at long retention intervals,
retrieval strength is positively related to arousal (see
Fig. 8.5).   Retrieval strength can be measured by any of
the conventional retention measures, whereas storage
strength can only be inferred.

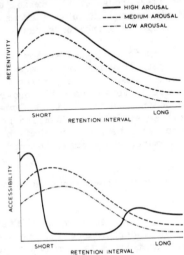

Fig. 8.5.   Item retentivity and accessibility
as a function of item arousal.   Adapted
from Levonian (1972).

Levonian's hypothesis has the advantage over Walker's
theory that it can accommodate various relationships between
item arousal and short-term retention.   For example,
consider those experiments where items are divided into the
two categories of high arousal and low arousal.   The
description of an item as low or high in arousal is relative
to the range of item arousal found in any particular
experiment.   If the high-arousal items actually fall into
the medium-arousal range, whereas the low-arousal items fall
into the low-arousal range, then the theory predicts that
memory performance at short retention intervals will be
better for the so-called high-arousal items.   However, if
the high-arousal items fall in the high-arousal range, then
they will be poorly recalled at short retention intervals.

The lack of any satisfactory method for assigning items
to Levonian's proposed division into high, medium, and low
arousal is an embarrassment for the theory.   In addition,
little is said about the factors producing the arousal-
retentivity and arousal-accessibility functions.
Furthermore, like Berlyne (1967), Levonian appears to
assume that retention test performance at long retention
intervals reflects the underlying storage strength, an
assumption disconfirmed by M. W. Eysenck (e.g., 1975b).

Summary

In spite of continuing uncertainty about the most
appropriate definition and measurement of arousal, it is
clear that several replicable findings have been obtained.
Of the various theories put forward, Walker's action-
decrement theory, which argues that high arousal leads to
greater consolidation of the trace but to greater short-term
inhibition of retrieval, does not account satisfactorily for
the data and is definitely inadequate.

Hypotheses relating arousal to levels or types of
processing (e.g., Schwartz, 1975a, 1975b) seem more
promising.   It is assumed that one of the major determinants
of item arousal is the depth or thoroughness of an item's
encoding, thus providing a simple interpretation of the
common finding that long-term retention is superior for high-
arousal items.   It is also assumed that high levels of
subject arousal have the effect of inducing the subject to
encode the physical attributes of to-be-learned material at
the expense of the semantic attributes.   However, while
several findings are consistent with this latter assumption,
the author considers that determination of the attributes
that are encoded is more flexible than suggested by this
hypothesis.   Furthermore, it is probable that the
hypothesis is limited in potential applicability to
situations where there is considerable time pressure (e.g.,
due to fast rates of presentation).

The theoretical approach that seems of most general
usefulness is that initiated by Easterbrook (1959): high
arousal reduces the number of cues that are utilized.   The
hypothesis has been revised by Broadbent (1971), who argued
that high arousal increases the bias towards dominant
sources of information, and extended to handle retrieval

data by the author.   Additional revisions have been
proposed by Walley and Weiden (1973), who have supplied a
speculative physiological underpinning for Easterbrook's
hypothesis, and who have proposed that high arousal produces
cognitive masking, which in turn reduces the possibility of
shared or parallel processing.

Arousal has a number of different effects on information
processing, and all the theories discussed in this chapter
provide incomplete accounts.   For example, Broadbent (1971)
found evidence that the ability to select relevant stimuli
is sometimes impaired by arousal.   He showed subjects an
array of red and white digits, and asked them to report as
many digits of a specified colour as possible.   Loud noise
produced a deterioration in performance.   On the other hand,
when selection or discrimination of relevant stimuli was
facilitated by instructing subjects to report all digits
regardless of colour, noise was associated with a slight
improvement in performance.

A further possible factor involved in the relationship
between arousal and memory is what is known as state-
dependent forgetting.   It has been found that forgetting is
greater when the subject's state on the retention test differs
from that at the time of learning, and is reduced when there
is congruence of state at input and at output.   While
Folkard et al. (1977) found no evidence for state-dependent
forgetting when they tested for story retention at the same
or a different time of day, it is possible that similar
states of arousal at input and test may enhance performance,
due to an increased number of salient retrieval cues.

CHAPTER 9

INTROVERSION-EXTRAVERSION, LEARNING, AND MEMORY

In the experimental investigation of the relationship between personality and memory, the assessment of personality has usually been by means of paper-and-pencil questionnaire techniques such as Cattell's Sixteen Personality Factor (SPF) test and the Eysenck Personality Inventory (EPI). These tests attempt to measure personality traits, i.e., relatively stable and consistent dispositions. The usual experimental approach has involved the comparison on some learning task of extreme scorers on a personality trait or dimension (e.g., anxiety or introversion-extraversion).

Several objections have been raised to the trait construct by Mischel (1968). He argued that people do not manifest the intra-individual consistency of behaviour across different situations that is predicted by trait and factor theorists. For example, Dudycha (1936) made several thousand naturalistic observations of college students, recording each student's time of arrival at classes, appointments, extra-curricular activities, vesper services, and entertainments. He obtained little evidence for a trait of punctuality, since the mean cross-situational correlation coefficient was only +.19. In other words, the punctual person in one situation might well not be so in another situation. Mischel noted that there appears to be a ceiling of about +.30 on cross-situational correlation coefficients, a finding he attributed to genuine behavioural variability rather than to imperfect methodology.

An important factor here is the question of response equivalence-classes. In general terms, individuals will appear more inconsistent, the more specific are the response classes employed. For example, Skinner (1938) obtained great response predictability in studies with rats where lever depression constituted a response class. If the pressure applied to the lever had been used to divide lever presses into several different response classes, it is probable that most of this predictability would have vanished. Liddell, James, and Anderson (1934) put a sheep

191

in a harness, placed her foot on a metal plate, rang a bell,
and administered an electric shock.   After a few trials, she
raised her hoof off the plate when the bell sounded.   Then
the wretched animal was turned upside down, so that her head
was on the metal plate.   When the bell sounded, she lifted
her head off the plate, and did not lift her hoof.   In this
simple case, it would be a remarkably obtuse experimenter who
claimed that this shows the inconsistency of sheep behaviour.
Since response categories are theoretically defined, apparent
behavioural inconsistencies may be replaced by predictability
when there is some theoretical understanding of the most
appropriate response classes or categories.

There are several strands of research indicating the
desirability of retaining the trait concept.   While the
prevalent but sterile and simplistic Skinnerian approach
attributes all individual differences to differences in
conditioning history, the evidence is strong that heredity is
of importance.   If this is so, then traits can be seen as
representing these hereditary influences.   Shields (1973)
has reviewed the experimental evidence from twin studies, and
concluded as follows:

> The most consistent finding is of a significant hered-
> itary component in extraversion-introversion.   Many
> studies also show the same with respect to a trait or
> factor that might be interpreted as neuroticism or as
> related to neuroticism, but the findings here are not so
> consistent (pp. 567-568).

One of the most thorough studies was by Shields (1962),
who used a forerunner of the Maudsley Personality Inventory
(MPI).   For the extraversion scale, he obtained intra-pair
correlations of +.61 for monozygotic twins reared apart,
+.42 for monozygotic twins reared together, and of -.17 for
dyzygotic twins reared together.   For neuroticism, the
correlations were +.53 for monozygotic twins reared apart,
+.38 for monozygotic twins reared together, and +.11 for
dyzygotic twins reared together.   Although the low
correlations for dyzygotic twins and the greater correlations
for monozygotic twins reared apart than together are
inconsistent with genetic theory, the general pattern of
results is indicative of some hereditary determination of
personality.   Jinks and Fulker (1970) re-analyzed Shields'
data, and the heritability estimates obtained by the
biometrical method of analysis were 54 per cent for

neuroticism and 67 per cent for extraversion.

A problem in many of the studies is that in certain respects the environment may be more similar for monozygotic twins than for dyzygotic twins. However, at least some of this difference may well be the result of genotype-environment interaction such as monozygotic twins selecting more similar environments. Scarr (1968) reported some very pertinent findings from pairs where the parents were mistaken about the zygosity of their twins. She compared 11 misclassified pairs with 40 correctly classified pairs, and concluded that, "differences in the parental treatment that twins receive are much more a function of the degree of their genetic relatedness than of parental beliefs about 'identicalness' and 'fraternalness'."

Since traits are claimed to be relatively permanent personality characteristics, longitudinal consistency is a necessary although not sufficient requirement for personality traits. Kagan and Moss (1962) and Schaefer and Bayley (1963) have reported substantial consistency of individual differences in social behaviour from infancy to adolescence. For example, Schaefer and Bayley obtained stability coefficients for behaviour ratings of friendliness from 69 months to adolescence of +.20 for females and of +.52 for males.

It is probable that some of the apparent inconsistency of an individual's behaviour across different situations is due to the existence of interactions between traits and situational factors. Behaviour can plausibly be viewed as a joint function of situational determinants and individual characteristics, and trait theorists have frequently been criticized for their relative lack of interest in situational factors. This issue was investigated by Endler and Hunt in a series of studies (e.g., Endler & Hunt, 1966, 1968, 1969; Endler, Hunt, & Rosenstein, 1962). They constructed a questionnaire called the S-R Inventory of Anxiousness, which permits the assessment of the relative contributions of situations, responses, and individual differences to self-reported anxiousness. For each of 11 situations (e.g., 'You are going on a roller coaster'), college students were asked to indicate their reactions in terms of 14 specific response modes (e.g., 'mouth gets dry', 'having loose bowels'). Analysis of variance indicated that the contributions of situations and of individual differences

were approximately equal and quite small in comparison with
the variance contributed by the interaction between
situations and individual differences.

Bowers (1973) located 11 studies that had evaluated the
relative magnitude of person and situational influences on
behaviour.   On average, 12.71 per cent of the variance was
due to persons, far less than anticipated on a thoroughgoing
trait theory, 10.17 per cent was due to situations, and 20.77
per cent of the variance was due to the interaction between
persons and situations.   Golding (1975) has made two
important observations about these data: (1) while the
omega-squared ratios used in these studies do technically
index the percentage total variation, they are inappropriate
as measures of the general significance of situations or
persons;   (2)   the large person by situation interactions
need interpretation.   Mischel (1968) argued that these
interactions reflected the 'idiosyncratic' organization of
behaviour within individuals, whereas Bowers seemed to think
that the obtained interactions could be meaningfully
decomposed into replicable patterns that were not highly
idiosyncratic.   The current evidence is unclear, so that
while a trait-state theorist would argue that individual
differences in states produce most of the observed person by
situation interaction, this may or may not be true.

A further difficulty with the trait approach is that
traits are often construed as hypothetical entities that
cause behaviour.   Since traits are indexed by subjects'
responses on a questionnaire, theories relating personality
traits to behaviour on some task tend to be of the response-
response variety, i.e., basically correlational in nature.
Causal relationships between traits and behaviour could more
readily be inferred if it were possible to manipulate a
subject's personality experimentally.   Since such control is
lacking, it is extremely difficult to decide whether observed
differences in behaviour between groups differing in some
personality trait are attributable to differences in that
trait or to some other difference between the groups.

One solution to some of the problems is to obtain separate
measures of a subject's traits and of his state or mood, as,
for example, in the State Trait Anxiety Inventory (STAI) of
Spielberger, Gorsuch, and Luschene (1969).   Anxiety as a
trait is measured by asking the subjects whether they
sometimes or often feel anxious in a given situation, and

anxiety as a state is measured by asking them whether they feel anxious at that moment in time. Similar state measures have been investigated by Nowlis (1966) with his Mood Adjective Check List (MACL) and Thayer (1967) with his Activation-Deactivation Adjective Check List (ADACL). Both of these latter tests require the subject to indicate the extent to which various adjectives (e.g., angry, tense, activated) apply to him at that moment.

Theoretically, it may be assumed that a subject's mood or state is jointly determined by his personality traits and by the situational context, so that state measures take account of the impact of the situation on the individual whereas trait measures do not. It might be expected that state measures would be more predictive of task performance than would trait measures, and Spielberger, O'Neil, and Hanse (1972) found in several experiments that state anxiety was more closely related to learning than was trait anxiety.

An interesting problem is whether personality traits can be construed as merely affecting the probability that someone will be in a particular mood or state. As one would expect, there is reasonable evidence that people high in trait anxiety have a greater probability than those low in trait anxiety of being in an anxious mood or state (e.g., Green, 1964; Spielberger, 1972), but the relationship between the trait of introversion-extraversion and mood is less clear. However, Christie and Venables (1973) found that extraverts were significantly more aggressive, activated, and nonchalant than introverts on the MACL. If traits only affect the probability of moods, then groups of subjects with different personalities but the same mood should perform equivalently, whereas groups with the same personalities but different moods should perform differently. Future research is likely to see much more emphasis being devoted to trait-state interactions.

Extraversion and Arousal

A high proportion of the researchers investigating the relationship between introversion-extraversion and memory have assumed that introverts are more aroused than extraverts (e.g., H. J. Eysenck, 1967, 1973). A full evaluation of this assumption requires consideration of both behavioural and physiological data.

The physiological evidence will be reviewed in the light
of the hypothesis (H. J. Eysenck, 1967) that, "skin
conductance and alpha activity are measures of extraversion"
(p. 170). Gale (1973) has reviewed the EEG findings,
noting that most investigators have argued that high
amplitude and low frequency of alpha are indicative of low
arousal, whereas low amplitude and high frequency reflect
high arousal. The results from the various studies are by
no means consistent, due to the existence of several
methodological inadequacies. One problem is that
researchers in this area commonly instruct their subjects to
'do nothing', an instruction that fails to control adequately
the subjects' behaviour.

Of the sixteen studies discussed by Gale, seven
supported the hypothesis that introverts are more aroused
than extraverts, three supported the opposite hypothesis, and
six found non-significant differences in EEG between
introverts and extraverts. In addition, a recent study by
Travis, Kondo, and Knott (1974) found no difference in
alpha between introverts and extraverts. Gale suggested
that the studies finding that introverts were more aroused
than extraverts involved situations producing moderate levels
of arousal. The studies failing to obtain these results
involved tasks where the subjects were either interested in
the task, or bored, so that the extraverts aroused
themselves, possibly via the use of imagery. It is likely
that further enlightenment about the relationship between
introversion-extraversion and the EEG will require much
greater attention to possible subject-situation interactions.

Inconsistency also characterizes the results obtained from
studies investigating aspects of electrodermal activity.
Crider and Lunn (1971) recorded the spontaneous fluctuation
rate and the speed of orienting response habituation of the
palmar skin potential, and measured extraversion by means of
the Minnesota Multiphasic Personality Inventory (MMPI).
They obtained significant correlations of -.48 between
extraversion and speed of habituation, and of -.38 between
extraversion and fluctuations. On the other hand, Coles,
Gale, and Kline (1971) also considered the relationship
between extraversion (measured by the EPI) and electrodermal
activity during habituation, but with different results.
Although introverts produced more spontaneous responses than
extraverts, there was no difference between these two groups
in speed of habituation or tonic conductance. Koriat,

Averill, and Malmstrom (1973) recorded skin conductance and heart rate during habituation, and observed no differences in physiological responding between introverts and extraverts.

Further studies of physiological responses during habituation were carried out by Mangan and O'Gorman (1969) and by Sadler, Mefferd, and Houck (1971). In both studies, there was evidence for an interaction between extraversion and neuroticism, in which stable introverts and neurotic extraverts took longer to habituate physiologically than did neurotic introverts or stable extraverts.

Nielsen and Petersen (1976) found that basal level skin conductance was unrelated to extraversion as measured by the EPI. However, extraverted subjects exhibited fewer and smaller electrodermal responses than introverted subjects to moderately intense stimuli.

In earlier work, Bronzhaft, Hayes, Welch, and Koltur (1960) related personality and GSR in students, obtaining a non-significant correlation with extraversion, and Burdick (1966) obtained a non-significant correlation of -.24 between extraversion and spontaneous GSR activity. Opton and Lazarus (1967) exposed their subjects to threat of shock and to a film containing harrowing incidents in a wood mill. They recorded both skin conductance and heart rate, but found no differences between introverts and extraverts on either measure.

There are a few additional studies which have looked at other physiological measures. Shagass and Kerenyi (1958) found that the sedation threshold (the amount of sodium amytal required to produce certain EEG changes) was considerably greater in introverts than in extraverts. Smith (1973) found that resting frontalis electromyographic (EMG) levels were unrelated to extraversion as measured by the EPI, whereas Matus (1974) obtained a significant negative correlation of -.45 between frontalis EMG and extraversion. Bull and Nethercott (1972) persuaded their subjects to take 150 steps on and off a box, and recorded heart rate both before and after the task. Extraversion as measured by the EPI was unrelated to heart rate. Finally, Blake (1967) noted that the body temperature of introverts was higher than that of extraverts during the morning and early afternoon, whereas the body temperature of extraverts was higher than that of introverts during the evening.

There are several reasons for the inconclusive nature of
the experimental evidence, but the main deficiency has been
that most studies have investigated a single physiological
response in a single experimental situation.   Since
physiological measures are affected by interactions between
personality traits and situations, the question "Are
introverts more physiologically aroused than extraverts?"
has no unequivocal answer.   The type of research which may
be required is exemplified by a study done by Opton and
Lazarus (1967).   They used two experimental situations
(threat of shock and a stressful film), and in one analysis
divided subjects into two main groups: those who responded
physiologically more to the film than to the threat of shock,
and those who responded more to the threat of shock (i.e., an
intra-individual analysis).   There was a tendency for those
subjects showing more stress to the film than to the threat
of shock to be introverted.   Future research might benefit
from more consideration of differential reactions of subjects
to environmental factors and from less attention to absolute
differences between the physiological responses of
personality groups.

There are additional advantages with the Opton and
Lazarus approach.   For example, there is much evidence
(e.g., Lacey, 1967) of individual response specificity, i.e.,
most subjects are characteristically more physiologically
responsive on some measures than others, but subjects differ
in terms of their patterns of physiological responsivity.
The use of a research design involving ipsative or intra-
individual comparisons rather than purely inter-individual
or normative comparisons minimizes the problem of individual
response specificity.   Opton and Lazarus analyzed their
data both in terms of inter-group differences in arousal and
in terms of intra-subject variations in the pattern of
physiological response to different situations, and obtained
significant differences only when considering intra-subject
data.

Much of the behavioural evidence suggesting that
introverts are functionally more aroused than extraverts has
been reviewed by H. J. Eysenck (1967).   He reported
supportive data from the fields of motivation, conditioning,
perception, psychopharmacology, vigilance, and learning.   He
interpreted the results as indicating that an intermediate
level of arousal was both optimal for performance and was
actively preferred by subjects.   A relatively direct test of

this hypothesis is to give subjects the opportunity to
increase or decrease the amount of arousal-inducing
stimulation which they receive. Since, theoretically,
introverts are more aroused than extraverts, it is more
likely that introverts will want to decrease the level of
stimulation, whereas extraverts are more likely to seek
increases in the level of stimulation.

In an early experiment, Weisen (1965) used an operant
conditioning procedure in which reinforcement for button-
pressing was either a 3-second period of light and sound
stimulation ('onset' condition) or a 3-second period of
relief from light and sound stimulation ('offset' condition).
As predicted, extraverts pressed more frequently in the
onset condition and introverts more frequently in the offset
condition.   In a similar study, Davies, Hockey, and Taylor
(1969) allowed subjects to press during a vigilance task for
either the onset or the offset of varied sounds.   The
extraverts pressed more frequently in the onset condition,
but less frequently in the offset condition.

Gale (1969) allowed subjects in a mild sensory deprivation
situation to obtain four different sound reinforcements by
pressing buttons.   Extraverts engaged in significantly more
button-pressing than introverts, and they also made more
changes among the sources of stimulation.   Hill (1975) gave
introverted and extraverted subjects a monotonous task to
perform, and found that extraverts introduced more variety
than introverts into their pattern of responses.   Hill
suggested that this was an attempt on the part of extraverts
to increase the amount of stimulation received.

In sum, there is reasonable evidence that extraverts
behave as if they were less aroused than introverts, and,
indeed, Farley and Farley (1967) obtained a significant
correlation between extraversion and sensation-seeking as
measured by the Sensation-Seeking Scale (Zuckerman, Kolin,
Price, & Zoob, 1964).   Extraversion seems to consist of the
two components of sociability and impulsivity (S. B. G.
Eysenck & H. J. Eysenck, 1963), where sociability implies a
desire for stimulation from other people, and impulsivity
implies a wish for stimulation from other environmental
stimuli and from actions.

There are several different ways in which the personality
dimension of introversion-extraversion might be related to

arousal.   Most theoretical accounts (e.g., H. J. Eysenck,
1967) assume that introverts are chronically more aroused
than extraverts, and that introverts and extraverts have the
same optimal level of arousal.   A slightly different theory
would propose that introverts and extraverts do not differ in
their basal, or resting, levels of arousal, but that the
consequences of stimulation are different for the two
personality groups: "High cortical arousal (introversion)
can be seen to act as an amplifying valve for incoming
sensory stimulation, compared with the average degree of
arousal (ambiversion)" (H. J. Eysenck, 1971, p. 69).   A
third theoretical possibility (shown in Fig. 9.1) is that the

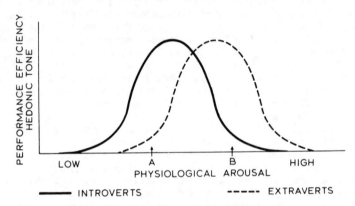

Fig. 9.1. Optimal-level theory's
explanation of behavioural differences
between introverts and extraverts.

arousal levels of introverts do not normally differ from those
of extraverts, but that the optimal level of arousal is lower
for introverts than it is for extraverts.   This possibility
handles an otherwise anomalous trend in the experimental
findings: the behavioural evidence that introverts are more
aroused than extraverts is much stronger than the
physiological evidence.   On this theory, introverts and
extraverts at point A in Fig. 9.1 would be equally aroused
physiologically, but the introvert would be closer to his
optimal level of arousal.   However, at point B on the
arousal continuum, while introverts and extraverts would

again be equivalently aroused physiologically, extraverted
subjects would now be closer to their optimal arousal level.

Obviously the three theories discussed above are similar
enough that much of the experimental evidence fails to
discriminate among them.   The crucial difference is that the
optimal-level theory predicts that performance differences
would be found between introverts and extraverts equated for
level of physiological arousal.   Unfortunately, few studies
have included both physiological and behavioural measures.
However, relevant evidence was obtained by M. W. Eysenck
(1974a, 1975c, 1975d).   He indexed arousal by means of
Thayer's ADACL.   In none of these studies did introverts
appear to be more aroused than extraverts; if anything, the
trend was in the opposite direction.   In all of these
studies, introverts and extraverts were divided into low- and
high-arousal groups;   characteristically, introverts
performed better when lowly aroused, whereas extraverts
performed better when highly aroused.   Although any
conclusions can only be tentative, since the ADACL was given
before rather than during task performance, the results
suggest that substantial performance differences can be
obtained between groups of introverts and extraverts of equal
arousal level.

The exact relationship between introversion-extraversion
and arousal has not been clarified by the work on learning
and memory.   In order to facilitate communication, the
results of many of the experiments will be interpreted by
assuming that introverts are chronically more aroused than
extraverts.   In all cases, the results could as well, or
better, be interpreted in terms of the optimal-level theory.
The discussion of the relevant evidence will be relatively
succinct, since a complete review is available (M. W.
Eysenck, 1976c).

It is appropriate to consider the research literature
under the two separate headings of episodic and semantic
memory, since Tulving (1972) presented evidence indicating
that the two kinds of memory function in different ways.
These terms were defined as follows by Tulving (1972):
"Episodic memory refers to memory for personal experiences
and their temporal relations, while semantic memory is a
system for receiving, retaining, and transmitting information
about meaning of words, concepts, and classification of
concepts" (pp. 401-402).

Episodic Memory

Two major hypotheses relating the dimension of
introversion-extraversion and verbal learning have been
examined experimentally. The first hypothesis is that
extraverts will show faster learning than introverts in tasks
which are 'difficult' or which involve response competition,
but that this disadvantage will be attenuated in tasks which
are 'easy' or which involve little or no response
competition. The second hypothesis is H. J. Eysenck's
(1967) modification of Walker's (1958) action-decrement
theory, which was discussed in detail in the previous chapter.
The hypothesis states that the period of consolidation is
longer for introverts than for extraverts, with the result
that the short-term retention of extraverts exceeds that of
introverts, but introverts manifest better long-term
retention.

Task Difficulty

The hypothesis relating introversion-extraversion to task
difficulty has been examined in several studies (Allsopp &
H. J. Eysenck, 1974, 1975; Bone, 1971; M. W. Eysenck,
1975c; Howarth, 1969a, 1969b; Jensen, 1964; McLaughlin &
H. J. Eysenck, 1967; Purohit, 1966; Shanmugan & Santhanam,
1964; Siegman, 1957). Of these eleven studies, only three
failed to obtain the predicted findings (Allsopp & H. J.
Eysenck, 1975; M. W. Eysenck, 1975c; Purohit, 1966).
However, in spite of the weight of evidence in favour of the
hypothesis, it is not clear exactly why introverts should be
at a disadvantage on difficult tasks. Various possible
interpretations have been suggested, as follows:-

(1) Weiner (1966) and Weiner and Schneider (1971)
have argued that experiments frequently involve a confounding
of task difficulty level with subjective feelings of success
and failure. It is possible that performance on a difficult
task results in a feeling of failure due to the relatively
slow rate of learning, whereas performance on an easy task
produces success feelings because of the speed of mastery.
In support of this hypothesis, Tennyson and Wooley (1971)
found that the mean level of state anxiety was significantly
higher following a difficult task than following an easy
task.   While Weiner and Weiner and Schneider investigated
the personality variable of anxiety rather than extraversion,
they unconfounded the factors of task difficulty and success-

failure, and obtained evidence that the subjective feelings of success or failure were more related to the performance of different personality groups than was task difficulty.

(2) The learning differences between introverts and extraverts may reflect differences in encoding processes. One possibility is simply that introverts take longer than extraverts to discover suitable verbal and imaginal mediators, and that difficult tasks may increase this time difference. Farley and Kumar (unpublished) presented nonsense syllable-digit paired-associates to their subjects, and instructed them to write down the way in which they might remember each pair. While there were no differences as a function of personality in the types of transformation applied to the paired-associates, the introverts took nearly twice as long to write down their mediators. However, it is unclear whether this difference is due to faster information processing by the extraverts, or whether extraverts are simply less cautious in responding.

Schwartz (1975a, 1975b) argued that high arousal orients memory towards the physical characteristics of verbal material, while adversely affecting memory for its semantic aspects. He found that neurotic introverts were more affected by the phonemic characteristics of words and less affected by the semantic characteristics than other personality groups. The notion that introverts and extraverts may utilize qualitatively different processing strategies is an exciting one, but the exact mechanisms involved are not clear. Although Schwartz appeared to believe that the effects obtained are due to differences in retrieval strategies, it is more likely that they are due to differences in initial encoding. For example, Schwartz (1975b) found that neurotic introverts were far less likely than other personality groups to recall the words of a categorized word list presented in random order in their categories, and Rundus (1971) found that a key determinant of the amount of semantic organization in recall was the extent to which subjects rehearsed the items in categories during presentation.

If the hypothesis put forward by Schwartz is interpreted as implying that high levels of arousal inhibit deeper levels of processing, then a reasonable deduction is that high arousal will have a detrimental effect on imaginal processing. There is some evidence suggesting that

extraverts may be better able than introverts to utilize
imaginal processing. For example, Eusę and Haney
(unpublished) obtained scores of image controllability and
clarity from the Gordon Test (Gordon, 1949), and of
introversion-extraversion from the EPI, and discovered that
extraverts had significantly greater image control and
clarity than introverts.   Gale, Morris, Lucas, and
Richardson (1972) obtained a significant correlation between
the Betts Vividness of Imagery Scale and extraversion, with
extraverts reporting more vivid imagery than introverts.

Morris and Gale (1974) also found that vivid imagery was
more prevalent among extraverts, and in addition noticed a
non-significant tendency for extraverts to recall more words
than introverts in an immediate test of incidental free
recall.   Since individual differences on the Betts
questionnaire have been found to correlate with performance
on memory tasks (e.g., Morris & Gale; Sheehan, 1966b), it is
possible that the advantage of extraverts over introverts in
short-term retention might be due to the more effective use
of imaginal mediation by extraverts.   However, Morris and
Gale asked their subjects to rate all the presented words at
the conclusion of the experiment for the amount of imagery
which they had induced during their initial presentation, and
found that this measure of experienced imagery did not
correlate with extraversion.

The relationship between introversion-extraversion and
imagery becomes confused when one considers other studies
such as those of Costello (1957) and Richardson (1969).
Costello compared dysthymics (very introverted neurotic
patients) and hysterics (slightly introverted neurotic
patients), and found that dysthymics had vivid, uncontrolled
imagery, whereas hysterics had weak, uncontrolled imagery.
Richardson found in his initial studies that introverted
neurotics had vivid, uncontrolled imagery, whereas extraverted
neurotics had weak, uncontrolled imagery, but he was unable
to replicate these findings.   Huckabee (1974) asked
introverts and extraverts to rate the ease with which
abstract and concrete nouns evoked images.   Introversion-
extraversion was significantly correlated with imagery for
both abstract nouns (-.20) and concrete nouns (-.49), i.e.,
high imagery scores were more likely to be obtained by
introverts.

A problem with the above studies is that imagery was

assessed by means of questionnaire techniques, which are probably inadequate (see Chapter 3). A potentially more fruitful approach is that of Voicu and Vranceanu (1975). They divided their subjects into physiologically hyper-reactive and hypo-reactive groups, and asked them to learn lists of pictures and words in conditions of quiet or of noise. Noise only had a significant detrimental effect on the picture learning of hyper-reactive subjects. An implication is that high arousal (noise plus hyper-reactivity) somehow interfered with or inhibited imaginal processing of the pictorial stimuli.

(3) In general terms, the differences in the performance of introverts and extraverts on easy and difficult tasks can be interpreted in terms of the Yerkes-Dodson Law (e.g., McLaughlin & H. J. Eysenck, 1967). However, although most of the findings support the prediction of the Yerkes-Dodson Law that the optimal level of arousal should be inversely related to task difficulty, the 'Law' provides no explanation of this relationship.

(4) There is experimental evidence (e.g., Cameron & Myers, 1966) that extraverts are less cautious than introverts. It is possible that the superior short-term retention of extraverts is attributable to their greater readiness to produce responses of whose correctness they are uncertain. The most obvious deduction from this hypothesis is that extraverts should produce more changes and errors than introverts. McLaughlin and Kary (1972) found that extraverts made more correct responses and more errors on a recognition test than introverts. Forrest (1963) asked subjects to recall a series of drawings, and described those who tended to produce exaggerated descriptions of the drawings as 'sharpeners'. He found that the sharpeners were highly significantly more extraverted than the 'levelers' (i.e., those who did not produce exaggerated descriptions). Gauld and Stephenson (1967) required their subjects to recall a story as accurately as possible, and obtained a significant negative correlation between conscientiousness (possibly related to introversion) and the number of errors introduced into the recall attempt.

M. W. Eysenck (1976b) made the point that the errors made by subjects might be due either to genuine memorial distortions or to deliberate invention of material to fill in gaps in their memories. In order to study memory per se, he

investigated the recall of a passage under instructions
emphasizing the need for accuracy.   In contrast to the
findings of Forrest (1963) and of Gauld and Stephenson (1967),
he found that highly activated introverts produced the
largest number of errors and distortions.   This finding
suggests that the poor short-term recall of introverts is not
due to a high response criterion, but it must be noted that
errors could be due either to inaccurate encoding or a low
response criterion.

Evidence more consistent with theoretical expectations was
obtained in recent unpublished work done with Chris
Gillespie.   Subjects were allocated to groups on the basis
of their scores on the extraversion scale of the EPI and the
General Activation scale of Thayer's ADACL.   A signal-
detection analysis of recognition-memory performance
indicated that activated extraverts had stored more
information than the other groups, and that introverts
adopted more stringent response criteria than extraverts,
especially during the early stages of the continuous
recognition task.

It may be of value to relate individual differences in
response criteria to an hypothesis developed by Gray (1972).
On the basis of a considerable volume of research, he
concluded that "we may regard the dimension of introversion-
extraversion as a dimension of susceptibility to
punishment and non-reward: the greater the degree of
introversion, the greater is this susceptibility" (p. 194).
In recent research, Gupta (1976) investigated individual
differences in verbal operant conditioning under various
conditions of positive and negative reinforcement.
Introverted subjects consistently showed more conditioning
than extraverted subjects with negative reinforcement,
suggesting that introverts are more susceptible to
punishment.   There was also some evidence that extraverts
were more affected than introverts by reward.   It is thus
possible that the nature and direction of any differences
between introverts and extraverts in response criteria will
depend upon the rewards and punishments associated with hits,
misses, correct rejections, and false alarms.

(5) M. W. Eysenck (1975c) argued that an
important difference between introverts and extraverts might
be in the speed of retrieval of to-be-remembered information.
He recorded the recall speed of subjects learning easy and

difficult lists of paired associates, and noticed that those
subjects having intermediate levels of arousal (high
activation extraverts and low activation introverts) had
faster response latencies than those of low (low activation
extraverts) or high (high activation introverts) levels of
arousal.   He concluded that previous studies had
confounded storage and retrieval effects.   The generally
superior performance of extraverts to introverts in other
studies, usually involving short retrieval periods, may be
due both to the slower speed of retrieval of introverts and
to the better learning of extraverts.

In order to investigate the effects of introversion-
extraversion on retrieval unconfounded by storage differences,
M. W. Eysenck (1975d) equated the degree of learning of
introverts and extraverts.   Subjects learned each of two
categorized word lists to a criterion of two successive
perfect recalls of the members of each category in their
correct serial order.   The subjects were then probed with
a category name and an item-position cue, and had to respond
appropriately as quickly as possible.   The results
conformed closely to those of M. W. Eysenck (1975c), with
extraverts responding more rapidly under high activation,
whereas the reverse was the case for introverted subjects.

M. W. Eysenck (e.g., 1975b, 1975c) has proposed that high
arousal has the effect of biasing the subject's search
processes towards readily accessible, or functionally
dominant, information more than is the case with lower levels
of arousal.   As task difficulty increases, so does the
accessibility of the required information decrease.   This
hypothesis centres the effects of introversion-extraversion
in the retrieval stage, and leads to the prediction that
introverts should be at a considerable disadvantage to
extraverts with the relatively inaccessible information and
the short retrieval periods used in many of the studies, a
prediction supported by the evidence.   A further prediction
is that, if sufficient time for retrieval is allowed, any
advantage of extraverts over introverts should be attenuated.
Both predictions were supported by M. W. Eysenck (1975c):
a moderate level of arousal was associated with faster
responding than high arousal, but an analysis of the number
of failures to produce the correct response during the ten
seconds allowed for recall indicated no effects of
extraversion or of activation.   Furthermore, on the easy
list, where the correct responses were presumably becoming

more accessible over trials, the response latency
advantage of high arousal subjects increased over trials.

Retention Interval

H. J. Eysenck (1967, 1973) combined Walker's action-
decrement theory with the notion that introverts are
chronically more aroused than extraverts, and deduced that
the short-term retention of extraverts would exceed that of
introverts, but that the position would be reversed for
long-term retention. Modest support for this hypothesis
derives from several of the studies already discussed, in
which extraverts usually performed better than introverts
at the short retention intervals used.

The crucial prediction on the H. J. Eysenck-Walker
hypothesis is that there should be a significant extraversion
by retention interval interaction. The relevant studies
are discussed in detail by M. W. Eysenck (1976c). The
predicted interaction has been obtained in a number of
studies (Howarth 7 H. J. Eysenck, 1968; McLean, 1968;
Osborne, 1972; Skanthakumari, 1965), but there are some
negative results (Berlyne & Carey, 1968; McLaughlin, 1968;
McLaughlin & Kary, 1972).

One difficulty with these studies is that it is hard to
decide whether the results obtained are a function of
subject arousal at input, subject arousal at output, or a
combination of both. An additional possibility is that
introverts are more likely to rehearse the stored information
during the long retention intervals than are extraverts.
The only strong evidence for the hypothesis is the subject
arousal by retention interval interaction. It would be
desirable if those factors thought to affect consolidation
were included in the experiments in this area, since they
should theoretically have differential effects on introverts
and extraverts.

Incidental Learning

Some of the studies reviewed in the previous chapter
(Davies & Jones, 1975; Hockey & Hamilton, 1970) produced
results supporting Easterbrook's (1959) hypothesis that
heightened arousal reduces the range of cue utilization. As
applied to human learning and memory, the prime deduction
receiving experimental investigation is that high levels of

arousal should have a detrimental effect on incidental
learning.   The notion that introverts are functionally more
highly aroused than extraverts would be supported indirectly
if it were found that introverts manifested less incidental
learning than extraverts.   This hypothesis was investigated
by Imam (1974).   He presented subjects with nonsense
syllables enclosed in geometrical figures, having instructed
them to learn the nonsense syllables.   The incidental task
involved matching each nonsense syllable with the shape in
which it had been enclosed during learning.   There was no
difference in incidental learning as a function of
introversion-extraversion.   However, an unsatisfactory
aspect of this experiment was that there was no guarantee
that the subjects actually perceived the incidental material.

In an interesting study, M. C. Eysenck (in preparation)
investigated the incidental learning of attribute information.
The subjects were instructed to process the material either
phonemically or semantically, and were then unexpectedly
given a recognition test involving synonym pairs and
homophone pairs.   Incidental learning, in the sense of
learning other than that specified in the instructions, is
necessary to select the appropriate synonym after semantic
instructions or to select the appropriate homophone after
phonemic instructions.   As expected, introverts showed less
incidental learning than extraverts, presumably because they
processed a smaller number of word attributes than extraverts.
However, while this finding accords with Easterbrook's
hypothesis, there is some question as to whether the results
should be interpreted in arousal terms, since activation as
measured by Thayer's ADACL was unrelated to performance.   If
subsequent work confirms the view that introverts process
fewer attributes or features than extraverts, this would
provide a potential explanation for the frequent superiority
of extraverts in short-term recall.

Semantic Memory

The majority of studies investigating the relationship
between introversion-extraversion and semantic memory have
used tests of verbal or word fluency, such as asking subjects
to write down as many words as possible within a certain
interval of time fulfilling some criterion (e.g., animal
names; words starting with the letter G).   In the first
such study, Cattell (1934) asked his subjects to write down

two-syllable words during a period of two-and-a-half minutes.
Surgency, a personality trait resembling extraversion,
correlated +.30 with fluency. Although some subsequent
studies have failed to obtain any significant relationship
between extraversion and fluency (e.g., Hofstaetter, O'Connor,
& Suziedelis, 1957; Rim, 1954), most studies have found that
extraverts recall more words than introverts (e.g., DiScipio,
1971a; Gewirtz, 1948; White, 1968).

These early studies provided practically no theoretical
account of the findings. Accordingly, M. W. Eysenck (1974a)
attempted a more systematic investigation of the phenomenon.
Subjects were asked to retrieve items from five different
categories, and were permitted to shift category at any time.
Extraverts recalled significantly more words than introverts,
and there was a highly significant interaction between
extraversion and general activation (Thayer, 1967), shown in
Fig. 9.2. An implication of this finding is that a high
level of arousal, as represented by high activation
introverts, has a detrimental effect on retrieval from
semantic memory.

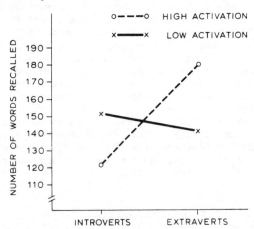

Fig. 9.2. Number of items retrieved as a function
of introversion-extraversion and general activation.
Based on data in M. W. Eysenck (1974a).

A further finding was that the extent to which recall was
organized or clustered in terms of the semantic categories
was strongly related to recall performance. The existence of

a significant interaction between extraversion and general
activation for clustering, paralleling that for the recall
data, indicated that some of the individual differences in
recall might be attributable to differences in organization.

M. W. Eysenck (1974c) argued that there was a methodological problem in the previous studies of personality
differences in semantic memory, since it is probable that
subjects search through their previous emissions in order to
avoid repeating responses. The greater cautiousness of
introverts (Cameron & Myers, 1966) may mean that they perform
more re-checks than extraverts, and thus have less effective
time available for retrieval from semantic memory. In order
to obviate this difficulty, M. W. Eysenck (1974c) used
semantic memory tasks requiring only a single response on any
given trial. On recall trials, subjects produced a word
from a specified category beginning with a designated letter
(e.g., article of furniture-T), and on recognition trials
they decided whether or not a word belonged to a specified
category. Extraverts responded considerably faster than
introverts on recall trials, but there was no difference
between them on recognition trials. Fuller analysis of the
results involved dividing both recall and recognition trials
into those involving easy, or high dominance, items, and those
using difficult, or low dominance, items. The optimal level
of subject arousal varied inversely with the difficulty of the
retrieval task. In a subsequent study, using the same
recall and recognition tasks, but manipulating arousal by
means of general activation and white noise, M. W. Eysenck
(1975b) obtained comparable results.

Several alternative hypotheses can be proposed to account
for the various findings:-

(1) It is possible that introverts retrieve
information as rapidly as extraverts, but that they take
longer to decide whether the retrieved information is correct,
due to their greater cautiousness. However, the recognition
memory task used by M. W. Eysenck (1974c) revealed no
difference in response latencies between introverts and
extraverts, showing that undue cautiousness does not always
slow the responding of introverts. Furthermore, analyses of
the error scores on the recall and recognition tasks used by
M. W. Eysenck (1974c) indicated that, while introverts tended
to produce fewer errors than extraverts, the difference was
not significant.

(2) The simplest hypothesis is that the
frequent inferiority of introverts in retrieval from semantic
memory is due to introverts searching more slowly than
extraverts through semantic memory.   However, this hypothesis
would need elaboration to account for the significant three-
way interaction of extraversion, activation, and item
dominance on recall trials found by M. W. Eysenck (1974c), in
which intermediate levels of arousal produced the greatest
response speeds with high-dominance items, whereas subject
arousal was negatively related to speed with low-dominance
items.   Furthermore, M. W. Eysenck (1974a) used a long
retrieval period in a fluency task (12 minutes), and subjects
apparently recalled as many items as they could, in view of
the generally small number of items recalled during the last
two or three minutes of the retrieval period.   In spite of
the ample time available for retrieval, extraverts recalled
many more words than introverts.   Finally, the rapid initial
retrieval rate of introverts in that experiment suggested
that they do not necessarily have a slower search rate than
extraverts.

(3) It has been suggested (e.g., Bieri, 1970)
that cognitive complexity is greater in introverts than in
extraverts, and this difference in complexity might be
reflected in differences in semantic memory organization.
It might, for example, be the case that it is more difficult
to search for information that is organized complexly, and
that introverts organize information in a more complex manner
than extraverts.   It is true that it is difficult to
unconfound storage and retrieval factors in studies of
semantic memory, since we have to infer the storage
characteristics of semantic memory on the basis of retrieval
measures.   However, it seems improbable that storage
differences could explain all the findings, since the
effects of white noise and of general activation on
performance in semantic memory tasks are presumably on
search and retrieval processes.

(4) A different hypothesis which may be
applicable to the verbal fluency data is that introverts are
more likely than extraverts to experience problems
associated with sampling with replacement when retrieving
information from semantic memory.   Several pieces of
evidence indicate that retrieval of an item of information
increases its strength, and enhances the probability of its
subsequent recall (e.g., Roediger, 1973, 1974; Rundus, 1973).

If retrieval increases the strength of retrieved information more for introverts than extraverts, then introverts would be more susceptible to re-retrieval of items. An alternative mechanism by which introverts might experience repeated retrievals of items is through their relative failure to discriminate between previously retrieved and non-retrieved items. In the verbal fluency situation, the rapid initial recall rate of introverts followed by their marked reduction in recall rate follows from the hypothesis, since problems of sampling with replacement will increase during the course of the retrieval period. The finding that introverts had recalled half of what they would finally recall earlier in the retrieval period than extraverts is also consistent with the hypothesis.

The information that is sampled with replacement probably consists both of individual words and of attributes common to several words (e.g., ferocity and size of animals, Rips, Shoben, & Smith, 1973). In a re-analysis of the data of M. W. Eysenck (1974a), the author investigated the bursts of responses produced by introverts and extraverts, defining a burst as two or more successive responses where all the inter-response times (IRTs) are among the fastest 25 per cent of IRTs produced by that subject. The assumption is that the items within a burst are related and share common attributes (cf., Mandler, 1975; Pollio, 1964). The main finding was that activated introverts produced many fewer bursts than extraverts, but actually had more words per burst on average. The conclusion is that introverts find it more difficult to retrieve attributes defining categorical subsets than do extraverts, possibly due to their re-sampling of attributes already retrieved.

(5) As was noted in the previous chapter, some of the findings on speed of retrieval from semantic memory (e.g., M. W. Eysenck, 1974c, 1975b) can be accounted for by a theory put forward by Walley and Weiden (1973). On their hypothesis, high arousal causes cognitive masking and reduces the possibility of shared or parallel processing. If introverts are more aroused than extraverts and thus less able to process in parallel, this would imply that they would be at a disadvantage in any task involving the processing of several different items of information, as is presumably true of the low-dominance recall items used by M. W. Eysenck.

In sum, the differences between introverts and extraverts

in semantic memory tasks could be due to at least five
factors: (1) introverts search through semantic memory more
slowly than extraverts; (2) information in semantic memory
is less efficiently organized in introverts than in
extraverts; (3) introverts are more likely to re-retrieve
information from semantic memory; (4) introverts are more
cautious than extraverts about emitting information which
they have retrieved; and (5) introverts are more susceptible
than extraverts to cognitive masking, and thus have a higher
probability of processing serially. There is some
experimental evidence inconsistent with factors (1) and (4),
and factor (2) is hard to test. The remaining factors, three
and five, seem best to account for the available data. They
can both be seen as more specific versions of the hypothesis
proposed by M. W. Eysenck (1976a): "High arousal has the
effect of biasing the subject's search process towards
readily accessible, or functionally dominant, stored
information more than is the case with lower levels of
arousal" (p. 401).

At a more speculative level, the hypothesis that high
arousal increases the natural bias of the subject's search
process towards readily accessible stored information appears
to be potentially applicable to the study of humour
appreciation and of divergent thinking. The comprehension
and appreciation of humour depends upon the retrieval of
relevant information from semantic memory, much of it of a
relatively inaccessible nature. Similarly, divergent
thinking also requires the retrieval of non-dominant
information from semantic memory.

An interesting information-processing theory of humour has
recently been proposed in slightly different forms by a
number of investigators (e.g., Jones, 1970; Shultz, 1970;
Suls, 1972). The basic assumption is that the comprehension
and appreciation of humour involves a biphasic sequence of
incongruity and resolution. Jokes often contain an
incongruity which serves to arouse or surprise the listener
as well as information which can be used to resolve the
incongruity and reduce his level of arousal. The listener
appreciates the joke to the extent that he detects and
resolves its incongruity. The relative unfunniness of a
joke one has heard before or a cartoon one has seen before
(e.g., Martin, 1905) is due to the fact that once we have
resolved an incongruity, we may subsequently fail to detect,
and be aroused by, the joke's incongruity.

In many jokes, the incongruity depends on the relationship between the last- or punch-line and the preceding part of the joke. For example, consider the following W. C. Fields joke: "Do you believe in clubs for young people?" "Only when kindness fails."   There is an apparent incongruity between the question and the answer, which depends on the fact that most subjects will initially interpret the homograph 'clubs' in its semantic interpretation of 'social groups'. The joke is appreciated when the subject subsequently retrieves the alternative semantic interpretation of clubs, meaning large sticks. Shultz (1974) pointed out that jokes can also involve phonological and syntactical ambiguities. For example, consider the following joke: "Can you tell me how long cows should be milked?" "They should be milked the same as short ones, of course." Chortle! Chortle! Here the initial grammatical bracketing of (how long) (cows) becomes (how) (long cows).

There is reasonable empirical support for the theory. Jones (1970) noted that cartoon humour was a linear function of the degree of incongruity perceived in cartoons. Shultz (1974) asked subjects to indicate the order in which they processed the various elements in verbal jokes. As predicted by the theory, subjects usually detected initially the first element of the incongruity and the biased meaning of the ambiguous element (e.g., clubs meaning social groups). This was followed by detection of the second element of the incongruity and then, finally, the hidden meaning of the ambiguous element (e.g., clubs as large sticks). The biased meaning of the ambiguous element is relatively dominant and readily accessible in semantic memory, whereas the hidden meaning of the ambiguous element is non-dominant and inaccessible. In the light of the findings reported earlier in the chapter, the prediction follows that high arousal or introversion would facilitate retrieval of the biased meaning of the ambiguous element of a joke, but would inhibit retrieval of the hidden meaning of the ambiguity. Thus high subject arousal should lengthen the time required to perceive humour.

Retrieval from semantic memory is also involved in the performance of tests of divergent thinking, such as the Uses test (in which subjects must think of as many uses as possible for a common object). Hargreaves and Bolton (1972) factor analyzed the results from 15 divergent and non-

divergent tests.   The divergent tests loaded primarily on
two factors, both of which were factorially distinct from
I.Q.   Verbal tests of divergent thinking loaded on one
factor, whereas non-verbal tests of divergent thinking
loaded on the other.   Hargreaves and Bolton concluded that
divergent tests measure an integrated range of abilities.

The relationship between divergent thinking and arousal
remains unclear.   Hudson (1968) failed to obtain a
significant correlation between convergence-divergence and
extraversion, and DiScipio (1971b) found that introversion-
extraversion was unrelated to performance on each of three
tests of divergent-thinking ability.   More negative findings
were obtained by Soueif and El-Sayed (1970), who considered
several measures of divergent thinking and of personality.
Over 90 per cent of the linear correlations between
divergent thinking and personality did not differ
significantly from zero.   However, further analysis did
reveal the existence of some complex interactional effects
among the personality variables (e.g., for introverts and
ambiverts but not extraverts, some of the divergent-test
measures were positively correlated with ego integration).

More promising results were obtained by Martindale and
Greenough (1973).   They presented tests of convergent and
divergent thinking under conditions of low arousal (relaxation), medium arousal (ego-involving instructions), and
high arousal (white noise).   Arousal had a slight, but non-
significant, enhancing effect on convergent-test performance,
and a significant detrimental effect on divergent-test
performance.   The notion that high arousal inhibits
divergent thinking has received indirect support from a
number of studies of incidental learning (e.g., Mendelsohn
& Griswold, 1964, 1966; Laughlin, 1967; Laughlin, Doherty,
& Dunn, 1968).   In these studies, those subjects performing
well on tests of divergent-thinking ability showed more
incidental learning than those showing less divergent-
thinking ability.   This finding, combined with Easterbrook's
hypothesis that arousal restricts the range of cue
utilization, suggests that subjects good at divergent thinking
may be less aroused than those less good.   The intriguing
implication is that people who are highly aroused are
relatively unable to make effective use of information at the
level of subsidiary awareness, whether the information is in
the external or the internal environment.

There is also some evidence that performance on tests of divergent thinking is detrimentally affected if the tests are given in an arousing, evaluative, context. For example, Boersma and O'Bryan (1968) gave tests of divergent-thinking ability to schoolchildren nine and ten years old under either formal or informal conditions, and found that the children doing the tests under informal, non-evaluative, conditions scored significantly higher on both non-verbal and verbal tests.

In sum, there is some evidence that high arousal has a detrimental effect on divergent thinking, and it is plausible to suppose that the tendency for high arousal to produce a search process biased towards accessible sources of information is at least partially responsible. There may also be some interesting relationships between divergence and episodic memory. Sacks and M. W. Eysenck (1976) presented concrete and abstract sentences followed by a recognition test, and obtained a significant interaction between abstractness-concreteness and convergence-divergence, in which concrete sentences were better recognized than abstract sentences by convergers, but there was no difference for divergers. They attributed this interaction to the greater ability of divergers to discover the several interpretations of a single nominal stimulus held to be inherent in abstract, but not concrete, sentences. On Easterbrook's hypothesis, the divergers' ability to process a wide range of semantic interpretations may be partially due to their low level of arousal.

Summary

The experimental evidence indicates that there are relatively consistent differences in learning and memory as a function of introversion-extraversion. In most cases, extraverts show more rapid learning than introverts on difficult tasks, such as those involving response competition; extraverts tend to recall better than introverts at short retention intervals, whereas the opposite is the case at long retention intervals; and extraverts retrieve information faster than introverts from episodic and semantic memory. Furthermore, there are clear parallels between the results obtained by investigators concerning themselves with arousal and learning and those dealing with introversion-extraversion and learning. There is some important link

between introversion-extraversion and arousal, although the
precise nature of the link has not been established.
However, a reasonable assumption is that the optimal level
of physiological arousal is lower in introverts than in
extraverts.

A major criticism of the research literature relates to
the nature of the tasks used and the explanatory accounts
offered for the results. As Johnson (1974) has pointed out,
recent theoretical and conceptual developments in the study
of human memory have only just started to permeate the
literature on personality differences in memory. Relatively
few of the studies discussed in this chapter have been
concerned with psychological processes. Nevertheless,
recent research has suggested that introverts tend to process
fewer of the attributes of to-be-learned material than
extraverts at the time of input, and that introverts
experience greater difficulty than extraverts at retrieving
relatively inaccessible information at output. In addition,
there is suggestive evidence that introverts and extraverts
differ in their response criteria. These findings indicate
the limited value in merely comparing retention-test
performance of introverts and extraverts without also
obtaining information about the processes producing memory-
performance differences.

CHAPTER 10

ANXIETY, NEUROTICISM, AND MEMORY

Several hundred studies have looked at the effects of individual differences in anxiety on learning, usually measuring anxiety by means of a self-report questionnaire. Although several different questionnaires have been utilized in this research, the Manifest Anxiety Scale (MAS; Taylor, 1953) has been the most widely used. In spite of the fact that there is relatively little agreement on the definition of the concept of anxiety, the various measures are comparable. For example, H. J. Eysenck and S. B. G. Eysenck (1969) found that the second-order factor of anxiety obtained from Cattell's Sixteen Personality Factor Test correlated substantially with the neuroticism scale of the Eysenck Personality Inventory (EPI), and Sherrill, Salisbury, Friedman, and Horowitz (1968) obtained a correlation of +.65 between scores on the neuroticism scale of the short-form Maudsley Personality Inventory (MPI) and the MAS. In a large-scale study, Templer (1971a, 1971b) factor analyzed data from several personality questionnaires, including the MPI, the MAS, and the IPAT Anxiety Scale Questionnaire. The inter-correlations among the IPAT, the MAS, and the neuroticism scale of the MPI were all of the order of +.6 to +.8. Furthermore, all three measures loaded heavily on the anxiety factor extracted from the data, and had only small loadings on the extraversion factor.

Proper interpretation of anxiety-test scores is open to doubt. For example, Edwards, Cone, and Abbott (1970) have pointed out that most of the items on the MAS are keyed for socially undesirable responses. Their study indicated that high scorers on the MAS may simply be those who are prepared to admit to socially undesirable modes of behaviour. In contrast, the finding that patients with chronic anxiety states score considerably higher than normals on questionnaire measures of anxiety (e.g., Kelly & Walter, 1968) provides evidence that the measures possess some validity.

Although most of the major questionnaire measures of
anxiety treat it as a unidimensional trait, there is
increasing evidence that a rather more complex
conceptualization is necessary. For example, it seems
probable that there is a valid distinction between state
anxiety, a transitory emotional condition, and trait anxiety,
a relatively stable personality characteristic. Cicero
(see Lewis, 1970) originated the distinction, which at a
rather later date was developed by Cattell and Scheier (1958,
1961) and by Spielberger (1966). Spielberger, Gorsuch, and
Lushene (1970) have devised the State Trait Anxiety
Inventory (STAI), claiming that state anxiety is
"characterized by subjective, consciously perceived feelings
of tension and apprehension, and heightened autonomic
nervous system activity" (p. 3), whereas trait anxiety
"refers to relatively stable individual differences in
anxiety proneness" (p. 3).

Additional refinements to the anxiety concept have been
proposed by Endler in a series of articles (e.g., Endler &
Shedletsky, 1973; Shedletsky & Endler, 1974; Endler,
Magnusson, Ekehammar, & Okada, 1976). He noted that most
trait measures of anxiety, including the MAS and the STAI,
are primarily concerned with inter-personal or ego-
threatening aspects of trait anxiety. Endler and
Shedletsky (1973) compared performance on the trait scale of
the STAI and the S-R Inventory of Anxiousness, which
assesses trait anxiety for three classes of situations
(inter-personal threats, physical danger, and ambiguous
threats). The STAI correlated significantly higher with the
inter-personal situation scales than with the physical danger
or ambiguous threat situation scales. Endler et al. (1976)
factor analyzed data from the S-R Inventory of General Trait
Anxiousness, the STAI, and the Behavioural Reactions
Questionnaire, and obtained two major factors (inter-personal
threat and physical danger). The trait measure of the STAI
loaded approximately .80 on the inter-personal threat factor
and .25 on the physical danger factor. In other analyses,
Endler et al. obtained evidence for at least three anxiety
reaction factors: somatic distress, psychic distress, and
absence of curiosity.

If there are discriminable facets of trait anxiety, this
could help to account for some of the complexities in the
literature. For example, it has been assumed that trait
anxiety interacts with situational stress to produce state

anxiety, so that high trait-anxiety subjects will respond
with more state anxiety than low trait-anxiety subjects in a
stressful situation.   Some evidential support has been
provided by Hodges (1968), Hodges and Spielberger (1969),
O'Neil, Spielberger, and Hansen (1969), and Rappaport and
Katkin (1972), all of whom found differential responding on
state anxiety measures for high and low trait-anxiety
subjects under ego-involving conditions.   On the other hand,
several studies (e.g., Hodges, 1968; Hodges & Spielberger,
1966; Katkin, 1965) have found that situations that do not
pose a 'psychological threat' to self-esteem (e.g., physical
danger) are not perceived as any more threatening by high
trait-anxiety individuals than by those low on trait anxiety.
In these studies, trait anxiety has been measured by
questionnaires dealing with reactions to inter-personal
threat.   It appears to be the case that there are trait-
situation interactions such that maximal state anxiety occurs
where there is congruence between the type of threat
provided by the situation and the relevant facet of trait
anxiety.   Several of the studies on the effects of anxiety
on learning discussed later are consistent with this
hypothesis.

Spence and Spence

The first major learning theory to consider the
relationship between anxiety and learning was put forward by
Spence (Spence, 1958; Spence & Spence, 1966).   In essence,
habit strength, or trace strength, and drive were said to
multiply together to produce excitatory potential.   The
habit of greatest strength in any particular situation will
manifest itself in performance, provided that the level of
excitatory potential produced by that habit when multiplied
by drive exceeds the response threshold.   It was further
assumed that the level of drive was a function of a
persistent emotional response aroused by aversive stimuli.
Among the determinants of this emotional response are
conditions producing heightened emotional drive, such as ego-
involving instructions or shock, and the subject's emotional
responsiveness, measurable by the MAS.   The emotional
response not only partially determines the amount of drive
(D), but also produces drive stimuli.   These drive stimuli
in turn will lead to task-irrelevant behaviour.   Figure 10.1
overleaf provides a simplified version of the theory as it
applies to learning.

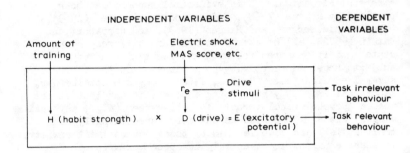

Fig. 10.1. Spence's theory of learning.
Adapted from H. J. Eysenck (1973).

A major prediction from the theory stems from the fact
that any increase in drive will increase the difference in
probability of two responses differing in initial strength.
Thus an increase in drive will cause the stronger of two
competing responses to become still stronger. This would
presumably increase the efficiency of performance on tasks
such as simple conditioning, where the correct response has
no close competitor. However, on more complex tasks, where
the correct response has to be discriminated from some other
strongly competing response or responses, an increase in
drive would make the error responses still stronger relative
to the correct response, thus leading to a decrement in
performance. In more modern terminology, Spence and Spence
(1966) argued that drive and anxiety had their effects
primarily on retrieval processes. It is important to note
that drive does not affect directly either storage
(represented by habit strength), or the degree of caution
used by the subject when deciding whether or not to respond
(represented by the response threshold).

The major instrument which has been used to investigate
individual differences in emotional responsiveness has been
the MAS, which is a self-report, paper-and-pencil
questionnaire. The items on the MAS were selected from

those on the Minnesota Multiphasic Personality Inventory (MMPI) on the basis of clinical impression of how well they fitted Cameron's (1947) definition of anxiety. As Jessor and Hammond (1957) pointed out, the MAS elicits verbal responses about other, non-verbal, responses indicative of emotional responsiveness. The MAS is only an appropriate measure of drive if the verbal responses are accurate. Kimble and Posnick (1967) re-wrote the MAS, preserving the formal elements of each question, but eliminating its anxiety-related content, and found that this new measure correlated substantially with the original MAS. This suggests that the MAS might be measuring something other than anxiety. Furthermore, it has been suggested (e.g., H. J. Eysenck, 1973) that the MAS is factorially complex, since it correlates about +.6 to .7 with Eysenck's neuroticism factor, and -.3 to .4 with his extraversion factor (Sherrill et al., 1968).

In spite of the above doubts about the validity of the MAS, there are a very considerable number of published articles investigating the relationship between the MAS and learning. Since fairly comprehensive reviews are available (H. J. Eysenck, 1973; Spence & Spence, 1966), only selected parts of this literature will be considered here. In studies of eyelid conditioning, where there are presumably no strong competing responses, the prediction is that high levels of anxiety will increase the probability of obtaining the conditioned response. Spence (1964) reported that this prediction was confirmed in 21 out of 25 independent comparisons of high- and low-anxiety subjects as measured by the MAS.

Studies considering the effects of anxiety on verbal learning have largely used paired-associate tasks, mainly because a certain amount of control is possible over the number and strengths of competing responses. In some studies, subjects received non-competitive paired-associate lists in which the stimulus and response terms were selected so as to minimize the similarity among them. Since there should be no strong competing responses, the prediction is that the high-anxiety group should become increasingly superior to the low-anxiety group as learning progresses. Three studies using this type of list (Spence, 1958; Taylor, 1958; Taylor & Chapman, 1955) obtained this result, but two did not (Kamin & Fedorchak, 1957; Lovaas, 1960). On a slightly different type of non-competitive paired-associate

list, in which there was an initial associative connection
between the members of each pair, high-anxiety subjects are
again predicted to learn more rapidly than low-anxiety
subjects.   The results are generally confirmatory (Besch,
1959; Spence, Farber, & McFann, 1956a; Spence, Taylor, &
Ketchel, 1956b; Standish & Champion, 1960).

With competitive paired-associate lists, in which some of
the stimulus items are initially more closely associated
with response terms other than the responses with which they
are paired in the list, the prediction is that high levels of
anxiety will initially strengthen strong, incorrect,
responses, leading to poor performance.   This prediction has
been supported several times (e.g., Ramond, 1953; Spence et
al., 1956a, 1956b; Standish & Champion, 1960).   The theory
also predicts that, as learning progresses and the correct
responses become stronger than the incorrect responses, high-
anxiety subjects should surpass low-anxiety subjects.
Standish and Champion (1960) confirmed this prediction.

Saltz (1970) made the interesting suggestion that high-
anxiety subjects on the MAS are sensitive to failure and
anticipation of failure (i.e., ego threat), whereas low-
anxiety subjects are sensitive to stress induced by pain.
Experimentally, the results indicate that failure feedback
and electric shock are not equivalent methods of increasing
emotional responsiveness, although the theory of Spence and
Spence (1966) suggests that they are.   With failure
information given to subjects, the usual finding is that
there is an interaction between anxiety level and failure,
with the performance of high-anxiety subjects being inferior
under failure as compared to non-failure, whereas the
performance of low-anxiety subjects experiencing failure
varies from being slightly superior to being inferior to the
non-failure subjects (e.g., Gordon & Berlyne, 1954; Lucas,
1952; Sarason, 1957; Walker, 1961).   Theoretically, it is
assumed that high-anxiety subjects are more likely to respond
to the ego-threat of learning that they have performed
poorly by generating drive stimuli that lead to task-
irrelevant behaviour.   In the case of electric shock, high-
anxiety subjects appear to be less detrimentally affected
than low-anxiety subjects, even with competitive tasks (e.g.,
Besch, 1959; Chiles, 1958).   This result, which is contrary
to the theory of Spence and Spence, suggests that low-
anxiety subjects are more sensitive than high-anxiety subjects
to the effects of painful stimulation, or shock.

Saltz (1970) argued that the sensitivity of high-anxiety subjects to anticipation of failure might help to explain other findings:

> Massive competition typically increases the difficulty level of the material. Thus, the superior performance of low-anxious subjects on such tasks may indicate that these subjects are relatively unaffected by the threat of failure involved in difficult materials, while high-anxious subjects, being more sensitive to failure, find difficult material more stressful (p. 571).

In other words, Saltz claimed that there was a confounding of variables in the literature, with easy, non-competitive, tasks tending to be associated with feelings of success, whereas difficult, competitive, tasks are associated with failure.

While Spence and Spence (1966) emphasized the task-complexity variable, Saltz (1970) proposed that success-failure is more important. Weiner (1966) and Weiner and Schneider (1971) unconfounded these two variables by giving their subjects false social norms indicating that they were succeeding at a difficult verbal learning task or failing at an easy learning task. Under these conditions, subjects high in anxiety performed better on the difficult task and worse on the easy task than subjects low in anxiety.

It is thus clear that learning tasks differ in important ways other than the number and strengths of competing incorrect responses. This conclusion is reinforced by a study (Tennyson & Wooley, 1971) in which subjects were given a measure of transient levels of anxiety (the anxiety-state scale of the STAI) after concept acquisition tasks on both difficult and easy materials. They found that the mean level of state anxiety following the difficult task was significantly higher than the mean obtained after the easy task. Spielberger, O'Neil, and Hansen (1972) also found that difficult learning tasks increased state anxiety much more than easy tasks, particularly during the initial stages of learning.

Although the above findings indicate that the Spence-Spence theory is over-simplified, it is not clear that the alternative, cognitive theory analysis (Weiner, 1972), based on feelings of success and failure, is generally valid.

It suggests that performance on learning tasks is dependent
on the difficulty of the task, whereas much of the evidence
(e.g., Spence et al., 1956a; Taylor, 1958; Taylor &
Chapman, 1955) supports the contention of Spence and Spence
that number and strength of incorrect responses is the more
important factor.   In addition, when a learning task
comprises both easy and difficult components, Weiner's theory
predicts that the subject rapidly oscillates between feelings
of success and failure as easy and difficult items are
presented to him.   This seems implausible.

   In sum, the evidence is generally favourable to the
hypothesis that high-anxiety subjects should perform better
than low-anxiety subjects where the dominant response is
correct, whereas low-anxiety subjects should, at least
initially, be superior where the dominant response is
incorrect.   It should be noted, however, that several
studies have failed to ensure that the dominant response was
incorrect under the 'difficult' condition (Hill, 1957).   The
theory is inadequate in several ways.   One deficiency relates
to the assumption that the response threshold is the same for
high- and low-anxiety subjects.   Since high drive has the
effect of raising additional items above the threshold, the
prediction must follow that high-anxiety subjects would
recall more items than low-anxiety subjects in a test of free
recall.   Mueller (1976a) failed to find any differences in
free recall between high- and low-anxiety subjects in several
experiments, and non-significant differences were also
reported by Rogers and Battig (1972).   Mueller (1976b)
actually found that low-anxiety subjects showed considerably
higher levels of free recall than high-anxiety subjects.

   Goulet and Mazzei (1969) investigated the response
threshold more directly in a paired-associate learning task.
From their data, they calculated what they termed a
'confidence threshold' for each paired associate, defined as
the trial on which a response was first given to the stimulus
member of the pair, whether or not the response was correct.
Contrary to the Spence-Spence model, low-anxiety subjects
tended to produce responses on earlier trials than high-
anxiety subjects, and thus had a lower confidence or response
threshold.   Goulet and Mazzei concluded: "The high-anxiety
subjects may withhold responding until fairly confident of the
stimulus-response pairings, whereas low-anxiety subjects may
require a lower degree of confidence and thus respond earlier
in practice where a lower degree of associative strength

exists between stimuli and responses" (p. 251).

A second problem relates to the fact that the great majority of studies investigating effects of anxiety have used short anticipation intervals of between two and four seconds, i.e., when a stimulus is presented, the subject must produce the correct response rapidly. There is evidence that anxiety has somewhat different effects on speed of response from the effects on probability of a correct response. For example, Straughan and Dufort (1969) found no differences between high- and low-anxiety subjects in probability of recall, whether or not they had received relaxation instructions. However, there was a significant interaction between anxiety and relaxation in speed of correct responding, with subjects who were low in anxiety being slowed by relaxation instructions, whereas the performance of subjects high in anxiety was facilitated. Similarly, Standish and Champion (1960) found significant differences in response speed among high-, medium-, and low-anxiety subjects on a paired-associate task after performance had become error-free. Further experimental consideration of the discrepant effects of anxiety and stress on probability and speed of response seems desirable.

A third problem relates to the question as to whether individuals scoring high on the MAS are chronically higher in emotional responsiveness than those scoring low. The evidence is much more consistent with the notion that high- and low-MAS scorers only differ in anxiety under conditions of ego threat. If this is the case, then the MAS is obviously not an entirely suitable measure of emotional responsiveness. As Spielberger, O'Neil, and Hansen (1972) pointed out, the concept of A-state seems logically more closely associated with drive than does A-trait. They reported the results of several experiments relating anxiety as measured by the STAI to performance on computer-assisted learning. In three separate experiments, there were no significant relationships between trait anxiety and performance, whereas each experiment produced a significant negative relationship between state anxiety and difficult-task performance. The non-significant findings with trait anxiety occurred in spite of the fact that those scoring high on trait anxiety generally scored higher than those scoring low on trait anxiety on the measure of state anxiety.

In one of the experiments reported by Spielberger et al.

(1972), the subjects received either neutral or negative
feedback during the learning of difficult concepts in
mathematics.   Measures of state anxiety were taken before
the task, and at three points during the task.   As can be
seen in Fig. 10.2, the stress induced by negative feedback
produced a much larger increase in A-state for those subjects
high in A-trait than for those low in A-trait.   In this
experiment, high A-state was associated with a high
incidence of errors, especially during the later stages of
learning.

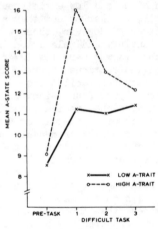

Fig. 10.2. Anxiety-state scores as a function
of anxiety-trait and negative feedback. Adapted
from Spielberger, O'Neil, and Hansen (1972).

One obvious advantage of the approach adopted by
Spielberger et al. is that it provides a method of measuring
changes in anxiety occurring during the performance of the
task.   However, there is the difficulty of distinguishing
between the effects of anxiety on performance, and those of
performance on anxiety.

A fourth problem is of more fundamental importance.
While Spence and Spence (1966) hypothesized that anxiety
affected retrieval or performance rather than learning, the
experimentation in this area has very largely failed to
address itself directly to this assumption.   An obvious
approach would be to separate presentation and test trials in

time, and to present stressful stimulation (e.g., electric shock, ego-threatening instructions) either at input or at output.   According to models of the Spence-Spence type, the effects of stress at output should be greater than at input. However, Straughan and Dufort (1969) used this approach, presenting relaxation instructions either prior to list input or prior to recall, and found that the interactional effects of anxiety and relaxation on recall speed were greater when relaxation preceded acquisition.

Zubrycki and Borkowski (1973) investigated the effects of anxiety on storage and retrieval in a study in which subjects were presented with eight words, belonging to either two or four different categories.   Subjects then counted backwards, followed by free recall and then cued recall. Overall, low-anxiety subjects recalled more words than high-anxiety subjects.   However, the dependent variable of most interest was cued recall minus free recall.   On the assumption (Tulving & Pearlstone, 1966) that cueing reduces the retrieval problem, and provides a more accurate estimate of storage, a large discrepancy between cued and free recall would indicate difficulties in retrieval.   In fact, the enhancing effect of cueing was greater for low-anxiety than for high-anxiety subjects, indicating that low-anxiety subjects were significantly superior to high-anxiety subjects in storage.

Recent Research

Mueller (1976a) argued that there were at least two different effects that anxiety might have on learning and storage: quantitative and qualitative.   Quantitatively, the effects of anxiety on learning have been investigated most thoroughly with the digit-span task.   While variable results have been reported, several studies have found that situationally-induced stress has a detrimental effect on digit-span performance (e.g., Dunn, 1968; Griffiths, 1958; Hodges, 1968; Moldawsky & Moldawsky, 1952; Pyke & Agnew, 1963).   The interpretation of this result is complicated by the fact that digit span appears to involve an amalgam of primary and secondary memory (Craik, 1971a).   There is no simple relationship between anxiety and digit-span performance.   For example, Hodges and Spielberger (1969) found that digit span was negatively related to the level of trait anxiety, whereas Knox and Grippaldi (1970) observed the best digit-span performance in those with a medium level of

state and trait anxiety.   Hodges and Durham (1972) obtained
an interaction between intelligence and anxiety with high
intelligence enhancing digit-span performance for high-
anxiety subjects, but having a detrimental effect on low-
anxiety subjects.   Mueller (1976a) found no effects of
anxiety on digit span in several studies.   The evidence
suggests that stress and high levels of state anxiety have a
detrimental effect on digit span, whereas trait anxiety has
negligible effects.

There have been remarkably few attempts to account
theoretically for the effects of anxiety on span performance.
Baddeley and Hitch (1974) argued that short-term memory
comprises a central 'work space' of limited capacity which
controls the use of a more peripheral 'articulatory loop'.
This implies that anxiety might affect either or both of these
processes.   Folkard (1976), discussing his own work on the
effects of arousal on short-term memory, concluded that
arousal reduced subvocal activity and thus the use of the
articulatory loop during short-term memory tasks, but had
little, if any, effect on the work space.   Folkard has
manipulated arousal by means of induced muscle tension and
time of day rather than through individual differences in
anxiety, so that his hypothesis may or may not be relevant to
the anxiety literature.   However, at the very least, an
experimental determination of whether anxiety affects
primarily the articulatory loop or the central work space
seems desirable.

Possible qualitative effects of anxiety on learning were
also investigated by Mueller (1976a).   He linked Easterbrook's
(1959) hypothesis with Craik and Lockhart's (1972) depth-of-
processing hypothesis, and argued that anxious or aroused
subjects would utilize fewer of the available attributes
when encoding information.   This notion was considered in a
series of experiments on free recall.   In the first
experiment, Mueller used both categorized and associatively
related word lists presented in random order.   Although
there were no significant differences in recall, either from
primary memory or from secondary memory, there were differences
in the organization of recall.   On both types of list,
high-anxiety subjects initially demonstrated less clustering
in recall than low-anxiety subjects, but this difference was
reduced as learning progressed.   These findings indicate
that high-anxiety subjects are less likely to use semantic
features of presented material during learning, but do not

reveal what organizational methods they are using.   As
Postman (1972) has noted, there are a variety of alternative
bases of organization, such as recall in the order of
presentation (cf., Mandler, 1969).

In a further experiment, Mueller used a list of unrelated
words presented on each of several trials, and again found no
difference in free recall between high- and low-anxiety
subjects.   In terms of subjective organization (the tendency
for subjects to recall words in the same order on adjacent
trials; Tulving, 1962), high-anxiety subjects initially
showed less organization of output than did low-anxiety
subjects.

In a final experiment, Mueller (1976a) presented subjects
with lists of words that were either phonemically or
categorically related.   High-anxiety subjects clustered less
on both lists initially, and, in addition, they also had a
lower level of recall.   In a subsequent study, they (i.e.,
high-anxiety subjects) again recalled less than low-anxiety
subjects (Mueller, 1976b).   Many of the list words were
phonemically or semantically related to other list words,
and high-anxiety subjects manifested much less phonemic and
semantic clustering than low-anxiety subjects.   Bartel,
DuCette, and Wolk (1972) also found that subjects apparently
high in anxiety showed less clustering in recall of a
categorized word list than did low-anxiety subjects.

Although the finding that the free recall of high-anxiety
subjects is less semantically organized than that of low-
anxiety subjects is well established, the proper interpretation of this result is unclear.   Mueller (1976a) argued that
high-anxiety subjects manifest restricted encoding of to-be-
remembered material, and yet the nature of the encoding
process used by high-anxiety subjects is unknown.   It is
possible, for example, that high-anxiety subjects are
organizing the input either imaginally or conceptually, in
ways which the clustering measures fail to reveal.
Furthermore, it is not necessarily the case that the effects
of anxiety on clustering occur at the encoding stage.
Borges (1972) presented categorized word lists with either
zero or twelve items intervening between successive category
members, and found equivalent levels of recall and clustering
under both conditions.   However, the twelve-item spacing
group took twice as long for free recall as the zero-item
spacing group.   The natural interpretation of the data is

that the zero-item spacing group organized semantically
during encoding, whereas the twelve-item spacing group
organized semantically at the time of recall.   A suitable
method for investigating Mueller's hypothesis is the overt
rehearsal technique (Rundus, 1971): if anxiety affects
encoding, the overt rehearsal patterns of high-anxiety
subjects during list presentation should show less semantic
organization than those of low-anxiety subjects.

Anxiety and Intelligence

A continual problem in work investigating the effects of
individual differences on learning and memory is the
possibility that a specified individual difference variable
may erroneously appear to affect learning because it is
correlated with some second variable that actually does
affect learning.   For example, it is possible that some of
the detrimental effects of high anxiety on memory are due to
uncontrolled differences in intelligence.   Grice (1955) and
Kerrick (1955) both reported that the MAS scores of
American Air Force basic trainees were negatively and
significantly correlated with a variety of measures of
intelligence.   However, several other studies (e.g., Dana,
1957; Klugh & Bendig, 1955; Spielberger, 1958) failed to
find any relationship between anxiety and intelligence.   At
least part of the difference in results is probably
attributable to the mean intellectual ability levels of the
samples used: the studies reporting no relationship
usually used college students.   Spielberger (1958) obtained
empirical evidence that negative correlations between
measures of anxiety and intelligence were more prevalent in
samples containing a sizeable proportion of subjects with
low ability.   Since the great majority of studies
investigating anxiety differences in learning have used
college students as subjects, it is unlikely that there was a
serious confounding of anxiety and intelligence in most of
the published literature.

Within the general framework of the Spence-Spence model,
there is a second aspect to the relationship between anxiety
and intelligence.   As Spielberger (1966) noted:-

> Materials of average difficulty may actually be quite
> easy for bright students; for less able students, such
> materials might be extremely difficult and, in some
> cases, beyond the student's learning capacity.   Thus,

task difficulty would seem to depend on both the intrinsic complexity of the materials to be learned and the intellectual ability of the student (p. 377).

A reasonable prediction is that the detrimental effects of high anxiety on complex, competitional, tasks would be attenuated in the case of highly intelligent subjects. Spielberger (1966) considered the effects of anxiety on complex learning task (academic achievement), and found that high-anxiety students obtained poorer grades than low-anxiety students in the middle range of ability. However, among the cleverest of the students, there was some evidence that high anxiety increased academic achievement. The most appropriate interpretation of this finding is unclear. While Spielberger argued that high ability reduces the number of competing erroneous responses which are elicited, it seems equally plausible to assume that high ability reduces the anxiety experienced in difficult learning situations. Spielberger has extended his findings to paired-associate learning (Gaudry & Spielberger, 1970), where he found that, early in learning, high anxiety facilitated performance for intelligent subjects and impaired performance for dull subjects relative to their low-anxiety counterparts.

Physiology

In spite of the argument by Spence and Spence (1966) that the relationship (if any) between measures of emotional responsiveness and physiological indices of arousal was irrelevant to their theoretical position, there have been several theoretical attempts to relate anxiety and arousal (e.g., H. J. Eysenck, 1973; Mueller, 1976a). Experimentally, the evidence is somewhat confusing. Part of the problem is that inter-correlations among the various physiological measures are fairly low, with individuals varying considerably from measure to measure in their position with respect to other individuals (Lacey & Lacey, 1958). In addition, the various questionnaire measures of anxiety used in the relevant studies tend to inter-correlate at reasonable levels, but are clearly not entirely equivalent.

Smith (1973) found that the resting frontalis EMG level correlated positively with trait anxiety as measured by Cattell's IPAT Anxiety Scale Form A, suggesting that high-anxiety subjects are chronically aroused. However, he

failed to find a significant relationship between frontalis
muscle tension and state anxiety on the Nowlis Adjective
Check List.   On the other hand, Forrest and Kroth (1971)
found no difference in blood pressure prior to a stressful
task as a function of scores on the MAS and the STAI.
During the stressful task, however, high A-state subjects on
the STAI had higher systolic blood pressure than medium and
low A-state subjects, and high A-trait subjects and high-MAS
scorers had higher diastolic blood pressure than medium
scorers.   Somewhat surprisingly, the diastolic blood
pressure of low scorers on the A-trait scale and the MAS was
as high as that of high-anxiety subjects, possibly because
low-anxiety subjects tend to avoid anxiety-evoking situations
and so have not developed coping mechanisms to handle stress.
Rappaport and Katkin (1972) recorded the GSRs of high- and
low-MAS scorers during a non-stressful situation or during
exposure to ego-involving stress.   There was no GSR
difference as a function of anxiety in the absence of stress,
but high-anxiety subjects showed a significant increase in
GSR rate under stress compared to low-anxiety subjects.
Bull and Nethercott (1972) found that anxiety was unrelated to
basal heart rate, but negatively related to physiological
recovery after performing the Harvard Step Test.

   Some studies have found no significant relationships
between anxiety and physiological measures.   For example,
Katkin (1965) found no difference in GSR between high- and
low-anxiety scorers on the MAS, under conditions of rest or
of threat of electric shock.   Kilpatrick (1972)
investigated the tonic and phasic electrodermal activity of
high and low A-trait subjects selected on the basis of STAI
scores.   The subjects performed a complex cognitive task
after neutral or stressful instructions, but no physiological
differences between the high- and low-anxiety subjects were
obtained.

   In the electrodermal research, three measures of arousal
have been proposed: level of skin conductance, number of
spontaneous fluctuations, and amplitude of the skin
conductance response elicited by specific stimuli.   Stern
and Janes (1973) surveyed 20 studies, and found that none of
these measures correlated with trait anxiety.   Some of the
negative findings may have been due to absence of stress in
the experimental settings of some of the investigations.
For example, Koepke and Pribram (1966) recorded spontaneous
fluctuations in a non-stressful situation, and Neva and

Hicks (1970) measured spontaneous fluctuations in high- and low-MAS scorers during induced muscle tension, which would hardly seem to constitute an emotion-arousing situation.

Nielsen and Petersen (1976) may have induced some stress in their subjects by presenting white noise at 105 db. They found that subjects scoring high on Willoughby's measure of trait anxiety showed more spontaneous fluctuations and had a higher skin conductance level. Furthermore, the neuroticism scale of the EPI correlated positively with the number of spontaneous fluctuations.

It is doubtful whether most of the studies have used the most appropriate methodology. Martin and Sroufe (1970), in their review of the evidence, concluded:-

> The implications are (1) that the individual's characteristic pattern of autonomic response must be taken into account before degree of anxiety relative to other individuals can be inferred, and (2) that relative changes in different autonomic responses within the same individual tend to be correlated, and each response may have some validity for reflecting anxiety level (p. 225).

In one of the better studies, Mandler, Mandler, Kremen, and Sholitan (1961) obtained non-significant correlations between the MAS and 11 individual autonomic measures. However, when each subject's highest autonomic response was used as his score, this correlated +.60 with the MAS score.

In spite of the apparent inconsistency of the findings, it does appear to be the case that high-anxiety subjects are more likely to be more physiologically aroused than low-anxiety subjects under stressful conditions than under resting or non-stressful conditions (e.g., Bull & Nethercott, 1972; Forrest & Kroth, 1971; Nielsen & Petersen, 1976; Rappaport & Katkin, 1972). In other words, the physiological evidence suggests that anxious people are not chronically highly aroused, but are so only in certain situations. Saltz's (1970) hypothesis that high-anxiety subjects are more sensitive to ego-threat, whereas low-anxiety subjects are sensitive to pain would suggest that those high in trait anxiety should be more physiologically aroused than low-anxiety subjects when ego-threatened but not when shocked. The findings of Katkin (1965) and Rappaport and Katkin (1972) are consistent with this hypothesis, but those of Forrest and

Kroth (1971) are not.

In a recent study, Glover and Cravens (1974) required
high-anxiety and low-anxiety subjects to participate in a
complex verbal learning task under neutral conditions, pain
stress, or failure stress. As might be expected on Saltz'
hypothesis, the high-anxiety subjects exposed to failure and
the low-anxiety subjects exposed to pain showed the lowest
levels of learning. The state-anxiety scale of the STAI
indicated that the state-anxiety scores of high-anxiety
subjects exposed to failure were elevated in comparison with
the neutral controls, whereas the scores of low-anxiety
subjects in the failure condition were not. Surprisingly,
pain stress did not affect the anxiety-state scores of either
anxiety group.

A more extensive review of the evidence on Saltz'
hypothesis is given by Spielberger (1972). A possible
interpretation of these results is provided by Shedletsky and
Endler (1974). They argued that trait anxiety is complex
and multi-dimensional, and that measuring instruments such
as the MAS and the trait-anxiety scale of the STAI are the
outcomes of an over-simplified, uni-dimensional, approach.
They concluded as follows: "Trait anxiety must be viewed as
encompassing threat of physical danger and ambiguity in
addition to interpersonal threat" (p. 524).

Arousal, Anxiety, and Learning
Several investigators have assumed that high-anxiety
subjects are more aroused than low-anxiety subjects, and that
theoretical statements about the effects of arousal will
extrapolate to anxiety. For example, Easterbrook (1959)
hypothesized that high levels of arousal are associated with
a restricted range of cue utilization. Zaffy and Bruning
(1966) related Easterbrook's hypothesis to learning
performance of high- and low-anxiety subjects. They gave
subjects a learning task in the presence of no cues,
irrelevant cues, or relevant ones. They contended that the
reduction of cue utilization in high-anxiety subjects would
mean that their performance would be less affected by the
additional cues than would the performance of low-anxiety
subjects. As predicted, the enhancement effect of relevant
cues and the detrimental effect of irrelevant cues were
greater in low-anxiety subjects.

Further evidence was obtained by Miller and Dost (1964),
who required their subjects to sort words into their
alphabetical order, under either incidental or intentional
learning conditions.   With instructions only to
alphabetize the words, high-anxiety subjects alphabetized
more efficiently than low-anxiety subjects, but showed less
incidental learning.   Conversely, when subsequently
instructed to learn the words while sorting, high-anxiety
subjects showed a greater disruption in sorting speed than
did low-anxiety subjects, but a greater improvement in the
number of words learned.   These findings are consistent with
the notion that anxiety, like arousal, leads to attentional
narrowing.

Mueller (1976a), as we have seen, has attempted to extend
Easterbrook's hypothesis, arguing that anxious or aroused
subjects will utilize fewer of the available attributes in
encoding stimuli for memory.   He found in several
experiments that high-anxiety subjects demonstrated less
semantic clustering in free recall than low-anxiety subjects.
The linkage between anxiety and arousal in this case is
strengthened by an experiment performed by Hörmann and
Osterkamp (1966), in which they found that white noise
significantly reduced clustering in free recall.

The Spence-Spence model can be regarded in some ways as an
elaboration of the Yerkes-Dodson Law (Broadhurst, 1959).
This hypothesis argues that there is an inverted U-shaped
function relating motivation or arousal and performance, with
intermediate levels of arousal being associated with the
highest levels of performance.   In addition, it was
suggested that the optimal level of arousal decreased as
task difficulty increased.   While Spence and Spence believed
that the number and strength of competing responses were more
important determinants of performance than task difficulty
per se, the general similarity of the two hypotheses is
obvious.   Indeed, Malmo (1957) argued that most of the data
obtained with the MAS could be satisfactorily explained by
assuming that the relationship between drive and performance
takes the form of an inverted-U.   However, the Yerkes-Dodson
Law is a purely descriptive statement of the anticipated
empirical relationships among three variables, and is in need
of theoretical underpinning of the kind provided by Spence
and Spence (1966).   The important point to note is the
general similarity of results between studies investigating
anxiety and studies investigating arousal more directly (e.g.,

Courts, 1942; Wood & Hokanson, 1965).

One of the major theories relating arousal and memory is Walker's (1958) action-decrement theory. This theory, which was discussed in more detail in Chapter 8, predicts that low arousal should be associated with better recall than high arousal at short retention intervals, but that high arousal should lead to better recall at long retention intervals. A reasonable prediction is that there should be an interaction between anxiety and retention interval under ego threat, with high anxiety leading to poor short-term retention but to good long-term retention. In spite of the prevalent assumption that high-anxiety subjects are more aroused than low-anxiety subjects, there appears to be little work linking Walker's theory with anxiety.

H. J. Eysenck (1973) has suggested that a complex relationship exists between anxiety and arousal. He noted that the MAS correlates with both extraversion and neuroticism, and argued that arousal should be separated into two components, cortical arousal (identified with personality differences in extraversion) and autonomic activation (identified with personality differences in neuroticism). More specifically, he proposed that introversion was responsible for the drive properties of high-anxiety subjects, whereas neuroticism, when aroused through some manipulation of the experimental situation, produced the drive stimuli that led to task-irrelevant performance. The evidence certainly indicates that individual differences in neuroticism are commonly less important in determining retention-test performance than are differences in extraversion, as this theory seems to imply. Moreover, there is some evidence that the introversion component of the MAS is primarily responsible for the performance differences of high-anxiety and low-anxiety subjects (e.g., Willoughby, 1967).

A related, but somewhat different, explanation for the fact that introversion-extraversion is a more generally important determinant of memory than is neuroticism or anxiety is favoured by the author. The optimal-level theory, which argues that the optimal level of arousal is lower in introverts than extraverts, but that introverts and extraverts are usually equally aroused physiologically, leads to the prediction that introverts and extraverts will usually be at different distances from optimal arousal, and will thus

perform differently.   On the other hand, the main effect of
high trait anxiety or high neuroticism is to increase the
arousing effects of situational threat.   Thus anxiety should
not affect learning and memory when situational threat is not
involved.   Furthermore, since a mood or state of anxiety is
associated with more substantial conscious awareness than is
true of an introverted mood or state, it may well be that a
major consequence of state anxiety is to distract attention
away from the to-be-learned material.   The evidence relevant
to this hypothesis is considered in the next section.

Direction-of-attention Theory

A plausible interpretation of some of the detrimental
effects of anxiety upon learning and memory was originally
proposed by Mandler and Sarason (1952).   They distinguished
between task-relevant responses and self-oriented responses,
the latter representing a class of generalized responses
which are readily evoked in a test situation, and which
interfere with the learning of specific task-relevant
responses.   According to Mandler and Sarason, these self-
oriented responses "may be manifested as feelings of
inadequacy, helplessness, heightened somatic reaction,
anticipations of punishment or loss of status and esteem, and
implicit attempts at leaving the test situation" (p. 166).
Theoretically, it was assumed that high-anxiety subjects
produced substantially more of these task-irrelevant responses
than low-anxiety subjects, and that attention was thereby
distracted from the to-be-learned material.   In order to
examine these hypotheses, Mandler and Sarason devised a Test
Anxiety Questionnaire (TAQ), on the argument that a test
relating specifically to the subject's reactions to testing
situations would be more predictive than a general anxiety
questionnaire of his performance in such situations.

Evidence that the incidence of self-oriented responses is
related to anxiety was obtained by Mandler and Watson (1966).
They administered a series of digit-symbol tasks to groups of
low- and high-TAQ scorers.   In response to the post-
experimental question, "How often during the testing did you
find yourself thinking how well, or how badly, you seemed to
be doing" (p. 276), high test-anxiety subjects reported
markedly greater occurrence of such thoughts than did the low
test-anxiety subjects.   Neale and Katahn (1968) replicated
these results.

Ganzer (1968) considered the effects of audience presence
and test anxiety on serial learning. A record was kept of
the frequency and content of all of the subject's task-
irrelevant comments while they were working on the task.
The main finding was that "high TAS (Test Anxiety Scale)
scorers, especially in the Observed condition, emitted more
than any other group. Content analysis revealed that the
comments were mostly of a self-evaluative or apologetic
nature" (p. 194).

Liebert and Morris (1967) and Doctor and Altman (1969)
noted that factor-analytic investigation of the TAQ indicated
that test anxiety comprised the two separable components of
worry and emotionality. Worry was conceptualized as
cognitive expression of concern about one's level of
performance, whereas emotionality referred to the autonomic
arousal aspect of anxiety. Doctor and Altman asked their
subjects to answer worry and emotionality items from the TAQ
in terms of their current feelings immediately prior to an
important examination. While both worry and emotionality
were negatively correlated with examination performance,
worry was the stronger determinant of poor performance.

Similarly, Morris and Liebert (1970) found that
correlations between worry scores and final examination
grades, with emotionality partialled out, were negative and
significant. Correlations between emotionality scores and
grades, with worry partialled out, were non-significant. It
is plausible to assume that worry exerts its detrimental
effect on performance by distracting attention away from
task-relevant sources of information.

Wine (1971) has reviewed some of the evidence favouring
an attentional interpretation of the detrimental effects of
anxiety on learning, and she mentioned an interesting
unpublished study conducted by her on test-anxious students.
Three forms of treatment of test anxiety were compared: self-
explorational; attentional; and attentional plus relaxation.
The attentional condition involved giving the subjects
intensive practice in dealing with test anxiety, accompanied
by instructions to focus fully on the tasks and to try to
inhibit self-relevant thinking. The attentional training
produced significant positive changes on questionnaire
measures of test-related anxiety, the Wonderlic Personnel
Tests, and a digit-symbol test, and these changes were not
increased by adding relaxation training. The self-

explorational condition did not affect any of the measures.

In sum, there is a reasonable amount of evidence
indicating that a state of anxiety is attention-demanding,
and that acquisition of to-be-learned material by the highly
anxious subject is detrimentally affected by a division of
attention between self-relevant and task-relevant information.
One consequence of the attentional lability of highly anxious
subjects would presumably be a high level of behavioural
variability, and several investigators have noted a
relationship between anxiety and variability.   For example,
Fiske (1957) found that behavioural variability was
associated with being rated, both by the self and by
observers, as anxious, depressed, retiring, and detached.

However, while it is clear that anxiety increases the
incidence of self-evaluative thoughts, there is no compelling
evidence that this actually causes performance decrement.
An attentional account of the adverse effects which anxiety
has on task performance would be more persuasive if
experimental paradigms permitting more direct measurement of
attention were utilized.   One prediction from an attentional
hypothesis is that most of the time the rate of information
acquisition should be unaffected by anxiety.   Only during
those time periods when anxious subjects are generating self-
evaluative thoughts should anxiety exert a detrimental effect
on learning.

Semantic Memory

Since the Spence-Spence model hypothesizes that anxiety
affects performance rather than learning, the use of semantic
memory tasks would seem to be relevant when evaluating the
model.   However, the findings are somewhat sparse and
inconsistent.   Three main predictions seem to follow from
the Spence-Spence model as applied to word association data.
The first is that high-anxiety subjects should produce more
dominant, or primary, word associations than low-anxiety
subjects.   The second is that high-anxiety subjects should
respond faster than low-anxiety subjects.   The third is that
high-anxiety subjects should produce more associations than
low-anxiety subjects in continuous word association.

In fact, none of these predictions has been satisfactorily
confirmed.   Jenkins (1960) found that the number of primary
responses on the word-association test was negatively related

to an overall measure of maladjustment derived from the MMPI.
Nakamura and Wright (1965) found no difference in response
commonality as a function of differences in MAS score.
Sarason (1959) observed that situational stress created by
emphasizing the evaluative aspects of the word-association
test situation produced relatively low commonality scores
among high test-anxiety subjects. Kanfer (1960) reported
that high-anxiety and low-anxiety subjects on the MAS did not
differ in terms of the number of primary associates produced.
Innes (1972) obtained a significant negative relationship
between the neuroticism scale of the EPI and the number of
primary associates produced.

The variability in the findings may be due to the relative
lack of experimental control present in the word-association
test situation.   Subjects are free to adopt a variety of
retrieval strategies, and also have the choice as to whether
to emit the first associate retrieved.   More consistent
results might be obtained if there were more experimental
constraint over the type of associate to be produced (e.g.,
synonyms, antonyms, etc.).   The assumption that the primary
associate as indicated by word association norms is the
dominant or strongest associate for both high- and low-
anxiety subjects may be in error.   It might well be more
interesting to consider the speed of emission of associates.

With the method of continuous word association, the results
are more encouraging.   Davids and Eriksen (1955) found a
significant positive correlation between MAS score and the
number of associations produced.   Johnson and Lim (1964)
found that high-anxiety subjects showed a greater tendency to
produce more associations to words rated as 'good' than to
those rated as 'bad' than did low-anxiety subjects, a result
replicated by Innes (1971).   Innes also found that high-
anxiety subjects produced more cohesive associative clusters
with positively evaluated words than with negatively
evaluated words, whereas low-anxiety subjects showed equal
cohesion with both sets of words.

In verbal fluency tasks, subjects are required to produce
as many exemplars of a specified category (e.g., articles of
furniture) as they can as rapidly as possible.   The prediction from the Spence-Spence model is that more responses will
be above threshold for high-anxiety than for low-anxiety
subjects.   The evidence does not appear to support this
prediction.   Gewirtz (1948) found no relationship between the

personality variables of emotional control and emotional excitability on the one hand and verbal fluency on the other. DiScipio (1971a) observed no main effect of neuroticism on word fluency, but there was a significant interaction between extraversion and neuroticism, in which stable extraverts were more fluent than neurotic extraverts, but stable introverts were less fluent than neurotic introverts. M. W. Eysenck (1974a) noted that word fluency was not affected by neuroticism, nor was it affected by scores on the high-activation scale of Thayer's ADACL, a state measure related to anxiety. Thus there is very little evidence that anxiety is positively related to verbal fluency. Indeed, as we saw in Chapter 9, it is primarily extraversion which has been found to be associated with fluency.

Since normal speech requires the retrieval of information from semantic memory, it may prove fruitful to examine the speech patterns of anxious and non-anxious people. Ramsay (1968) found no difference in the length of silence between utterances as a function of neuroticism. Lalljee and Cook (1975) discovered that the incidence of ritualized speech (e.g., 'I mean') increased when subjects were discussing anxiety-evoking topics, possibly because anxiety reduces the speed with which information can be retrieved from semantic memory.

It is surprising that so little work has been done on anxiety differences in semantic memory. The great advantage of investigating semantic memory is that individual differences in performance are unlikely to be due to encoding or storage factors, but are presumably due to retrieval or response criterion factors.

Summary

The emphasis in the literature on introversion-extraversion and anxiety has been justified by the discovery of several replicable findings and by the theoretical relationships between these variables and physiology. Logically, it seems preferable to start by working with large, second-order factors, such as introversion-extraversion and anxiety, rather than with small, inconsistent first-order factors.

As with the work on extraversion, the major inadequacy of

the research on anxiety has been the failure to determine
more precisely the effects of anxiety on the various
information-processing stages.   It is very surprising, for
example, that so few of the considerable number of studies
done to test the theories of Spence (1958) and of Spence and
Spence (1966) have directly evaluated the notion that anxiety
affects only the retrieval stage.   Recent work has indicated
that anxiety affects the amount of encoding (e.g., Holdges &
Spielberger, 1969; Pyke & Agnew, 1963), the type of
encoding (e.g., Bartel et al., 1972; Mueller, 1976a), the
speed of retrieval (Straughan & Dufort, 1969), and response
caution (Goulet & Mazzei, 1969).   Since, broadly speaking,
the effects of anxiety on all these factors is to reduce
performance, it is obvious that merely finding detrimental
effects of anxiety on performance is unrevealing about the
exact processes involved.

There are tantalizing similarities among the results
obtained from studies of arousal, introversion-extraversion,
and anxiety, and theories such as those of Yerkes and Dodson
(1908), Easterbrook (1959), and Walker (1958) all seem
applicable to some extent to the different sets of studies.
One of the advantages of considering work in all three areas
is that this allows for cross-fertilization.   For example,
an obviously interesting study could evaluate the relevance
of Walker's hypothesis to anxiety.

In spite of the similarities, it is probable that
important differences could be found if they were looked for.
Wachtel (1967) drew a distinction between the breadth of
allocation of attention and the stability of allocation over
time, and there is some evidence (Callaway & Stone, 1960)
that arousal decreases both the breadth and the stability of
attention.   Perhaps introversion primarily affects the
breadth of attention, whereas anxiety affects both the
breadth and the stability of attention.   The notion that
anxiety increases the lability of attention is supported by
the evidence (Wine, 1971) that anxiety leads subjects to
attend both to task-relevant and task-irrelevant information
(e.g., feelings of inadequacy).

CHAPTER 11

AGEING AND MEMORY

There are two major problems that confront the researcher investigating the effects of age on learning and memory, one methodological and the other interpretative. The methodological problem is that the easiest, and most frequently used, experimental approach to the study of ageing is the cross-sectional method, in which different age groups are tested at the same point in time. With this approach, differences among the various age groups could be due to actual effects of age, to generation or cohort differences, or to a combination of both. This problem can be solved along the lines proposed by Schaie (1970) and Schaie and Strother (1968), by re-examining a cross-sectional sample after a reasonable interval of time. This cross-sectional method allows one to unconfound age and cohort differences. Schaie and Strother concluded that most of the cross-sectional differences which they obtained represented differences between cohorts rather than true age changes. Until experimenters regularly use the cross-sequential method, conclusions about age differences must remain tentative.

The interpretative problem stems from the fact that chronological age, while undoubtedly a powerful variable, has the disadvantage of being non-psychological in nature and of failing to be under experimental control. Since individuals differ in personality, motivation, health, and cognitive processes as a function of age, a simple demonstration of age-related changes is of little value. Moreover, different studies have employed various samples of old subjects, ranging from highly intelligent 55-year-olds to senile 90-year-olds. In general, age-related changes are much more likely to be found with older and less able samples, so that age-related deficits are more interesting if obtained with intelligent subjects of late middle age.

In spite of the problems, a number of replicable findings have been obtained. A selective review of these findings is

245

to be found in this chapter, together with a more theoretical
discussion of some of the main hypotheses that have been
advanced.   More detailed summaries of the relevant
literature are available elsewhere (e.g., Arenberg, 1973;
Botwinick, 1973; M. W. Eysenck, 1974d).

Experimental Findings

Short-term Memory

A considerable variety of experimental techniques has been
used to study age differences in short-term memory (STM),
using the term STM in the atheoretical sense to refer to
situations in which there is a short input-output interval.
The techniques used include dichotic listening tasks,
single-channel tasks, free recall, digit span, the Brown-
Peterson technique, running memory span, and the Hebb
paradigm.   Details of these paradigms and the relevant
findings are given by M. W. Eysenck (1974d).

The major finding (or non-finding) has been that there are
few effects of age on STM performance.   An absence of age
changes in performance has been found, at least under certain
conditions, for the primary memory component of free recall
(Craik, 1968a), the running memory span (Talland, 1967), the
Brown-Peterson task (Keevil-Rogers & Schnore, 1969;
Kriaiciunas, 1968; Talland, 1967), memory span (Bromley,
1958; Drachman & Leavitt, 1972; Gilbert, 1941; Gilbert &
Levee, 1971).   Other studies of memory span (Taub, 1968,
1972b; Taub & Grieff, 1967; Taub & Walker, 1970) and those
on dichotic listening tasks (Caird, 1966; Craik, 1965; Inglis, 1964, 1965; Inglis & Ankus, 1965; Inglis & Caird,
1963; Mackay & Inglis, 1963) have found no age-related
deficits with the stimuli recalled first, but have found
significant effects of age on the stimuli recalled second.

Age decrements are more pronounced with visual
presentation of the material than with auditory presentation
(McGhie, Chapman, & Lawson, 1965; Taub, 1972a).   The
effects of rate of presentation are variable: Fraser (1958)
found that old subjects were only at a disadvantage with slow
rates of presentation, whereas Taub (1966, 1968, 1972a)
found that both age groups showed equivalent improvement with
a reduction in the rate of presentation.   In another
experiment, Taub (1972a) found that old subjects recalled
better with a slow rate of presentation, whereas young

subjects recalled better with a fast rate of presentation.
Since the effects of presentation rate are variable, and the
differences that variations in the presentation rate have on
decay, rehearsal, and other processing strategies are
unknown, little can be concluded about the effects of
presentation rate.

The most general conclusion that can be drawn from these
studies is that ageing has little effect on the ability to
retain information over short intervals of time.   However,
if the subjects must recall some of the information while
simultaneously retaining the rest of the information, then an
age deficit in retention of the last-recalled items is found.
Unfortunately, few of the studies have investigated the
processing strategies of young and old subjects in STM tasks,
so that it is not known whether young and old subjects are
processing the stimuli in comparable fashion, nor is it
known whether the various STM tasks used require similar
forms of information processing.   Shulman (1970) argued that
phonemic features of the input are encoded more rapidly than
semantic features, and that the fast rates of presentation
used in STM tasks lead subjects to concentrate on phonemic
processing.   Shulman (1971) reviewed the experimental
evidence on coding processes in the STM of young adults,
and concluded that phonemic processing is usually importantly
involved in STM tasks.   Thus a reasonable hypothesis is that
young and old subjects are equally capable of phonemically
encoding to-be-learned information (M. W. Eysenck, 1974b),
but that old subjects are more susceptible to interference,
particularly when two tasks must be performed simultaneously.

Evidence that the nature of the encoding processes may be
an important factor in determining whether or not there are
age-related changes in STM comes in a study by Heron and
Craik (1964).   They equated young and old groups on digit
span in the Finnish language, and then investigated age-
related differences in digit span in the subjects' native
language of English.   In this latter condition, old subjects
were significantly inferior to young subjects, possibly
because old subjects were less able than young subjects to
use the greater organizational and encoding opportunities
afforded by the more meaningful material.

Paired-associate and Serial Learning
Several studies of paired-associate learning (e.g.,

Arenberg, 1965, 1967a, 1967b; Canestrari, 1963, 1968) and
serial learning (e.g., Eisdorfer, 1965, 1968; Eisdorfer,
Axelrod, & Wilkie, 1963) have found that older subjects are
significantly inferior to younger subjects in speed of
learning.   However, the age deficit is attenuated when
either presentation time or the time available for responding
is increased.   More specifically, various studies have
indicated that a shorter anticipation interval (decreased
response time) rather than a shorter presentation interval
(decreased association time) is responsible for lowered
performance in the elderly (Canestrari, 1963; Eisdorfer
et al., 1963; Hulicka, Sterns, & Grossman, 1967; Monge &
Hultsch, 1971).   It is clearly possible to practice recall
during the presentation of an item, and to learn during the
anticipation interval, so that we cannot assume that learning
takes place only during presentation and retrieval only
during the anticipation interval.   It would appear that the
differential effects of presentation- and anticipation-
interval variations on young and old subjects will only be
clarified by studies more directly investigating the nature
of the processes occurring during these intervals.
However, the evidence is consistent with the notion that
old subjects require longer to retrieve stored information
than young subjects.

Several studies have found that old subjects make more
omission and fewer commission errors than young subjects
(e.g., Taub, 1967).   This suggests that old subjects are
more cunning or cautious in their production of responses.
Leech and Witte (1971) rewarded some of their old subjects
for making commission errors, and found that this had the
effect of reducing omission errors and facilitating learning.
Unfortunately Leech and Witte did not test young subjects, so
it is not known whether rewarding commission errors would
reduce the age deficit in learning.   However, the hypothesis
that old subjects are more cautious than young subjects
merits further research.

Most of the studies of paired-associate and serial
learning differ from the STM studies in that more material
was presented for learning, the retention intervals were
longer, the presentation rate was slower, and more
meaningful material was presented.   While few attempts have
been made to isolate which of these factors is responsible
for the different results obtained in the two sets of studies,
there is evidence (e.g., Hulicka & Grossman, 1967; Hulicka,

Sterns, & Grossman, 1967) that semantic and imaginal
processing is associated with rapid learning of paired
associates, so that an intriguing hypothesis is that ageing
does not affect phonemic processing, and thus age changes in
STM are not obtained, whereas ageing does have a detrimental
effect on semantic and imaginal processing, so that age
deficits in paired-associate and serial learning are found.
This hypothesis is discussed at greater length later in this
chapter.

Semantic Memory

Most of the few studies on age changes in semantic memory
have either considered the size of vocabulary as a function
of age, or have measured various aspects of word fluency.
Tests of vocabulary commonly reveal few or no changes with
advancing age (Fox, 1947; Lewinski, 1948; Shakow &
Goldman, 1938; Thorndike & Gallup, 1941).   Some studies
have even found progressive improvement in vocabulary size up
to the age of sixty or so (e.g., Garfield & Blek, 1952;
Trembly, 1964).   Although it is of interest to note the
virtual absence of age differences in vocabulary across the
adult life-span, interpretation of this finding is difficult,
since the relevant learning experiences of the subjects are
completely beyond the control of the experimenter.   However,
the considerably greater exposure to language which old
people have had probably enables them to compensate for their
general deterioration in performance.

Studies of word or verbal fluency have usually involved
tasks requiring subjects to produce as many words as possible
satisfying some constraint (e.g., belonging to a particular
category).   Vocabulary-test scores are frequently used to
equate young and old groups on storage of information in
semantic memory.   Several of these studies have obtained
significant age-related decrements in performance (Bilash &
Zubek, 1960; Birren, 1955; Birren, Riegel, & Robbin, 1962;
Riegel, 1959; Riegel & Birren, 1966; Schaie, 1958;
Strother, Schaie, & Horst, 1957).   Schaie and Strother
(1968) found substantial decrements in performance with
increasing age on both a cross-sectional and a longitudinal
analysis of their data.

There are some methodological and interpretative problems
in these studies on fluency.   For instance, the slower
writing speed of the older subjects may have been a factor in

their low levels of performance.   Drachman and Leavitt
(1972) required oral recall of words in each of five
categories of nouns, and found no significant decrement with
age.   Another possibility is that the greater cautiousness
of old people (e.g., Slater & Scarr, 1964) may make them more
liable to scan their previous responses to ensure that they
do not repeat themselves, in which case older subjects have
less time available for retrieval.   Additionally, recall
involves the retrieval of information as well as a decision
as to the appropriateness of what is retrieved (Kintsch,
1970).   The inferior performance of old subjects in verbal
fluency tasks could be due to a slowing of the retrieval
process, the decision process, or both.

In a recent study, M. W. Eysenck (1975a) attempted to
distinguish between the retrieval and decision components of
performance in semantic memory tasks.   His results indicated
that older people perform the search and retrieval processes
as fast, or faster, than young subjects, but require longer
to make decisions.   Additional evidence for a slowing of the
decision process with age in semantic-memory tasks comes
from a study by Fozard, Nuttall, and Waugh (1972), in which
they found a small but significant decline in vocabulary on a
timed, multiple-choice, test with increasing age.

If the findings from studies of paired-associate and
serial learning can be taken as illustrative of the effects
of ageing on episodic memory, then episodic memory is more
affected by age than is semantic memory.   However, Tulving's
(1972) distinction between episodic and semantic memory is
related to other conceptual distinctions.   For example,
Cattell (1943) distinguished between fluid and crystallized
ability, and M. D. Eysenck (1945, 1946) applied this
conceptualization to her innovative findings in work on cases
of senile dementia.   One of her major findings was that
deterioration was more marked with fluid ability than with
crystallized ability.   While the precise relationship
between the semantic-episodic and the crystallized-fluid
dichotomies is unclear, the more general applicability of the
crystallized-fluid distinction suggests that subsequent work
on ageing and memory should continue the extremely promising
line of work initiated by M. D. Eysenck.

Learning and Retention

In the great majority of the early studies on ageing and memory, it is impossible to determine whether the low levels of performance obtained by the older subjects are attributable to inadequate registration of the input (i.e., poor learning) or to a high level of forgetting during the retention interval. The distinction clearly has some importance, since attempts to improve the memory of old people would vary according to whether learning or retention defects were suspected. Experimentally, assessments of the relation between ageing and retention have usually involved an attempt to base age-group comparisons upon material which has been learned to an equivalent extent by the various age groups. However, several methodological problems are involved in the attempt to equalize the initial degree of learning (Goulet, 1972).

The first problem is that age is negatively correlated with speed of learning throughout the adult life-span, so that older subjects typically require several learning trials more than younger subjects in order to reach the same criterion of mastery. The conventional method of continuing the learning trials to a criterion of one perfect repetition of the to-be-remembered material has the disadvantage that no account is taken of the 'overlearning' that may occur after an item can be recalled with a probability of one.

An alternative approach, proposed by Underwood (1964), is to equate samples on the degree of projected learning, discontinuing the learning trials before list mastery has occurred. One problem here is that increases in performance in a learning task over trials will reflect both a specific transfer component from earlier trials with the same materials, and a non-specific transfer component, due to increased general familiarity with the requirements of the task. The equating of different age groups on projected learning may reflect nothing other than the pooled but differential effects of these two components at each age for which retention is being measured.

Furthermore, all studies which have attempted to equate the extent to which the material has been learned by various age groups have concentrated solely on the quantitative aspects of learning (i.e., the number of items correctly

recalled). However, there is strong evidence that the
learning processes of elderly and young subjects may be
qualitatively different, with elderly subjects less likely to
utilize imaginal and verbal mediators than young subjects
(e.g., Canestrari, 1968; Hulicka & Grossman, 1967).   If,
for example, old and young subjects both learn the
consonant string CPFC to criterion, but significantly more of
the young subjects have stored this string as 'Crystal Palace
Football Club', then the similarity of performance would
seem to be concealing an important difference in what has
actually been learned.

Finally, it must be noted that learning is being indexed
in terms of performance, and it would almost certainly be
incorrect to suppose that a one-to-one correspondence exists
between learning and performance.   It may be that the
relationship between learning and performance differs as a
function of age; speculatively, the allegedly greater
cautiousness of the elderly might mean that performance
becomes an increasingly inadequate index of learning as a
function of age.

Some of the problems can be overcome by appropriate
experimental controls.   For example, sufficient prior
practice on tasks similar to the critical task can reduce the
impact of non-specific transfer effects by ensuring that all
groups have reached the asymptote of learning-to-learn.
Similarly, the use of instructions telling all subjects to
use verbal or imaginal mediators, or the supplying of these
by the experimenter, should help to reduce qualitative
differences in what is learned by subjects of different age
groups.

The modal experimental finding is that there are no age
changes in retention, provided that young and old subjects
are equated for learning (Davis & Obrist, 1966; Desroches,
Kaiman, & Ballard, 1966; Gladis & Braun, 1958; Hulicka,
1965; Hulicka & Weiss, 1965; Moenster, 1972; Wimer &
Wigdor, 1958).   Furthermore, there is some evidence (e.g.,
Wickelgren, 1975a) that there are no age differences in the
rate of forgetting even when the various groups of subjects
are not equated for learning.   In addition, Suci, Davidoff,
and Braun (1962) found age changes in retention under an
interference condition, but no age changes under control
conditions, and Wimer (1960) and Hulicka and Rust (1964)
observed that young subjects showed superior retention to old

subjects.   It is unfortunate that little attention has been
paid to the processing strategies used by the subjects in
these studies.   It is possible that the task used in many of
the studies (paired-associate learning of unrelated items)
is learned in rote fashion by young and old subjects.   In
the Hulicka and Rust and Wimer studies, however, the young
subjects processed the material in more complex ways than the
old subjects, and this difference in processing may well have
produced the age differences in retention.   A testable
hypothesis is that age changes in retention will only be
found on learning tasks where there are age-related
differences in processing strategies.   With tasks requiring
complex processing, such as paragraph-memory tasks, age
differences in retention would be expected, whereas there
would be no age differences in retention of a digit- or letter
series.

Theoretical Considerations

   Age differences in learning and retention certainly arise
from a multiplicity of causes.   However, three of the major
theoretical approaches have emphasized different causal
factors.   Processing-deficit hypotheses argue that age-
related decrements in learning and retention are due
primarily to the unwillingness or inability of old subjects
to process the to-be-remembered material as thoroughly as
young subjects.   Retrieval-deficit hypotheses argue that
ageing is associated principally with increased difficulty
in the retrieval of stored information.   Motivational
hypotheses argue that the motivational level of old subjects
in learning situations is supra-optimal.   While these three
theoretical approaches are considered separately, it is
clear that they are not mutually exclusive.   For example,
supra-optimal motivation will presumably manifest itself
either in a processing deficit or a retrieval deficit, and it
is possible that old subjects experience both processing and
retrieval deficits.

Processing-deficit Hypotheses
   It has frequently been assumed (e.g., Craik, 1968b;
Hultsch, 1969, 1971) that older subjects are less able than
younger subjects to organize or structure to-be-learned
material.   A more general version of this hypothesis was
provided by M. W. Eysenck (1974b), who suggested that older

subjects are inferior to younger subjects at the more complex
forms of information processing, including semantic,
conceptual, and imaginal processing.   Since the degree, or
depth, of information processing is a major determinant of
retention (Craik & Lockhart, 1972), this hypothesis provides
a potential explanation for age-related deficits in
retention.   This hypothesis has been investigated in three
separate ways.   The first approach relies upon the use of
dependent variables to measure the nature of processing, over
and above the conventional dependent variables of correct
responses and trials to criterion.   The second approach
attempts to induce various types of processing by means of
appropriate instructional manipulations.   The third
approach compares age effects on different tasks which differ
in their processing requirements and potentialities.   The
first two approaches have frequently been considered in the
same study, so they will be discussed together.

Laurence (1966) found that old subjects showed inferior
free recall of an unrelated word list to young subjects, but
that age had no effect on subjective organization of recall.
She argued that the subjective organization index might not
adequately reflect organizational processes, since rigid
adherence to an invariant order of output would produce a
high subjective organization score.

In contrast, Hultsch (1974) found that old subjects were
significantly inferior to young subjects at subjective
organization of output in a free-recall study.   However,
subjects of all ages obtained higher organization scores on
the second list than on the first, implying that the
processing deficit commonly manifested by old subjects may be
reduced if they have the opportunity to re-acquire some of
the higher-order skills necessary for effective learning.
However, this conclusion may apply only to intelligent, well-
educated subjects such as those used by Hultsch.

Denney (1974) presented her subjects with free-recall
lists.   The middle-aged subjects recalled considerably more
words than the elderly subjects, and also showed much more
categorical clustering.   In fact, the elderly subjects
showed no evidence of clustering.

Rowe and Schnore (1971) found that concrete paired
associates were better recalled than abstract paired
associates by subjects of all ages, but that old subjects had

the lowest level of overall performance. Post-experimental
questioning indicated that old subjects were less likely to
have used verbal or imaginal mediation than the middle-aged
or young subjects.

Hulicka and Grossman (1967) gave their subjects
conventional instructions, imagery instructions,
experimenter-supplied verbal mediators, or experimenter-
supplied verbal mediators plus imagery instructions. The
paired-associate learning performance of the young subjects
was much better than that of the old subjects, and several
findings suggested that this age-related deficit was due, in
part, to a processing deficit. With conventional
instructions, the old subjects reported the use of mediators
only half as often as the young subjects (for 36 per cent
versus 68 per cent of the pairs). Old subjects reported the
use of verbal mediators more frequently than young subjects
(for 26 per cent versus 17 per cent of the pairs). Pairs
learned by mediation were significantly better remembered
than pairs learned without mediation, particularly for the
old subjects. Instructions to use mediators resulted in a
slightly greater percentage improvement in the learning
scores of the old subjects (13.3 per cent versus 6.7 per cent
improvement). It is possible that, given more prolonged
practice, old subjects could be trained to use mediational
techniques with a high degree of efficiency.

Hulicka et al. (1967) informed their subjects that it
would be easier to learn paired associates if an image or
phrase were selected to link the words of each pair together.
As in the Hulicka and Grossman (1967) study, old subjects
were more likely than young subjects to report using verbal
mediation, but considerably less likely to report using
imaginal mediation. Overall, old subjects used mediational
techniques less frequently than young subjects (for 72 per
cent versus 86 per cent of the pairs), and the old subjects
showed a substantial learning deficit.

Canestrari (1968) gave subjects a paired-associate learning
task under control conditions, or with phrases incorporating
the stimulus and response terms, or with drawings
representing the paired associates. While the young
subjects performed equivalently under all conditions, the old
subjects showed greatly improved performance under both
visual and verbal mediator conditions. Presumably a
processing deficit was partially responsible for the poor

performance of the old subjects under the control conditions.

Treat and Reese (1976) found that young subjects outperformed old subjects on a paired-associate learning task when standard instructions were given.   However, instructions to form an interactive image of the two items in each pair led to improved performance, and eliminated the age-related deficit.

Hultsch (1969) gave his subjects a free-recall task. The initial instructions were either conventional, or they stressed the advantages of organizing the information, or they suggested that the list could be organized alphabet-ically.   Young subjects recalled more than middle-aged subjects.   When the subjects were divided into high and low verbal facility groups on the basis of a vocabulary test, there was a significant interaction between age and instructions for the low verbal facility subjects.   In this interaction, the middle-aged subjects were significantly inferior to the young subjects under the conventional and organizational instructions, but not under the alphabetical instructions.   The implication of this finding is that the middle-aged subjects found it more difficult than the young subjects to organize the presented information efficiently unless they were provided with a suitable method of organization.

Hultsch (1971) asked subjects either to inspect a list of words or to sort the words into between two and seven categories prior to free recall.   The sorting condition led to better free recall than the inspection condition, and there was a significant interaction between age and conditions in which old subjects benefited more from the sorting condition.   Mandler (1967) has used the number of sorting categories as an index of organization, but Hultsch found no difference in the number of categories used as a function of age, possibly because most subjects at all ages used six or seven categories.   Additionally, Hultsch used a superior sample with respect to verbal facility and education. While Hultsch claims that the results support the hypothesis that age deficits in free recall can be reduced when organization is facilitated, it should be noted that no evidence was presented as to the extent of organization under the inspection condition.

M. W. Eysenck (1974b) argued that studies using

instructional manipulations in an intentional-learning
paradigm (e.g., Canestrari, 1968; Hulicka & Grossman, 1967)
suffered from the methodological problem that it is
difficult to induce subjects to use sub-optimal learning
strategies.   Furthermore, earlier studies used a restricted
range of instructional conditions.   Accordingly, M. W.
Eysenck (1974b) asked subjects to perform one of four
orienting tasks, followed by an unexpected test for free
recall.   The four tasks involved counting the number of
letters in each word, finding words rhyming with the list
words, finding appropriate modifying adjectives for the list
words, and rating the vividness of the images produced by
each word.   The major finding was a significant interaction
between age and orienting task, in which age had no effect
on recall with the letter-counting and rhyming tasks, but
did with the adjective and imagery tasks (see Fig. 11.1).
The conclusion drawn was that age does not affect low-level
processing, whether orthographic (letter-counting task) or
phonemic (rhyming task), but does affect deep processing,
whether semantic (adjective task) or imaginal (imagery task).

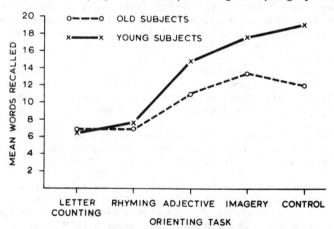

Fig. 11.1. Recall as a function
of age and processing task. Based
on Data in M. W. Eysenck (1974b).

    Lauer (1975) has replicated and extended these findings.
Subjects were instructed to respond to each of a list of
nouns with either its category name, an associated word, a
rhyme, a letter description, or in any manner they wished.

They subsequently received free recall, cued recall, and
recognition tests.   For free and cued recall, the young
were superior to the old on semantic-processing tasks but not
on physical-processing tasks.   The results were rather
different on the recognition test.   The young showed
superior recognition overall, and this was especially marked
on the physical tasks.   She concluded that age deficits are
"localized primarily in deeper semantic levels of processing,
reflecting insufficient elaboration by the elderly of
semantic traces with consequent difficulties in
retrievability" (p. 1).

Three of the studies (Hulicka & Grossman, 1967; Hulicka
et al., 1967; Rowe & Schnore, 1971) have obtained evidence
that old subjects are less likely than young subjects to
report the use of mediational techniques, even when
instructed to employ such techniques.   Old subjects were
particularly reluctant to utilize imaginal mediation.   In
these studies, however, the use of mediational techniques was
inferred from post-experimental questioning of the subjects.
Subjects may forget their learning strategies during the time
interval between learning and post-experimental questioning,
they may claim to have used mediation more frequently than
they actually did (due to the 'demand' characteristics of the
situation), or they may not be completely aware of the
techniques which they have used.   If old subjects report
less use of mediation, it could always be argued that this
merely reflects poorer retention of mediational techniques by
old subjects, rather than less frequent use of mediation.

Those studies which have compared the subjective
organization of young and old groups have often been
unsuccessful in finding age differences.   M. W. Eysenck
(1974b), Hultsch (1971), and Laurence (1966) all found no
difference in organization between young and old groups;
only the Denney (1974) and Hultsch (1974) studies have
obtained an age-related organizational deficit.   However,
M. W. Eysenck and Hultsch both used samples of high verbal
facility, and Laurence suggested that the subjective
organization index she used might be a very imprecise
measure of the organization that occurred.   It may be noted
that most of these studies were concerned with semantically-
based organization.   Since Hulicka and Grossman (1967) and
Hulicka et al. (1967) found that old people were at a
disadvantage to young people with respect to imaginal
mediation rather than verbal, or semantic, mediation, it

would be interesting to investigate free recall for pictures.
Frost (1971) presented young adults with pictures in various
orientations, and found that recall was organized according
to visual similarities. Possibly old subjects would show
little evidence of such a visually-based organizational
ability.

Most of the studies discussed so far indicate that old
subjects are less likely than young subjects to utilize
efficient information-processing strategies under normal
instructional conditions. An important question is whether
or not this processing deficit is reversible when suitable
instructions are given to young and old subjects. The
evidence indicates that the old do have the ability to use
more efficient processes if suitably instructed (Canestrari,
1968; Hulicka & Grossman, 1967; Hultsch, 1969, 1971; Treat
& Reese, 1976).

A number of studies have investigated age differences
across several learning tasks. An obvious difficulty in
accounting for the results of such studies is that it is
extremely hard to specify the critical differences between
the processes involved in different tasks. Two of the main
hypotheses in this area have been put forward by Ruch (1934)
and by Craik (1968b). Ruch predicted that older subjects
would show the least deficit when the task involved learning
which was compatible with habitual behaviour. Craik
hypothesized that old subjects would be at a greater
disadvantage when dealing with material that was highly
amenable to chunking.

Ruch's (1934) subjects learned pairs of logically related
words, nonsense materials (arbitrary equations of the form
E x Z = G), and interference materials (false equations of the
form 3 x 5 = 6). The age-related deficit was greatest for
the interference material, less for the nonsense task, and
least for the familiar word associates. Since the
interference task appeared least compatible with habitual
behaviour and the familiar word associates the most
compatible, Ruch concluded that the experimental results
favoured his hypothesis. However, rather contrary to the
hypothesis, he also found that all age groups performed
better on the interference material than on the nonsense
task.

Korchin and Basowitz (1957) replicated Ruch's (1934) study.

The old group was significantly worse than the young group on all three paired-associate learning tasks. The old subjects were especially at a disadvantage with the nonsense and interference paired associates, but they had no greater difficulty with the interference than with the nonsense paired associates. Further evidence that older subjects find it difficult to re-organize existing habits comes in a study of serial learning by Kay (1951), in which elderly subjects showed considerable difficulty in unlearning their incorrect responses.

Gilbert (1941), in a classic study, took 11 measures of memory from young and old subjects. The smallest age deficits were obtained on digit-span tasks, and on other tasks involving immediate retention. Subsequent retention tests indicated that the age-related deficit was rather greater for paired associates than for the retention of a paragraph. Since a paragraph would seem to be more 'amenable to chunking' than paired associates, this finding is contrary to Craik's (1968b) hypothesis. An additional interesting finding was that the most intelligent old subjects, as measured by the Terman vocabulary test, showed less loss than the old group considered as a whole, not only when compared with the entire young group, but also when compared with a sub-sample of the young group matched for intellectual level.

Somewhat different results emerged from a study by Gilbert and Levee (1971). Although they also found little age-related decrement in digit-span performance, they found a greater deficit in the retention of paragraphs than of paired associates. Performance on a test involving imagery (memory for designs) showed a decline similar to that for paired associates. They concluded, in line with Craik's (1968b) hypothesis, that the greatest age-related loss occurred in that type of meaningful verbal memory which is most frequently encountered in everyday life.

Heron and Craik (1964) matched young and old subjects for their digit span, presenting the digits in a foreign language. The young subjects were significantly better than the old subjects on a subsequent digit-span task in their native language, possibly because the organizational potential was greater with the more familiar material, and the young subjects were better able to exploit it.

Craik and Masani (1967) required their subjects to recall meaningful sentences, scrambled proverbs, and lists of colour names. The relative inferiority of the old subjects was more marked with the meaningful sentences and the scrambled proverbs than with the colour names. Craik (1968b) argued that the colour names were less amenable to chunking or organization than the other learning materials, but there may well be additional salient differences among these three tasks. In a second experiment, Craik and Masani presented strings of words varying in their approximation to English connected discourse, and found that the relative disadvantage of old subjects increased as the word strings became more meaningful, especially for those subjects low in verbal facility. However, the differences in 'meaningfulness' of the various word strings are a complex amalgam of differences in grammaticality, differences in associative relatedness, and differences in semantic coherence (Johnson, 1968). Furthermore, the results might be due to age differences in either storage or retrieval.

In subsequent work using similar materials, Craik and Masani (1969) argued that the number of adopted chunks recalled (i.e., groups of words for which the sequence in recall is the same as at input) could be regarded as an index of retrieval efficiency, whereas the number of words per adopted chunk measured coding efficiency. Since age affected the number of chunks recalled but did not affect the number of words per chunk, Craik and Masani concluded that there are important age-related differences in retrieval.

Craik (1968b) asked for free recall of digits, English county names, animal names, or unrelated words. In spite of apparent differences in amenability to chunking of these various types of material, the interaction between age and type of material was not significant.

Laurence (1967a) found that young and old adults both recalled more words from lists of related than of unrelated words, but the major finding was an age by list type interaction, in which old subjects were at more of a disadvantage on the unrelated lists than on the related ones. She argued that previous learning and experience were more directly relevant to learning the related lists.

Superficially, the various findings seem irreconciliable.

For example, Craik (1968b) has fairly consistently found
that age-related deficits are more pronounced with material
which is familiar and meaningful, whereas Korchin and
Basowitz (1957), Laurence (1967a), and Ruch (1934)
found the opposite.   Additionally, some studies have
compared old and young subjects with respect to their ability
to learn paired-associate lists varying in terms of the
intra-pair associative strength (Canestrari, 1966; Kausler
& Lair, 1966; Ross, 1968; Zaretsky & Halbertstam, 1968).
In all these studies, the old subjects were at a greater
disadvantage with lower associative-strength pairs.   The
implication is that old subjects performed better with the
more meaningful pairs.

Such contradictions are extremely likely to be found in
studies which concentrate on inter-task differences without
any clear conceptualization of the salient ways in which the
processing involved in the various tasks differ from each
other.   The terminology has been quite remarkably loose and
amorphous: tasks apparently differ in their 'meaningfulness',
in their 'amenability to chunking', in the extent to which
they are 'compatible with habitual behaviour', but these
task differences are never unequivocally shown to be the
major aspects of task differences.   Thus, for example,
Gilbert and Levee (1971) argued that a major difference
between paragraph and paired-associate recall was that the
former task used more 'meaningful' material than the latter.
However, the two tasks also differ in intrinsic interest, in
presentation rates, in quantity of information, in
redundancy, in grammaticality, in the subject's freedom to
recall thematically, and so on.

An hypothesis which may offer some scope for reconciling
the various findings starts with the distinction (cf.,
Goulet, 1972) between specific and non-specific transfer.
It is highly probable that subjects in all the learning
situations discussed in this chapter made heavy use of
previously acquired information.   The hypothesis is as
follows: old subjects are considerably less likely than
young subjects to make use of non-specific sources of
transfer (i.e., higher-order habits, skills, and strategies),
but age differences in specific sources of transfer will be
relatively small.   There is much evidence that the old
make less use of non-specific mnemonic strategies such as
imaginal and verbal mediation (e.g., Canestrari, 1968;
M. W. Eysenck, 1974b; Hulicka et al., 1967).   In studies

where old subjects are at less of a disadvantage on the more
meaningful materials, specific transfer of simple associative
links appears necessary for successful performance on the
meaningful material (e.g., Canestrari, 1966; Kausler & Lair,
1966; Ruch, 1934).

As we have seen previously, processing-deficit hypotheses
offer a potential explanation for the finding that age
differences are much less on STM tasks than on other learning
tasks.   If STM tasks primarily involve low-level phonemic
processing, then no age-related processing deficit will
appear.   On other tasks, involving deeper levels of
processing (e.g., semantic), age-related processing deficits
will occur, and lead to age differences in retention (M. W.
Eysenck, 1974b).

Retrieval-deficit Hypotheses

There is a considerable body of evidence indicating that
failures of recall can be due either to storage failures or
to retrieval failures (e.g., Tulving & Pearlstone, 1966).
It is thus possible that the inferior levels of recall
observed in old subjects could be due primarily to age-
related changes in the efficiency of the retrieval
mechanism, rather than to age-related changes in the
storage mechanism.   This retrieval-deficit hypothesis has
been investigated experimentally in various ways including
recall-recognition comparisons, cued-noncued free recall
comparisons, speed-of-retrieval studies, and studies using
the measures of signal-detection theory.

The rationale behind the method of recall-recognition
comparisons is that retrieval processes are far more heavily
implicated in recall than in recognition.   Thus if the old
show inferior recall to young subjects, but do not differ in
recognition, then one may conclude that their low level of
recall is attributable to a retrieval rather than a storage
deficit.   However, if old subjects show both inferior
recall and recognition, then the implication is that they
suffer primarily from a storage deficit.   Unfortunately,
the exact differences between the processes involved in
recall and in recognition remain obscure.   Tulving and
Thomson (1973) have produced evidence indicating that, at
least in some circumstances, there is a substantial retrieval
component involved in recognition, and Underwood (1972) has
argued that recall and recognition may differ in terms of the

word attributes necessary for successful performance.

In the initial experiments by Schonfield (1965) and by Schonfield and Robertson (1966), it was found that recall performance declined consistently and significantly with age, but that there was no deterioration with age in recognition performance. However, a 'ceiling' effect may have been operating on the recognition task, since for no age group did mean recognition performance fall below 80 per cent. Furthermore, the subjects were of superior intelligence, which may help to explain the lack of a recognition performance decrement with increasing age.

McNulty and Caird (1966) pointed out that only partial information about each item is required to mediate successful recognition. Thus older subjects may have learned fewer whole items than younger subjects, and thus be inferior at recall, but may have retained sufficient partial information about most items to perform well on a recognition test.

An appropriate procedure for testing the McNulty-Caird hypothesis would be to use a number of recognition tests in which the difficulty level of the recognition test was manipulated. If old subjects have, in fact, learned less about the list items than young subjects, then this inferiority should manifest itself on the more difficult recognition items. Hartley and Marshall (1967) gave old subjects 'easy' and 'difficult' recognition tests, and found that recognition performance was unaffected by the nature of the distractors. They concluded that, if partial learning were occurring, then performance should have been superior in the condition with dissimilarity between the correct and incorrect alternatives. However, all subjects received the list followed by the difficult recognition test after the list followed by the easy recognition test, so that uncontrolled practice effects may have been operative.

Erber (1974) argued that the lack of significant age-related deficits in recognition might be due to the use of easy recognition tests. Accordingly, she used a relatively difficult recognition test, together with tests of recall. Her major finding was a highly significant age deficit on the recognition task, in addition to the anticipated age deficit on the recall task.

Kapnick (1971) attempted to vary the difficulty of word recognition by manipulating list length. While performance varied inversely with list length, there was no effect of age. However, he used a relatively easy recognition test.

Harwood and Naylor (1969) used both recall and recognition tests at various retention intervals. When the recognition test was delayed for four weeks after learning, an age deficit was obtained. However, the age deficit for recognition was less than that for recall.

Some of the experimental evidence discussed in Chapter 2 indicates that a greater depth of processing is necessary for recall than for recognition. For example, phonemic coding often leads to reasonable recognition performance, but extremely poor recall. Old subjects, who apparently find imaginal and semantic processing difficult (e.g., Hulicka & Grossman, 1967) will be at a great disadvantage in recall situations, where deep levels of processing are necessary (M. W. Eysenck, 1974b). However, the processing capacities of old subjects will suffice for most recognition situations, unless the discrimination between new and old items is made difficult (Erber, 1974). More direct support for the hypothesis would require the manipulation of processing strategies, followed by tests of recall and recognition.

The work on cued-noncued free recall comparisons derives from studies by Tulving and Pearlstone (1966) and Tulving and Osler (1968), in which subjects were presented with category names and category instances, but were told that they would only be asked to recall the category instances. At test, the subject received either conventional noncued free recall or free recall aided by visual presentation of all the category names. Cued recall was considerably higher than noncued recall, and it was argued that some of the retrieval problems associated with noncued recall had been obviated by the category cues. Applied to the question as to the reasons for the inferior retention of the old, a storage deficit would be predicted to lead to inferior cued and noncued recall for the old compared to younger subjects, whereas a retrieval deficit would be predicted to lead to inferior noncued recall for older subjects, and a relatively greater improvement with cueing for older subjects.

Laurence (1967b) presented a categorized word list, and

discovered that only the old subjects benefited from
category cues at recall.   Old and young adults did not
differ in terms of their cued recall performance.   Drachman
and Leavitt (1972) presented a list of unrelated words for
several trials.   Subjects were either uncued or given the
initial letters of the list words as cues.   Cued recall was
significantly superior to noncued recall, but cueing did not
provide a relatively greater recall advantage for the old
subjects.   It should be noted that the Drachman and Leavitt
findings are not conclusive.   Although the old subjects
derived little advantage from the alphabetical cues, it is
possible that they would have shown substantial increases in
recall if different retrieval cues (e.g., other list items)
had been used.   In order to obtain a maximally accurate
estimate of the number of words stored, it would seem to be
highly desirable to use a variety of retrieval cues.   Since
the Drachman and Leavitt and the Laurence studies both used
a single form of retrieval cue, it is probable that their
studies under-estimated the amount of information stored.

In a recent study, Hultsch (1975) obtained evidence that
old subjects experience problems both of storage and of
retrieval.   He presented categorized word lists under cued
or noncued free recall conditions, and found that cueing
led to a greater increase in the number of categories
recalled by old than by young subjects, suggesting an age-
related retrieval deficit.   However, the old subjects
recalled significantly fewer words per category than young
subjects, and cueing did not benefit the old subjects more
than the young, indicating an age-related storage deficit.

It is clear that young and old people frequently store
more information than they can retrieve, but whether the
disparity between what can be stored and what can be
retrieved is greater in old people has not been clearly
established.   At the other end of the age scale, M. W.
Eysenck and Baron (1974) compared the cued and noncued recall
of five- and eight-year-old children.   They found that
cueing enhanced the recall performance of the younger children
more than that of the older children, indicating that the low
levels of recall shown by young children may be due, in part,
to problems of retrieval rather than of storage alone.

If old subjects do suffer from retrieval difficulties,
then one might anticipate that they would have slower speed of
retrieval of information, as well as a lower probability of

retrieval. Some of the studies on paired-associate
learning reviewed in an earlier section of this chapter
found evidence that old subjects retrieve the response terms
of paired associates more slowly than young subjects (e.g.,
Canestrari, 1963; Monge & Hultsch, 1971). However, the
slower retrieval speed of old subjects may have been due to
their lesser degree of storage of the paired associates.

Some studies have investigated age changes in speed of
retrieval while attempting to ensure adequate learning of the
material by young and old. In essence, the subject learns a
short list of items, followed by one or more probes. If the
probe corresponds to a list item, the subject responds 'yes'
as quickly as possible, but if it does not, he responds 'no'.
Work using this paradigm is discussed at greater length in
Chapter 5. The evidence is sometimes taken to indicate
(Sternberg, 1969) that the subject performs a serial
exhaustive scan of the list items on all trials. All the
studies using this paradigm with old subjects (Anders &
Fozard, 1973; Anders, Fozard, & Lillyquist, 1972; Eriksen,
Hamlin, & Daye, 1973; Kirsner, 1972a) have found that old
subjects perform this serial exhaustive scan more slowly than
young subjects. Kirsner (1972a), however, argued that age
changes on this task could be due to changes in perceptual
or response factors rather than memorial factors.
Accordingly, he also used a naming task, in which subjects
had merely to name the probe, rather than to decide whether
it had appeared in the list. On the argument that the
naming task and the retrieval task differed primarily in
terms of memory comparison, Kirsner assumed that the
difference between the retrieval and naming latencies
provided a direct estimate of the memorial component of
retrieval latency. With this corrected latency measure, he
found a reduction in age changes in retrieval, suggesting
that there was some influence of perceptual and response
factors on the uncorrected latency measure. In addition, it
is not definitely known whether young and old subjects in
these experiments learned the stimulus materials to an
equivalent extent.

Recently, some investigators have started to utilize the
measures of signal-detection theory in order to distinguish
between age-related effects on storage and on retrieval.
Gordon and Clark (1974a) presented a paragraph of connected
discourse, followed by a recognition memory test. The older
subjects performed at a lower level than the younger subjects,

due to age differences in sensitivity rather than in
response criterion.   While there are doubts about the
interpretation of these measures, particularly in memory
experiments where the assumptions of signal-detection theory
are clearly violated, these findings indicate that the older
subjects suffered from a storage deficit rather than a
retrieval deficit.   Similar results in recognition memory
for lists of words and nonsense syllables were obtained by
Gordon and Clark (1974b).   However, Craik (1971b)
investigated recognition performance from primary and
secondary memory, and found no age effect on sensitivity.

The most reasonable conclusion is that old subjects find
retrieval more difficult than young subjects.   The semantic-
memory studies of word fluency also suggest the same
conclusion, although they are methodologically suspect (M. W.
Eysenck, 1975a).   However, none of the studies has provided
unequivocal evidence in favour of a retrieval-deficit account
of age-related differences in retention.   The reason for
this is that it has so far proved impossible to ensure that
storage of the to-be-learned information has been equated
across age groups both quantitatively and qualitatively.

Motivational Hypotheses
   Motivational and personality factors need to be considered,
because there is fairly strong evidence for age-related
differences in some non-cognitive factors.   Bendig (1960),
using the Guilford Zimmerman Temperament Survey, Calden and
Hokanson (1959), using the Minnesota Multiphasic Personality
Inventory, and Gutman (1966), using the Maudsley Personality
Inventory, have all obtained evidence that people tend to
become more introverted with increasing age.   Additionally,
Craik (1964) found a decrease in sociability among his older.
subjects, and Slater and Scarr (1964) found a decrease in
impulsivity in older people.   Since there is some evidence
that introverts are characterized by higher levels of arousal
than extraverts (e.g., Gale, 1973), this personality change
may be important.   There is also some evidence that older
people are more neurotic than younger people (Gutman, 1966),
but Vassiliou, Georgas, and Vassiliou (1967) found no
relationship between age and scores on the Taylor Manifest
Anxiety Scale.

Motivational factors have been studied in some detail by
Eisdorfer and his co-workers.   Powell, Eisdorfer, and

Bogdonoff (1964) required young and old subjects to learn a
serial list.   Before, during, and after learning, blood
samples were collected, and subsequently analyzed for plasma
free fatty acid content.   The old subjects made more errors
on the learning task than did the young subjects.
Throughout the study, the plasma free fatty acid levels of
the old subjects were significantly higher than those of the
young subjects.   Both groups of subjects demonstrated a
considerable rise in the plasma free fatty acid levels
following the initiation of the learning task.   Since plasma
free fatty acid level is used as an index of autonomic
activation, it is possible that the poor learning of the old
group was, in part, attributable to a supra-optimal level of
arousal (Eisdorfer, 1967).

   Troyer, Eisdorfer, Bogdonoff, and Wilkie (1967) used a
serial rote learning task with either a four- or a ten-
second stimulus presentation interval under three conditions:
no stress; maximal stress, produced by fasting, needle
puncture, blood sampling, and electrical monitoring of heart
rate and respiration; and adaptation to stress, in which the
stressors of the maximal stress condition were applied both
on the day prior to learning, and in conjunction with the
learning task.   Only old people were used in this study.
The three experimental groups performed equivalently at the
four-second stimulus exposure interval, possibly because the
fast pacing induced a high degree of stress.   The effects of
stress were noticeable at the ten-second stimulus exposure
interval, where the no-stress group made considerably fewer
errors than either of the stress groups.   Unfortunately the
failure to use groups of young subjects means that the
implications of this study for an interpretation of age-
related differences in memory are unclear.

   Eisdorfer, Nowlin, and Wilkie (1970) required old people
to learn a serial list.   Measures of heart rate, GSR, and
plasma free fatty acid levels were taken several times during
the experimental session.   Half the subjects received
propranolol, a drug which largely mitigates the
physiological concomitants of central nervous system arousal.
The three physiological measures taken during the experiment
indicated that the drug group was less highly aroused than
the placebo control group.   The main finding was that the
drug group made significantly fewer errors on the learning
task than the control group.   This finding is consistent
with the hypothesis that the learning deficit of old people

is partially due to a supra-optimal level of arousal.

Ross (1968) presented young and old people with paired
associates of high and low associative strength.
Motivational factors were manipulated by means of the
instructions, which were neutral, supportive, or challenging.
As can be seen in Fig. 11.2, the old subjects took
significantly longer to reach criterion than the young
subjects with paired associates of high associative strength,
but there were no effects of the instructional variable.
With paired associates of low associative strength, the old
subjects were at a considerable disadvantage.   The young
subjects were again unaffected by the instructions given,
whereas old subjects performed worst under the most arousing
conditions (challenging instructions) and best under the
least arousing conditions (supportive instructions).

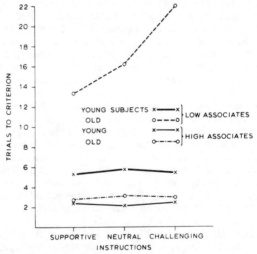

Fig. 11.2. Trials to criterion as a
function of age, associative strength,
and instructions. Based on data in Ross (1968).

These results can be interpreted by assuming that old
subjects tend to be more aroused than young subjects, and that
the learning of low associative strength paired associates is
a more difficult task than the learning of high associative
strength paired associates.   According to the Yerkes-Dodson
Law (Broadhurst, 1959), the optimal level of arousal varies

inversely with task difficulty.   On the easy task, the
optimal level of arousal is high, so that the old subjects
are not at an enormous disadvantage.   On the difficult task,
the optimal level of arousal is low, so that the old subjects
perform poorly, especially when given the arousing
instructions.

   Thompson and Wilson (1966) took EEG recordings from
exceptionally intelligent old subjects during rest control,
eyes open, and repetitive photic stimulation.   At a later
date, these same subjects participated in a paired-associate
learning task.   Good and poor learners on the paired-
associate task were compared in terms of EEG activity.   In
the rest control records, the poor learners tended to have
more slow waves than the good learners.   During eye opening
and photic stimulation, the good learners had significantly
more beta waves than the poor learners, but alpha changes
resulting from the stimulation conditions were comparable for
both groups.   Thompson and Wilson claimed modest support for
the hypothesis that more aroused old subjects learn better
than those less aroused.   However, the failure to take
physiological recordings concurrently with the learning task
makes it difficult to come to any firm conclusions.

   The somewhat limited experimental evidence indicates that
old people may be chronically more highly aroused than
young people (e.g., Bendig, 1960; Craik, 1964).   Direct
physiological recording suggests that old subjects may tend
to be over-aroused in the learning situation (e.g.,
Eisdorfer et al., 1970; Powell et al., 1964), a conclusion
consistent with findings from studies using instructional
manipulations (e.g., Ross, 1968; Troyer et al., 1967).   The
hypothesis that old subjects are more aroused than young
subjects in learning situations is applicable to several of
the major findings.   For example, Schwartz (1975a, 1975b)
has found that high levels of arousal lead to greater
processing of the physical characteristics of to-be-learned
material together with less processing of the semantic
characteristics.   The substantial evidence that old subjects
show less imaginal and semantic processing than young
subjects may thus be partially due to the effects of high
arousal on processing strategies.   Furthermore, high arousal
slows down the speed of recall or retrieval (M. W. Eysenck,
1974c, 1975b), and old subjects retrieve information more
slowly than young subjects (e.g., Anders & Fozard, 1973).
High arousal has detrimental effects on paired-associate

learning (M. W. Eysenck, 1975c), and old subjects perform
worse than young subjects in word fluency tests (e.g.,
Bilash & Zubek, 1960; Birren, 1955).   On word fluency
tests, introverts produce fewer words than extraverts
(Cattell, 1934; White, 1968), and old people tend to be
more introverted than young people (e.g., Bendig, 1960;
Gutman, 1966).   Although it may seem unlikely that
differences in arousal level between old and young can
account for more than a small proportion of age-related
learning differences, it is clear that more research should
examine carefully the hypothesis that one source of age-
related differences in memory lies in uncontrolled variations
in arousal level as a function of age.

Summary

The general pattern of results in the experimental
literature is that age-related deficits are prevalent in
long-term or secondary memory, but are less noticeable in
short-term memory and in semantic memory.   Since deep levels
of encoding, such as semantic and imaginal processes, are
especially consequential determinants of long-term retention,
it is reasonable to hypothesize (M. W. Eysenck, 1974b) that
old subjects are inferior to younger subjects at the more
complex forms of information processing, including imaginal,
semantic, and conceptual levels of processing.   The evidence
reviewed in this chapter has provided strong support for this
hypothesis.

If it were the case that older people form memory traces
which are less variegated and rich than those formed by
younger people, then it is clear (Tulving & Watkins, 1975)
that one consequence would be that successful retention-test
performance would occur to a more restricted range of
retrieval cues with increasing age.   Since most of the
findings supporting the retrieval-deficit hypothesis are of
this type, they are necessarily inconclusive.

One of the factors leading to less thorough processing by
the old may be supra-optimal arousal, but the evidence is not
conclusive.   Lauer (1975) found age-related decrements in
retention in spite of the fact that older subjects reported
less anxiety than young subjects.   Furthermore, anxiety
level was unrelated to memory performance among older subjects
with a mean age of 70 years.

In sum, while there are undoubtedly many determinants of age decrements in memory, the evidence is most consistent with the hypothesis that deep and elaborate encoding occurs decreasingly among older people, and that this is the prime cause of age-related deficits in secondary memory.

CHAPTER 12

INTELLIGENCE AND MEMORY

As a generalization, researchers interested in cognition and information processing have ignored individual differences whereas those concerned with individual differences in intelligence have typically been uninterested in theoretical conceptualizations of the processes involved in intelligent behaviour. Part of the difference between the two approaches is that the focus of cognitive theorists is at a relatively molecular level, whereas that of psychometrists is much more molar. Cattell (1971) has expressed this point rather well:

> Not nearly enough steps and aspects of the learning and recall process - such as immediate committing to memory, rate of fading, mode of retrieval, and other manifestations important to the memorizing processes - have been used by psychometrists, who have tended instead to confine themselves to some total learning effect (p. 42).

Guilford (1956, 1971) was one of the first to appreciate the need for a proper theoretical superstructure in the intelligence field. He argued that intelligence-test items differed in terms of content (figural, symbolic, semantic, and behavioural), in terms of operations (evaluation, convergent production, divergent production, memory, and cognition), and in terms of products (units, classes, relations, systems, transformations, and implications). In his structure-of-intellect model, Guilford used content, operation, and product as parameters of a three-dimensional model. Theoretically, the four kinds of contents, five kinds of operations, and six kinds of products could generate 120 factors, of which Guilford claims to have identified about one hundred. However, Guilford's product classes could easily be replaced by others with equally good claims, and the content categories are neither exhaustive nor mutually independent. Furthermore, it is clear that Guilford has investigated extremely narrow and specific factors, choosing tests for the sole purpose of fitting a

subjective framework.   In effect, a very specific factor is
made to appear more consequential by multiplying the number
of separate tests in a small, specialized, area.   In
addition, it is likely that many test items involve different
content at different stages along the road to solution.

   Cattell (1971) has proposed a process model of intelligence
which represents an advance on that put forward by Guilford.
In his Ability Dimension Analysis Chart (ADAC), he identified
12 dimensions belonging to three domains.   Domain A concerns
three Action Phases: involvement of input; involvement of
internal processing and storage;   and involvement of output.
Domain C is Content, and comprises two dimensions:
involvement of experiential-cultural dimensions (e.g.,
verbal, numerical, spatial);   and involvement of neural-
organizational dimensions (e.g., visual, tactile).   Domain P
concerns Process Parameters, and has seven dimensions:
demand in terms of complexity of relation eduction;   demand
in terms of multiplexity of sets;   amount of committing to
memory;   amount of retentive ability involved;   amount of
retrieval activity;   flexibility versus firmness;   and speed
demand.   Any ability may involve complex combinations of
these 12 dimensions (e.g., it may involve separate content at
input, storage, and output).   While it is as yet uncertain
how successful this model will be, it is more immediately
appealing than the Guilford model, and the dimensions
postulated overlap more substantially with the concepts of
modern information-processing theory than is the case with
previous models.   As will become apparent, much of the
research in this area has potential relevance to the Cattell
model.

   The approaches discussed in the remainder of this chapter
represent a sampling of those proposed in the literature.
Some researchers have argued that important intelligence-
memory relationships may be based upon the type of information
involved.   For example, Paivio (1971a) claimed that the
intelligence factors of verbal and spatial ability are
differentially involved in various memory tasks, depending
upon the involvement of verbal and imaginal processing.   On
the other hand, Earl Hunt has argued for a more empirical
approach, in which the investigator compares subjects low and
high on an intelligence factor on a large variety of memory
tasks, and looks for those aspects of information processing
on which the intelligence groups differ to the greatest
extent.

At a more theoretical level, Witkin has proposed that people with different cognitive styles (field dependence versus field independence) will differ with respect to their attention to, and learning of, certain kinds of information. Ellis has argued that those differing in intelligence also differ in the extent to which they use rehearsal processes during learning, and Jensen has claimed that differences in intelligence are less important when learning is of a simple, rote, nature than when it involves complex transformations of the input. Most of these approaches are complementary, in the sense that the processes emphasized are not mutually exclusive.

Spatial and Verbal Ability

There is quite strong evidence for the existence of an intelligence factor of spatial ability (cf., Vernon, 1971), and it appears to have a powerful hereditary determination. Vandenberg (1967) reviewed the relevant evidence, and concluded that spatial ability was as much, or more, heritable than verbal ability, and less related to environmental factors such as education or socio-economic status. Evidence for a clear separation between spatial and verbal ability was obtained by DiVesta, Ingersoll, and Sunshine (1971). In two factor-analytic experiments, they identified verbal and spatial abilities as orthogonal factors.

Several researchers have hypothesized that differences in learning and memory between those high and low in spatial ability should be dependent upon the extent to which the stimulus materials permit the use of imaginal processing. For example, Kuhlman (1960) compared high and low spatial ability children matched for intelligence. She found that those high in spatial ability were more accurate at reproducing geometrical forms from memory.

Stewart (1965) compared students of high and low spatial ability on several memory tasks. The two groups of students were matched on intelligence. In a paired-associate task, picture-digit and word-digit pairs were used. The picture-digit pairs were learned faster by those high than by those low in spatial ability, whereas the reverse was the case for the word-digit pairs. Similar results were obtained in a study of recognition memory for words and pictures. High spatial ability subjects performed better than low ability subjects on picture recognition, and the opposite was true

for word recognition. Moreover, analysis of the errors
suggested that those high in spatial ability were more
likely to code a word as a picture than were lows, whereas
lows were more likely to code a picture as a word than highs.
In a free recall experiment, however, low spatial ability
subjects recalled more than highs, and this finding was not
qualified by an interaction with the vividness of the words
comprising the list.

Further negative evidence was obtained by Paivio, Rogers,
and Smythe (1968). They studied free recall of words and
pictures. Pictures were recalled better than words, but
those high and low in spatial ability did not differ
significantly in their recall of either type of stimulus.

Ernest and Paivio (1969) found that spatial ability was
unrelated to paired-associate learning. However, high-
imagery subjects showed superior incidental learning to low-
imagery subjects.

A rather different relationship between spatial ability
and memory is suggested by the work of Ernest and Paivio
(1971), DiVesta and Ross (1971), and Klee and M. W. Eysenck
(1973). Ernest and Paivio found that imagery or spatial
ability did not affect the speed with which subjects formed
images to concrete words. However, high-imagery subjects
formed images to abstract words significantly faster then
low-imagery subjects. DiVesta and Ross found that high-
imagery subjects had an advantage over low imagers when the
stimulus members of paired associates were of low rated
imagery, but there was less difference when the stimulus was
of high rated imagery. Klee and M. W. Eysenck found that
high imagers comprehended abstract sentences much faster than
low imagers, but there was less difference on concrete
sentences.

Although some relationships between spatial ability and
memory performance have been obtained, they are neither
particularly strong nor consistent. Several reasons may be
advanced for this:-

(1) Tests of spatial ability typically involve
complex manipulations of imaginal processing, and this may
differ from the rather simpler forms of imaginal processing
involved in, for example, paired-associate learning.
(2) While it has frequently been assumed (e.g.,

Paivio, 1971a) that words of high vividness or concreteness
tend to be processed imaginally, this assumption has not
gone unchallenged (e.g., Baddeley, Grant, Wight, & Thomson,
1975).
          (3) The studies by DiVesta and Ross (1971) and
Klee and M. W. Eysenck (1973) suggest that certain types of
material may consistently evoke imaginal processing in both
high and low imagers, which might reduce the correlation
between spatial ability and memory.
          (4) Differences in spatial ability may be
associated with personality differences, and this confounding
may obscure the relationship between spatial ability and
memory.   Barton, Cattell, and Silverman (1974) gave students
Cattell's 16 P. F. and Thurstone's Primary Mental Abilities
test.   A comparison of male subjects high on verbal but low
on spatial ability with those low on verbal and high on
spatial ability indicated that the former subjects tended to
be more conscientious, tender-minded, guilt prone, and
conservative.

Hunt's Empirical Approach

A recent attempt to integrate work on intelligence and on
information processing has been made by Hunt and his co-
workers (Hunt, Frost, & Lunneborg, 1973; Hunt, Lunneborg, &
Lewis, 1975).   In both studies, the strategy has been to
examine differences in performance on standard memory tasks
as a function of individual differences in intelligence.
The memory tasks are selected so as to measure some of the
major aspects of information processing.   Interest centres
in locating some tasks where differences in intelligence are
very important, combined with other tasks where such
differences play no role.

Subjects in the 1973 study were selected from University of
Washington undergraduate students who had taken the
Washington Pre-College battery, from which a Verbal Ability
Composite score and a Quantitative Ability Composite score
were extracted.   Those selected for the study had both
composite scores in the extreme quartiles (i.e., top 25 per
cent or bottom 25 per cent) for their entering class.

Of the seven tasks used, high quantitative-ability (QA)
students only outperformed low QA students on three.   In a
continuous paired-associate task devised by Atkinson and
Shiffrin (1968), it was found that the rate of loss of

retrievable information was significantly lower for subjects
in the high QA groups.   In the Brown-Peterson paradigm,
involving retaining a consonant trigram over a period of a
few seconds filled with counting backwards, high QA scorers
showed consistently better performance than low QA scorers.
Additional testing revealed that this was so, despite the
fact that quantitative ability was unrelated to digit span.
The third significant difference between high and low QA
scorers was on retention of paired associates.   Subjects
learned a list of paired associates to criterion, and were
then tested for retention five weeks later.   High QA
subjects made significantly fewer errors on this retention
test than did low QA subjects.   The tentative conclusion was
that there is a relationship between resistance to interference and quantitative ability, although the mechanism
producing this relationship is not known.

High verbal-ability (VA) subjects differed from low VA
subjects on five of the tasks.   One task involved free
recall of a list of words belonging to a limited number of
semantic categories, presented in either categorized or
random fashion.   There were no group differences in the
number of words recalled, and semantic clustering (i.e.,
adjacent recall of members of the same category) was
uniformly high when the list was presented in categorized
fashion.   However, the high VA subjects showed a marked drop
in the amount of clustering when the list was presented in
random order, whereas the low VA subjects continued to
cluster.   One reason for this anomalous finding may be that
the list comprised ten words from each of three categories,
with the limited list organization leading the high VA
subjects to impose their own idiosyncratic organization on
the material.

Another task involved the name matching and physical
matching tasks developed by Posner.   In the name match
condition, the subject responds 'same' if two letters have
the same name (e.g., AA or aA); in the physical match
condition, the subject responds 'same' only if the two
letters are physically identical (e.g., AA or aa).   While
there were no group differences in physical matching, high VA
subjects were faster than low VA subjects in name matching,
suggesting that high VA subjects had faster name access.

In other experiments, high VA subjects showed greater
release from proactive inhibition than low VA subjects, high

VA scorers had a significantly faster rate of search than
low VA scorers in the Sternberg paradigm, and verbal ability
was related to speed of acquisition of a list of paired
associates.   Overall, Hunt et al. (1973) concluded that
there was a relationship between speed of short-term memory
processes and verbal ability.   Probably the most interesting
finding was that individual differences in intelligence
interacted in predictable ways with treatment effects in
several of the most widely used paradigms in contemporary
memory research.   Thus, while a priori one might have
predicted that high intelligence would be associated with a
uniform superiority on memory tasks, this was not the way
the results turned out.   Furthermore, larger interactions
might have been obtained if a more heterogeneous sample had
been investigated.

   Intuitively, it is not surprising that verbal ability is
related to performance on memory tasks involving verbal
material.   However, operationally, verbal ability is
measured by a person's knowledge of the meanings of words,
syntactical rules, and semantic relations among the concepts
denoted by words, whereas memory tasks are usually designed
so that extra-experimental knowledge will not systematically
affect performance, i.e., performance depends only on
information known to all the subjects.   In other words,
intelligence tests tend to measure a rather static ability to
display relevant knowledge, whereas memory tasks are
concerned with more active processes.   Given these
differences of emphasis, the discovery of relationships
between test performance and memory-task performance is a
worthwhile enterprise.

   Hunt et al. (1975) compared the performance of high and
low VA subjects on a number of laboratory tasks.   The first
experiment replicated the earlier finding using the Posner
paradigm, namely that the advantage of high VA subjects was
mainly on name matching trials.   In the second experiment,
high VA scorers learned lists of words better than low VA
scorers, but the two groups did not differ with respect to
lists of nonsense syllables.   In the third experiment, high
VA subjects showed superior performance in the Brown-
Peterson short-term memory paradigm.   In the fourth
experiment, subjects were required to indicate which of two
speech or non-speech sounds had been presented first.   There
was a highly significant interaction between verbal ability
and type of stimulus: verbal ability was positively related

to accuracy of performance with speech stimuli, but
unrelated to performance with non-speech stimuli.   In the
fifth experiment, subjects read an assertion about a picture,
then looked at a picture, and decided as rapidly as possible
whether the assertion was true with respect to the picture.
Under several conditions, there were no differences as a
function of verbal ability, but the low verbals took much
longer than the high verbals to comprehend, and to make a
decision about, negative statements.   In the final
experiment, subjects did addition problems to the base 7, 12,
or 26.   The advantage shown by the high VA subjects increased
as the problems became more difficult,i.e., as the base of the
number system increased.

The above findings, together with those obtained by Hunt
et al. (1975) from a factor-analytic study, indicated that
high verbals have a number of advantages over low verbals.
For example, as revealed by performance on the Posner matching
task, high verbals have the ability to extract the meaning
rapidly from a physical representation.   Performance in the
Brown-Peterson paradigm suggested that high verbals have the
ability to retain over short intervals of time the order of
stimulus presentation.   The Sternberg and arithmetical
calculation data indicate that high-verbal subjects are more
rapid in the manipulation of information in short-term
memory.

Although the evidence obtained by Hunt et al. only reveals
a correlation between verbal ability and certain aspects of
memory-task performance, it is reasonable to assume that high
VA subjects possess more information about the linguistic
aspects of their culture because they are faster at various
components of information processing, rather than the
reverse.   The major failure of the Hunt approach is that the
theoretical import of several of the findings is in doubt.
For example, it has been found that high verbals apparently
had a faster rate of scan than low verbals in the Sternberg
paradigm.   As we saw in Chapter 5, the interpretation of
results in the Sternberg paradigm is very difficult.   This
slope difference could be due (a) to group differences in
response caution;   (b) to differences in speed of the
exhaustive serial scan;   (c) to more efficient encoding of
the stimuli by high verbals;   or (d) to faster parallel
processing by high verbals.   It is probable that a series of
studies investigating the relationship between verbal ability
and Sternberg-paradigm performance will be needed to

elucidate the slope difference between high and low verbals.

Field Dependence

The concept of 'field dependence' was introduced into psychology by Witkin and his associates (Witkin, Lewis, Hertzman, Machover, Meissner, & Wapner, 1954; Witkin, Dyk, Faterson, Goodenough, & Karp, 1962). They found that subjects showed a certain amount of consistency in their performance on several perceptual tasks such as the Rod-and-Frame Test (RFT) and the Embedded Figures Test (EFT). Under difficult perceptual conditions, field-independent subjects were less likely than field-dependent subjects to show distortions and inaccuracies in perception. Subsequent work has indicated that field-dependent and field-independent subjects, as indexed by performance on tasks such as the RFT and the EFT, appear to differ in personality, motivation, cognitive style, and other characteristics. Witkin et al. (1962) described field-dependent people as less 'psychologically differentiated' from others and from the external environment than field-independent people. The former are said to rely heavily in their functioning on external cues, whereas the latter are more responsive to self-generated cues and are less dependent on external stimuli.

Successful experimental investigation of the correlates of field dependence obviously requires the availability of suitable methods for measuring field dependence. While the RFT and the EFT have possibly been used more frequently than other tests for this purpose, several other perceptual tests have also been used. Arbuthnot (1972) reviewed some of the evidence on the inter-correlations of the various measures of field dependence. Of 21 correlations between the RFT and Witkin's original 24-item individually administered EFT, the mean correlation coefficient was +.54, indicating that these two tests share only 29 per cent of their variance. Studies correlating the RFT and Jackson's shortened 12-item form of Witkin's EFT reported a mean correlation coefficient of +.37, and thus a shared variance of about 14 per cent. Other inter-correlations with different tests tended to produce still lower correlation coefficients, indicating that there are considerable measurement problems with the concept of field dependence.

It has frequently been suggested that field dependence is

related to various personality traits and dimensions.   For
example, Witkin et al. (1962) hypothesized that field-
dependent people tend to have poorly developed control and
defence mechanisms, and to express greater anxiety than
field-independent people.   Vernon (1972) proposed the
following hypothesis: "In many respects, the field
independent sounds like the introvert, the dependent like the
extravert" (p. 376).   Evans (1967) obtained a correlation of
+.39 between extraversion on the MPI and the EFT, i.e.,
field-dependent subjects tended to be extraverted.   However,
Fine (1972), Fuhrer, Baer, and Cowan (1973), and Pearson
(1972) all failed to find any relationship between
extraversion and field dependence.

The hypothesis of Witkin et al. (1962) relating field
dependence and anxiety has been investigated in a number of
studies.   Adeval, Silverman, and McGough (1968), Dargel and
Kirk (1973), Fine (1972), and Fuhrer et al. (1973) all
reported non-significant correlations between anxiety or
neuroticism and field dependence.   Nevertheless, it is
possible that there is a more complex relationship between
field dependence and personality.   Fine argued as follows:

It appears that the field-dependent introvert is an
individual with a strong orientation toward or need for
external stimulation and with a 'built-in' inability to
get it.   'Neurotic' behaviour appears to be at least
one possible outcome of this conflict between two
incompatible personality dimensions within a given
individual (p. 941).

He obtained supportive evidence in each of several
experiments.

There is apparently a substantial overlap between field
independence and tests of intelligence.   This relationship
is likely to be attenuated with above average, homogeneous,
groups of the kind used by Witkin et al. (1962).   Dubois
and Cohen (1970) quoted correlations of up to +.56 between
intelligence and the EFT, and of up to +.35 between
intelligence and the RFT in college women.   Vernon (1972)
carried out a factor-analytical study among eighth-grade
children, using a variety of tests of field dependence,
together with tests of personality, divergent thinking, and
intelligence.   The major finding was that the factor
extracted from the battery of tests of field dependence was

not distinct from general intelligence and spatial ability.

In sum, field dependence is a somewhat amorphous and
intractable concept.   The various tests proposed for its
measurement do not correlate very highly with each other, and
it is likely that field-independent subjects are more
intelligent than field-dependent subjects.   This background
indicates that one should view the work on field-dependence
and memory with caution.

Predictions from Witkin's theories as to differences in
memorial functioning between field-dependent and field-
independent subjects have not tended to be characterized by
precise utilization of the hypothetico-deductive method.
Witkin et al. (1962) suggested that field-dependent subjects,
being in need of support and guidance from others, are
particularly attentive to facial characteristics and
expressions, which provide useful cues to other people's
moods and attitudes.   Crutchfield, Woodworth, and Albrecht
(1956) tested Air Force officers, who had previously stayed
at assessment centres, for the accuracy of their recall of
other residents of the centre.   They found that the number
of correct identifications of fellow residents was
significantly related to field dependence.   Messick and
Damarin (1964) found that field-dependent subjects
outperformed field-independent subjects in the incidental
recognition of photographs of human faces.   It is possible
that this finding is due in part to the fact that women tend
to be more field-dependent than men.   Given the usual
superiority of field-independent subjects on perceptual and
cognitive tasks, it is interesting to find situations in
which the opposite occurs.

Other studies have investigated incidental learning with
different results.   Witkin et al. (1962) found that field-
independent subjects were superior both in incidental recall
of words from the Stroop Colour Word Test, and in incidental
recognition of Thematic Apperception Test cards.   An
attempted reconciliation of these discrepant findings is to
be found in a series of articles by Eagle and his associates
(Eagle, Fitzgibbons, & Goldberger, 1966; Eagle, Goldberger,
& Breitman, 1969; Fitzgibbons, Goldberger, & Eagle, 1965).
The incidental material used in their studies was divided
into social words (i.e., words having clear relevance for
social interaction) and neutral words (i.e., words having no
particular relevance for social interaction).

The main finding was that field-dependent subjects were superior to field-independent subjects in the recall and recognition of social stimuli. With neutral stimuli, the results tended to favour the field-independent subjects. Since Crutchfield et al. (1956) and Messick and Damarin (1964) used socially-relevant stimuli, their results are consistent with those of Eagle. Furthermore, the recent failure of Imam (1973) to find any differences in incidental recognition between field-dependent and field-independent subjects is explicable in view of his stimulus materials, which were geometric forms and nonsense syllables.

In most of the Eagle studies, there was a tendency for the field-independent subjects to perform the experimenter-designated task more efficiently than the field-dependent subjects, but partial correlations revealed that this difference was not responsible for the incidental-learning findings. The overall pattern of results suggests that field-independent subjects may have a narrower range of cue utilization than field-dependent subjects. According to Easterbrook (1959), high arousal tends to reduce cue utilization, and would thus restrict incidental learning. Silverman and McGough (1971) found that field-dependent subjects were more highly aroused than field-independent subjects under conditions of uncertainty, as represented by a rest interval prior to the experiment, but field-independent subjects were more aroused when specific stimuli were presented.

Additional evidence that arousal may be related to field dependence was obtained by Callaway (1959) and by Oltman (1964). Callaway found an increase in field independence after administering stimulant drugs (amobarbital and methamphetamine), and Oltman found that white noise increased field independence. It is plausible that performance on tests of field dependence, which usually involve a conflict between relevant and irrelevant cues, should be related to arousal. However, even if a difference in arousal level between field-dependent and field-independent subjects were found, it is not clear how an arousal-based interpretation would explain the differential effects of field dependence on retention of neutral and social stimuli.

As Johnson (1974) has indicated, the major inadequacy of the work relating cognitive style and memory is the failure

to adopt an information-processing approach. Differences in
retention-test performance between field-dependent and
field-independent people could be due to differences in
attention, short-term store capacity, rehearsal strategies,
depth of processing, time course of consolidation, retrieval,
or degree of caution in responding.

Ellis' Rehearsal-deficit Hypothesis

Ellis (1970) proposed the rehearsal strategy deficit
hypothesis, according to which the inferior memory performance
of low-intelligence subjects is, in large measure,
attributable to inefficient use of rehearsal techniques.
Since, according to Atkinson and Shiffrin (1968), the main
effect of rehearsal is to increase the secondary memory
storage of information, a reasonable deduction from the
theory is that differences in intelligence should affect
secondary rather than primary memory. Fagan and Binzley
(1970) compared the multi-trial free recall performance of
average and retarded adolescents in one experiment, and
superior and average children in a second. In both
experiments, the higher-I.Q. group recalled significantly
more. Furthermore, this recall superiority occurred only
over the initial portions of the serial-position curve, and
there was no difference between the groups at terminal serial
positions. This suggests that higher levels of intelligence
are associated with superior secondary memory, but not
primary memory.

More direct evidence that differences in intelligence are
related to differences in rehearsal strategies was obtained
by Fagan (1972). He compared the single-trial free recall
performance of superior and average intelligence groups under
instructions to rehearse overtly. In confirmation of the
results of Fagan and Binzley (1970), the effects of
differences in intelligence were most clearly seen in the
initial and middle serial positions. The more intelligent
subjects showed more overt rehearsal, especially over the
initial and middle portions of the list. When the subjects
were divided into active rehearsers (i.e., concurrent
rehearsal of present and previous items) and passive
rehearsers (i.e., rehearsal of present item only), it was
found that many of the superior-intelligence subjects were
active rehearsers.

Belmont and Butterfield (1969) presented normal and

retarded subjects with a serial list followed by a probe,
with the subjects instructed to indicate the original
location of the probe.   In order to index rehearsal
strategies, the subjects were allowed to present the serial
list at their own chosen speed.   Retarded subjects
typically presented the list to themselves very rapidly,
suggesting that they were not rehearsing the stimulus
material.   While about half the normal children performed in
similar fashion, the other half showed a gradual increase in
presentation time over the initial serial positions.   This
is indicative of a cumulative-rehearsal strategy.

If the poor levels of recall obtained by low-intelligence
subjects are due to inefficient rehearsal techniques, then
instructions in the use of efficient rehearsal strategies
might enhance their levels of recall.   Kellas, Ashcraft, and
Johnson (1973) investigated multi-trial free recall
performance in mildly retarded adolescents.   Half the
subjects received normal instructions, whereas the other
half was instructed to rehearse the material cumulatively.
The rehearsal-instructed subjects learned the list in fewer
trials than the non-instructed subjects, indicating that
retarded subjects can successfully process information for
retrieval from secondary memory when they have used an
active rehearsal strategy.   Similar results were obtained by
Luszcz and Bacharach (1975), who found that training retarded
subjects to use a cumulative-rehearsal strategy improved
their recognition-memory performance.

It has been established that some of the memory-
performance differences among groups varying in intelligence
are due to differences in rehearsal strategy.   Although the
researchers in this area have not distinguished between the
quantitative (i.e., the amount) and the qualitative (i.e.,
the patterning) aspects of rehearsal, it is probable that
both are important.   The finding of Jensen and Frederisen
(1973) that intelligence was more related to free recall of
categorized than of non-categorized word lists indicates that
the successful patterning of rehearsal, based upon an
appreciation of the inter-relationships existing among words,
may be especially difficult for those of low intelligence.
There is, in addition, the point that a basis for this line
of research was the Atkinson and Shiffrin (1968) model.   As
we saw in Chapter 2, recent research has indicated that
amount of rehearsal is a rather less consequential
determinant of memory performance than Atkinson and Shiffrin

supposed.

It is likely that rehearsal processes are more closely
related to memory performance in those tasks requiring the
verbatim recall of words presented at a fast rate than in
tasks involving comprehension of semantically related
material.   It is worth noting that the majority of studies
obtaining evidence in support of Ellis' rehearsal-deficit
hypothesis have used a single paradigm, i.e., free recall.
Some attempt should be made to establish the applicability of
the hypothesis to other experimental situations.

Jensen's Theory

Spearman (1923), in his classic work on intelligence,
defined noegenetic action as that leading to new mental
content and anoegenetic as thinking which deals only with
reproduction or recognition.   Jensen (1970) argued for a
related distinction between two levels of ability, asserting
of Level I ability that it,

> is characterized especially by the lack of any need of
> elaboration, transformation or manipulation of the input
> in order to arrive at the output.   The input need not
> be referred to other past learning in order to issue
> effective output...Level II ability, on the other hand,
> is characterized by transformation and manipulation of
> the stimulus prior to making the response (pp. 155-156).

Level II ability is seen as corresponding to the general
factor of intelligence.   Some laboratory tasks, such as
conditioning, digit span, and simple associative learning,
involve Level I ability, whereas other tasks (e.g., complex
conceptual learning and abstract problem solving) involve
Level II ability.   Some tasks (e.g., paired-associate
learning) can be learned either through the use of Level I or
Level II abilities.   The crucial difference between Level I
and Level II tasks is in the complexity of the cognitive
demands involved, rather than merely task difficulty.   For
example, repeating ten digits is a difficult task, but it
only involves Level I ability.

An obvious prediction is that intelligence should be more
related to performance on complex tasks involving Level II
ability than on simple tasks involving Level I ability.
Rohwer (1967) compared lower-class Negro children with middle-

class white children.   Although these groups differed in
I.Q. by 18 points on average, they showed no significant
differences in serial learning, paired-associate learning, or
digit span.   Jensen and Frederiksen (1973) compared lower-
class Negro and upper-middle-class white children on free
recall of categorized and non-categorized word lists.   It
was argued that successful performance on a categorized word
list, especially if the words were presented in random order,
would require clustering of the members of each category, a
Level II ability.   Less plausibly, it was argued that
learning of non-categorized word lists would tend to involve
only Level I ability.   As had been predicted, the more
intelligent group showed more of an advantage on the
categorized lists presented in random order than on the
non-categorized lists.

Jensen and Figueroa (1975) argued that backward digit
span, while it depends upon the Level I ability involved in
forward digit span, also requires transformation of the input
prior to output, a Level II ability.   It was predicted that
intelligence would correlate more highly with backward digit
span than with forward digit span.   For both white and black
groups of children, backward digit span was significantly more
correlated with I.Q. than was found for forward digit span.

Jensen (1970) elaborated on his Level I-Level II
distinction by arguing that there is a hierarchical
relationship between the two levels of ability, in that the
development of Level II ability depends functionally upon
Level I ability, whereas the reverse is not true.   Thus
Level II problems such as Raven's matrices items involve
retaining information in memory (i.e., Level I) while mental
operations are performed on it (i.e., Level II).   The most
obvious prediction from this formulation is that there would
be very few individuals with high Level II ability combined
with low Level I ability, whereas there would be many people
with high Level I ability but low Level II ability (e.g.,
idiot savants).   Some support for this hypothesis was
discussed by Matarazzo (1972) in connection with the digit-
span test of the Wechsler intelligence test: "Ordinarily, an
adult who cannot repeat at least four or five digits is
either organically impaired or mentally retarded.
Nevertheless, mental retardates sometimes do well on the
Memory Span Test" (p. 205).

Jensen (1974) investigated the hierarchical relationship

further in a study where black and white children were
tested on a Level I task (digit span) and a Level II task
(Lorge-Thorndike I.Q.).   While whites and blacks matched for
intelligence were similar in terms of memory score on the
digit-span task, the reverse was not the case.   Blacks and
whites matched for digit span showed extremely large
differences in I.Q., with whites consistently having the
higher I.Q.'s.   In other words, the findings suggested that
if subjects have the intelligence, they also have the memory,
whereas if they have the memory, they do not necessarily have
the intelligence.

Jensen (1974) also tested another prediction of the
hierarchical hypothesis, namely that the variability of
memory scores should decrease systematically going from low
to high levels of intelligence.   The prediction was partially
supported by the data.   However, Durning (1968) correlated
performance on the Armed Forces Qualification Test (AFQT),
for a sample of Navy recruits, with digit span, and found no
greater variance on digit memory for low AFQT scorers than
for high scorers.   She suggested that the proposed
hierarchical relationship between Level I and Level II might
apply only to children.

In sum, the notion that general intelligence is more
closely related to complex memory tasks than to simple ones is
intuitively reasonable and supported by much of the evidence.
However, Jensen has placed undue emphasis upon the general
factor of intelligence.   It is certainly the case that there
is substantial evidence for a general factor, as Guilford
(1964) demonstrated.   He examined more than 7,000 correlation
coefficients among intellectual measures.   In spite of the
fact that many of these data were collected from
homogeneous groups of subjects, he found that more than 80
per cent of these correlation coefficients were significantly
greater than zero.   However, there are also strong arguments
for postulating other, less general, factors such as verbal-
educational and spatial-mechanical (e.g., Vernon, 1965).

A further difficulty with the Jensen approach is that the
level or type of ability involved in a particular learning
task is less constant than Jensen imagined, varying as a
function of individual differences and stage of practice.
For example, Labouvie, Frohring, Baltes, and Goulet (1974)
investigated multi-trial free recall of unrelated pictorial
stimuli with immediate or delayed recall.   It was

hypothesized that the conceptual strategy of subjective
organization of the material would be employed more under
delayed recall conditions and increasingly over trials, and
that the correlation between intelligence and memory
performance would reflect the extent to which subjective
organization was occurring. As predicted, intelligence was
more strongly related to memory performance under delayed
than immediate recall conditions, and on the later
acquisition trials.

Unfortunately, subsequent work by Labouvie-Vief, Levin,
and Urberg (1975) failed to replicate these findings.
However, some support for the notion that the relationship
between performance on a particular task and intelligence is
not constant was obtained. Subjects learned a list of
paired associates under standard conditions, under speeded
conditions (i.e., fast presentation), or strategy conditions
(i.e., subjects were instructed to imagine an interaction
involving each to-be-associated pair). It was hypothesized
that the speeded condition would increase the use of rote
activity, whereas the strategy condition would maximize the
use of conceptual activity. As predicted, the correlation
between intelligence and learning in the strategy condition
was +.51; in the speeded condition, it was -.06.

Das (1973) claimed that level I abilities typically involve
sequential or serial processing of information, whereas level
II abilities require simultaneous or parallel processing.
Two factor-analytical studies of various memory and
intelligence tasks each produced a factor representing
parallel processing and a factor representing serial
processing. However, Das assumed that visual tasks lead to
parallel processing, whereas auditory tasks produce
successive processing. Thus his parallel-processing factor
might equally well be described as a spatial-ability factor,
and his serial-processing factor as a verbal-ability factor.
Furthermore, the assumption that imaginal processing is
necessarily parallel and verbal processing sequential is not
consistent with some of the relevant experimental data (see
Chapter 3).

Summary

The investigation of inter-relationships between
intelligence and information processing would be of relatively

minor interest if differences in intelligence were associated
only with quantitative differences in performance.   However,
several studies have found significant interactions between
individual differences in intelligence and treatment effects.
As Hunt et al. (1973) pointed out,

> Quite without theory, the existence of an interaction
> between treatment effects and subject characteristics
> establishes a problem for the experimentalist.   The
> logic of most experimental studies assumes that the
> 'error term' represents measurement error and is
> randomly distributed over observations (p. 115).

Since the general factor of intelligence is of such
pervasive influence, the literature is full of dozens of
significant empirical associations between intelligence and
almost every aspect of information processing.   This makes
it difficult to decide which findings are of theoretical
consequence.   Furthermore, in spite of the sparcity of
relevant data, it is likely that there are relatively few
simple linear relationships between intelligence and aspects
of information processing.   For example, consider the
relationship between verbal ability and learning.   Differences in quantity of rehearsal may be more apparent between
those low and intermediate in verbal ability, whereas
differences in patterning of rehearsal (e.g., semantic
clustering) may be greater between those intermediate and
high in verbal ability than between those low and
intermediate.

A theoretical approach that would be consistent with some
of those discussed in this chapter is one based on the depth
or levels of processing approach.   The basic hypotheses are
that more intelligent subjects differ from less intelligent
subjects more with respect to deep levels of processing than
shallow levels, and that intelligence is related to the speed
and efficiency with which the attributes or features of
presented material are encoded.   The theories of Ellis and
Jensen represent cognate approaches.   An appropriate
technique to use would be the Tulving and Watkins (1975)
reduction method described in Chapter 4.   The prediction is
that richer, multi-attribute, memory traces are formed by
more intelligent subjects.

To date, most investigators have concentrated on the
effects of intelligence on the acquisition of information.

However, it is likely that intelligence also affects the
speed with which information can be retrieved, and Hunt et al.
have obtained some relevant evidence.   Gaudry and Spielberger
(1970) asked subjects to learn easy paired associates, and
measured the speed of correct recall.   Both during
acquisition and after complete learning had occurred, the
more intelligent subjects recalled much faster than the less
intelligent subjects.

REFERENCES

Aaronson, D. (1976) Performance theories for sentence coding: Some qualitative observations, J. exp. Psychol.: Hum. Percept. Perform. 2, 42-55.

Aaronson, D., and Scarborough, H. S. (1976) Performance theories for sentence coding: Some quantitative evidence, J. exp. Psychol.: Hum. Percept. Perform. 2, 56-70.

Adams, J. A. (1967) Human Memory, McGraw-Hill, London.

Adeval, G., Silverman, A. J., and McGough, W. E. (1968) MMPI findings in field-dependent and field-independent subjects, Percept. mot. Skills 26, 3-8.

Allport, D. A. (1975) Critical notice: The state of cognitive psychology, Q. Jl. exp. Psychol. 27, 141-152.

Allsopp, J. F., and Eysenck, H. J. (1974) Personality as a determinant of paired-associates learning, Percept. mot. Skills 39, 315-324.

Allsopp, J. F., and Eysenck, H. J. (1975) Extraversion, neuroticism, and verbal reasoning ability as determinants of paired-associates learning, Br. J. Psychol. 66, 15-24

Anders, T. R. (1971) Retrospective reports of retrieval from short-term memory, J. exp. Psychol. 90, 251-257.

Anders, T. R. (1973) A high-speed self-terminating search of short-term memory, J. exp. Psychol. 97, 34-40.

Anders, T. R., and Fozard, J. L. (1973) Effects of age upon retrieval from primary and secondary memory, Developm. Psychol. 9, 411-415.

Anders, T. R., Fozard, J. L., and Lillyquist, T. D. (1972) Effects of age upon retrieval from short-term memory, Developm. Psychol. 6, 214-217.

Anderson, J. R., and Bower, G. H. (1971) On an associative trace for sentence memory, J. verb. Learn. verb. Behav. 10, 673-680.

Anderson, J. R., and Bower, G. H. (1972a) Configural properties in sentence memory, J. verb. Learn. verb. Behav. 11, 594-605.

Anderson, J. R., and Bower, G. H. (1972b) Recognition and retrieval processes in free recall, Psychol. Rev. 79, 97-123.

Anderson, J. R., and Bower, G. H. (1973) Human Associative Memory, Wiley, London.

295

Anderson, J. R., and Bower, G. H. (1974) A propositional
theory of recognition memory, Mem. Cogn. 2, 406-412.

Anderson, J. R., and Reder, L. M. (1974) Negative
judgments in and about semantic memory, J. verb. Learn.
verb. Behav. 13, 664-681.

Anderson, R. C., and Hidde, J. L. (1971) Imagery and
sentence learning, J. educ. Psychol. 62, 526-530.

Anisfeld, M. (1969) False recognition produced by semantic
and phonetic relations under two presentation rates,
Psychon. Sci. 17, 366-367.

Arbuthnot, J. (1972) Cautionary note on measurement of
field independence, Percept. mot. Skills 35, 479-488.

Archer, B. U., and Margolin, R. (1970) Arousal effects in
intentional recall and forgetting, J. exp. Psychol. 86,
8-12.

Arenberg, D. (1965) Anticipation interval and age
differences in verbal learning, J. abnorm. soc. Psychol.
70, 419-425.

Arenberg, D. (1967a) Age differences in retroaction, J.
Geront. 22, 88-91.

Arenberg D. (1967b) Regression analysis of verbal learning
on adult age at two anticipation intervals, J. Geront.
22, 411-414.

Arenberg, D. (1973) Cognition and ageing: Verbal learning,
memory, and problem solving, in C. Eisdorfer and M. P.
Lawton (Eds.), The Psychology of Adult Development and
Ageing, APA, Washington

Atkinson, R. C., Herrmann, D. J., and Wescourt, K. T. (1974)
Search processes in recognition memory. In R. L. Solso
(Ed.), Theories in Cognitive Psychology: The Loyola
Symposium, Erlbaum, Potomac, Md.

Atkinson, R. C., and Juola, J. F. (1972) Search and
decision processes in recognition memory, Tech. Rep. No.
194, Stanford Univ.

Atkinson, R. C., and Juola, J. F. (1973) Factors
influencing speed and accuracy of word recognition. In
S. Kornblum (Ed.), Attention and Performance, Vol. IV,
Academic Press, London.

Atkinson, R. C., and Shiffrin, R. M. (1968) Human memory:
A proposed system and its control processes. In K. W.
Spence and J. T. Spence (Eds.), The Psychology of
Learning and Motivation: Advances in Research and Theory,
Vol. 2, Academic Press, London.

Atwood, G. (1971) An experimental study of visual
imagination and memory, Cogn. Psychol. 2, 290-299.

Aube, M., and Murdock, B. (1974) Sensory stores and high-speed scanning, Mem. Cogn. 2, 27-33.

Ausubel, D. P. (1962) A subsumption theory of meaningful verbal learning and retention, J. gen. Psychol. 66, 213-244.

Bacon, S. J. (1974) Arousal and the range of cue utilization, J. exp. Psychol. 102, 81-87.

Baddeley, A. D. (1972a) Retrieval rules and semantic coding in short-term memory, Psychol. Bull. 78, 379-385.

Baddeley, A. D. (1972b) Human memory. In P. C. Dodwell (Ed.), New Horizons in Psychology, Vol. 2, Penguin, Harmonsworth.

Baddeley, A. D., and Ecob, J. R. (1970) Reaction time and short-term memory: A trace strength alternative to the high-speed scanning hypothesis, Tech. Rep. No. 13, Univ. Calif., San Diego.

Baddeley, A. D., Grant, S., Wight, E., and Thomson, N. (1975) Imagery and visual working memory. In P. M. A. Rabbitt and S. Dornic (Eds.), Attention and Performance, Vol. V, Academic Press, London.

Baddeley, A. D., and Hitch, G. (1974) Working memory. In G. H. Bower (Ed.), Recent Advances in Learning and Motivation, Vol. VIII, 47-89.

Baddeley, A. D., Thomson, N., and Buchanan, M. (1975) Word length and the structure of short-term memory, J. verb. Learn. verb. Behav. 14, 575-589.

Bahrick, H. P. (1969) Measurement of memory by prompted recall, J. exp. Psychol. 79, 213-219.

Bahrick, H. P. (1970) Two-phase model for prompted recall, Psychol. Rev. 77, 215-222.

Banks, W. P., and Atkinson, R. C. (1974) Accuracy and speed strategies in scanning active memory, Mem. Cogn. 2, 629-636.

Banks, W. R. (1970) Signal detection theory and human memory, Psychol. Bull. 74, 81-99.

Barclay, J. R., Bransford, J. D., Franks, J. J., McCarrell, N. S., and Nitsch, K. (1974) Comprehension and semantic flexibility, J. verb. Learn. verb. Behav. 13, 471-481.

Baron, J. (1973) Phonemic stage not necessary for reading, Q. Jl. exp. Psychol. 25, 241-246.

Bartel, H., DuCette, J., and Wolk, S. (1972) Category clustering in free recall and locus of control, J. gen. Psychol. 87, 251-257.

Bartlett, F. (1932) Remembering, Cambridge Univ. Press, Cambridge.

Battig, W. F., and Montague, W. E. (1969) Category norms

for verbal items in 56 categories: A replication and
extension of the Connecticut Category Norms, J. exp.
Psychol. 80, No. 3, Part 2.

Beatty, J., and Kahneman, D. (1966) Pupillary changes in
two memory tasks, Psychon. Sci. 5, 371-372.

Begg, I., and Clark, J. M. (1975) Contextual imagery in
meaning and memory, Mem. Cogn. 3, 117-122.

Begg, I., and Paivio, A. (1969) Concreteness and imagery in
sentence meaning, J. verb. Learn. verb. Behav. 8, 821-
827.

Belmont, J. M., and Butterfield, E. C. (1969) The relations
of short-term memory to development and intelligence.   In
L. P. Lipsitt and H. W. Reese (Eds.), Advances in Child
Development and Behaviour, Vol. 4, New York, Academic
Press.

Bendig, A. W. (1960) Age differences in the interscale
factor structure of the Guilford-Zimmerman Temperament
Survey, J. consult. Psychol. 24, 134-138.

Bennett, G. K., Seashore, H. G., and Wesman, A. G. (1963)
Differential Aptitude Tests (Grades 8-13 and adults),
Psychological Corporation, New York.

Berlyne, D. E. (1967) Arousal and reinforcement.   In D.
Levine (Ed.), Nebraska Symposium on Motivation, Univ.
Nebraska Press, Lincoln, Neb.

Berlyne, D. E., Borsa, D. M., Craw, M. A., Gelman, R. S., and
Mandell, E. E. (1965) Effects of stimulus complexity and
induced arousal on paired-associate learning, J. verb.
Learn. verb. Behav. 4, 291-299.

Berlyne, D. E., and Carey, S. T. (1968) Incidental learning
and the timing of arousal, Psychon. Sci. 13, 103-104.

Berry, R. N. (1962) Skin conductance levels and verbal
recall, J. exp. Psychol. 63, 275-277.

Besch, N. F. (1959) Paired-associates learning as a function
of anxiety level and shock, J. Personality 27, 116-124.

Betts, G. H. (1909) The Distribution and Functions of
Mental Imagery, Teachers College, Columbia, New York.

Bieri, J. (1970) Cognitive structures in personality.   In
H. M. Schroder and P. Suedfeld (Eds.), Personality Theory
and Information Processing, Ronald Press, New York.

Bilash, I., and Zubek, J. P. (1960) The effects of age on
factorially 'pure' mental abilities, J. Geront. 15, 175-
182.

Binet, A. (1966) Mnemonic virtuosity: A study of chess
players (translated by M. L. Simmel and S. B. Barron),
Genet. Psychol. Monogr. 74, 127-162.

Birenbaum, G. (1930) Das Vergessen einer Vornahme.

Isolierte seelische Systeme und dynamische Gesamtbereiche. Psychol. Forsch. 13, 218-284.

Birren, J. E. (1955) Age changes in speed of simple responses and perception and their significance for complex behaviour. In Old Age in the Modern World, Livingstone, London.

Birren, J. E., Riegel, K. F., and Robbin, J. S. (1962) Age differences in continuous word associations measured by speech recordings, J. Geront. 17, 95-96.

Bjork, R. A., and Whitten, W. B. (1974) Recency-sensitive retrieval processes in long-term free recall, Cogn. Psychol. 6, 173-189.

Blake, M. J. F. (1967) Relationship between circadian rhythm of body temperature and introversion-extraversion, Nature, Lond. 215, 896-897.

Blumenthal, A. L. (1967) Prompted recall of sentences, J. verb. Learn. verb. Behav. 6, 203-206.

Blumenthal, A. L., and Boakes, R. (1967) Prompted recall of sentences, J. verb. Learn. verb. Behav. 6, 674-676.

Bobrow, S. A., and Bower, G. H. (1969) Comprehension and recall of sentences, J. exp. Psychol. 80, 455-461.

Boersma, F. J., and O'Brien, K. (1968) An investigation of the relationship between creativity and intelligence under two conditions of testing, J. Personality 36, 341-348.

Bone, R. N. (1971) Interference, extraversion and paired-associate learning, Br. J. soc. clin. Psychol. 10, 284-285.

Borges, M. A. (1972) The random vs. blocked effect in categorized recall: An analytic solution. Unpubl. Ph.D. thesis, Univ. Calif., San Diego.

Botwinick, J. (1973) Age and Behaviour, Springer, New York.

Bousfield, W. A., and Barclay, W. D. (1950) The relationship between order and frequency of occurrence of restricted associative responses, J. exp. Psychol. 40, 643-647.

Bousfield, W. A., and Rosner, S. R. (1970) Free versus uninhibited recall, Psychon. Sci. 20, 75-76.

Bousfield, W. A., and Sedgewick, C. H. W. (1944) An analysis of sequences of restricted associative responses, J. gen. Psychol. 30, 149-165.

Bousfield, W. A., Sedgewick, C. H. W., and Cohen, B. H. (1954) Certain temporal characteristics of the recall of verbal associates, Am. J. Psychol. 67, 111-118.

Bower, G. H. (1967) A multicomponent theory of the memory trace. In K. W. Spence and J. T. Spence (Eds.), The Psychology of Learning and Motivation: Advances in

Research and Theory, Vol. 1, Academic Press, London.

Bower, G. H. (1970) Imagery as a relational organizer in associative learning, J. verb. Learn. verb. Behav. 9, 529-533.

Bower, G. H. (1972) Mental imagery and associative learning. In L. Gregg (Ed.), Cognition in Learning and Memory, Wiley, New York.

Bower, G. H., and Bostrum, A. (1968) Absence of within-list PI and RI in short-term recognition memory, Psychon. Sci. 10, 211-212.

Bower, G. H., Clark, M. C., Lesgold, A. M., and Winzenz, D. (1969) Grouping operations in free recall, J. verb. Learn. verb. Behav. 8, 481-493.

Bower, G. H., Karlin, M. B., and Dueck, A. (1975) Comprehension and memory for pictures, Mem. Cogn. 3, 216-220.

Bower, G. H., Munoz, R., and Arnold, P. G. (1972) On distinguishing semantic and imaginal mnemonics, unpubl. manuscript.

Bower, G. H., and Winzenz, D. (1970) Comparison of associative learning strategies, Psychon. Sci. 20, 119-120.

Bowers, K. S. (1973) Situationism in psychology: An analysis and a critique, Psychol. Rev. 80, 307-336.

Bransford, J. D., Barclay, J. R., and Franks, J. J. (1972) Sentence memory: A constructive versus interpretive approach, Cogn. Psychol. 3, 193-209.

Bransford, J. D., and Johnson, M. K. (1972) Contextual prerequisities for understanding: Some investigations of comprehension and recall, J. verb. Learn. verb. Behav. 11, 717-726.

Bregman, A. S. (1968) Forgetting curves with semantic, phonetic, graphic, and contiguity cues, J. exp. Psychol. 78, 539-546.

Briggs, G. E., and Swanson, J. M. (1970) Memory retrieval and central functions in human information processing, J. exp. Psychol. 86, 296-308.

Broadbent, D. E. (1958) Perception and Communication, Pergamon Press, London.

Broadbent, D. E. (1971) Decision and Stress, Academic Press, London.

Broadbent, D. E., and Broadbent, M. H. P. (1975) The recognition of words which cannot be recalled. In P. M. A. Rabbitt and S. Dornic (Eds.), Attention and Performance, Vol. V, Academic Press, London.

Broadhurst, P. L. (1959) The interaction of task difficulty

and motivation: The Yerkes-Dodson Law revived, Acta
psychol. 16, 321-338.

Bromley, D. B. (1958) Some effects of age in short-term
learning and remembering, J. Geront. 13, 398-406.

Bronzhaft, A., Hayes, R., Welch, L., and Koltuv, M. (1960)
Relationship between PGR and measures of extraversion,
ascendance, and neuroticism, J. Psychol. 50, 193-195.

Brooks, L. R. (1967) The suppression of visualization by
reading, Q. Jl. exp. Psychol. 19, 289-299.

Brooks, L. R. (1968) Spatial and verbal components of the
act of recall, Can. J. Psychol. 22, 349-368.

Brooks, L. R. (1970) An extension of the conflict between
visualization and reading, Q. Jl. exp. Psychol. 22, 91-
96.

Brooks, L. R. (1972) Unpubl. work.

Brown, J. (1968) Reciprocal facilitation and impairment of
free recall, Psychon. Sci. 10, 41-42.

Brown, R., and McNeill, D. (1966) The 'tip of the tongue'
phenomenon, J. verb. Learn. verb. Behav. 5, 325-337.

Bruce, D., and Crowley, J. J. (1970) Acoustic similarity
effects on retrieval from secondary memory, J. verb.
Learn. verb. Behav. 9, 190-196.

Bruner, J. S., Olver, R. R., and Greenfield, P. M. (1966)
Studies in Cognitive Growth, Wiley, New York.

Bruning, J. L., Capage, J. E., Kozuh, G. F., Young, P. F.,
and Young, W. E. (1968) Socially induced drive and
range of cue utilization, J. Person. soc. Psychol. 9,
242-244.

Bugelski, B. R. (1970) Words and things and images, Am.
Psychol. 25, 1002-1012.

Bull, R. H. C., and Nethercott, R. E. (1972) Physiological
recovery and personality, Br. J. soc. clin. Psychol. 11,
297.

Burdick, J. A. (1966) Autonomic lability and neuroticism,
J. psychosom. Res. 9, 339-342.

Burrows, D., and Okada, R. (1971) Serial position effects
in high speed memory search, Percept. Psychophys. 10,
305-308.

Buschke, H. (1975) Short-term retention, learning, and
retrieval from long-term memory. In D. Deutsch and J. A.
Deutsch (Eds.), Short-term Memory, Academic Press,
London.

Buschke, H., and Lenon, R. (1969) Encoding homophones and
synonyms for verbal discrimination and recognition,
Psychon. Sci. 14, 269-270.

Butter, M. J. (1970) Differential recall of paired

302   References

associates as a function of arousal and concreteness-
imagery levels, J. exp. Psychol. 84, 252-256.

Byrne, B. (1974) Item concreteness vs. spatial organization
as predictors of visual imagery, Mem. Cogn. 2, 53-59.

Caird, W. K. (1966) Ageing and short-term memory, J.
Geront. 21, 295-299.

Calden, C., and Hokanson, J. E. (1959) The influence of age
on MMPI responses, J. clin. Psychol. 15, 194-195.

Callaway, E. (1959) The influence of amobarbital
(amylobarbitone) and methamphetamine on the focus of
attention, J. ment. Sci. 105, 382-392.

Callaway, E., and Stone, G. (1960) Re-evaluating the focus
of attention. In L. Uhr and J. G. Miller (Eds.), Drugs
and Behaviour, Wiley, New York.

Cameron, N. (1947) The Psychology of Behaviour Disorders,
Houghton Mifflin, New York.

Cameron, R., and Myers, J. L. (1966) Some personality
correlates of risk taking, J. gen. Psychol. 74, 51-60.

Canestrari, R. E. (1963) Paced and self-paced learning in
young and elderly adults, J. Geront. 18, 165-168.

Canestrari, R. E. (1966) The effects of commonality on
paired-associate learning in two age groups, J. genet.
Psychol. 108, 3-7.

Canestrari, R. E. (1968) Age changes in acquisition. In
G. A. Talland (Ed.), Human Ageing and Behaviour,
Academic Press, New York.

Caramazza, A., Hersh, H., and Torgerson, W. S. (1976)
Subjective structures and operations in semantic memory,
J. verb. Learn. verb. Behav. 15, 103-117.

Castillo, D. M., and Gumenik, W. E. (1972) Sequential
memory for familiar and unfamiliar forms, J. exp. Psychol.
95, 90-96.

Cattell, R. B. (1934) Temperament tests: II. Tests, Br.
J. Psychol. 24, 20-49.

Cattell, R. B. (1943) The measurement of adult intelligence,
Psychol. Bull. 40, 153-193.

Cattell, R. B. (1971) Abilities: Their Structure, Growth
and Action, Houghton Mifflin, Boston.

Cattell, R. B., and Scheier, I. H. (1958) Factors in
personality change: A dimension of the condition-response
incremental design and application to the 69 personality
response measures and three stimulus conditions, Advance
Publication No. 9, Urbana, Illinois.

Cattell, R. B., and Scheier, I. H. (1961) The Meaning and
Measurement of Neuroticism and Anxiety, Ronald, New York.

Cermak, G., Schnorr, J. Buschke, H., and Atkinson, R. C.
(1970) Recognition memory as influenced by differential
attention to semantic and acoustic properties of words,
Psychon. Sci. 19, 79-81.

Chase, W. G., and Clark, H. H. (1972) Mental operations in
the comparison of sentences and pictures. In L. W.
Gregg (Ed.), Cognition in Learning and Memory, Wiley,
New York.

Chiles, W. D. (1958) Effects of shock-induced stress on
verbal performance, J. exp. Psychol. 56, 159-165.

Chomsky, N. (1965) Aspects of the Theory of Syntax, M.I.T.
Press, Cambridge Mass.

Christie, M. J. (1974) Individual differences in the
psychophysiological stress response. Paper presented at
the B.P.S. conference, Social section, Univ. York.

Christie, M. J., and Venables, P. H. (1973) Mood changes in
relation to age, EPI scores, time and day, Br. J. soc.
clin. Psychol. 12, 61-72.

Clark, H. H. (1973) The language-as-fixed-effect fallacy:
A critique of language statistics in psychological
research, J. verb. Learn. verb. Behav. 12, 335-359.

Clark, H. H., and Chase, W. G. (1972) On the process of
comparing sentences against pictures, Cogn. Psychol. 3,
472-517.

Clark, H. H., and Lucy, P. (1975) Understanding what is
meant from what is said: A study in conversationally
conveyed requests, J. verb. Learn. verb. Behav. 14, 56-
72.

Clifton, C., and Birenbaum, S. (1970) Effects of serial
position and delay of probe in a memory scan task, J. exp.
Psychol. 86, 69-76.

Clifton, C., and Gutschera, K. (1971) Evidence for
hierarchical search processes in a recognition memory task,
J. verb. Learn. verb. Behav. 10, 528-541.

Cofer, C. N. (1967) The specificity of individual
differences in learning. In R. M. Gagne (Ed.), Learning
and Individual Differences, Merrill, Columbus, Ohio.

Coles, M. G. H., Gale, A., and Kline, P. (1971) Personality
and habituation of the orienting reaction: Tonic and
response measures of electrodermal activity, Psychophysiol. 8, 54-63.

Collins, A. M., and Quillian, M. R. (1969) Retrieval time
from semantic memory, J. verb. Learn. verb. Behav. 8,
240-248.

Collins, A. M., and Quillian, M. R. (1970) Does category
size affect categorization time?, J. verb. Learn. verb.

Behav. 9, 432-438.

Coltheart, M. (1975) Iconic memory: A reply to Professor
Holding, Mem. Cogn. 3, 42-48.

Conrad, C. (1972) Cognitive economy in semantic memory,
J. exp. Psychol. 92, 149-154.

Corballis, M. C. (1967) Serial order in recognition and
recall, J. exp. Psychol. 74, 99-105.

Corballis, M. C. (1975) Access to memory: An analysis of
recognition time. In P. M. A. Rabbitt and S. Dornic (Eds.)
Attention and Performance, Vol. V, Academic Press,
London.

Corballis, M. C., Kirby, J., and Miller, A. (1972) Access to
elements of a memorized list, J. exp. Psychol. 94, 185-
190.

Cornsweet, D. M. (1969) Use of cues in the visual periphery
under conditions of arousal, J. exp. Psychol. 80, 14-18.

Corteen, R. S. (1969) Skin conductance changes and word
recall, Br. J. Psychol. 60, 81-90.

Costello, C. G. (1957) The control of visual imagery in
mental disorder, J. Ment. Sci. 103, 840-849.

Courts, F. A. (1942) The influence of practice on the
dynamogenic effect of muscular tension, J. exp. Psychol.
30, 504-511.

Craik, F. I. M. (1964) An observed age difference in
responses to a personality inventory, Br. J. Psychol. 55,
453-462.

Craik, F. I. M. (1965) The nature of the age decrement in
performance on dichotic listening tasks, Q. Jl. exp.
Psychol. 17, 227-240.

Craik, F. I. M. (1968a) Two components in free recall, J.
verb. Learn. verb. Behav. 7, 996-1004.

Craik, F. I. M. (1968b) Short-term memory and the ageing
process. In G. A. Talland (Ed.), Human Ageing and
Behaviour, Academic Press, London.

Craik, F. I. M. (1971a) Primary memory, Br. med. Bull. 27,
232-236.

Craik, F. I. M. (1971b) Age differences in recognition
memory, Q. Jl. exp. Psychol. 23, 316-323.

Craik, F. I. M. (1973) A 'levels of analysis' view of
memory. In P. Pliner, L. Krames, and T. Alloway (Eds.),
Communication and Affect, Academic Press, London.

Craik, F. I. M., and Jacoby, L. L. (1975) A process view of
short-term retention. In F. Restle (Ed.), Cognitive
Theory, Vol. I, Erlbaum Associates, Potomac, Maryland.

Craik, F. I. M., and Lockhart, R. S. (1972) Levels of
processing: A framework for memory research, J. verb.

Learn. verb. Behav. 11, 671-684.

Craik, F. I. M., and Masani, P. A. (1967) Age differences in the temporal integration of language, Br. J. Psychol. 58, 291-299.

Craik, F. I. M., and Masani, P. A. (1969) Age and intelligence differences in coding and retrieval of word lists, Br. J. Psychol. 60, 315-319.

Craik, F. I. M., and Tulving, E. (1975) Depth of processing and the retention of words in episodic memory, J. exp. Psychol.: Gen. 1, 268-294.

Crain, D. D., and DeRosa, D. V. (1974) Retrieval of information from multiple ensembles in short-term memory, Mem. Cogn. 2, 255-260.

Crider, A., and Lunn, R. (1971) Electrodermal lability as a personality dimension, J. exp. Res. Person. 5, 145-150.

Crowder, R. G. (1975) Inferential problems in echoic memory. In P. M. A. Rabbitt and S. Dornic (Eds.), Attention and Performance, Vol. V, Academic Press, London.

Crowne, D. P., and Marlowe, D. (1964) The Approval Motive: Studies in Evaluative Dependence, Wiley, New York.

Crutchfield, R. S., Woodworth, D. G., and Albrecht, R. E. (1958) Perceptual performance of effective persons, USAF WADC Tech. Note, No. 58-60.

Dana, R. H. (1957) Manifest anxiety, intelligence, and psychopathology, J. consult. Psychol. 21, 38-40.

Danks, J. H., and Sorce, P. A. (1973) Imagery and deep structure in the prompted recall of passive sentences, J. verb. Learn. verb. Behav. 12, 114-117.

Dargel, R., and Kirk, R. E. (1973) Note on the relation of anxiety to field dependency, Percept. mot. Skills 37, 218.

Das, J. P. (1973) Structure of cognitive abilities: Evidence for simultaneous and successive processing, J. educ. Psychol. 65, 103-108.

Davids, A. H., and Eriksen, C. W. (1955) The relationship of manifest anxiety to association productivity and intellectual attainment, J. consult. Psychol. 19, 219-222.

Davies, D. R., Hockey, G. R. J., and Taylor, A. (1969) Varied auditory stimulation, temperament differences and vigilance performance, Br. J. Psychol. 60, 455-457.

Davies, D. R., and Jones, D. M. (1975) The effects of noise and incentive upon attention in short-term memory, Br. J. Psychol. 66, 61-68.

Davies, G., and Proctor, J. (1976) The recall of concrete

and abstract sentences as a function of interpolated task, Br. J. Psychol. 67, 63-72.

Davis, S. H., and Obrist, W. D. (1966) Age differences in learning and retention of verbal material, Cornell J. soc. Relations 1, 95-103.

Dean, P. J. (1971) Organizational structure and retrieval processes in long-term memory. Unpubl. Ph.D. thesis, Univ. Calif., San Diego.

Deese, J. (1959) On the prediction of occurrence of particular verbal intrusions in immediate recall, J. exp. Psychol. 58, 17-22.

Deese, J. (1961) From the isolated verbal unit to connected discourse. In C. N. Cofer (Ed.), Verbal Learning and Verbal Behaviour, McGraw-Hill, London.

Deese, J. (1962) On the structure of associative meaning, Psychol. Rev. 69, 161-175.

Deese, J. (1965) The Structure of Associations in Language and Thought, J. Hopkins, Baltimore.

Demetrescu, M., Demetrescu, M., and Iosif, G. (1965) The tonic control of cortical responsiveness by inhibitory and facilitatory diffuse influences, EEC clin. Neurophysiol. 18, 1-24.

Den Heyer, K., and Barrett, B. (1971) Selective loss of visual and verbal information in STM by means of visual and verbal interpolated tasks, Psychon. Sci. 25, 100-102.

Denney, N. W. (1974) Clustering in middle and old age, Developm. Psychol. 10, 471-475.

Desroches, H. F., Kaiman, B. D., and Ballard, H. T. (1966) Relationship between age and recall of meaningful material, Psychol. Rep. 18, 920-922.

DeVilliers, P. A. (1974) Imagery and theme in recall of connected discourse, J. exp. Psychol. 103, 263-268.

Di Scipio, W. J. (1971a) Divergent thinking: A complex function of interacting dimensions of extraversion-introversion and neuroticism-stability, Br. J. Psychol. 62, 545-550.

Di Scipio, W. J. (1971b) Divergent thinking and personality measures of English and American education majors, J. genet. Psychol. 119, 99-107.

Di Vesta, F. J., Ingersoll, G., and Sunshine, P. (1971) A factor analysis of imagery tests, J. verb. Learn. verb. Behav. 10, 471-479.

Di Vesta, F. J., and Ross, S. M. (1971) Imagery ability, abstractness, and word order as variables in recall of adjectives and nouns, J. verb. Learn. verb. Behav. 10, 686-693.

Doctor, R. M., and Altman, F. (1969) Worry and
emotionality as components of test anxiety, with
replication and further data, Psychol. Rep. 24, 563-568.

Donaldson, W., and Murdock, B. B. (1968) Criterion change
in continuous recognition memory, J. exp. Psychol. 76,
325-330.

Doob, L. W. (1964) Eidetic images among the Ibo, Ethnol.
3, 357-363.

Doob, L. W. (1965) Exploring eidetic imagery among the
Kamba of Central Kenya, J. soc. Psychol. 67, 3-22.

Doob, L. W. (1966) Eidetic imagery: A cross-cultural will-
o'-the-wisp?, J. Psychol. 63, 13-34.

Dornic, S. (1975) Some studies on the retention of order
information. In P. M. A. Rabbitt and S. Dornic (Eds.),
Attention and Performance, Vol. V, Academic Press, London.

Drachman, D. A., and Leavitt, J. (1972) Memory impairment
in the aged: Storage versus retrieval deficit, J. exp.
Psychol. 93, 302-308.

Dubois, T. E., and Cohen, W. (1970) Relationship between
measures of psychological differentiation and intellectual
ability, Percept. mot. Skills 31, 411-416.

Dudycha, G. J. (1936) An objective study of punctuality in
relation to personality and achievement, Archs. Psychol.,
N. Y. 204, 1-319.

Dunn, J. A. (1968) Anxiety, stress, and the performance of
complex intellectual tasks: A new look at an old question,
J. consult. clin. Psychol. 32, 669-673.

Durning, S. (1968) Unpubl. report.

D'Zurilla, T. (1965) Recall efficiency and mediating
cognitive events in 'experimental repression', J. Person.
soc. Psychol. 3, 253-256.

Eagle, M., Fitzgibbons, D., and Goldberger, L. (1966) Field
dependence and memory for relevant and irrelevant
incidental stimuli, Percept. mot. Skills 23, 1035-1038.

Eagle, M., Goldberger, L., and Breitman, M. (1969) Field
dependence and memory for social vs. neutral and relevant
vs. irrelevant incidental stimuli, Percept. mot. Skills
29, 903-910.

Easterbrook, J. A. (1959) The effect of emotion on cue
utilization and the organization of behaviour, Psychol.
Rev. 66, 183-201.

Ebbinghaus, H. (1885) Memory, Teachers College, New York.

Edwards, A. L., Cone, J. D., and Abbott, R. D. (1970)
Anxiety, structure, or social desirability?, J. consult.
clin. Psychol. 34, 236-238.

Egan, J. P. (1958) Recognition memory and the operating characteristic, AFCRC TN, 58-51, AD, 52650, Hearing and Communication Lab., Indiana Univ.

Eisdorfer, C. (1965) Verbal learning and response time in the aged, J. genet. Psychol. 107, 15-22.

Eisdorfer, C. (1967) New dimensions and a tentative theory, Gerontol. 7, 14-18.

Eisdorfer, C. (1968) Arousal and performance: Experiments in verbal learning and a tentative theory. In G. A. Talland (Ed.), Human Ageing and Behaviour, Academic Press, New York.

Eisdorfer, C., Axelrod, S., and Wilkie, F. L. (1963) Stimulus exposure time as a factor in serial learning in an aged sample, J. abnorm. soc. Psychol. 67, 594-600.

Eisdorfer, C., Nowlin, J., and Wilkie, F. L. (1970) Impairment of learning in the aged by modification of autonomic nervous system activity, Science, N. Y. 170, 1327-1329.

Ellis, N. R. (1970) Memory processes in retardates and normals. In N. R. Ellis (Ed.), International Review of Research in Mental Retardation, Vol. 4, New York, Academic Press.

Endler, N. S., and Hunt, J. McV. (1966) Sources of behavioural variance as measured by the S-R Inventory of Anxiousness, Psychol. Bull. 65, 336-346.

Endler, N. S., and Hunt, J. McV. (1968) S-R Inventories of hostility and comparisons of the proportions of variance from persons, responses, and situations for hostility and anxiousness, J. Person. soc. Psychol. 9, 309-315.

Endler, N. S., and Hunt, J. McV. (1969) Generalizability of contributions from sources of variance in the S-R Inventories of Anxiousness, J. Personality 37, 1-24.

Endler, N. S., Hunt, J. McV., and Rosenstein, A. J. (1962) An S-R Inventory of Anxiousness, Psychol. Monogr. 76 (17, Whole No. 536).

Endler, N. S., Magnusson, D., Ekehammar, B., and Okada, M. (1976) The multidimensionality of state and trait anxiety, Scand. J. Psychol. 17, 81-96.

Endler, N. S., and Shedletsky, R. (1973) Trait versus state anxiety, authoritarianism and ego threat versus physical threat, Can. J. behav. Sci. 5, 347-361.

Erber, J. T. (1974) Age differences in recognition memory, J. Geront. 29, 177-181.

Eriksen, C. W., Hamlin, R. M., and Daye, C. (1973) Ageing adults and rate of memory scan, Bull. psychon. Soc. 1, 259-260.

Ernest, C. H., and Paivio, A. (1971) Imagery and verbal
associative latencies as a function of imagery ability,
Can. J. Psychol. 25, 83-90.

Estes, W. K., and DaPolito, F. (1967) Independent variation
of information storage and retrieval processes in paired-
associate learning, J. exp. Psychol. 75, 18-26.

Evans, F. J. (1967) Field dependence and the Maudsley
Personality Inventory, Percept. mot. Skills 24, 526.

Eysenck, H. J. (1967) The Biological Basis of Personality,
C. C. Thomas, Springfield.

Eysenck, H. J. (1971) Editor's introduction. In H. J.
Eysenck (Ed.), Readings in Extraversion-Introversion,
Vol. 3, Staples, London.

Eysenck, H. J. (1973) Personality, learning, and 'anxiety'.
In H. J. Eysenck (Ed.), Handbook of Abnormal Psychology,
Pitman, London.

Eysenck, H. J., and Eysenck, S. B. G. (1969) The Structure
and Measurement of Personality, Routledge and Kegan Paul,
London.

Eysenck, M. C. (In preparation) Incidental learning as a
function of activation, extraversion, and neuroticism.

Eysenck, M. D. (1945) An exploratory study of mental
organization in senility, J. Neurol. Neurosurg. Psychiat.
8, 15-21.

Eysenck, M. D. (1946) The psychological aspects of ageing
and senility, J. ment. Sci. 92, 171-181.

Eysenck, M. W. (1974a) Extraversion, arousal, and retrieval
from semantic memory, J. Personality 42, 319-331.

Eysenck, M. W. (1974b) Ageing, learning, and memory,
unpubl. manuscript.

Eysenck, M. W. (1974c) Individual differences in speed of
retrieval from semantic memory, J. Res. Person. 8, 307-
323.

Eysenck, M. W. (1974d) Age differences in incidental
learning, Developm. Psychol. 10, 936-941.

Eysenck, M. W. (1975a) Retrieval from semantic memory as a
function of age, J. Geront. 30, 174-180.

Eysenck, M. W. (1975b) Effects of noise, activation level,
and response dominance on retrieval from semantic memory,
J. exp. Psychol.: Hum. Learn. Mem. 1, 143-148.

Eysenck, M. W. (1975c) Arousal and speed of recall, Br. J.
soc. clin. Psychol. 14, 269-277.

Eysenck, M. W. (1975d) Extraversion, arousal, and speed of
retrieval from secondary storage, J. Personality 43,
390-401.

Eysenck, M. W. (1976a) Arousal, learning, and memory,

Psychol. Bull. 83, 389-404.

Eysenck, M. W. (1976b) Extraversion, activation, and the recall of prose, Br. J. Psychol. 67, 53-61.

Eysenck, M. W. (1976c) Extraversion, verbal learning, and memory, Psychol. Bull. 83, 75-90.

Eysenck, M. W. (1977) Levels of processing: A critique, Br. J. Psychol. 68.

Eysenck, M. W. (In preparation) First letters as retrieval cues from semantic memory.

Eysenck, M. W. (In preparation) The reverse tip-of-the-tongue phenomenon.

Eysenck, M. W., and Baron, C. R. (1974) Effects of cueing on recall from categorized word lists, Developm. Psychol. 10, 665-666.

Eysenck, M. W., and Eysenck, M. C. (In preparation) Effects of encoding distinctiveness on recall and recognition.

Eysenck, S. B. G., and Eysenck, H. J. (1963) On the dual nature of extraversion, Br. J. soc. clin. Psychol. 2, 46-55.

Fagan, J. F. (1972) Rehearsal and free recall in children of superior and average intelligence, Psychon. Sci. 28, 352-354.

Fagan, J. F., and Binzley, V. (1970) Free recall in children of superior, average, and retarded I.Q., Gatlinburg Conference on Mental Retardation, Gatlinburg, Tenn.

Farley, F., and Farley, S. V. (1967) Extraversion and stimulus-seeking motivation, J. consult. Psychol. 31, 215-216.

Fine, B. J. (1972) Field-dependent introvert and neuroticism: Eysenck and Witkin united, Psychol. Rep. 31, 939-956.

Fischler, I., Rundus, D., and Atkinson, R. C. (1970) Effects of overt rehearsal procedures on free recall, Psychon. Sci. 19, 249-250.

Fiske, D. W. (1957) An intensive study of variability scores, Educ. psychol. Measmt. 17, 453-465.

Fitzgibbons, D., Goldberger, L., and Eagle, M. (1965) Field dependence and memory for incidental material, Percept. mot. Skills 21, 743-749.

Folkard, S. (1976) The reduction of subvocal activity under stress, and its effect on information processing and memory, Proceedings of the XXI International Congress of Psychology, Paris.

Folkard, S., Monk, T. H., Bradbury, R., and Rosenthall, J.

(1977) Time of day effects in school children's immediate and delayed recall of meaningful material, <u>Br. J. Psychol.</u> 68.

Forrest, D. W. (1963) Relationship between sharpening and extraversion, <u>Psychol. Rep.</u> 13, 564.

Forrest, M., and Kroth, J. A. (1971) Psychometric and physiological indices of anxiety, <u>J. clin. Psychol.</u> 27, 40-42.

Forrin, B., and Cunningham, K. (1973) Recognition time and serial position of probed items in short-term memory, <u>J. exp. Psychol.</u> 99, 272-279.

Foss, D. J., and Harwood, D. A. (1975) Memory for sentences: Implications for human associative memory, <u>J. verb. Learn. verb. Behav.</u> 14, 1-16.

Foss, D. J., and Lynch, R. H. (1969) Decision processes during sentence comprehension: Effects of surface structure on decision times, <u>Percept. Psychophys.</u> 5, 145-148.

Fozard, J. L., Nuttall, R. L., and Waugh, N. C. (1972) Age-related differences in mental performance, <u>Ageing hum. Developm.</u> 3, 19-43.

Fraser, D. C. (1958) Decay of immediate memory with age, <u>Nature, Lond.</u> 182, 1163.

Freedman, J. L., and Loftus, E. F. (1971) Retrieval of words from long-term memory, <u>J. verb. Learn. verb. Behav.</u> 10, 107-115.

Freedman, J. L., and Loftus, E. F. (1974) Retrieval of words from well-learned sets: The effect of category size, <u>J. exp. Psychol.</u> 102, 1085-1091.

Freud, S. (1915) Repression. In <u>Freud's Collected Papers</u>, Vol. IV, Hogarth, London.

Freud, S. (1943) <u>A General Introduction to Psychoanalysis</u>, Garden City, New York.

Frost, N. (1971) Clustering by visual shape in the free recall of pictorial stimuli, <u>J. exp. Psychol.</u> 88, 409-413.

Frost, N. (1972) Encoding and retrieval in visual memory tasks, <u>J. exp. Psychol.</u> 95, 317-326.

Fuhrer, M. J., Baer, P. E., and Cowan, C. O. (1973) Orienting responses and personality variables as predictors of differential conditioning of electrodermal responses and awareness of stimulus relations, <u>J. Person. soc. Psychol.</u> 27, 287-296.

Gagne, R. M. (1967) <u>Learning and Individual Differences</u>, Merrill, Columbus, Ohio.

Gale, A. (1969) "Stimulus hunger": Individual differences in operant strategy in a button-pressing task, Behav. Res. Ther. 7, 265-274.

Gale, A. (1973) The psychophysiology of individual differences: Studies of extraversion and the EEG. In P. Kline (Ed.), New Approaches to Psychological Measurement, Wiley, London.

Gale, A., Morris, P. E., Lucas, B., and Richardson, A. (1972) Types of imagery and imagery types: An EEG study, Br. J. Psychol. 63, 523-531.

Galton, F. (1883) Inquiries into Human Faculty and its Development, MacMillan, London.

Ganzer, V. J. (1968) Effects of audience presence and test anxiety on learning and retention in a serial learning situation, J. Person. soc. Psychol. 8, 194-199.

Gardiner, J. M. (1974) Levels of processing in word recognition and subsequent free recall, J. exp. Psychol. 102, 101-105.

Gardiner, J. M., Craik, F. I. M., and Birtwistle, J. (1972) Retrieval cues and release from proactive inhibition, J. verb. Learn. verb. Behav. 11, 778-783.

Gardiner, J. M., Craik, F. I. M., and Bleasdale, F. A. (1973) Retrieval difficulty and subsequent recall, Mem. Cogn. 1, 213-216.

Gardiner, J. M., and Klee, H. (1976) Memory for remembered events: An assessment of output monitoring in free recall, J. verb. Learn. verb. Behav. 15, 227-234.

Garfield, S. L., and Blek, L. (1952) Age, vocabulary level, and mental impairment, J. consult. Psychol. 16, 395-398.

Gaudry, E., and Spielberger, C. D. (1970) Anxiety and intelligence in paired-associate learning, J. educ. Psychol. 61, 386-391.

Gauld, A., and Stephenson, G. M. (1967) Some experiments relating to Bartlett's theory of remembering, Br. J. Psychol. 58, 39-50.

Geis, M. F., and Winograd, E. (1974) Norms of semantic encoding variability for fifty homographs, Bull. psychon. Soc. 3, 429-431.

Gewirtz, J. L. (1948) Studies in word-fluency. II. Its relation to eleven items of child behaviour, J. genet. Psychol. 72, 177-184.

Gilbert, J. C. (1941) Memory loss in senescence, J. abnorm. soc. Psychol. 36, 73-86.

Gilbert, J. C., and Levee, R. F. (1971) Patterns of declining memory, J. Geront. 26, 70-75.

Gladis, M., and Braun, H. W. (1958) Age differences in transfer and retroaction as a function of intertask response similarity, J. exp. Psychol. 55, 25-30.

Glanzer, M., and Cunitz, A. R. (1966) Two storage mechanisms in free recall, J. verb. Learn. verb. Behav. 5, 351-360.

Glanzer, M., Gianutsos, R., and Dubin, S. (1969) The removal of items from short-term storage, J. verb. Learn. verb. Behav. 8, 435-447.

Glanzer, M., Koppenaal, L., and Nelson, R. (1972) Effects of relations between words on short-term storage and long-term storage, J. verb. Learn. verb. Behav. 11, 403-416.

Glanzer, M., and Razel, M. (1974) The size of the unit in short-term storage, J. verb. Learn. verb. Behav. 13, 114-131.

Glass, A. L., and Holyoak, K. J. (1975) Alternative conceptions of semantic theory, Cogn. 3, 313-339.

Glover, C. B., and Cravens, R. W. (1974) Trait anxiety, stress, and learning: A test of Saltz' hypothesis, J. Res. Person. 8, 243-253.

Goggin, J., and Wickens, D. D. (1971) Proactive interference and language change in short-term memory, J. verb. Learn. verb. Behav. 10, 453-458.

Golding, S. L. (1975) Flies in the ointment: Methodological problems in the analysis of the percentage of the variance due to persons and situations, Psychol. Bull. 82, 278-288.

Goldstein, A. G., and Chance, J. E. (1971) Visual recognition memory for complex configurations, Percept. Psychophys. 9, 237-241.

Gomulicki, B. R. (1953) Recall as an abstractive process, Unpubl. Ph.D. thesis, Oxford Univ.

Gomulicki, B. R. (1956) Recall as an abstractive process, Acta psychol. 12, 77-94.

Gordon, R. (1949) An investigation into some of the factors that favour the formation of stereotyped images, Br. J. Psychol. 39, 156-167.

Gordon, S. K., and Clark, W. C. (1974a) Application of signal detection theory to prose recall and recognition in elderly and young adults, J. Geront. 29, 64-72.

Gordon, S. K., and Clark, W. C. (1974b) Adult age differences in word and nonsense syllable recognition memory and response criterion, J. Geront. 29, 659-665.

Gordon, W. M., and Berlyne, D. E. (1954) Drive-level and flexibility in paired-associate nonsense syllable learning, Q. Jl. exp. Psychol. 6, 181-185.

Goulet, L. R. (1972) New directions for research on ageing and retention, J. Geront. 27, 52-60.

Goulet, L. R., and Mazzei, J. (1969) Verbal learning and confidence thresholds as a function of test anxiety, intelligence, and stimulus similarity, J. exp. Res. Person. 3, 247-252.

Gray, J. A. (1972) The psychophysiological nature of introversion-extraversion: A modification of Eysenck's theory. In V. D. Nebylitsyn and J. A. Gray (Eds.), Biological Bases of Individual Behaviour, London, Academic Press.

Green, R. F. (1964) The measurement of mood, Tech. Rep., Office of Naval Research.

Greene, J. (1972) Psycholinguistics: Chomsky and Psychology, Penguin, Harmondsworth.

Gregg, V. (1976) Word frequency, recognition and recall. In J. Brown (Ed.), Recall and Recognition, Wiley, London.

Grice, G. R. (1955) Discrimination reaction time as a function of anxiety and intelligence, J. abnorm. soc. Psychol. 50, 71-74.

Griffith, D., and Johnston, W. A. (1973) An information-processing analysis of visual imagery, J. exp. Psychol. 100, 141-146.

Griffiths, J. (1958) The effect of experimentally induced anxiety on certain subtests of the Wechsler-Bellevue, Diss. Abstrs. 18, 655-656.

Grober, E. H., and Loftus, E. F. (1974) Semantic memory: Searching for attributes vs. searching for names, Mem. Cogn. 2, 413-416.

Groot, A. D. de (1966) Perception and memory versus thought: Some old ideas and recent findings. In B. Kleinmuntz (Ed.), Problem Solving, Wiley, New York.

Gruneberg, M. M., Smith, R. L., and Winfrow, P. (1973) An investigation into response blockaging, Acta psychol. 37, 187-196.

Gruneberg, M. M., and Sykes, R. N. (1969) Acoustic confusion in long term memory, Acta psychol. 29, 293-296.

Guilford, J. P. (1956) The structure of intellect, Psychol. Bull. 53, 267-293.

Guilford, J. P. (1964) Zero intercorrelations among tests of intellectual abilities, Psychol. Bull. 61, 401-404.

Guilford, J. P. (1971) Some misconceptions of factors, Psychol. Bull. 77, 392-396.

Gupta, B. S. (1976) Extraversion and reinforcement in

verbal operant conditioning, Br. J. Psychol. 67, 47-52.

Gutman, G. M. (1966) A note on the MPI: Age and sex differences in extraversion and neuroticism in a Canadian sample, Br. J. soc. clin. Psychol. 5, 128-129.

Halff, H. M., Ortony, A., and Anderson, R. C. (1976) A context-sensitive representation of word meanings, Mem. Cogn. 4, 378-383.

Hall, J. F. (1954) Learning as a function of word frequency, Am. J. Psychol. 67, 138-140.

Hamilton, P., Hockey, G. R. J., and Quinn, J. G. (1972) Information selection, arousal and memory, Br. J. Psychol. 63, 181-189.

Hargreaves, D. J., and Bolton, N. (1972) Selecting creativity tests for use in research, Br. J. Psychol. 63, 451-462.

Hart, J. T. (1965) Memory and the feeling-of-knowing experience, J. educ. Psychol. 56, 208-216.

Hart, J. T. (1966) Methodological note on feeling-of-knowing experiments, J. educ. Psychol. 57, 347-349.

Hartley, J., and Marshall, I. S. (1967) Ageing, recognition and partial learning, Psychon. Sci. 9, 215-216.

Harwood, E., and Naylor, G. F. K. (1969) Recall and recognition in elderly and young subjects, Aust. J. Psychol. 21, 251-257.

Haveman, J., and Farley, F. H. (1969) Arousal and retention in paired-associate, serial, and free learning, Tech. Rep. No. 91, Wisconsin Research and Development Centre for Cognitive Learning, Contract OE 5-10-154, U. S. Office of Education, Department of Health, Education, and Welfare.

Haviland, S., and Clark, H. (1974) What's new? Acquiring new information as a process in comprehension, J. verb. Learn. verb. Behav. 13, 512-521.

Heron, A, and Craik, F. I. M. (1964) Age differences in cumulative learning of meaningful and meaningless material, Scand. J. Psychol. 5, 209-217.

Herriot, P. (1974) Attributes of Memory, Methuen, London.

Hill, A. B. (1975) Extraversion and variety-seeking in a monotonous task, Br. J. Psychol. 66, 9-13.

Hill, W. F. (1957) Comments on Taylor's "Drive theory and manifest anxiety", Psychol. Bull. 54, 490-493.

Hockey, G. R. J. (1970) Signal probability and spatial location as possible bases for increased selectivity in noise, Q. Jl. exp. Psychol. 22, 37-42.

Hockey, G. R. J. (1973) Changes in information-selection patterns in multisource monitoring as a function of induced arousal shifts, J. exp. Psychol. 101, 35-42.

Hockey, G. R. J., and Hamilton, P. (1970) Arousal and information selection in short-term memory, Nature, Lond. 226, 866-867.

Hodges, W. F. (1968) Effects of ego threat and threat of pain on state anxiety, J. Person. soc. Psychol. 8, 364-372.

Hodges, W. F., and Durham, R. L. (1972) Anxiety, ability, and digit span performance, J. Person. soc. Psychol. 24, 401-406.

Hodges, W. F., and Spielberger, C. D. (1969) Digit span: An indicant of trait or state anxiety?, J. consult. clin. Psychol. 33, 430-434.

Hofstaetter, P. R., O'Connor, J. P., and Suziedelis, A. (1957) Sequences of restricted associative responses and their personality correlates, J. gen. Psychol. 57, 219-227.

Hogan, R. M., and Kintsch, W. (1971) Differential effects of study and test trials on long-term recognition and recall, J. verb. Learn. verb. Behav. 10, 562-567.

Holding, D. H. (1975) Sensory storage reconsidered, Mem. Cogn. 3, 31-41.

Hollenberg, C. K. (1970) Functions of visual imagery in the learning and concept formation of children, Child Dev. 41, 1003-1015.

Holmes, D. S. (1972) Repression or interference? A further investigation, J. Person. soc. Psychol. 22, 163-170.

Hörmann, H., and Osterkamp, U. (1966) Uber den Einfluss von kontinuierlichem Lärm auf die Organisation von Gedächtnisinhalten, Z. exp. angew. Psychol. 13, 31-38.

Horowitz, L. M., and Manelis, L. (1972) Toward a theory of redintegrative memory: Adjective-noun phrases. In G. H. Bower (Ed.), The Psychology of Learning and Motivation: Advances in Research and Theory, Vol. VI, Academic Press, New York.

Howarth, E. (1969a) Personality differences in serial learning under distraction, Percept. mot. Skills 28, 379-382.

Howarth, E. (1969b) Extraversion and increased interference in paired-associate learning, Percept. mot. Skills 29, 403-406.

Howarth, E., and Eysenck, H. J. (1968) Extraversion, arousal, and paired-associate recall, J. exp. Res. Person. 3, 114-116.

Huckabee, M. W. (1974) Introversion-extraversion and imagery, Psychol. Rep. 34, 453-454.

Hudson, L. (1968) _Frames of Mind_, Methuen, London.

Hulicka, I. M. (1965) Age differences for intentional and incidental learning and recall scores, _J. Am. Geriatr. Soc._ 13, 639-648.

Hulicka, I. M., and Grossman, J. L. (1967) Age-group comparisons for the use of mediators in paired-associate learning, _J. Geront._ 22, 46-51.

Hulicka, I. M., and Rust, L. D. (1964) Age-related retention deficit as a function of learning, _J. Am. Geriatr. Soc._ 11, 1061-1065.

Hulicka, I. M., Sterns, H., and Grossman, J. L. (1967) Age-group comparisons of paired-associate learning as a function of paced and self-paced association and response times, _J. Geront._ 22, 274-280.

Hulicka, I. M., and Weiss, R. L. (1965) Age differences in retention as a function of learning, _J. consult. Psychol._ 29, 125-129.

Hultsch, D. F. (1969) Adult age differences in the organization of free recall, _Developm. Psychol._ 1, 673-678.

Hultsch, D. F. (1971) Adult age differences in free classification and free recall, _Developm. Psychol._ 4, 338-343.

Hultsch, D. F. (1974) Learning to learn in adulthood, _J. Geront._ 29, 302-308.

Hultsch, D. F. (1975) Adult age differences in retrieval: Trace-dependent and cue-dependent forgetting, _Developm. Psychol._ 11, 197-201.

Humphrey, G. (1951) _Thinking: An Introduction to its Experimental Psychology_, Methuen, London.

Hunt, E., Frost, N., and Lunneborg, C. (1973) Individual differences in cognition: A new approach to intelligence. In Bower, G. H. (Ed.), _Advances in Learning and Motivation_ Vol. 7, Academic Press, London.

Hunt, E., Lunneborg, C., and Lewis, J. (1975) What does it mean to be high verbal?, _Cogn. Psychol._ 7, 194-227.

Huttenlocher, J. (1968) Constructing spatial images: A strategy in reasoning, _Psychol. Rev._ 75, 550-560.

Hyde, T. S. (1973) Differential effects of effort and type of orienting task on recall and organization of highly associated words, _J. exp. Psychol._ 99, 111-113.

Hyde, T. S., and Jenkins, J. J. (1969) Differential effects of incidental tasks on the organization of recall of a list of highly associated words, _J. exp. Psychol._ 82, 472-481.

Imam, A. (1973) Incidental learning: IV. A function of field dependence, Pak. J. Psychol. 6, 7-23.

Imam, A. (1974) Extraversion and incidental learning, Pak. J. Psychol. 7, 41-54.

Indow, T., and Togano, K. (1970) On retrieving sequence from long-term memory, Psychol. Rev. 77, 317-331.

Inglis, J. (1964) Influence of motivation, perception and attention on age-related changes in short-term memory, Nature, Lond. 204, 103-104.

Inglis, J. (1965) Immediate memory, age and brain function. In A. T. Welford and J. E. Birren (Eds.), Behaviour, Ageing, and the Nervous System, Thomas, Springfield.

Inglis, J., and Ankus, M. N. (1965) Effects of age on short-term storage and serial rote learning, Br. J. Psychol. 56, 183-195.

Inglis, J., and Caird, W. K. (1963) Age differences in successive responses to simultaneous stimulation, Can. J. Psychol. 17, 98-105.

Innes, J. M. (1971) Word association, associative structure and manifest anxiety, Br. J. Psychol. 62, 519-525.

Innes, J. M. (1972) The relationship of word-association commonality response set to cognitive and personality variables, Br. J. Psychol. 63, 421-428.

Jacoby, L. L. (1974) The role of mental contiguity in memory: Registration and retrieval effects, J. verb. Learn. verb. Behav. 13, 483-496.

Jacoby, L. L. (1975) Physical features vs. meaning: A difference in decay, Mem. Cogn. 3, 247-251.

James, W. (1890) Principles of Psychology, Vol. 1, Holt, New York.

James, W. (1892) Psychology, Holt, New York.

Jenkins, J. J. (1960) Commonality of association as an indicator of more general patterns of verbal behaviour. In T. A. Sebeok (Ed.), Style in Language, Wiley, London.

Jensen, A. (1964) Individual differences in learning: Interference factor, Cooperative Research Project No. 1867, Office of Education, U. S. Department of Health, Education, and Welfare.

Jensen, A. (1970) Hierarchical theories of mental ability. In B. Dockrell (Ed.), On Intelligence, Ontario Institute for Studies in Education, Toronto.

Jensen, A. (1974) Interaction of Level I and Level II abilities with race and socioeconomic status, J. educ. Psychol. 66, 99-111.

Jensen, A., and Frederiksen, J. (1973) Free recall of

categorized and uncategorized lists: A test of the
Jensen hypothesis, J. educ. Psychol. 3, 304-312.

Jensen, A., and Figueroa, R. A. (1975) Forward and backward
digit span interaction with race and I.Q.: Predictions
from Jensen's theory, J. educ. Psychol. 67, 882-893.

Jessor, R., and Hammond, K. R. (1957) Construct validity
and the Taylor Manifest Anxiety Scale, Psychol. Bull.
54, 161-170.

Jinks, J. L., and Fulker, D. W. (1970) A comparison of the
biometrical genetical, MAVA and classical approaches to
the analysis of human behaviour, Psychol. Bull. 73, 311-
349.

Johnson, J. H. (1974) Memory and personality: An
information processing approach, J. Res. Person. 8,
1-32.

Johnson, M. K., Bransford, J. D., Nyberg, S. E., and Cleary,
J. J. (1972) Comprehension factors in interpreting
memory for abstract and concrete sentences, J. verb.
Learn. verb. Behav. 11, 451-454.

Johnson, N. F. (1965) The psychological reality of phrase
structure rules, J. verb. Learn. verb. Behav. 4, 469-
474.

Johnson, N. F. (1968) Sequential verbal behaviour. In T.
R. Dixon and D. L. Horton (Eds.), Verbal Behaviour and
General Behaviour Theory, Prentice-Hall, Englewood Cliffs.

Johnson, R. C., and Lim, D. (1964) Personality variables in
associative production, J. gen. Psychol. 71, 349-350.

Johnson-Laird, P. N. (1974) Experimental psycholinguistics.
In M. R. Rosenzweig and L. W. Porter (Eds.), Annual
Review of Psychology, Vol. 25, Annual Reviews Inc.,
Palo Alto.

Johnson-Laird, P. N., Robins, C., and Velicogna, L. (1974)
Memory for words, Nature, Lond. 251, 704-705.

Johnson-Laird, P. N., and Stevenson, R. (1970) Memory for
syntax, Nature, Lond. 227, 412-413.

Jones, G. V. (1976) A fragmentation hypothesis of memory:
Cued recall of pictures and of sequential position, J.
exp. Psychol.: Gen. 105, 277-293.

Jones, J. (1970) Cognitive factors in the appreciation of
humour: A theoretical and experimental analysis, unpubl.
Ph.D. thesis, Yale Univ.

Kagan, J., and Moss, H. (1962) Birth to Maturity, Wiley,
New York.

Kahneman, D. (1973) Attention and Effort, Prentice-Hall,
London.

Kahneman, D., Beatty, J., and Pollack, I. (1967) Perceptual deficit during a mental task, *Science, N.Y.* 157, 218-219.

Kahneman, D., and Peavler, W. S. (1969) Incentive effects and pupillary changes in associative learning, *J. exp. Psychol.* 79, 312-318.

Kahneman, D., Tursky, B., Shapiro, D., and Crider, A. (1969) Pupillary, heart rate and skin resistance changes during a mental task, *J. exp. Psychol.* 79, 164-167.

Kamin, L. J., and Fedorchak, O. (1957) The Taylor scale, hunger, and verbal learning, *Can. J. Psychol.* 11, 212-218.

Kanfer, F. H. (1960) Word association and the drive hypothesis of anxiety, *J. clin. Psychol.* 16, 200-204.

Kaplan, R., and Kaplan, S. (1969) The arousal-retention interval interaction revisited: The effects of some procedural changes, *Psychon. Sci.* 15, 84-85.

Kaplan, S., and Kaplan, R. (1968) Arousal and memory: A comment, *Psychon. Sci.* 10, 291-292.

Kapnick, P. (1971) Age and recognition memory, unpubl. Ph.D. thesis, Washington Univ. St. Louis.

Katkin, E. S. (1965) Relationship between manifest anxiety and two indices of autonomic stress, *J. Person. soc. Psychol.* 2, 324-333.

Kausler, D. H., and Lair, C. V. (1966) Associative strength and paired-associate learning in elderly subjects, *J. Geront.* 21, 278-280.

Kay, H. (1951) Learning of a serial task by different age groups, *Q. Jl. exp. Psychol.* 3, 166-183.

Keevil-Rogers, P., and Schnore, M. M. (1969) Short-term memory as a function of age in persons of above average intelligence, *J. Geront.* 24, 184-188.

Kellas, G. A., Ashcraft, M. H., and Johnson, N. S. (1973) Rehearsal processes in the short-term memory performance of mildly retarded adolescents, *Am. J. ment. Defic.* 77, 670-679.

Kellas, G. A., Ashcraft, M. H., Johnson, N. S., and Needham, S. (1973) Temporal aspects of storage and retrieval in free recall of categorized lists, *J. verb. Learn. verb. Behav.* 12, 499-511.

Kellas, G. A., McCauley, C., and McFarland, C. E. (1975) Re-examination of externalized rehearsal, *J. exp. Psychol. Hum. Learn. Mem.* 1, 84-90.

Kelly, D. H. W., and Walter, C. J. S. (1968) The relationship between clinical diagnosis and anxiety, assessed by forearm blood flow and other measurements,

Br. J. Psychiat. 114, 611-626.

Kennedy, R. A., and Wilkes, A. L. (1969) Analysis of storage and retrieval processes in memorizing simple sentences, _J. exp. Psychol._ 80, 396-398.

Kerrick, J. S. (1955) Some correlates of the Taylor Manifest Anxiety Scale, _J. abnorm. soc. Psychol._ 50, 75-77.

Kilpatrick, D. G. (1972) Differential responsiveness of two electrodermal indices to psychological stress and performance of a complex cognitive task, _Psychophysiol._ 9, 218-226.

Kimble, G. A., and Posnick, G. M. (1967) Anxiety?, _J. Person. soc. Psychol._ 7, 108-110.

Kintsch, W. (1968) Recognition and free recall of organized lists, _J. exp. Psychol._ 78, 481-487.

Kintsch, W. (1970) Models for free recall and recognition. In D. A. Norman (Ed.), _Models of Human Memory_, Academic Press, London.

Kintsch, W. (1972a) Notes on the structure of semantic memory. In E. Tulving and W. Donaldson (Eds.), _Organization of Memory_, Academic Press, London.

Kintsch, W. (1972b) Abstract nouns: Imagery versus lexical complexity, _J. verb. Learn. verb. Behav._ 11, 59-65.

Kintsch, W., and Buschke, H. (1969) Homophones and synonyms in short-term memory, _J. exp. Psychol._ 80, 403-407.

Kirsner, K. (1972a) Developmental changes in short-term recognition memory, _Br. J. Psychol._ 63, 109-117.

Kirsner, K. (1972b) Naming latency facilitation: An analysis of the encoding component in recognition reaction time, _J. exp. Psychol._ 95, 171-176.

Klee, H. (1975) Imagery in the comprehension and construction of sentences, unpubl. Ph.D. thesis, Univ. London.

Klee, H., and Eysenck, M. W. (1973) Comprehension of abstract and concrete sentences, _J. verb. Learn. verb. Behav._ 12, 522-529.

Kleinsmith, L. J., and Kaplan, S. (1963) Paired-associate learning as a function of arousal and interpolated interval, _J. exp. Psychol._ 65, 190-193.

Kleinsmith, L. J., and Kaplan, S. (1964) Interaction of arousal and recall interval in nonsense syllable paired-associate learning, _J. exp. Psychol._ 67, 124-126

Kleinsmith, L. J., Kaplan, S., and Tarte, R. D. (1963) The relationship of arousal to short- and long-term recall,

Can. J. Psychol. 17, 393-397.

Klugh, H. E., and Bendig, A. W. (1955) The Manifest
    Anxiety and ACE Scales and college achievement, J.
    consult. Psychol. 19, 487.

Knox, W. J., and Grippaldi, R. (1970) High levels of state
    or trait anxiety and performance on selected verbal WAIS
    subtests, Psychol. Rep. 27, 375-379.

Koepke, J. E., and Pribram, K. H. (1966) Habituation of
    GSR as a function of stimulus duration and spontaneous
    activity, J. comp. physiol. Psychol. 61, 442-448.

Kolers, P. A., and Ostry, D. J. (1974) Time course of loss
    of information regarding pattern analyzing operations,
    J. verb. Learn. verb. Behav. 14, 599-612.

Korchin, S. H., and Basowitz, H. (1957) Age differences in
    verbal learning, J. abnorm. soc. Psychol. 54, 64-69.

Koriat, A., Averill, J. R., and Malmstrom, E. J. (1973)
    Individual differences in habituation: Some methodological
    and conceptual issues, J. Res. Person. 7, 88-101.

Koriat, A., and Lieblich, I. (1974) What does a person in a
    "TOT" state know that a person in a "don't know" state
    doesn't know?, Mem. Cogn. 2, 647-655.

Kosslyn, S. M. (1973) Scanning visual images: Some
    structural implications, Percept. Psychophys. 14, 90-94.

Kriaicunas, R. (1968) The relationship of age and
    retention-interval activity in short-term memory, J.
    Geront. 23, 169-173.

Kuhlman, C. K. (1960) Visual imagery in children, unpubl.
    Ph.D. thesis, Radcliffe College.

Labouvie, G. V., Frohring, W. R., Baltes, P. B., and Goulet,
    L. R. (1973) Changing relationship between recall
    performance and abilities as a function of stage of
    learning and timing of recall, J. educ. Psychol. 64,
    191-198.

Labouvie-Vief, G., Levin, J. R., and Urberg, K. A. (1975)
    The relationship between selected cognitive abilities and
    learning: A second look, J. educ. Psychol. 67, 558-569.

Lacey, J. I. (1967) Somatic response patterning and stress:
    Some revisions of activation theory. In M. H. Appley and
    R. Trumbull (Eds.), Psychological Stress, Appleton-
    Century-Crofts, New York.

Lacey, J. I., and Lacey, B. C. (1958) Verification and
    extension of the principle of autonomic response-
    stereotypy, Am. J. Psychol. 71, 50-73.

Lakoff, G. (1972) Hedges: A study in meaning criteria and
    the logic of fuzzy concepts. Papers from the eighth

regional meeting, Chicago Linguistics Soc., Chicago.

Lalljee, M., and Cook, M. (1975) Anxiety and ritualized speech, Br. J. Psychol. 66, 299-306.

Landauer, T. K., and Freedman, J. L. (1968) Information retrieval from long-term memory: Category size and recognition time, J. verb. Learn. verb. Behav. 7, 291-295.

Landauer, T. K., and Meyer, D. E. (1972) Category size and semantic-memory retrieval, J. verb. Learn. verb. Behav. 11, 539-549.

Lauer, P. A. (1975) The effects of different types of word processing on memory performance in young and elderly adults, unpubl. Ph.D. thesis, Univ. Colorado, Boulder, Colorado.

Laughlin, P. R. (1967) Incidental concept formation as a function of creativity and intelligence, J. Person. soc. Psychol. 5, 115-119.

Laughlin, P. R., Doherty, M. A., and Dunn, R. F. (1968) Intentional and incidental concept formation as a function of motivation, creativity, intelligence, and sex, J. Person. soc. Psychol. 8, 401-409.

Laurence, M. W. (1966) Age differences in performance and subjective organization in the free-recall learning of pictorial material, Can. J. Psychol. 20, 388-399.

Laurence, M. W. (1967a) A developmental look at the usefulness of list categorization as an aid to free recall, Can. J. Psychol. 21, 153-165.

Laurence, M. W. (1967b) Memory loss with age: A test of two strategies for its retardation, Psychon. Sci. 9, 209-210.

Lazar, G., and Buschke, H. (1972) Successive retrieval from permanent storage, Psychon. Sci. 29, 388-390.

Leech, S., and Witte, K. L. (1971) Paired-associate learning in elderly adults as related to pacing and incentive conditions, Developm. Psychol. 5, 180.

Levelt, W. J. M. (1970) A scaling approach to the study of syntactic relations. In G. B. Flores d'Arcais and W. J. M. Levelt (Eds.), Advances in Psycholinguistics, North-Holland.

Levinger, G., and Clark, J. (1961) Emotional factors in the forgetting of word associations, J. abnorm. soc. Psychol. 62, 99-105.

Levonian, E. (1967) Retention of information in relation to arousal during continuously-presented material, Am. educ. Res. J. 4, 103-116.

Levonian, E. (1972) Retention over time in relation to

arousal during learning: An explanation of discrepant
findings, _Acta psychol_. 36, 290-321.

Levy, B. A., and Murdock, B. B. (1968) The effects of
delayed auditory feedback and intralist similarity in
short-term memory, _J. verb. Learn. verb. Behav_. 7, 887-
894.

Levy, C. M., and Murphy, P. H. (1966) The effects of
alcohol on semantic and phonetographic generalization,
Psychon. Sci. 4, 205-206.

Lewinski, R. J. (1948) Vocabulary and mental measurement:
A quantitative investigation and review of research,
J. genet. Psychol. 72, 247-281.

Lewis, A. (1970) The ambiguous word "anxiety", _Internat. J.
Psychiatry_ 9, 62-79.

Liddell, H. S., James, W. T., and Anderson, O. D. (1934)
The comparative physiology of the conditioned motor reflex,
based on experiments with the pig, dog, sheep, goat, and
rabbit, _Compar. Psychol. Monogr_. 11, 1-89.

Liebert, R. M., and Morris, L. W. (1967) Cognitive and
emotional components of test anxiety: A distinction and
some initial data, _Psychol. Rep_. 20, 975-978.

Light, L. L. (1972) Homonyms and synonyms as retrieval cues,
J. exp. Psychol. 96, 255-262.

Light, L. L., and Carter-Sobell, L. (1970) Effects of
changed semantic context on recognition memory, _J. verb.
Learn. verb. Behav_. 9, 1-11.

Light, L. L., Kimble, G. A., and Pellegrino, J. W. (1975)
Comments on "Episodic memory: When recognition fails",
by Watkins and Tulving, _J. exp. Psychol.: Gen_. 1, 30-36.

Lockhart, R. S., Craik, F. I. M., and Jacoby, L. (1976)
Depth of processing, recognition, and recall. In J. Brown
(Ed.), _Recall and Recognition_, Wiley, London.

Loftus, E. F. (1973) Category dominance, instance
dominance, and categorization time, _J. exp. Psychol_. 97,
70-74.

Loftus, E. F., and Cole, W. (1974) Retrieving attribute and
name information from semantic memory, _J. exp. Psychol_.
102, 1116-1122.

Loftus, E. F., Freedman, J. L., and Loftus, G. R. (1970)
Retrieval of words from subordinate and superordinate
categories in semantic hierarchies, _Psychon. Sci_. 21,
235-236.

Loftus, E. F., and Suppes, P. (1972) Structural variables
that determine the speed of retrieving words from long-
term memory, _J. verb. Learn. verb. Behav_. 11, 770-777.

Loftus, G. R., and Bell, S. M. (1975) Two types of

information in picture memory, *J. exp. Psychol.: Hum. Learn. Mem.* 1, 103-113.

Loftus, G. R., and Loftus, E. F. (1974) The influence of one memory retrieval on a subsequent memory retrieval, *Mem. Cogn.* 2, 467-471.

Lovaas, O. I. (1960) The relationship of induced muscular tension, tension level, and manifest anxiety in learning, *J. exp. Psychol.* 59, 145-152.

Lucas, J. D. (1952) The interactive effects of anxiety, failure, and intra-serial duplication, *Am. J. Psychol.* 65, 59-66.

Luria, A. R. (1968) *The Mind of a Mnemonist* (translated by L. Solotaroff), Basic Books, New York.

Luszcz, M. A., and Bacharach, V. R. (1975) List organization and rehearsal instructions in recognition memory of retarded adults, *Am. J. ment. Defic.* 80, 57-62.

Mackay, H. A., and Inglis, J. (1963) The effect of age on a short-term auditory storage process, *Gerontologia* 8, 193-200.

Madison, P. (1956) Freud's repression concept: A survey and attempted clarification, *Int. J. Psycho-Anal.* 37, 75-81.

Magoun, H. W. (1963) *The Waking Brain*, Thomas, Springfield.

Malmo, R. B. (1957) Anxiety and behavioural arousal, *Psychol. Rev.* 64, 276-287.

Maltzman, I., Kantor, W., and Langdon, B. (1966) Immediate and delayed retention, arousal, and the orienting and defensive reflexes, *Psychon. Sci.* 6, 445-446.

Mandler, G. (1967) Organization and memory. In K. W. Spence and J. T. Spence (Eds.), *The Psychology of Learning and Motivation: Advances in Research and Theory*, Vol. 1, Academic Press, London.

Mandler, G. (1969) Input variables and output strategies in free recall of categorized words, *Am. J. Psychol.* 82, 531-539.

Mandler, G. (1972) Organization and recognition. In E. Tulving and W. Donaldson (Eds.), *Organization of Memory*, Academic Press, London.

Mandler, G. (1975) Memory storage and retrieval: Some limits on the reach of attention and consciousness. In P. M. A. Rabbitt and S. Dornic (Eds.), *Attention and Performance*, Vol. V, Academic Press, London.

Mandler, G., Mandler, J. E., Kremen, J., and Sholitan, R. D. (1961) The response to threat: Relations among verbal and physiological indices, Psychol. Monogr. 75, (Whole No. 513).

Mandler, G., Pearlstone, A., and Koopmans, H. S. (1969) Effects of organization and semantic similarity on recall and recognition, J. verb. Learn. verb. Behav. 8, 410-423.

Mandler, G., and Sarason, S. B. (1952) A study of anxiety and learning, J. abnorm. soc. Psychol. 47, 166-173.

Mandler, G., and Watson, D. L. (1966) Anxiety and the interruption of behaviour. In D. Spielberger (Ed.), Anxiety and Behaviour, Academic Press, London.

Mandler, G., and Worden, P. E. (1973) Semantic processing without permanent storage, J. exp. Psychol. 100, 277-283.

Mangan, G. L., and O'Gorman, J. G. (1969) Initial amplitude and rate of habituation of orienting reaction in relation to extraversion and neuroticism, J. exp. Res. Person. 3, 275-282.

Martin, B., and Sroufe, L. A. (1970) Anxiety. In C. G. Costello (Ed.), Symptoms of Psychopathology, Wiley, London.

Martin, L. J. (1905) Psychology of aesthetics: Experimental prospecting in the field of the comic, Am. J. Psychol. 16, 35-116.

Martindale, C., and Greenough, J. (1973) The differential effect of increased arousal on creative and intellectual performance, J. genet. Psychol. 123, 329-335.

Matus, I. (1974) Select personality variables and tension in two muscle groups, Psychophysiol. 11, 91.

May, J. E., and Clayton, J. N. (1973) Imaginal processes during the attempt to recall names, J. verb. Learn. verb. Behav. 12, 683-688.

Mazuryk, G. F. (1974) Positive recency in final free recall, J. exp. Psychol. 103, 812-814.

McCauley, C., and Kellas, G. (1974) Induced chunking: Temporal chunking of storage and retrieval, J. exp. Psychol. 102, 260-265.

McGhie, A., Chapman, J., and Lawson, J. S. (1965) Changes in immediate memory with age, Br. J. Psychol. 56, 69-75.

McLaughlin, R. J. (1968) Retention in paired-associate learning related to extraversion and neuroticism, Psychon. Sci. 13, 333-334.

McLaughlin, R. J., and Eysenck, H. J. (1967) Extraversion, neuroticism, and paired-associates learning, J. exp. Res. Person. 2, 128-132.

McLaughlin, R. J., and Kary, S. K. (1972) Amnesic effects

in free recall with introverts and extraverts, Psychon. Sci. 29, 250-252.

McLean, P. D. (1968) Paired-associate learning as a function of recall interval, personality and arousal, unpubl. Ph.D. thesis, London.

McLean, P. D. (1969) Induced arousal and time of recall as determinants of paired-associate recall, Br. J. Psychol. 60, 57-62.

McNamara, H. J., and Fisch, R. I. (1964) Effect of high and low motivation on two aspects of attention, Percept. mot. Skills 19, 571-578.

McNulty, J. A., and Caird, W. K. (1966) Memory loss with age: Retrieval or storage?, Psychol. Rep. 19, 229-230.

Mehler, J., Bever, T. G., and Carey, P. (1967) What we look at when we read, Percept. Psychophys. 2, 213-218.

Melton, A. W. (1967) Individual differences and theoretical process variables: General comments on the conference. In R. M. Gagne (Ed.), Learning and Individual Differences, Merrill, Columbus, Ohio.

Mendelsohn, G. A., and Griswold, B. B. (1964) Differential use of incidental stimuli in problem solving as a function of creativity, J. abnorm. soc. Psychol. 68, 431-436.

Mendelsohn, G. A., and Griswold, B. B. (1966) Assessed creativity potential, vocabulary level, and sex as predictors of the use of incidental cues in verbal problem solving, J. Person. soc. Psychol. 4, 423-431.

Messick, S., and Damarin, R. (1964) Cognitive style and memory for faces, J. abnorm. soc. Psychol. 69, 313-318.

Meyer, D. E., and Ellis, G. B. (1970) Parallel processes in word recognition, paper presented at the meeting of the Psychon. Sci. Soc., San Antonio.

Meyer, D. E., Schvaneveldt, R. W., and Ruddy, M. G. (1974) Functions of graphemic and phonemic codes in visual word-recognition, Mem. Cogn. 2, 309-321.

Miller, G. A. (1969) A psychological method to investigate verbal concepts, J. math. Psychol. 6, 169-191.

Miller, G. A. (1972) English verbs of motion: A case study semantics and lexical memory. In A. W. Melton and E. Martin (Eds.), Coding Processes in Human Memory, Winston, Washington, D. C.

Miller, G. A., and Selfridge, J. A. (1950) Verbal context and the recall of meaningful material, Am. J. Psychol. 63, 176-187.

Miller, M. E., and Dost, J. A. (1964) Stimulus vividness and anxiety level in intentional-incidental learning, Psychol. Rep. 14, 819-825.

Milles, K. (1969) The effect of a basis for stimulus classification in recognition reaction time, unpubl. master's thesis, Kent State Univ.

Mischel, W. (1968) *Personality and Assessment*, Wiley, New York.

Moenster, P. A. (1972) Learning and memory in relation to age, *J. Geront.* 27, 361-363.

Moldawsky, S., and Moldawsky, P. C. (1952) Digit span as an anxiety indicator, *J. consult. Psychol.* 16, 115-118.

Monge, R. H., and Hultsch, D. F. (1971) Paired-associate learning as a function of adult age and the length of the anticipation and inspection intervals, *J. Geront.* 26, 157-162.

Moray, N. (1967) Where is capacity limited? A survey and a model. In A. Sanders (Ed.), *Attention and Performance*, Vol. 1, North-Holland, Amsterdam.

Morgan, C. L. (1894) *An Introduction to Comparative Psychology*, Scott, London.

Morin, R. E., DeRosa, and Stultz, V. (1967) Recognition memory and reaction time, *Acta psychol.* 27, 298-305.

Morris, L. W., and Liebert, R. M. (1970) Relationship of cognitive and emotional components of test anxiety to physiological arousal and academic performance, *J. consult. clin. Psychol.* 35, 332-337.

Morris, P. E., and Gale, A. (1974) A correlational study of variables related to imagery, *Percept. mot. Skills* 38, 659-665.

Morris, P. E., and Stevens, R. (1974) Linking images and free recall, *J. verb. Learn. verb. Behav.* 13, 310-315.

Morton, J. (1970) A functional model for memory. In D. A. Norman (Ed.), *Models of Human Memory*, Academic Press, London.

Morton, J. (1975) Structuring experience - Some discussion points. In A. Kennedy and A. Wilkes (Eds.), *Studies in Long-Term Memory*, Wiley, London.

Morton, J., and Byrne, R. (1975) Organization in the kitchen. In P. M. A. Rabbitt and S. Dornic (Eds.), *Attention and Performance*, Vol. V, Academic Press, London.

Mowbray, G., and Rhodes, M. (1959) On the reduction of choice reaction times with practice, *Q. Jl. exp. Psychol.* 11, 16-23.

Mueller, J. H. (1976a) Anxiety and cue utilization in human learning and memory. In M. Zuckerman and C. D. Spielberger (Eds.), *Emotions and Anxiety: New concepts, Methods and Applications*, Erlbaum Associates, Potomac, Md.

Mueller, J. H. (1976b) Test anxiety, input modality, and levels of organization in free recall, Bull. psychon. Soc.

Müller, G. E. (1913) Zur Analyse der Gedächtnistätigkeit und des Vorstellungsverlaufes, Z. Psychol. 8,

Murdock, B. B. (1967) Recent developments in short-term memory, Br. J. Psychol. 58, 421-433.

Murdock, B. B. (1972) Short-term memory. In G. H. Bower (Ed.), The Psychology of Learning and Motivation: Advances in Research and Theory, Vol. 5, Academic Press, London.

Murdock, B. B. (1974) Human Memory: Theory and Data, Wiley, London.

Murray, D. J., and Newman, F. M. (1973) Visual and verbal coding in short-term memory, J. exp. Psychol. 100, 58-62.

Muscovitch, M., and Craik, F. I. M. (1976) Depth of processing, retrieval cues, and uniqueness of encoding as factors in recall, J. verb. Learn. verb. Behav. 15, 447-458.

Nakamura, C. Y., and Wright, H. D. (1965) Effects of experimentally induced low drive, response mode, and social cues on word association and response speed, J. exp. Res. Person. 1, 122-131.

Naus, M. J. (1974) Memory search of categorized lists: A consideration of alternative self-terminating search strategies, J. exp. Psychol. 102, 992-1000.

Naus, M. J., Glucksberg, S., and Ornstein, P. A. (1972) Taxonomic word categories and memory search, Cogn. Psychol. 3, 643-654.

Neale, J. M., and Katahn, M. (1968) Anxiety, choice and stimulus uncertainty, J. Personality 36, 235-245.

Neisser, U. (1967) Cognitive Psychology, Appleton, London.

Neisser, U. (1972) Changing conceptions of imagery. In P. W. Sheehan (Ed.), The Function and Nature of Imagery, Academic Press, New York.

Nelson, D. L., and Brooks, D. H. (1973a) Independence of phonetic and imaginal features, J. exp. Psychol. 97, 1-7.

Nelson, D. L., and Brooks, D. H. (1973b) Functional independence of pictures and their verbal memory codes, J. exp. Psychol. 98, 44-48.

Nelson, D. L., and Brooks, D. H. (1974) Relative effectiveness of rhymes and synonyms as retrieval cues, J. exp. Psychol. 102, 503-507.

Nelson, T. O., Metzler, J., and Reed, D. A. (1974) Role of

details in the long-term recognition of pictures and
verbal descriptions, J. exp. Psychol. 102, 184-186.

Neva, E., and Hicks, R. A. (1970) A new look at an old
issue: Manifest anxiety scale validity, J. consult. clin.
Psychol. 35, 406-408.

Newell, A. (1973) You can't play 20 questions with nature
and win. In W. G. Chase (Ed.), Visual Information
Processing, Academic Press, London.

Nielsen, T. C., and Petersen, K. E. (1976) Electrodermal
correlates of extraversion, trait anxiety and schizo-
phrenism, Scand. J. Psychol. 17, 73-80.

Norman, D. A. (1969) Memory and Attention: An Introduction
to Human Information Processing, Wiley, London.

Norman, D. A., and Rumelhart, D. E. (1970) A system for
perception and memory. In D. A. Norman (Ed.), Models of
Human Memory, Academic Press, London.

Norman, D. A., and Wickelgren, W. A. (1969) Strength theory
of decision rules and latency in retrieval from short-term
memory, J. math. Psychol. 6, 192-208.

Novik, N. (1974) Parallel processing in a word-nonword
classification task, J. exp. Psychol. 102, 1015-1020.

Novinski, L. S. (1972) A re-examination of the part/whole
effect in free recall, J. verb. Learn. verb. Behav. 11,
228-233.

Nowlis, V. (1966) Research with the Mood Adjective Check
List. In S. S. Tomkins and C. E. Izard (Eds.), Affect,
Cognition, and Personality, Tavistock, London.

Oltman, P. K. (1964) Field dependence and arousal, Percept.
mot. Skills 19, 441.

O'Neil, H. F., Spielberger, C. D., and Hansen, D. N. (1969)
Effects of state anxiety and task difficulty on computer-
assisted learning, J. educ. Psychol. 60, 343-350.

Opton, E. M., and Lazarus, R. S. (1967) Personality
determinants of psychophysiological response to stress:
A theoretical analysis and an experiment, J. Person. soc.
Psychol. 6, 291-303.

Osborne, J. W. (1972) Short- and long-term memory as a
function of individual differences in arousal, Percept.
mot. Skills 34, 587-593.

Osgood, C. E., Suci, G. J., and Tannenbaum, P. H. (1957)
The Measurement of Meaning, Univ. Illinois Press, Urbana.

Paivio, A. (1968) A factor-analytic study of word
attributes and verbal learning, J. verb. Learn. verb.
Behav. 7, 41-49.

Paivio, A. (1969) Mental imagery in associative learning
    and memory, *Psychol. Rev.* 76, 241-263.
Paivio, A. (1971a) *Imagery and Verbal Processes*, Holt,
    Rinehart, and Winston, London.
Paivio, A. (1971b) Imagery and language. In S. J. Segal
    (Ed.), *Imagery: Current Cognitive Approaches*,
    Academic Press, London.
Paivio, A., and Csapo, K. (1969) Concrete-image and verbal
    memory codes, *J. exp. Psychol.* 80, 279-285.
Paivio, A., and Csapo, K. (1971) Short-term sequential
    memory for pictures and words, *Psychon. Sci.* 24, 50-51.
Paivio, A., and Foth, D. (1970) Imaginal and verbal
    mediators and noun concreteness in paired-associate
    learning: The elusive interaction, *J. verb. Learn. verb.
    Behav.* 9, 384-390.
Paivio, A., and Madigan, S. A. (1970) Noun imagery and
    frequency in paired-associate and free-recall learning,
    Can. J. Psychol. 24, 353-361.
Paivio, A., Rogers, T. B., and Smythe, P. C. (1968) Why are
    pictures easier to recall than words?, *Psychon. Sci.* 11,
    137-138.
Paivio, A., and Yuille, J. C. (1969) Changes in
    associative strategies and paired-associate learning over
    trials as a function of word imagery and type of learning
    set, *J. exp. Psychol.* 79, 458-463.
Paivio, A., Yuille, J. C., and Madigan, S. A. (1968)
    Concreteness, imagery, and meaningfulness values for 925
    nouns, *J. exp. Psychol. Monogr. Suppl.* 76, (1, Part 2).
Pascal, G. R. (1949) The effect of relaxation upon recall,
    Am. J. Psychol. 62, 33-47.
Patterson, K. E. (1971) Retrieval limitations in
    categorized free recall, unpubl. Ph.D. thesis, Univ.
    Calif., San Diego.
Patterson, K. E. (1972) Some characteristics of retrieval
    limitation in long-term memory, *J. verb. Learn. verb.
    Behav.* 11, 685-691.
Patterson, K. E., Meltzer, R. H., and Mandler, G. (1971)
    Inter-response times in categorized free recall, *J. verb.
    Learn. verb. Behav.* 10, 417-426.
Pearson, P. R. (1972) Field dependence and social
    desirability response set, *J. clin. Psychol.* 28, 166-
    167.
Penfield, W. (1955) The permanent record of the stream of
    consciousness, *Acta psychol.* 11, 47-69.
Penfield, W. (1959) The interpretive cortex, *Science, N. Y.*
    129, 1719-1725.

Penfield, W. (1968) Engrams in the human brain, Proc. R. Soc. Med. 61, 831-840.

Penn, N. E. (1964) Experimental improvements on an analogue of repression paradigm, Psychol. Rec. 14, 185-196.

Peterson, L. R., and Peterson, M. J. (1959) Short-term retention of individual verbal items, J. exp. Psychol. 58, 193-198.

Pezdek, K., and Royer, J. M. (1974) The role of comprehension in learning concrete and abstract sentences, J. verb. Learn. verb. Behav. 13, 551-558.

Piaget, J., and Inhelder, B. (1966) L'Image Mentale chez L'Enfant, Presses Universitaires de France, Paris.

Pike, R. (1973) Response latency models for signal detection, Psychol. Rev. 80, 53-68.

Pollio, H. R. (1964) Composition of associative clusters, J. exp. Psychol. 67, 199-208.

Pollio, H. R., Richards, S., and Lucas, R. (1969) Temporal properties of category recall, J. verb. Learn. verb. Behav. 8, 529-536.

Popper, K. (1935) Logik der Forschung, Vienna.

Postman, L. (1961) The present status of interference theory. In C. N. Cofer (Ed.), Verbal Learning and Verbal Behaviour, McGraw-Hill, London.

Postman, L. (1972) A pragmatic view of organization theory. In E. Tulving and W. Donaldson (Eds.), Organization of Memory, Academic Press, London.

Postman, L., and Phillips, L. W. (1965) Short-term temporal changes in free recall, Q. Jl. exp. Psychol. 17, 132-138.

Postman, L., and Stark, K. (1969) The role of response availability in transfer and interference, J. exp. Psychol. 79, 1-10.

Postman, L., and Underwood, B. J. (1973) Critical issues in interference theory, Mem. Cogn. 1, 19-40.

Powell, A. H., Eisdorfer, C., and Bogdonoff, M. D. (1964) Physiologic response patterns observed in a learning task, Archs. gen. Psychiat. 10, 192-195.

Purohit, A. P. (1966) Levels of introversion and competitional paired-associate learning, J. Personality 34, 129-143.

Pyke, S., and Agnew, N. (1963) Digit span performance as a function of noxious stimulation, J. consult. Psychol. 27, 281.

Pylyshyn, Z. W. (1973) What the mind's eye tells the mind's brain: A critique of mental imagery, Psychol. Bull. 80, 1-24.

Ramond, C. K. (1953) Anxiety and task as determiners of verbal performance, J. exp. Psychol. 46, 120-124.

Ramsay, R. W. (1968) Speech patterns and personality, Lang. Speech 11, 54-63.

Rappaport, H., and Katkin, E. S. (1972) Relationships among manifest anxiety, response to stress, and the perception of autonomic activity, J. consult. clin. Psychol. 38, 219-224.

Raser, G. A. (1972) False recognition as a function of encoding dimension and lag, J. exp. Psychol. 93, 333-337.

Raymond, B. (1969) Short-term and long-term storage in free recall, J. verb. Learn. verb. Behav. 8, 567-574.

Reder, L. M., Anderson, J. R., and Bjork, R. A. (1974) A semantic interpretation of encoding specificity, J. exp. Psychol. 102, 648-656.

Reed, A. V. (1976) List length and the time course of recognition in immediate memory, Mem. Cogn. 4, 16-30.

Reeves, F. B., and Bergum, B. O. (1972) Perceptual narrowing as a function of peripheral cue relevance, Percept. mot. Skills 35, 719-724.

Reitman, W. (1970) What does it take to remember? In D. A. Norman (Ed.), Models of Human Memory, Academic Press, London.

Richardson, A. (1969) Mental Imagery, Routledge and Kegan Paul, London.

Richardson, J. T. E. (1975a) Imagery, concreteness, and lexical complexity, Q. Jl. exp. Psychol. 27, 211-223.

Richardson, J. T. E. (1975b) Concreteness and imageability, Q. Jl. exp. Psychol. 27, 235-249.

Richardson, J. T. E., and Baddeley, A. D. (1975) The effect of articulatory suppression in free recall, J. verb. Learn. verb. Behav. 14, 623-629.

Riegel, K. F. (1959) A study of verbal achievements of older persons, J. Geront. 14, 453-456.

Riegel, K. F., and Birren J. E. (1966) Age differences in verbal associations, J. genet. Psychol. 108, 153-170.

Rim, Y. (1954) Perseveration and fluency as measures of introversion-extraversion in abnormal subjects, J. Personality 23, 324-334.

Rips, L. J., Shoben, E. J., and Smith, E. E. (1973) Semantic distance and the verification of semantic relations, J. verb. Learn. verb. Behav. 12, 1-20.

Roediger, H. L. (1973) Inhibition in recall from cueing with recall targets, J. verb. Learn. verb. Behav. 12, 644-657.

Roediger, H. L. (1974) Inhibiting effects of recall, Mem. Cogn. 2, 261-269.

Rogers, J. L., and Battig, W. F. (1972) Effect of amount of prior free recall learning on paired-associate transfer, J. exp. Psychol. 92, 373-377.

Rohwer, W. D. (1967) Social class differences in the role of linguistic structures in paired-associate learning: Elaboration and learning proficiency, Basic Research Project No. 5-0605, Contract No. OE 6-10-273, U. S. Off. Educ., Washington, D. C.

Rosch, E. (1974) Universals and cultural specifics in human categorization. In R. Breslin, W. Loner, and S. Bochner (Eds.), Cross-cultural Perspectives, Sage, London.

Ross, E. (1968) Effects of challenging and supportive instructions in verbal learning in older persons, J. educ. Psychol. 59, 261-266.

Rowe, E. J., and Schnore, M. M. (1971) Item concreteness and reported strategies in paired-associate learning as a function of age, J. Geront. 26, 470-475.

Rubenstein, H., Garfield, L., and Millikan, J. A. (1970) Homographic entries in the internal lexicon, J. verb. Learn. verb. Behav. 9, 487-494.

Rubenstein, H., Lewis, S. S., and Rubenstein, M. A. (1971) Evidence for phonemic recoding in visual word recognition, J. verb. Learn. verb. Behav. 10, 645-657.

Ruch, F. L. (1934) The differentiative effects of age upon human learning, J. gen. Psychol. 11, 261-286.

Rundus, D. (1971) Analysis of rehearsal processes in free recall, J. exp. Psychol. 89, 63-77.

Rundus, D., and Atkinson, R. C. (1970) Rehearsal processes in free recall, a procedure for direct observation, J. verb. Learn. verb. Behav. 9, 99-105.

Sachs, J. S. (1967) Recognition memory for syntactic and semantic aspects of connected discourse, Percept. Psychophys. 2, 437-442.

Sacks, H. V., and Eysenck, M. W. (1976) Convergence-divergence and the learning of concrete and abstract sentences, Br. J. Psychol. 67.

Sadler, T. G., Mefferd, R. B., and Houck, R. L. (1971) The interaction of extraversion and neuroticism in orienting response habituation, Psychophysiol. 8, 312-318.

Salthouse, T. A. (1974) Using selective interference to investigate spatial memory representations, Mem. Cogn. 2, 749-757.

Saltz, E. (1970) Manifest anxiety: Have we misread the

data?, Psychol. Rev. 77, 568-573.

Salzberg, P. M. (1976) On the generality of encoding specificity, J. exp. Psychol.: Hum. Learn. Mem. 2, 586-596.

Santa, J. L., and Lamwers, L. L. (1974) Encoding specificity: Fact or artifact?, J. verb. Learn. verb. Behav. 13, 412-423.

Santa, J. L., and Lamwers, L. L. (1976) Where does the confusion lie? Comments on the Wiseman and Tulving paper, J. verb. Learn. verb. Behav. 15, 53-58.

Sarason, I. G. (1957) The effect of anxiety and two kinds of failure on serial learning, J. Personality 25, 383-392.

Sasson, R. Y. (1971) Interfering images at sentence retrieval, J. exp. Psychol. 89, 56-62.

Sasson, R. Y., and Fraisse, P. (1972) Images in memory for concrete and abstract sentences, J. exp. Psychol. 94, 149-155.

Scarr, S. (1969) Social introversion-extraversion and genetic and environmental bias in twin studies, Eugen. Qu. 15, 34-40.

Schaefer, W. S., and Bayley, N. (1963) Maternal behaviour, child behaviour and their inter-correlations from infancy through adolescence, Monogr. Soc. Res. Child Developm. 28 (3, Serial No. 87), 1-127.

Schaeffer, B., and Wallace, R. (1969) Semantic similarity and the comparison of word meanings, J. exp. Psychol. 82, 343-346.

Schaeffer, B., and Wallace, R. (1970) The comparison of word meanings, J. exp. Psychol. 86, 144-152.

Schaie, K. W. (1958) Rigidity-flexibility and intelligence: A cross-sectional study of the adult life span from 20 to 70 years, Psychol. Monogr. 72 (No. 9).

Schaie, K. W. (1970) A reinterpretation of age-related changes in cognitive structure and functioning. In L. R. Goulet and P. B. Baltes (Eds.), Life-span Developmental Psychology: Research and Theory, Academic Press, London.

Schaie, K. W., and Strother, C. R. (1968) A cross-sequential study of age changes in cognitive behaviour, Psychol. Bull. 70, 671-680.

Schalling, D., Levander, S., and Wredenmark, P. (1975) Unpubl. manuscript.

Schonfield, D., and Robertson, B. (1966) Memory storage and ageing, Can. J. Psychol. 20, 228-236.

Schönpflug, W., and Beike, P. (1964) Einprägen und Aktivierung bei gleichzeitiger Variation der Absichtlichkeit des Lernens und der Ich-Bezogenheit des Lernstoffs, *Psychol. Forsch.* 27, 366-376.

Schulman, A. I. (1971) Recognition memory for targets from a scanned word list, *Br. J. Psychol.* 62, 335-346.

Schvaneveldt, R. W., and Meyer, D. E. (1973) Retrieval and comparison processes in semantic memory. In S. Kornblum (Ed.), *Attention and Performance*, Vol. IV, Academic Press, London.

Schwartz, R. M., and Humphreys, M. S. (1974) Recognition and recall as a function of instructional manipulations of organization, *J. exp. Psychol.* 102, 517-519.

Schwartz, S. (1974) Arousal and recall: Effects of noise on two retrieval strategies, *J. exp. Psychol.* 102, 896-898.

Schwartz, S. (1975a) The effects of arousal on recall, recognition, and the organization of memory, unpubl. manuscript.

Schwartz, S. (1975b) Individual differences in cognition: Some relationships between personality and memory, *J. Res. Person.* 9, 217-225.

Seamon, J. G. (1972) Imagery codes and human information retrieval, *J. exp. Psychol.* 96, 468-470.

Segal, S. J. (1971) Processing of the stimulus in imagery and perception. In S. J. Segal (Ed.), *Imagery: Current Cognitive Approaches*, Academic Press, London.

Segal, S. J., and Fusella, V. (1970) Influence of imaged pictures and sounds on detection of visual and auditory signals, *J. exp. Psychol.* 83, 458-464.

Shagass, C., and Kerenyi, A. B. (1958) Neurophysiologic studies of personality, *J. nerv. ment. Dis.* 126, 141-147.

Shakow, D., and Goldman, R. (1938) The effect of age on the Stanford-Binet vocabulary score of adults, *J. educ. Psychol.* 29, 241-256.

Shallice, T., and Warrington, E. K. (1970) Independent functioning of verbal memory stores: A neuropsychological study, *Q. Jl. exp. Psychol.* 22, 261-273.

Shanmugan, T. E., and Santhanam, M. C. (1964) Personality differences in serial learning when interference is presented at the marginal visual level, *J. Ind. Acad. appl. Psychol.* 1, 25-28.

Shapiro, B. J. (1969) The subjective estimation of relative word frequency, *J. verb. Learn. verb. Behav.* 8, 248-251.

Shedletsky, R., and Endler, N. S. (1974) Anxiety: The state-trait model and the interaction model, *J. Personality* 42, 511-527.

Sheehan, P. W. (1966a) Accuracy and vividness of visual

images, <u>Percept. mot. Skills</u> 23, 391-398.

Sheehan, P. W. (1966b) Functional similarity of imaging to perceiving: Individual differences in vividness of imagery, <u>Percept. mot. Skills</u> 23, 1011-1033.

Shepard, R. N. (1967) Recognition memory for words, sentences, and pictures, <u>J. verb. Learn. verb. Behav.</u> 6, 156-163.

Shepard, R. N., and Chipman, S. (1970) Second-order isomorphism of internal representations: Shapes of states, <u>Cogn. Psychol.</u> 1, 1-17.

Sherrill, D., Salisbury, J. L., Friedman, S. T., and Horowitz, B. (1968) Interrelationships among manifest anxiety, extraversion and neuroticism under two scoring conditions, <u>Psychol. Rep.</u> 22, 1255-1256.

Shields, J. (1962) <u>Monozygotic Twins Brought up Apart and Brought up Together</u>, Oxford University Press, London.

Shields, J. (1973) Heredity and psychological abnormality. In H. J. Eysenck (Ed.), <u>Handbook of Abnormal Psychology</u>, Pitman, London.

Shiffrin, R. M. (1970) Memory search. In D. A. Norman (Ed.), <u>Models of Human Memory</u>, Academic Press, London.

Shiffrin, R. M., and Atkinson, R. C. (1969) Storage and retrieval processes in long-term memory, <u>Psychol. Rev.</u> 76, 179-193.

Shiffrin, R. M., and Schneider, W. (1974) An expectancy model for memory search, <u>Mem. Cogn.</u> 2, 616-628.

Shuell, T. J. (1969) Clustering and organization in free recall, <u>Psychol. Bull.</u> 72, 353-374.

Shulman, H. G. (1970) Encoding and retention of semantic and phonemic information in short-term memory, <u>J. verb. Learn. verb. Behav.</u> 9, 499-508.

Shulman, H. G. (1971) Similarity effects in short-term memory, <u>Psychol. Bull.</u> 75, 399-414.

Shultz, T. R. (1970) Cognitive factors in children's appreciation of cartoons: Incongruity and its resolution, unpubl. Ph.D. thesis, Yale.

Shultz, T. R. (1974) Order of processing in humour appreciation, <u>Can. J. Psychol.</u> 28, 409-420.

Siegman, A. W. (1957) Some relationships of anxiety and introversion-extraversion to serial learning, unpubl. Ph.D. thesis, Ann Arbor.

Silverman, A. J., and McGough, W. E. (1971) Perceptual relationships to peripheral venous tone, <u>J. psychosom. Res.</u> 15, 199-205.

Simpson, P. J. (1972) High-speed memory scanning: Stability and generality, <u>J. exp. Psychol.</u> 96, 239-246.

Skanthakumari, S. R. (1965) Personality differences in the rate of forgetting, J. Ind. Acad. appl. Psychol. 2, 39-47.

Skinner, B. F. (1938) The Behaviour of Organisms, Appleton-Century-Crofts, New York.

Slamecka, N. J. (1968) An examination of trace storage in free recall, J. exp. Psychol. 76, 504-513.

Slamecka, N. J. (1969) Testing for associative storage in multitrial free recall, J. exp. Psychol. 81, 557-560.

Slamecka, N. J., Moore, T., and Carey, S. (1972) Part-to-whole transfer and its relation to organization theory, J. verb. Learn. verb. Behav. 11, 73-82.

Slater, P. E., and Scarr, H. A. (1964) Personality in old age, Genet. Psychol. Monogr. 70, 229-269.

Smith, A. D., D'Agostino, P. R., and Reid, L. S. (1970) Output interference in long-term memory, Can. J. Psychol. 24, 85-87.

Smith, E. E., Shoben, E. J., and Rips, L. J. (1974) structure and process in semantic memory, Psychol. Rev. 81, 214-241.

Smith, R. P. (1973) Frontalis muscle tension and personality, Psychophysiol. 10, 311-312.

Snodgrass, J. G., and Antone, G. (1974) Parallel versus sequential processing of pictures and words, J. exp. Psychol. 103, 139-144.

Snodgrass, J. G., Volvovitz, R., and Walfish, E. R. (1972) Recognition memory for words, pictures, and words + pictures, Psychon. Sci. 27, 345-347.

Soueif, M. I., and El-Sayed, A. M. (1970) Curvilinear relationships between creative thinking abilities and personality trait variables, Acta psychol. 34, 1-21.

Spearman, C. (1923) The Nature of 'Intelligence' and the Principles of Cognition, MacMillan, London.

Spence, J. T., and Spence, K. W. (1966) The motivational components of manifest anxiety: Drive and drive stimuli. In C. D. Spielberger (Ed.), Anxiety and Behaviour, Academic Press, London.

Spence, K. W. (1958) A theory of emotionally based drive (D) and its relation to performance in simple learning situations, Am. Psychol. 13, 131-141.

Spence, K. W. (1964) Anxiety (drive) level and performance in eyelid conditioning, Psychol. Bull. 61, 129-139.

Spence, K. W., Farber, I. E., and McFann, H. H. (1956a) The relation of anxiety (drive) level to performance in competitional and non-competitional paired-associates learning, J. exp. Psychol. 52, 296-305.

Spence, K. W., Taylor, J., and Ketchel, R. (1956b) Anxiety (drive) level and degree of competition in paired-associates learning, J. exp. Psychol. 52, 306-310.

Spielberger, C. D. (1958) On the relationship between anxiety and intelligence, J. consult. Psychol. 22, 220-224.

Spielberger, C. D. (1966) The effects of anxiety on complex learning and academic achievement. In C. D. Spielberger (Ed.), Anxiety and Behaviour, Academic Press, London.

Spielberger, C. D. (1972) Anxiety as an emotional state. In C. D. Spielberger (Ed.), Anxiety: Current Trends in Theory and Research, Vol. 1, Academic Press, London.

Spielberger, C. D., Gorsuch, R., and Luschene, R. (1969) The State Trait Anxiety Inventory (STAI) test manual form X, Consulting Psychologists Press, Palo Alto.

Spielberger, C. D., O'Neil, H. F., and Hansen, D. N. (1972) Anxiety, drive theory, and computer-assisted learning. In B. A. Maher (Ed.), Progress in Experimental Personality Research, Vol. 6, Academic Press, London.

Standing, L., Conezio, J., and Haber, R. N. (1970) Perception and memory for pictures: Single-trial learning of 2560 visual stimuli, Psychon. Sci. 19, 73-74.

Standish, R. R., and Champion, R. A. (1960) Task difficulty and drive in verbal learning, J. exp. Psychol. 59, 361-365.

Steriade, M. (1970) Ascending control of thalamic and cortical responsiveness. In C. C. Pfeiffer and J. R. Smythies (Eds.), International Review of Neurobiology, Vol. 12, Academic Press, London.

Stern, J. A., and Janes, C. L. (1973) Personality and psychopathology. In W. F. Prokasy and D. C. Raskin (Eds.), Electrodermal Activity in Psychological Research, Academic Press, London.

Sternberg, S. (1966) High-speed scanning in human memory, Science, N. Y. 153, 652-654.

Sternberg, S. (1969) Memory scanning: Mental processes revealed by reaction-time experiments, Am. Scient. 57, 421-457.

Stewart, J. C. (1965) An experimental investigation of imagery, unpubl. Ph.D. thesis, Toronto.

Straughan, J. H., and Dufort, W. H. (1969) Task difficulty, relaxation, and anxiety level during verbal learning and recall, J. abnorm. Psychol. 74, 621-624.

Strother, C. R., Schaie, K. W., and Horst, P. (1957) The relationship between advanced age and mental abilities, J. abnorm. soc. Psychol. 55, 166-170.

Suci, G. H., Davidoff, M. D., and Braun, J. C. (1962) Interference in short-term retention as a function of age. In C. Tibbitts and W. Donahue (Eds.), Social and Psychological Aspects of Ageing, Columbia University Press, New York.

Sulin, R. A., and Dooling, D. J. (1974) Intrusion of a thematic idea in retention of prose, J. exp. Psychol. 103, 255-262.

Suls, J. M. (1972) A two-stage model for the appreciation of jokes and cartoons: An information-processing analysis. In J. H. Goldstein and P. E. McGhee (Eds.), The Psychology of Humour, Academic Press, London.

Talland, G. A. (1967) Age and the immediate memory span, Gerontol. 7, 4-9.

Taub, H. A. (1966) Visual short-term memory as a function of age, rate of presentation, and schedule of presentation, J. Geront. 21, 388-391.

Taub, H. A. (1967) Paired associates learning as a function of age, rate, and instructions, J. genet. Psychol. 107, 43-48.

Taub, H. A. (1968) Age differences in memory as a function of rate of presentation, order of report, and stimulus organization, J. Geront. 23, 159-164.

Taub, H. A. (1972a) A comparison of young adult and old groups on various digit span tasks, Developm. Psychol. 6, 60-65.

Taub, H. A. (1972b) A further study of ageing, short-term memory, and complexity of stimulus organization, J. genet. Psychol. 120, 163-164.

Taub, H. A., and Grieff, S. (1967) Effects of age on organization and recall of two sets of stimuli, Psychon. Sci. 7, 53-54.

Taub, H. A., and Walker, J. B. (1970) Short-term memory as a function of age and response interference, J. Geront. 25, 177-183.

Taylor, J. A. (1953) A personality scale of manifest anxiety, J. abnorm. soc. Psychol. 48, 285-290.

Taylor, J. A. (1958) The effects of anxiety level and psychological stress on verbal learning, J. abnorm. soc. Psychol. 57, 55-60.

Taylor, J. A., and Chapman, J. P. (1955) Paired-associate learning as related to drive, Am. J. Psychol. 68, 671.

Templer, A. J. (1971a) A study of the relationship between anxiety and extraversion-introversion, Psychol. Afric. 14, 20-31.

Templer, A. J. (1971b) The relationship between self-report measures of anxiety and extraversion-introversion: A reconsideration, Psychol. Afric. 14, 161-169.

Tennyson, R. D., and Woolley, F. R. (1971) Interaction of anxiety with performance on two levels of task difficulty, J. educ. Psychol. 62, 463-467.

Thayer, R. E. (1967) Measurement of activation through self-report, Psychol. Rep. 20, 663-678.

Thayer, R. E. (1970) Activation states as assessed by verbal report and four psychophysiological variables, Psychophysiol. 7, 86-94.

Theios, J., Smith, P. G., Haviland, S. E., Traupmann, J., and Moy, M. C. (1973) Memory scanning as a serial self-terminating process, J. exp. Psychol. 97, 323-336.

Thompson, L. W., and Wilson, S. (1966) Electrocortical reactivity and learning in the elderly, J. Geront. 21, 45-51.

Thomson, D. M., and Tulving, E. (1970) Associative encoding and retrieval: Weak and strong cues, J. exp. Psychol. 86, 255-262.

Thorndike, E. L., and Woodworth, R. S. (1901) The influence of improvement in one mental function upon the efficiency of other functions, Psychol. Rev. 8, 247-261.

Thorndike, R. L., and Gallup, G. H. (1941) Verbal intelligence of the American adult, J. genet. Psychol. 30, 75-85.

Thorndyke, P. W. (1976) The role of inferences in discourse comprehension, J. verb. Learn. verb. Behav. 15, 437-446.

Tieman, D. G. (1972) Recognition memory for comparative sentences, unpubl. Ph.D. thesis, Stanford.

Townsend, J. T. (1971) A note on the identifiability of parallel and serial processes, Percept. Psychophys. 10, 161-163.

Travis, T. A., Kondo, C. Y., and Knott, J. R. (1974) Personality variables and alpha enhancement: A correlative study, Br. J. Psychiat. 124, 542-544.

Treat, N. J., and Reese, H. W. (1976) Age, pacing, and imagery in paired-associate learning, Developm. Psychol. 12, 119-124,

Treisman, A. M. (1964) The effect of irrelevant material on the efficiency of selective listening, Am. J. Psychol. 77, 533-546.

Treisman, A. M., and Tuxworth, J. (1974) Immediate and delayed recall of sentences after perceptual processing at different levels, J. verb. Learn. verb. Behav. 13, 38-44.

Trembly, D. (1964) Age and sex differences in creative thinking potential, Am. Psychol. 19, 516.

Troyer, W. G., Eisdorfer, C., Bogdonoff, M. D., and Wilkie, F. (1967) Experimental stress and learning in the aged, J. abnorm. Psychol. 17, 65-70.

Tulving, E. (1962) Subjective organization in free recall of 'unrelated' words, Psychol. Rev. 69, 344-354.

Tulving, E. (1966) Subjective organization and effects of repetition in multi-trial free-recall learning, J. verb. Learn. verb. Behav. 5, 193-197.

Tulving, E. (1967) The effects of presentation and recall of material in free-recall learning, J. verb. Learn. verb. Behav. 6, 175-184.

Tulving, E. (1968a) Theoretical issues in free recall. In T. R. Dixon and D. L. Horton (Eds.), Verbal Behaviour and General Behaviour Theory, Prentice-Hall, Englewood-Cliffs.

Tulving, E. (1968b) When is recall higher than recognition?, Psychon. Sci. 10, 53-54.

Tulving, E. (1972) Episodic and semantic memory. In E. Tulving and W. Donaldson (Eds.), Organization and Memory, Academic Press, London.

Tulving, E. (1974) Cue-dependent forgetting, Am. Scient. 62, 74-82.

Tulving, E., and Bower, G. H. (1974) The logic of memory representations. In G. H. Bower (Ed.), The Psychology of Learning and Motivation, Vol. 8, Academic Press, London.

Tulving, E., and Madigan, S. A. (1970) Memory and verbal learning. In Annual Review of Psychology, Vol. 20, Annual Reviews Inc., Palo Alto.

Tulving, E., and Osler, S. (1968) Effectiveness of retrieval cues in memory for words, J. exp. Psychol. 77, 593-601.

Tulving, E., and Pearlstone, Z. (1966) Availability versus accessibility of information in memory for words, J. verb. Learn. verb. Behav. 5, 381-391.

Tulving, E., and Psotka, J. (1971) Retroactive inhibition in free recall: Inaccessibility of information available in the memory store, J. exp. Psychol. 87, 1-8.

Tulving, E., and Thomson, D. M. (1971) Retrieval processes in recognition memory: Effects of associative context, J. exp. Psychol. 87, 116-124.

Tulving, E., and Thomson, D. M. (1973) Encoding specificity and retrieval processes in episodic memory, Psychol. Rev. 80, 352-373.

Tulving, E., and Watkins, M. J. (1975) Structure of memory traces, Psychol. Rev. 82, 261-275.

Turvey, M. T., and Egan, J. (1969) Contextual change and release from proactive interference in short-term memory, J. exp. Psychol. 81, 396-397.

Tversky, B. (1969) Pictorial and verbal encoding in a short-term memory task, Percept. Psychophys. 6, 225-233.

Tversky, B. (1973) Encoding processes in recognition and recall, Cogn. Psychol. 5, 275-287.

Tversky, B. (1974) Eye fixations in prediction of recognition and recall, Mem. Cogn. 2, 275-278.

Tzeng, O. J. L. (1973) Positive recency effect in delayed free recall, J. verb. Learn. verb. Behav. 12, 436-439.

Uehling, B. S. (1972) Arousal in verbal learning. In C. P. Duncan, L. Sechrest, and A. W. Melton (Eds.), Human Memory: Festschrift in Honour of Benton J. Underwood, Appleton-Century-Crofts, New York.

Uehling, B. S., and Sprinkle, R. (1968) Recall of a serial list as a function of arousal and retention interval, J. exp. Psychol. 78, 103-106.

Underwood, B. J. (1963) Stimulus selection in verbal learning. In C. N. Cofer and B. S. Musgrave (Eds.), Verbal Behaviour and Learning, McGraw-Hill, London.

Underwood, B. J. (1964) Degree of learning and the measurement of forgetting, J. verb. Learn. verb. Behav. 3, 112-129.

Underwood, B. J. (1969) Attributes of memory, Psychol. Rev. 76, 559-573.

Underwood, B. J. (1972) Are we overloading memory? In A. W. Melton and E. Martin (Eds.), Coding Processes in Human Memory, Winston, Washington, D. C.

Vandenberg, S. G. (1967) The nature and nurture of intelligence. In D. G. Glass (Ed.), Genetics, Rockefeller Univ. Press, New York.

Vassiliou, V., Georgas, J. G., and Vassiliou, G. (1967) Variations in manifest anxiety due to sex, age, and education, J. Person. soc. Psychol. 6, 194-197.

Vernon, P. E. (1965) Ability factors and environmental influences, Am. Psychol. 20, 723-733.

Vernon, P. E. (1971) Analysis of cognitive ability, Br. med. Bull. 27, 222-226.

Vernon, P. E. (1972) The distinctiveness of field independence, J. Personality 40, 366-391.

Voicu, C., and Vranceanu, M. (1975) Influence of the

dynamism of nervous processes on certain individual
memory differences, Rev. Roum. Sci. Sociales - Serie de
Psychol. 19, 13-20.

Wachtel, P. L. (1967) Conceptions of broad and narrow
attention, Psychol. Bull. 68, 417-429.

Walker, E. L. (1958) Action decrement and its relation to
learning, Psychol. Rev. 65, 129-142.

Walker, E. L. (1967) Arousal and the memory trace. In D.
P. Kimble (Ed.), The Organization of Recall, Acad.
Sciences, New York.

Walker, E. L., and Tarte, R. D. (1963) Memory storage as a
function of arousal and time with homogeneous and
heterogeneous lists, J. verb. Learn. verb. Behav. 2,
113-119.

Walker, R. E. (1961) The interaction between failure,
manifest anxiety, and task-irrelevant response in paired-
associate learning, unpubl. Ph.D. thesis, Northwestern
Univ.

Walley, R. E., and Weiden, T. D. (1973) Lateral inhibition
and cognitive masking: A neuropsychological theory of
attention, Psychol. Rev. 80, 284-302.

Wanner, H. E. (1968) On remembering, forgetting, and
understanding sentences: A study of the deep-structure
hypothesis, unpubl. Ph.D. thesis, Harvard.

Warrington, E. K. (1971) Neurological disorders of memory,
Br. med. Bull. 27, 243-247.

Watkins, M. J. (1973) When is recall spectacularly higher
than recognition?, J. exp. Psychol. 102, 161-163.

Watkins, M. J. (1974) Concept and measurement of primary
memory, Psychol. Bull. 81, 695-711.

Watkins, M. J., and Tulving, E. (1975) Episodic memory:
When recognition fails, J. exp. Psychol.: Gen. 1, 5-29.

Waugh, N. C. (1970) Retrieval time in short-term memory,
Br. J. Psychol. 61, 1-12.

Waugh, N. C., and Norman, D. A. (1965) Primary memory,
Psychol. Rev. 72, 89-104.

Weber, R. J., and Harnish, R. (1974) Visual imagery for
words: The Hebb test, J. exp. Psychol. 102, 409-414.

Weiner, B. (1966) The role of success and failure in the
learning of easy and complex tasks, J. Person. soc.
Psychol. 3, 339-344.

Weiner, B. (1972) Theories of Motivation: From Mechanism
to Cognition, Markham, Chicago.

Weiner, B., and Schneider, K. (1971) Drive versus
cognitive theory: A reply to Boor and Harmon, J. Person.

soc. Psychol. 18, 258-262.

Weisen, A. (1965) Differential reinforcing effects of onset and offset of stimulation on the operant behaviour of normals, neurotics, and psychopaths, unpubl. Ph.D. thesis, Univ. Florida.

Weist, R. M. (1972) The role of rehearsal: Recopy or reconstruct, J. verb. Learn. verb. Behav. 11, 440-445.

Wesner, C. E. (1972) Induced arousal and word-recognition learning by mongoloids and normals, Percept. mot. Skills 35, 586.

White, K. (1968) Anxiety, extraversion-introversion, and divergent thinking ability, J. creat. Behav. 2, 119-127.

Wickelgren, W. A. (1973) The long and the short of memory, Psychol. Bull. 80, 425-438.

Wickelgren, W. A. (1975a) Age and storage dynamics in continuous recognition memory, Developm. Psychol. 11, 165-169.

Wickelgren, W. A. (1975b) Alcoholic intoxication and memory storage dynamics, Mem. Cogn. 3, 385-389.

Wickelgren, W. A. (1975c) Dynamics of retrieval. In D. Deutsch and J. A. Deutsch (Eds.), Short-term Memory, Academic Press, London.

Wickens, D. D. (1970) Encoding categories of words: An empirical approach to meaning, Psychol. Rev. 77, 1-15.

Wickens, D. D. (1972) Characteristics of word encoding. In A. W. Melton and E. Martin (Eds.), Coding Processes in Human Memory, Winston, Washington, D. C.

Wickens, D. D., Born, D. G., and Allen, C. K. (1963) Proactive inhibition and item similarity in short-term memory, J. verb. Learn. verb. Behav. 2, 440-445.

Wilkinson, R. T., and Colquhoun, W. P. (1968) Interaction of alcohol with incentive and with sleep deprivation, J. exp. Psychol. 76, 623-629.

Williams, J. D. (1971) Memory ensemble selection in human information processing, J. exp. Psychol. 88, 231-238.

Willoughby, R. H. (1967) Emotionality and performance on competitional and non-competitional paired-associates, Psychol. Rep. 20, 659-662.

Wimer, R. E. (1960) Age differences in incidental and intentional learning, J. Geront. 15, 79-81.

Wimer, R. E., and Wigdor, B. T. (1958) Age differences in learning and retention, J. Geront. 13, 291-295.

Wine, J. (1971) Test anxiety and direction of attention, Psychol. Bull. 76, 92-104.

Wiseman, S., and Tulving, E. (1975) A test of confusion

theory of encoding specificity, *J. verb. Learn. verb. Behav.* 14, 370-381.

Wiseman, S., and Tulving, E. (1976) Encoding specificity: Relation between recall superiority and recognition failure, *J. exp. Psychol.: Hum. Learn. Mem.* 2, 349-361.

Witkin, H. A., Dyk, R. B., Faterson, H. F., Goodenough, D. R., and Karp, S. A. (1962) *Psychological Differentiation: Studies of Development*, Wiley, New York.

Witkin, H. A., Lewis, H. B., Hertzman, M., Machover, K., Meissner, P. B., and Wapner, S. (1954) *Personality Through Perception*, Harper and Row, New York.

Wood, C. G., and Hokanson, J. E. (1965) Effects of induced muscular tension on performance and the inverted U function, *J. Person. soc. Psychol.* 1, 506-510.

Wood, G. (1972) Organizational processes and free recall. In E. Tulving and W. Donaldson (Eds.), *Organization of Memory*, Academic Press, London.

Wood, G., and Clark, D. (1969) Instructions, ordering, and previous practice in free-recall learning, *Psychon. Sci.* 14, 187-188.

Wood, G., and Underwood, B. J. (1967) Implicit responses and conceptual similarity, *J. verb. Learn. verb. Behav.* 6, 1-10.

Woodworth, R. S. (1938) *Experimental Psychology*, Holt, New York.

Wyant, S., Banks, W. P., Berger, D., and Wright, P. W. (1972) Verbal and pictorial similarity in recognition of pictures, *Percept. Psychophys.* 12, 151-153.

Yerkes, R. M., and Dodson, J. D. (1908) The relation of strength of stimulus to rapidity of habit-formation, *J. comp. neurol. Psychol.* 18, 459-482.

Zaffy, D. J., and Bruning, J. L. (1966) Drive and the range of cue utilization, *J. exp. Psychol.* 71, 382-384.

Zangwill, O. L. (1956) A note on immediate memory, *Q. Jl. exp. Psychol.* 8, 140-143.

Zangwill, O. L. (1972) 'Remembering' revisited, *Q. Jl. exp. Psychol.* 24, 123-138.

Zaretsky, H. H., and Halbertstam, J. L. (1968) Age differences in paired-associate learning, *J. Geront.* 23, 165-168.

Zechmeister, E. R., and McKillip, J. (1972) Recall of place on the page, *J. educ. Psychol.* 63, 446-453.

Zeller, A. F. (1950a) An experimental analogue of

repression: I. Historical summary, _Psychol. Bull._ 47, 39-51.

Zeller, A. F. (1950b) An experimental analogue of repression: II. The effect of individual failure and success on memory measured by recall, _J. exp. Psychol._ 40, 411-422.

Zeller, A. F. (1951) An experimental analogue of repression: III. The effect of induced failure and success on memory measured by recall, _J. exp. Psychol._ 42, 32-38.

Zubrzycki, C. R., and Borkowski, J. G. (1973) Effect of anxiety on storage and retrieval processes in short-term memory, _Psychol. Rep._ 33, 315-320.

Zuckerman, M., Kolin, E. A., Price, L., and Zoob, I. (1964) Development of a sensation-seeking scale, _J. consult. Psychol._ 28, 447-482.

AUTHOR INDEX

SUBJECT INDEX

361

Picture memory,
 field dependence, 284
 parallel vs. serial
  processing, 56, 57
 phonemic similarity, 56
 spatial ability, 277
 vs. sentence memory, 122
 vs. word memory, 43.
Problem solving, 60.
Pupillary dilation, 96, 177,
 184.

R

Reading time, 115.
Recall,
 grouping, 112
 intentionality of learning,
  82
 interference effects, 93-95
 rehearsal, 87, 88
 speed of, 109-112
 word frequency, 81
 vs. recognition, 35, 72-75,
  78, 87, 157, 182, 263-265.
Recognition,
 anticipated test, 81
 attribute theory, 22
 context effects, 84
 direct vs. indirect, 85
 inference drawing, 34
 inferior to recall, 72-75
 latencies, 85, 98-109
 meaning vs. wording, 120
 phonemic information, 26, 27
 retrieval problems, 68, 69
 semantic information, 26, 27
 syntax vs. meaning, 115, 116.
Rehearsal,
 direct observation, 9, 10,
  20, 110, 232
 intelligence, 286-288
 recall vs. recognition, 87,
  88.
Relaxation, 181, 227.

Release effect, 18-20.
Response competition, 171, 184,
 185.
Retention interval, 80, 86,
 162, 171, 208.
Retrieval,
 arousal, 181-186
 complex retrieval, 97
 failure, 66-68
 neurological disorders, 13
 reconstruction and scanning,
  34
 rule formulation, 33, 34
 speed from semantic memory,
  150-153
 speed from short-term store,
  13
 stages involved, 33
 strategy differences, 78
 vs. storage, 61, 66-68.

S

Sampling with replacement,
 91, 94, 109, 110, 212, 213.
Scanlon, H., putative
 possessor of brain, 137.
Schema, 125.
Semantic differential, 23.
Semantic generalization, 178.
Semantic memory,
 arousal, 182-184, 209-214
 defined, 135, 201.
Short-term store,
 ageing, 246
 cross-situational generality,
  3
 digit span, 229
 displacement from, 6, 14
 free recall, 7, 111
 limited capacity, 6, 8, 9
 neurological disorders, 13,
  15
 phonemic coding, 7, 10, 11
 retention function, 13

DATE DUE